THE PRINTING PRESS AS AN AGENT OF CHANGE

*Communications and cultural
transformations in early-modern Europe*

Volume II

THE PRINTING PRESS
AS AN AGENT OF
CHANGE

*Communications and cultural
transformations in early-modern Europe*

Volume II

ELIZABETH L. EISENSTEIN

PROFESSOR OF HISTORY, UNIVERSITY OF MICHIGAN

CAMBRIDGE UNIVERSITY PRESS

CAMBRIDGE

LONDON · NEW YORK · MELBOURNE

Published by the Syndics of the Cambridge University Press
The Pitt Building, Trumpington Street, Cambridge CB2 1RP
Bentley House, 200 Euston Road, London NW1 2DB
32 East 57th Street, New York, NY 10022, USA
296 Beaconsfield Parade, Middle Park, Melbourne 3206, Australia

First published 1979

Printed in the United States of America
Typeset by Cambridge University Press
Printed and bound by Halliday Lithograph Company
West Hanover, Massachusetts

Library of Congress Cataloguing in Publication Data
Eisenstein, Elizabeth L.
The printing press as an agent of change.
Bibliography.
Includes index.
1. Printing–Influence.   2. Reformation.
3. Renaissance.   4. Technology and civilization.
I. Title.
Z124.E37   686.2   77-91083

ISBN 0 521 21967 1 volume I
ISBN 0 521 21969 8 volume II
ISBN 0 521 22044 0 set of two volumes

CONTENTS

PART THREE

THE BOOK OF NATURE TRANSFORMED

5

INTRODUCTION;
PROBLEMS OF PERIODIZATION

1. INTRODUCTION: 'THE GREAT BOOK OF NATURE' AND THE 'LITTLE BOOKS OF MEN'

Problems associated with the rise of modern science lend themselves to a similar argument. In other words, I think the advent of printing ought to be featured more prominently by historians of science when they set the stage for the downfall of Ptolemaic astronomy, Galenic anatomy or Aristotelian physics. This means asking for a somewhat more drastic revision of current guidelines than seems necessary in Reformation studies. In the latter field, the impact of printing may be postponed; but at least it is usually included among the agents that promoted Luther's cause. The outpouring of tracts and cartoons left too vivid and strong an impression for the new medium to be entirely discounted when investigating the Protestant Revolt. The contrary seems true in the case of the so-called 'scientific revolution.' Although a few authorities have suggested that sixteenth-century science was revolutionized by the 'cataclysmic' effect of printing, they do so by stressing a 'mass movement' which seems singularly unimpressive to other historians of science.[1] For exploitation of the mass medium was more common among prognosticators and quacks than among Latin-writing professional scientists, who often withheld their work from the press. When important treatises did appear in print, they rarely achieved the status of bestsellers. Given the limited circulation of works such as *De Revolutionibus* and the small number of readers able to understand them, it appears plausible to play down the importance of

[1] Price, *Science since Babylon*, pp. 98–9 stresses this popularizing theme and links the Reformation to it. See also passage cited in Conclusion, p. 691, below.

printing. Given the wider circulation of antiquated materials, many authorities are inclined to go even further and assign to early printers a negative, retrogressive role. 'There is no evidence that, except in religion, printing hastened the spread of new ideas...In fact the printing of medieval scientific texts may have delayed the acceptance of... Copernicus.'[2]

As the previous chapter may suggest, however, even in religion, the 'spread of new ideas' was only one of several new functions that deserve consideration. New functions performed by print affected orthodoxy as well as heresy. They changed the very nature of authority and authorship. They reoriented a sacred textual tradition. When seeking to understand scientific change we also need to look beyond the 'spread of new ideas' and to associate printers with other functions than popularization and propaganda. Textual traditions inherited from the Alexandrians, for example, were no more likely to continue unchanged after the shift from script to print than were scriptural traditions. For natural philosophers as for theologians, attempts at emendation and the pursuit of long-lived goals were likely to have a different outcome after printers replaced scribes.

At present, however, we are not only inclined to set the mass appeal of Lutheran tracts against the restricted appeal of Copernican treatises; we are also prone to discount textual traditions altogether when dealing with problems of scientific change. Conventional iconography encourages us to envisage Protestants with books in their hands (especially when we contrast them with Catholics holding rosaries). Early-modern scientists, however, are more likely to be portrayed holding plants or astrolabes than studying texts. Insofar as natural philosophers may have studied early printed editions of Ptolemy, Pliny, Galen or Aristotle,

---

[2] McLean, *Humanism and the Rise of Science*, p. 22. McLean's opinion is derived from the passage in Febvre and Martin, *L'Apparition* cited above (see chap. 1 n. 85, volume I). The thesis of retrogression was initially set forth by Sarton, 'The Scientific Literature,' pp. 62–8, and strongly upheld by Lynn Thorndike, *A History of Magic*, pp. 5–6. Sarton, in his later works: *Six Wings*, pp. 3, 116–19; *Appreciation*, pp. xi, 89–95; and 'The Quest,' p. 56; forcefully asserted that printing made possible scientific advance without abandoning the view that it also produced a 'retrograde' movement. His final verdict is probably best summed up in his own words as 'ambivalent.' See *Appreciation*, p. 168 and discussion of 'cultural lag' problem below, pp. 508. Sarton's scattered aperçus as well as Price's remark about 'cataclysmic' effects suggest the need to qualify the verdict that *all* historians of science have treated the advent of printing as unimportant given by Drake, 'Early Science and the Printed Book: The Spread of Science Beyond the University.' As its subtitle indicates, Drake's article, like Price's comments, connects printing with diffusion and vernacular translation. The limitations of this approach are noted in chap. 6 below.

they are usually accused of looking in the wrong direction. 'One would have thought that the breathtaking discoveries of the navigators would have turned attention from the little books of men to the great book of Nature but this happened much less often than one might expect.'[3] Yet how could the 'great book of Nature' be investigated, one is tempted to ask, without exchanging information by means of the 'little books of men?' The question is worth posing if only to bring out our own tendency to look in the wrong direction when considering the rise of modern science and related trends. It is partly because we envisage the astronomer gazing always at unchanging heavens and the anatomist taking human bodies as his only books, that the conceptual revolutions of the sixteenth century – which came before methods of star-gazing or dissection had been altered – seem peculiarly difficult to explain.

In this regard, the long-lived metaphorical image of by-passing other books in order to read in the book of nature, 'that universal and publick manuscript that lies expans'd unto the Eyes of all' is a source of deception which needs further analysis. Conventional treatments of this metaphor by intellectual and cultural historians provide fascinating excursions into the history of ideas but rarely pause over the problem of making freshly recorded observations available 'unto the Eyes of all.'

there are two Books from whence I collect my Divinity; besides that written one of God, another of His servant Nature, that universal and publick Manuscript, that lies expans'd unto the Eyes of all: those that never saw Him in the one, have discover'd Him in the other...Surely the Heathens know better how to joyn and read these mystical Letters than we Christians, who cast a more careless Eye on these common Hieroglyphicks and disdain to suck Divinity from the flowers of Nature.[4]

When Sir Thomas Browne compared the Bible with the book of nature, he was not only reworking a theme favored by Francis Bacon,[5]

---

[3] Sarton, *Six Wings*, p. 6.

[4] Thomas Browne, *Religio Medici* (1643), pt. I, chap. 16. Cited by Curtius, *European Literature*, p. 323 (where it is, confusingly, run in with a citation taken from the first part of chap. 15 of *Religio Medici*). See *Prose of Browne* (Endicott, ed.), p. 21.

[5] In the first book of *The Proficience and Advancement of Learning Divine and Humane* (1605) Bacon couples the 'book of God's word' with 'the book of God's work' and later refers to 'our Savior...laying before us the books or volumes to study if we will be secured from error: first the Scriptures...and then the creatures,' *Francis Bacon A Selection of His Works*, pp. 205, 242. Browne was using a 'Baconian technique...in calling Nature a Scripture,' according to Willey, *The Seventeenth Century Background*, p. 51. Since the same theme occurs

but was also drawing on earlier sources. According to Ernst Curtius, the same two 'books' were mentioned in medieval sermons and derive ultimately from very ancient Near Eastern texts. This lineage is viewed by Curtius as evidence of cultural continuity, and he uses it to argue against Burckhardt's thesis (or at least, against vulgarized versions of it). 'It is a favorite cliché...that the Renaissance shook off the dust of yellowed parchments and began instead to read in the book of nature or the world. But this metaphor itself derives from the Latin Middle Ages...'[6] The mere fact that references to a 'book of nature' appear in medieval Latin texts, however, is not a valid objection to the otherwise objectionable cliché. The persistence of old metaphors often masks major changes. In this case, all the changes that were entailed by the shift from script to print have been concealed. A seventeenth-century author, who coupled scripture with nature, might echo older texts. But both the real and metaphorical 'books' he had in mind were necessarily different from any known to twelfth-century clerks.

Thus when Saint Bernard referred to a 'book of nature,' he was not thinking about plants and planets, as Sir Thomas Browne was. Instead he had in mind monastic discipline and the ascetic advantages of hard work in the fields.[7] When his fellow monks celebrated natural fecundity, they also had pious ends in view. Many different vivid images were needed to serve as memory aids when learning moral lessons. 'Mankind is blind,' noted a fourteenth-century preacher's manual, containing excerpts drawn from works on natural history.

The human soul is forgetful in divine matters; but examples from nature are excellent devices to seize the memory in inescapable fashion...to fix men's thoughts upon the Creator...natural *exempla* are indispensable for preachers. Not only do they serve to capture the attention, but such examples are more meaningful than exhortation.[8]

The preacher in search of meaningful *exempla* was well served by the

in works by Bacon's contemporaries – such as Raleigh, Campanella and Galileo (whom Browne also read) the label 'Baconian' probably has to be cautiously applied. See e.g. relevant passage in Sir Walter Raleigh's *History of the World* (London, 1614) 1, 2, referring to 'Hieroglyphical Characters written on these large volumes of the firmament...also on the earth and the seas by the letters of...living creatures and plants' and citation from Galileo noted on p. 458, below. For philosophical background on the use of the theme by virtuosi, see Nelson, 'The Quest for Certitude,' pp. 363–72.   [6] Curtius, *European Literature*, p. 319.
[7] Leclercq, *The Love of Learning*, p. 135.
[8] Rouse and Rouse, 'The Texts called "Lumen Anime,"' p. 28. Paraphrased translation of preface to text composed *c.* 1332, by a compiler who may have been an Augustinian canon named Godfrey of Vorau.

abundance of variegated forms.[9] In medieval sermons, where didactic purposes came first, Scripture and nature were not separate but were intertwined. The latter, swathed in allegory, played a subservient role.

The remarks we find as to the behavior of animals...denote occasionally a certain sense of observation. Yet here again, allegories from the *Bestiary* are often superimposed on the things seen. In Nature, everything is symbolic. The symbols come either from biblical...or...classical tradition but they all have moral overtones.... works like the *Hortus deliciarum*...are used for teaching all the virtues through the imagery of the flowers that beautify a wholly spiritual garden. The meaning of the flowers and fruits lies...in their properties. No doubt few Western monks ever had any opportunity to see mandrake...or pomegranate but the plants which they did see, they saw through descriptions given by the *auctores*...[10]

When set against prefaces to medieval *florilegia*[11] Browne's reference to the 'heathens' who did not 'disdain' to 'suck Divinity' from real 'flowers of Nature' seems to indicate disenchantment with an earlier habit of mind. Much as Rabelais satirized those who assigned special 'virtues' to special plants, so too does Browne seem to be rejecting the literary allegorical conventions which had been cultivated by generations of monks.[12]

By the seventeenth century, the circumstances which had given rise to such conventions had been changed. Plant forms were no longer needed for memorizing moral lessons in Stuart England. When flowers

[9] The importance assigned to vivid, colorful and variegated objects in classical 'memory art' exercises is made clear by Yates, *The Art of Memory, passim*. She also describes how churchmen mobilized these arts to serve didactic Christian aims. How Erasmus prolonged this tradition by recommending the study of geography for oratory and composition is described by Watson, *The Beginnings of the Teaching of Modern Subjects in England*, p. 111.

[10] Leclercq, *The Love of Learning*, p. 137. It is important to note that this description is relevant to the Latin pulpit literature described by Curtius and characteristic of the monastic culture treated by Leclercq; but does not necessarily encompass the views of other medieval occupational groups, such as, e.g. merchants, woodcarvers, apothecaries *et al*. Late medieval natural philosophers were concerned with the properties of natural phenomena rather than their usefulness as mnemonic aids. Many other differences between scholastic and monastic views are underlined by Leclercq.

[11] Leclercq, *The Love of Learning*, pp. 186–7, discusses such prefaces. A typical example is offered by Herrade de Landsberg: 'This book was composed by me, a little bee...with the nectar from diverse flowers drawn from Holy Scripture...' Preface to *Hortus Deliciarum* attributed to Herrade de Landsberg (d. 1195) in Straub and Keller, *Herrade de Landsberg*, p. vi. The basic topos comparing the reader to a 'ruminating and selective' bee goes back at least to Plutarch and Basil. It also appears in one of Caxton's early prefaces. See Montgomery, 'William Caxton and the Beginnings of Tudor Critical Thought,' pp. 100–1. In transmuted form, it may be discerned in Matthew Arnold's celebrated discussion of 'sweetness and light.'

[12] Rabelais' satire, which appears in the seventh chapter of *Pantagruel* is discussed by Kline, 'Rabelais and the Age of Printing,' pp. 13 ff.

were associated with virtues or vices, it was more for poetic than for pedagogic effect. The Bible itself was no longer conveyed by a variety of 'mixed media' such as stained glass, altar-pieces, stone portals, choral music or mystery plays. Sacred stories could be more clearly separated from profane ones after the same authorized version had been placed in every parish church. To couple Bible reading and nature study, to link religious anthologies with botanical texts, no longer came naturally but required resorting to literary artifice, as is well demonstrated by Browne's Baroque prose.

When he reworked the old theme, did Browne have in mind a contrast between gardens of verses and real flower gardens? Was he underscoring the difference between 'Christian' florilegia and 'heathen' nature study? When he wrote of joining and reading 'mystical' letters or 'common Hieroglyphicks' was he referring to the heliocentric hypothesis, set forth in a treatise such as Thomas Digges' 'most auncient doctrine of Pythagoreans lately revived by Copernicus and by Geometricall Demonstrations approved'?[13] Did his paradoxical image of a 'universal public Manuscript' reflect an acquaintance with Galileo's celebrated reference to the 'grand book the universe which stands continually open to our gaze...written in the language of mathematics ...its characters are triangles, circles and other geometric figures'?[14]

Given the many levels of meaning that are compressed in his works, there is no easy way of answering such questions and several digressions would be required to attempt to reply. For my purpose it is enough to note that, whatever else was on his mind, Browne was familiar with the medium of print and with printed visual aids. In this regard, his book metaphors were based on objects Saint Bernard had never seen.

One might argue that this point is so obvious there is no need to restate it. Few surveys fail to remind us that science, like religion, underwent major changes during the early-modern era. Every schoolchild learns that the twelfth-century world picture was different from the seventeenth-century one. But beyond the textbook platitudes lies

[13] On Digges' treatise, see Koyré, *From the Closed World*, p. 35 and chap. 7 n. 146 below.

[14] From the *Assayer* (1623) in *Discoveries and Opinions of Galileo*, ed. and tr. by Stillman Drake, pp. 237-8. In the passage about his 'two books' cited above (n. 4), Browne relates the 'Scripture and Theology of the Heathens' to 'the naturall motion of the Sun' in contrast to the sun's 'Supernatural station' admired by 'the Children of Israel.' His cautious approach to Copernican views, his admiration for Galileo and his wide acquaintance with contemporary scientific literature are discussed by Chambers, 'Sir Thomas Browne.'

a vast literature of controversy over how to describe just what was different and how best to explain why a transformation occurred. In dealing with such questions I think there is much to be gained by placing more emphasis on the obvious, and pausing more carefully over the fact that the shift from script to print preceded a transformation of world views.

As things stand now, this seemingly obvious point is all too often obscured. To explain why Copernicus broke with the long prevailing geocentric theories; why observations made by Tycho Brahe and by William Harvey differed from those of previous investigators; why 'Galileo, Descartes and Newton were suddenly able to see well-known phenomena in a new way,' the historian of science, like the historian of the Reformation, is accustomed to consider a variety of factors. He is likely to pause over the 'problem of the Renaissance' and weigh the claims of Italians against Northerners, scholastics against lay humanists or Aristotelians against Platonists. Such 'novelties' as 'Neoplatonism,' the 'revival of ancient atomism' or the 'rediscovery of Archimedes' make demands on his attention.[15] As in dealing with the Reformation, he cannot overlook the possible significance of medieval 'precursors,' or the problems posed by individual 'genius.' He may be introduced, as are Lutheran scholars, to the findings of psychologists – not only to study the psychic life of 'young man, Newton,' but also to ponder the possibility of a collective 'gestalt-switch.'[16] He is also urged, mainly by Marxists, not to ignore socio-economic changes bearing on the commercial revolution and the rise of capitalism. He may well feel inclined to collaborate with sociologists and examine the 'Weber thesis' once again.[17] Whatever strategy is adopted however, the fifteenth-century communications revolution seems to require only the most casual glancing reference, if it is noticed at all.[18] Among new inventions or instruments, Galileo's telescope will loom larger than

---

[15] Thomas Kuhn, 'Science' (citations are from p. 78).

[16] Manuel, *A Portrait of Isaac Newton*; Thomas Kuhn, *The Structure of Scientific Revolutions*, pp. 111–14, 122–3.

[17] See especially Merton, *Science, Technology*. King, ('Reason, Tradition and the Progressiveness of Science') in discussing the approaches of Merton and Kuhn argues that 'the analysis of the formation [and] transmission...of research traditions' is a task for sociologists (p. 25). I hope this chapter will suggest why the help of historians is also needed.

[18] Basalla, *The Rise of Modern Science, External or Internal Factors?*, pp. ix–x, lists possible 'causal factors' currently proposed without mentioning the shift from script to print. As is suggested below, I think that the dichotomy implied by Basalla's subtitle would become less troublesome if more attention were given to the shift.

Gutenberg's movable type. If communications are considered in some detail, or the shift from script to print is assigned importance, the discussion is more likely to focus on seventeenth-century correspondence than on fifteenth-century books.

In most surveys dealing with early-modern science, European communications are handled in a way that postpones consideration of major change until the appearance of a periodical press, which replaced the 'letter box' of correspondents such as Friar Mersenne. Artificial barriers created by the practice of specializing in particular centuries often make it difficult to perceive cumulative continuous trends. In this instance, such barriers enclose the 'century of genius' in a way that seems to dam up a swelling stream of scientific publication and cut it off from the productive forces that brought it into the world. The development and improvement in postal service thus receives more attention than does the prior establishment of early printers' workshops, trade networks and book fairs.[19] 'During the seventeenth century, the printed word first assumed the importance which it is only now beginning to lose...The first of our learned journals the *Journal des Sçavans* and the *Philosophical Transactions* were both started in 1665.'[20]

These learned journals are singled out in standard accounts because they speeded up circulation of scientific news and enabled scattered virtuosi to keep abreast of each others' work. Periodical publication is thus viewed as a further extension of the kind of scientific reporting that had previously been conducted by handwritten correspondence.[21] It seems fair enough to place the shift from script to print in the seventeenth century when dealing with the limited topic of scientific journalism. But it is wrong to do this when one is concerned with the larger subject of the rise of modern science. Handwritten letters could keep correspondents informed about their colleagues' activities only up to a point. Handwriting was less helpful when it came to conveying actual research results. Doubtless news that Kepler was working on a new set of tables could be conveyed quite efficiently by handwritten

---

[19] On the 'rise of government postal services' as the one change in communications 'which truly deserves to be called revolutionary,' see Clark, *The Seventeenth Century*, p. 54. Similar emphasis on improved postal service (and better overland transportation) in promoting 'intercourse in the domain of thought' and facilitating 'the development of science' is in Merton, *Science, Technology*, p. 222.

[20] Vann (ed.), *Century of Genius*, part 1, 'The Medium and the Message,' p. 1.

[21] See e.g. Ornstein, *The Role of Scientific Societies*, p. 198.

correspondence. But this point does not apply to the *Rudolphine Tables* itself. When it came to distributing hundreds of copies of a work containing long lists of numbers, or diagrams, maps and charts, or even precise detailed verbal reports, hand-copying was vastly inferior to print. Kepler himself was well aware of the difference between manuscript and print.[22] As later discussion suggests, he was only one of many virtuosi who had made strenuous efforts to secure the services of printers. Even Mersenne took time out from letter-writing to help get Galileo's manuscripts to press. The historical significance of Galileo's trial is bound to be misconstrued if the printed word is held not to assume importance until the mid-1660s.[23] Since the printed word first assumed importance for the European scientific community in the 1470s when Regiomontanus established his Nuremberg press, the estimate is off by almost two hundred years.[24]

Doubtless the periodical publication which began in the 1660s affected the pace and character of scientific activities. Sociologists of science have good reason to argue that the functions performed by the new journals deserve close scrutiny.[25] At present, moreover, the scientific article and the scientific book often do seem to perform different functions; with the former playing a more innovative and the latter a more conservative role.[26] It is not clear, however, whether this holds true for nineteenth-century scientific publication, when significant innovative contributions by Lyell, Darwin, Maxwell and many others were made in books as well as in journals. The distinction, moreover, becomes ever more pointless as one moves back in time. It makes little

---

22 A long passage in praise of printing by Kepler, taken from a 1606 publication, is cited by Rosen, 'In defense of Kepler,' pp. 141–9.

23 On Kepler's struggles and activities of Mersenne and Galileo, see discussion in chap. 8 below.

24 Stillwell, *The Awakening Interest*, pp. 32–4 offers data on the output of Regiomontanus' press in the 1470s. For further discussion see pp. 586 ff below.

25 Merton and Zuckerman, 'Patterns of Evaluation in Science.'

26 The 'conservative' function performed by scientific *textbooks* is emphasized by Thomas Kuhn, *Structure of Scientific Revolutions*, pp. 136–7, even as the innovative function performed by periodical articles is stressed by Merton and Zuckerman, 'Patterns of Evaluation.' Both pass over the category of *innovative books*. That such books may still get published in the present century primarily as *monographs* is suggested by Anthony Parker, 'The Difficult Publishing Art of Persuading Scientists to Sit Down and Write Books,' pp. 813–14. He cites G. N. Watson's monograph on *Bessel Functions* as a case in point. Dirac's *Quantum Mechanics* might be added to the list. The pace of scientific publication has accelerated to the point where the circulation of 'pre-prints' has taken over the place previously occupied by the periodical press and Toulmin's paradoxical comment 'only out-of-date ideas ever actually get into print' seems cogent (Stephen Toulmin, *Human Understanding*, p. 275). In one sense, of course, the paradox has always held good. Unless composing is done with a compositor's stick, press work always involves some kind of 'lag.'

sense in the late seventeenth century, when Newton's *Principia* was published and the first issues of the *Transactions* appeared. When considering earlier works produced during the 'century of genius' or when tracing the full sequence of the Copernican Revolution, opposing books to journals not only fails to clarify any issues but also makes many things unnecessarily obscure.

However one may assess the role played by the learned journal in scientific activity, it should not lead to discounting 'the mere printing of a scientific work.' The learned journal probably did contribute significantly to a sharper definition of the professional scientist, to new divisions of intellectual labor and to the creation of a 'referee system.' But it did not usher in serial publication, the preservation of data, the 'shift from motivated secrecy to motivated public disclosure,' or a feedback from informed readers to responsive authors and editors.[27] These features were already taking shape before 1500 – in the age of incunabula. They ought to be placed *before* Copernicus and not after Galileo – if we want to understand how scientific data collection was transformed.

When set beside the consequences of the new mode of book production, moreover, the results of improvements in postal service or overland transport appear trivial indeed. Letters exchanged by Europeans in the early-modern era did not travel much more rapidly than had letters sent out in ancient Rome, but the information flow had nevertheless been transformed. It was not a more efficient postal service or better roads that distinguished the facilities available to seventeenth-century European astronomers from those enjoyed by the Alexandrians. (Nor was it a money economy or urbanization.) In seeking to explain why the *Almagest* remained authoritative as an astronomical text for some fourteen hundred years, whereas *De Revolutionibus* was surpassed in less than one hundred years, the replacement of scribe by printer must be examined first of all.

To insist that one must distinguish more sharply between a system of 'written' and one of 'printed' interchange, to insist that this difference is more important than that which separates a 'printed' book from a 'published' article is not merely to quibble over fine distinctions. If we seek to answer the question posed by Whitehead as to why the pace of a hitherto 'languid' search 'suddenly quickened in the sixteenth and

---

[27] Merton and Zuckerman, 'Patterns of Evolution,' p. 68.

seventeenth century,' then we have to be more careful and discriminating when considering how 'the mind of Europe' was prepared for its new adventure.

It is unnecessary to tell in detail the various incidents which marked the rise of science: the growth of wealth and leisure; the expansion of universities; the invention of printing; the taking of Constantinople; Copernicus; Vasco da Gama; Columbus; the telescope. The soil, the climate, the seeds were there, and the forest grew.[28]

Far from being unnecessary, I think it is essential to go into detail when discussing these assorted 'incidents,' and it is equally important to discriminate among them.

Every step of the remarkable 'adventure in ideas' which took educated Europeans from the *Almagest* to the *Principia* in less than two centuries was marked by the 'practice of merely putting manuscripts into print.' Because this practice was unknown before the fifteenth century, the ancients who had access to the special facilities for data collection provided in Alexandria, Pergamum and other great centers still had much to teach Europeans who lived in 1500. Given the difficulty of ensuring an adequate supply of specially trained copyists who could transcribe technical information, it is remarkable that a work such as the *Almagest* was preserved intact for so long an interval. Only the high priority Islam assigned to the study of astronomy can account for the work's preservation during those centuries when it was lost to the West. Islamic conquests embraced many ancient message centers. New observatories were constructed, old theories reformed and new data recorded by Arab astronomers. But no other great composition was produced to rival the authority possessed by the Alexandrian text in the Moslem world.[29]

Once recovered by the West and translated into Latin in the twelfth century, energies were necessarily absorbed there also in preserving and transmitting it. It was a very esoteric treatise throughout the age of scribes. Few copies of the full work were available at any one time.

---

[28] Whitehead, *Science and the Modern World*, pp. 27–8.
[29] The authority exerted by the *Almagest* among Arab astronomers is underlined by Sayili, *The Observatory in Islam*, p. 80, by Nasr, *Science and Civilization in Islam*, pp. 172–4, and by Watt, *The Influence of Islam on Medieval Europe*, pp. 24–5. All three point to numerous Arab critics and correctors of Ptolemy who seem to have played a role similar to the numerous scholastic critics of Aristotle in the West. Alternative models were occasionally proposed, additions and changes were often made but with the aim of explicating not discarding an inherited corpus of texts. On this point see also Pannekoek, *A History of Astronomy*, p. 169.

Few Western astronomers in any one generation were equipped to read the entire work or to instruct others in its use. The lifetimes of gifted astronomers were consumed, right down to Regiomontanus himself, making copies, recensions and epitomes of an initially faulty and increasingly corrupted twelfth-century translation from an Arabic text.

It is sometimes difficult to realize how much effort was needed to reconstitute the bodies of knowledge such as those of astronomy and arithmetic as they had been known in the ancient world. It was not a question of going beyond the ancients – the impulse to 'research' in the sense of extending the boundaries of scientific knowledge was only faintly stirring even in the twelfth century – but simply to learn what had been known and what the world had since lost was a stupendous task, demanding the labors of many scholars.[30]

For a full three hundred years *after* the twelfth century, the boundaries of scientific knowledge attained by Alexandrians continued to remain out of reach. The complete *Almagest* itself, it has been said, 'almost vanished from European astronomical literature until the sixteenth century.'[31] This may be somewhat overstated. In 1451 a new translation was made from the Greek; a carefully edited epitome based on the twelfth-century translation from Arabic was printed in 1496.[32] Nevertheless, the notion of an open-ended investigatory process, where increments of new information accumulate and the frontiers of the unknown recede, was still only 'faintly stirring' in the fifteenth century. The modern impulse to extend scientific knowledge had not yet been detached from the older impulse to retrieve and reconstitute it.

In the sixteenth century A.D. astronomers were still concerned with the very same problems that Ptolemy had tackled...To many people, this period of stagnation appears...inexcusably long, and they look for someone to blame ...To think in such terms is to miss two crucial points. The change-over to our modern views...called for a series of daring intellectual steps which could be taken only as new evidence gradually accumulated...This inevitably took time. In any case, the process could not begin at once. The

[30] Southern, *The Making of the Middle Ages*, p. 188.
[31] Ravetz, *Astronomy and Cosmology*, p. 21.
[32] George of Trebizond's translation from the Greek made in 1451 was printed in 1528. According to North, 'Medieval Background,' p. 8, Ravetz overstates the absence of knowledge of the complete *Almagest* until the sixteenth century. Gingerich's suggestion ('Crisis versus Aesthetic in the Copernican Revolution,' p. 88) that, in the 1460s, well-trained astronomers were just able to comprehend Ptolemy, seems fair enough.

young growth of Greek science, having been cut down...in Alexandria had to be transplanted.[33]

There is yet another 'crucial point' one must not miss when confronting the prolonged 'stagnation.' During the interval that elapsed between Ptolemy and Regiomontanus, new evidence was less likely to accumulate 'gradually' than to get corrupted or get lost and have to be retrieved or restored.[34] It is not so much 'stagnation' or even a slow rate of advance that needs explaining when dealing with conditions before printing. It is rather the manner in which a process of loss and corruption was temporarily arrested, and even on occasion reversed.

This reversal had occurred in ancient Alexandria where fresh data were preserved and did 'gradually accumulate' under the careful supervision of an élite corps of librarians.[35] Under these 'hothouse' conditions, fruitful work flourished for hundreds of years. Given such a long-lived collaborative enterprise and given its technical sophistication, one might question the notion of a 'young growth' and think instead about the unusual maturity that was achieved. The extensive facilities which made possible so much progress in mapping the earth and charting the planets seem to have been exceptional. Thereafter, some new ground was gained, but more old ground was lost. The feats of data collection achieved by ancient 'giants' remained beyond the reach of later 'dwarfs,' after the contents of Alexandrian libraries had been dispersed. Alexandrian achievements could not be surpassed, that is, until the process of textual transmission was transformed and data collection was placed on a new basis.

Once it is made clear that printing placed facilities which were

[33] Toulmin and Goodfield, *The Fabric of the Heavens*, p. 169. The significance of printing is more strongly asserted elsewhere in this book (see pp. 201–2) than in many other surveys.

[34] On the 'appallingly frequent scribal blunders...always present in medieval astronomical tables which have not been copied by astronomers' see Price (ed.) *The Equatorie of the Planetis*, p. 151. Note also references to frequent corruption of numerals as common scribal error and to 'contaminated' ms. tradition in Benjamin and Toomer, *Campanus of Novara*, pp. xii–xiii, n. 2.

[35] On this 'greatest library before the invention of printing' see Parsons, *The Alexandrian Library* who notes that the actual use made of it over the course of seven, possibly nine centuries, 'is still a virgin field of inquiry' (p. ix). Parsons' somewhat uncritical acceptance of ancient legends concerning Alexandria should be balanced against the more critical account by Pfeiffer, *History of Classical Scholarshp* (see especially pp. 236–7). Peiffer does note the absence of any central manuscript library on the scale of Alexandria even during the Renaissance (p. 110). When Zilsel, 'The Genesis of the Concept of Scientific Progress,' p. 328, discusses the lack of 'systematic organized collaboration' in antiquity he mentions Alexandria without appreciating its exceptional role and, here as elsewhere, fails to allow for the difference between conditions before and after print.

THE BOOK OF NATURE TRANSFORMED

superior to those of Alexandria at the disposal of learned men, it may become somewhat easier to explain why their activities had such unprecedented results. Belief in mathematical order, 'a habit of definite exact thought,' and concern with precise measurement need not necessarily be seen as late medieval novelties that require explanation. In some cases they may be regarded as long prevailing attitudes held by different groups that were weakly implemented throughout the age of scribes. For example, there is evidence in the field of astronomy that 'the ambition to achieve ever increasing standards of accuracy' was 'as strong in ancient Mesopotamia as it is in the modern world.'[36] Given Copernicus' profession, medieval scholasticism is no more needed than is Renaissance neo-Platonism to account for his desire to achieve a mathematically elegant scheme. 'Copernicus was a dedicated specialist. He belonged to the revived Hellenistic tradition of mathematical astronomy.'[37] However theologians and philosophers differed about cosmology, the professional astronomer had always assumed the universe was designed according to some form of mathematical order.

Thus one might supplement Whitehead's suggestion that scholasticism implanted a habit of 'definite exact thought' in the European mind by considering how this same habit was inculcated in astronomers of all cultures. The preservation of the *Almagest* was as important for Islam as it was for Christendom. Concern with precise description of celestial phenomena took different forms in different cultures, however. It is worth noting that the Christian calendar posed peculiar problems – just as polyglot Scriptures did. Fixing the date of Easter involved much more complicated issues, for example, than did the yearly celebration of Ramadan. When he examined Alexandrian texts and Arabic star maps or took advantage of new work in trigonometry, Copernicus was pursuing a course similar to that followed by previous generations of Christian astronomers who had been recruited by churchmen to solve calendrical problems. But he was freed from the task of copying tables and charts, and thus had released time for reading and reflecting. He was also supplied with more treatises, records and linguistic tools. His successors had even greater advantages in the form of paper tools.

'Why in the world' asks Herbert Muller, 'should men want to

36 Hoyle, *Astronomy*, p. 35.
37 Thomas Kuhn, *The Copernican Revolution*, p. 183. For further discussion see chap. 7 below.

measure...things precisely as they had not in the past? By the end of the sixteenth century, men had somehow developed the itch to know exact times, distances, rates, quantities...'[38] Muller is referring not to the study of the heavens but to more mundane, terrestrial activities associated with 'the publication of tables for calculation of interest,' the invention of decimals and logarithms, the 'spread of business habits of close reckoning.' The same question is often posed in connection with the high degree of precision achieved by the naked-eye observations of Tycho Brahe. Whatever activities were affected by exact measurement, a different approach to the problem is worth trying out. Here again, before assuming that new 'desires' had developed, we might look longer at the way old ones had been met. An Anglo-Norman 'algorism' of the fourteenth century consisting of 137 rhymed couplets, 'mostly octo-syllabic in Old French' indicates 'a practical spirit in the midst of bestiaries, computs, divination books, etc.'[39] Reciting rhymed couplets, however helpful as a mnemonic aid, does not lend itself as does studying notation to innovative higher mathematics. Heavy wooden tables are cumbersome compared with paper ones. Counting on one's fingers or even using an abacus did not encourage the invention of Cartesian coordinates. Leonardo Fibonacci, to be sure, compiled a 'book of the abacus' in the early thirteenth century, but it was a 'difficult task to memorize the tables the book contained' and 'not until the fifteenth century when Hindu numerals were spread by the printing press' did the systems outlined in the famous *Liber Abaci* achieve widespread use.[40]

It would seem that the first factor limiting the introduction into scientific practice of higher standards of observation and measurement...lay in the nature of science itself. Only when the concept of scientific research had changed was it possible to pay attention to the attainment of these higher standards...[41]

The very first limiting factor, however, was probably outside 'the nature of science' and was set by the difficulty of duplicating tables, charts, diagrams and maps. Before the advent of printing, to call for

[38] Muller, *Freedom in the Western World*, p. 239.
[39] Karpinski and Staubach, 'An Anglo Norman Algorism,' p. 126.
[40] Joseph and Frances Gies, *Leonardo of Pisa*, p. 98. The re-entry of the abacus marked an advance in the eleventh century, as noted by Southern, *Making of the Middle Ages*, pp. 186–7. The inconclusive struggle between abacists and algorists until the advent of printing and the victory of the latter thereafter is noted by Dantzig, *Number: the Language of Science*, pp. 33–4.
[41] A. R. Hall, *The Scientific Revolution*, p. 234.

more precise and uniform standards was to indulge in wishful thinking rather than contribute to research. The closest navigators and surveyors could come to universal common units was by using their own hands and feet, pacing across boat decks while at sea or across fields when on land.[42] Observation and measurement became more precise when man ceased to be the literal measure of things; when tables, charts and detailed records could be exactly reproduced and drawings to scale did not blur or smudge over time. After early printers had made available handbooks such as Simon Stevin's 'decimall arithmetike' or Leonard Digges' *A Booke Named Tectonicon* (the latter with a subtitle referring to 'exact measuring and speedie reckoning of all manner of Land, Squares, Timber, Stone, Steeples, Pillers, Globes'),[43] the old limits could be transcended and higher standards attained.

According to Crombie, 'the elements, both intellectual and practical, that came to produce the Scientific Revolution had been incubating in Western civilization for several centuries.'[44] One might elaborate this suggestion by emphasizing how many different groups within late medieval society placed a high value on achieving greater accuracy and more precise results. 'To astrologers, land-measurers, measurers of tapestry and wine casks and stereometricians, in general, mint masters and merchants all,' Simon Stevin addressed his new 'decimall arithmetike.'[45] In view of present tendencies to stress divisions between practical and theoretical, artisan and academic groups, it seems worth noting that Stevin's decimals, like Napier's logarithms, were just as helpful to professors of mathematics as to military engineers. The use of printed tables cut across other barriers which separated town from gown. Unlike rhymed verses in old French, the new forms of silent non-phonetic communication transcended distinctions between learned and vulgar tongues.

This point applies also to the new repeatable pictorial statements that became increasingly common in printed technical reference works. Like decimals and logarithms, woodcuts and engravings travelled

---

[42] On how man served as 'a measure for all things' see Dupree, 'The Pace of Measurement from Rome to America,' pp. 19–40, and Boas, *The Scientific Renaissance*, p. 204. See also Boas, pp. 35–6 for interesting description of how sailors envisaged a human figure (with head pointing North; feet pointing South; and arms pointing East and West) for the purposes of celestial navigation.

[43] Boas, *Scientific Renaissance*, p. 200 cites Leonard Digges' subtitle. This is the father of Thomas Digges whose description of Copernicus' doctrine is noted above, p. 458.

[44] See Crombie (ed.) *Scientific Change*, pp. 316 ff.

[45] Sarton, 'The First Explanation,' p. 160.

across linguistic frontiers, providing the life sciences with 'one common measure which speaks universally to all mankind' – in the words of Sir Joseph Banks describing pictures made by the artists who were sent with Captain Cook.[46] With regard to 'the veins, tools, vessels, sluices, machines, furnaces,' wrote Agricola, 'I have not only described them, but have also hired illustrators to delineate their forms, lest descriptions which are conveyed by words should either not be understood by the men of our times, or should cause difficulty to posterity.'[47] The descriptions of the Alexandrians had often caused difficulty to Western scholars partly because the texts of Ptolemy, Vitruvius, Pliny and others had been transmitted without pictures to accompany the often copied and translated words. Vitruvius refers to diagrams and drawings, but after the tenth century they were detached from Vitruvian texts.[48] Ptolemy's work on geography was retrieved, but any accompanying maps had been lost long before.[49] Simple pictograms had a better survival value. In the sixteenth century, when the difficulties created by scribal transmission were not fully appreciated, it often seemed as though earlier authorities had been arbitrarily and deliberately obscure.

Agricola protests against this arbitrary character in the name of knowledge that is communicable and whose language has the character of precision and intersubjectivity. There are many other books on this subject, but all are difficult to follow because the writers on these things use strange names which do not properly belong to the metals and because some of them employ now one name and now another although the thing itself changes not...[50]

Views of 'animals, plants, metals and stones' which had been transmitted for centuries became unsatisfactory to Agricola and his contem-

---

46 Bernard Smith, 'European Vision and the South Pacific,' p. 67 cites Sir Joseph Banks' remarks on the importance of engravings made from renderings of soil, rocks and plants observed on the expedition.

47 Cited by Paolo Rossi, Philosophy, Technology, p. 48.

48 Krinsky, 'Seventy-eight Vitruvius Manuscripts.' See also Zoubov, 'Vitruve et ses Commentateurs du XVIe Siècle,' pp. 69–70, concerning effort of illustrators to follow Vitruvius' description of the Tower of Winds in Athens. The effort to replace lost illustrations for Vitruvius and Ptolemy seems to me worth more attention as a powerful stimulus producing unexpected results. The invention of central perspective and of new map projection techniques, like that of the opera, may have resulted from attempts to redo what the ancients were (mistakenly) believed to have done before. See pp. 268 n, 281 above.

49 That the text of Ptolemy's Geography when recovered had long since lost all its maps as noted by Boas, Scientific Renaissance, p. 33. That the relatively small 500-copy first edition of the Geographia (Bologna, 1477) conveyed to many Italians and Germans their first sight of a map of any kind is noted by Bagrow, History of Cartography, p. 89.

50 Rossi, Philosophy, Technology, p. 53.

poraries. They attributed the deficiencies and inconsistencies they found to the 'linguistic barbarism' of the Gothic dark ages and to a prolonged 'lack of interest' in natural phenomena. Present evidence suggests that medieval natural philosophers were not lacking in curiosity. They were, however, lacking some essential investigative tools. Agricola's concern with 'communicable descriptive techniques' is certainly worth emphasizing but it also ought to be related to the new communications system of his day. The same point applies to Vesalius' 'acute sense of the importance of minutiae and...of precise and full reporting of observations.' Surely the new possibility of duplicating precise detailed reports alongside precise, detailed images deserves more attention when considering the shift that placed 'the traditional frames of...knowledge ...into a crisis situation.'[51] Similarly, the 'insistence that all experiments and observations be reported in full and naturalistic detail preferably accompanied by the names and credentials of witnesses'[52] needs to be related to the new kind of reporting that became possible only after the shift from script to print. As these comments may suggest, many different ancient and medieval scientific traditions were transformed by the capacity of printing to transmit records of observations without any loss of precision and in full detail. In view of the new equipment printing provided, it seems worth thinking longer about the new implementation of old aims before assuming that the significant change came from a shift of attitudes and goals. This approach, which seemed helpful when dealing with problems posed by the Reformation, ought to be equally useful when dealing with early-modern science.

By placing more emphasis on how print served to re-orient prevailing traditions, moreover, we might also be in a better position to relate religious and scientific changes to each other. Scriptural and scientific texts that had been transmitted by scribes were re-oriented at more or less the same time, under the aegis of printers. The fate of texts inherited from Aristotle, Galen and Ptolemy had something in common with that of texts inherited from Saint Jerome – a point to be discussed in the concluding chapter of this book.

[51] Rossi, *Philosophy, Technology*, pp. 47–9. In note 82 (p. 49), Rossi cites A. R. Hall on Vesalius and Sarton on how the new illustrations encouraged more awareness of 'stereotyped words.' But he does not deal explicitly with the way hand-copied illustrations had degenerated into stereotyped images before the advent of print.

[52] Thomas Kuhn, 'The Function of Measurement,' p. 192.

Insofar as Scripture and nature had been reoriented, their being coupled no longer meant the same thing. Browne kept up with the publications of the Royal Society and with the work of Bible scholars. Bible-reading and nature study were sufficiently distinguished in his mind that he could assign different functions and separate languages to each. Like his fellow virtuosi he was well aware of the thorny problems associated with deciphering God's words from ancient Hebrew texts.[53] Against the uncertain meanings and ambiguous allegories to be found in Scripture, he set the circles, triangles and other 'common hieroglyphicks' that 'heathen' philosophers – such as Euclid or Archimedes – knew how to join and read. When 'scriptural statements conflict with scientific truths,' notes Basil Willey, 'Browne will adhere unto Archimedes who speaketh exactly, rather than the sacred Text which speaketh largely.'[54]

In opposing Archimedes' formula to that provided by Solomon in the book of Chronicles, Sir Thomas Browne was not shaking off 'the dust of yellowed parchments' and taking a fresh look at the great outdoors. On the contrary he remained in the library with his eyes trained on old texts. But he *was* looking at texts which enabled Euclid and Archimedes to speak more 'exactly' (in Indo-Arabic numerals and by means of uniform diagrams) than had been the case before.[55] Similar analysis can be applied to the varied activities of the virtuosi who lived in Browne's day.

There is one very important feature of Kepler's actual procedure that I do not believe has ever come to light. It is, simply, that the hypotheses set forth were not developed inductively from an inspection of nature. Kepler was reading neither the Book of Nature nor the Book of Scripture but the books of ancient and contemporary writers...[56]

The notion that Renaissance men discarded 'dusty parchments' in favor of the 'book of nature' is not objectionable merely because previous book metaphors have been overlooked but mainly because the

[53] That Browne was thoroughly conversant with disputes over Hebrew vowel points and other controversies among seventeenth-century biblical scholars is shown in his tract, 'Of Language,' in *Prose of Browne* (Endicott, ed.) pp. 602 ff. In his introduction, Endicott also notes Browne's interest in Royal Society reports of Leeuwenhoek's work (p. xiii).

[54] Willey, *Seventeenth Century Background*, p. 68. The relevant passages are in Browne's *Pseudoxia Epidemica*, chap. 9 *Prose of Browne* (Endicott, ed.), p. 143.

[55] How a medieval copyist (of a twelfth-century Barcelona ms.) made Archimedes speak inexactly (by confusing a line drawn from point C to point L with a Roman numeral for 150) is noted by Clagett, *Archimedes*, p. 17.   [56] Westman, 'Kepler's Theory,' pp. 253–4.

investigation of natural phenomena has been misconstrued. The so-called cliché rests on a naive conception of scientific activity which is seen to consist of discarding old books or rejecting received opinion and making first-hand observations for oneself. 'He who wishes to explore nature must tread her books with his feet. Writing is learned from letters. Nature however by travelling from land to land: One land, one page. This is the Codex Naturae, thus must its leaves be turned.'[57] This naive view of science takes Browne's tricky image of a 'universal publick manuscript' at face value – as if any one observer could actually don 'seven-league boots' and see the whole world laid out before him, without recourse to maps and star catalogues, to atlases and travel guides; or, as if observations made in varied regions at different times did not have to be collected, preserved and correlated with each other, before plants or animals or minerals could be classified and compared; or finally, as if experiments did not have to be recorded in more than one notebook to be checked out and be of any scientific value at all.

sell your lands...burn up your books...buy yourself stout shoes, travel to the mountains, search the valleys, the deserts, the shores of the sea, and the deepest depressions of the earth; note with care the distinctions between animals, the differences of plants, the various kinds of minerals...Be not ashamed to study the astronomy and terrestrial philosophy of the peasantry. Lastly, purchase coal, build furnaces, watch and operate the fire...In this way and no other you will arrive at a knowledge of things and their properties.[58]

Insofar as it entails rejection of second-hand accounts and insistence on using one's own eyes, this naive view owes much to the arguments of sixteenth-century empiricists who set fresh observation and folk wisdom against the Latin book learning that was transmitted in the schools. The movement championed by these empiricists has been described by Whitehead as a 'recoil against the inflexible rationality of medieval thought.' 'The world required centuries of contemplation of irreducible and stubborn facts...after the rationalistic orgy of the middle ages...'[59]

To jump from the inflexibly rational schoolman to the nature-loving empiricist, however, is to pass over the intervening figure of the

[57] Cited from Paracelsus by Pagel and Rattansi, 'Vesalius and Paracelsus,' p. 316.
[58] Cited from Peter Severinus' *Idea Medicinae Philosophicae* (1660) by Debus, *English Paracelsians*, p. 20.   [59] Whitehead, *Science*, pp. 19; 28.

humanistic book-hunter. A 'recoil' against logic-chopping schoolmen had already occurred during the quattrocento, but it had often been on behalf of ancient authors and classical belles lettres rather than 'stubborn facts.'[60] Because of their attacks on scholasticism, their preference for examples over precepts and their interest in historical data, the quattrocento humanists are sometimes linked with sixteenth-century empiricists. Given the number of sixteenth-century humanists (such as Vives or Rabelais) who expressed empirical views, it seems that some sort of linkage did exist. Nevertheless, the humanist slogan, 'Back to the Sources!' led to Greek studies and library collections. It was quite compatible with fining professors who interpolated new material into fixed texts.[61] But it pointed in a different direction from the empiricist injunction to 'Burn up your books!' and learn from unlettered folk. 'The appearance of Paracelsus and the Aldine edition of Galen's works almost coincided...no two events could contrast more. Paracelsus had no use for the humanistic occupation with classical authors and with their words...to most of the humanistic Galenists Paracelsus and his whole following were an abomination.'[62] The humanist concern with rhetoric and the pursuit of eloquence, moreover, was not easily reconciled with the empiricist tendency to exalt the 'study of things' by deprecating the 'rabble of words.'[63]

All that is wanted is a certain power of observation. So will he observe the nature of things in the heavens in cloudy and clear weather, in the plains, on the mountains, in the woods. Hence he will seek out and get to know many things about those who inhabit those spots. Let him have recourse, for instance, to gardeners, husbandmen, shepherds, and hunters...For no man can possibly make all observations without help in such a multitude and variety of directions.[64]

It is noteworthy that Vives, even in this short passage, goes beyond a simple request for 'a certain power of observation' and in the end is

[60] Humanist objections to schoolmen posed by Salutati and his friends (who believed the cardinal sin was to argue without books or study of basic texts) are outlined by Gilbert, 'The Early Italian Humanists,' p. 219. The strongly anti-empirical position of Salutati vis-à-vis medical studies is brought out by Kemp, 'Il Concetto dell "Anima,"' p. 130.

[61] The case of John Geynes who was forced by the College of Physicians in 1559 to sign a recantation of his opinion that Galen was not infallible is cited by Debus, Science and Education, p. 6.

[62] Owsei Temkin, Galenism Rise and Decline of a Medical Philosophy, p. 132.

[63] Sir William Petty's dismissal of a 'rabble of words' is cited by R. F. Jones, Ancients and Moderns, p. 91. On the central role played by the pursuit of eloquence, see seminal essay by Gray, 'Renaissance Humanism.'

[64] Passage from Vives' De Anima (1538) cited by Haydn, The Counter Renaissance, p. 199.

envisaging a coordinator who correlates the findings of many observers. Still, he seems to think practical men unspoiled by book learning can provide adequate 'help.' The study of ancient languages aimed at mastery of technical literature produced by careful observers in the past finds no place in this program. Instead anti-intellectual and primitivist views are set forth which denounce all academic training, whether scholastic or humanist, or both. One authority has recently depicted the movement as directed against schoolmasters, textbooks and other restraints which print culture imposed.

When Libavius speaks of the Book of Nature he has in mind the clear-cut well ordered textbook of the class room. Croll's book on the other hand was...more mysterious...ultimately derived from the spoken word of God...intended for a largely illiterate audience with no access to the book of words...Paracelsus and Croll urge their followers to abandon the words ...in academic texts [and to] embrace the mentality of the illiterate peasant and artisan...[65]

In depicting the conflict between schoolmaster and Paracelsian, Hannaway appears to set the 'bourgeois' print culture of the former against the oral 'folk' culture of the latter. But this equation does not really work. For one thing, classroom procedures were geared to oral-aural modes of interchange – to dictation and recitation. For another thing, Croll (like Vives) belongs in the company of Renaissance scholars who were at home in the libraries and courts of princely patrons. He was affiliated with a court circle in Southern Bohemia which stood second only to that of Rudolph in Prague.[66] His major work, the *Basilica Chymica*, eventually issued by the Wechel press in Frankfurt, was designed for a Latin-reading, learned audience. It reflected a mentality which was quite remote from that of peasants and artisans. Paracelsus himself comes closer to being an autodidact and artisan-author. In this capacity he frequented the company of Basel printers, took full advantage of the new publicity system, and turned out a stream of publications – which suggests he had a flair for the metier of Aretino as well as for the healing arts. In short he too was a creature of print culture.

Attacking the academic establishment and satirizing pedants was indeed a common theme among Aretino's followers, the 'poligrafi' of

[65] Hannaway, *The Chemists and the Word*, p. 113.
[66] R. J. W. Evans, *Rudolf II and His World*, p. 142.

sixteenth-century Venice.[67] It seems plausible that students rather more than peasants provided the largest market for anti-establishment satires and polemics. (Do not many students belong within the category of 'bourgeois' print culture even when they chafe at the discipline that parents and teachers impose?) At all events, the sixteenth century did witness an unusually rich literary orchestration of anti-pedantic, primitivist themes which set the experience of simple folk against the foolishness of Latin pedants. The existence of a generalized rebellion against traditional academic pursuits and conventional bookish wisdom has been most amply illustrated by Hiram Haydn. Under the somewhat confusing rubric 'counter-Renaissance,' Haydn has collected a large number of citations from sixteenth-century theologians, philosophers, poets and other literati demonstrating that something more than either a 'recoil' from scholasticism or a rebellion against schoolmasters was at work.[68]

In my view the movement Whitehead describes as a 'recoil' and Haydn calls a 'counter-Renaissance' reflected disenchantment with those forms of teaching and book learning which had been inherited from the age of scribes. Insofar as memory training and 'slavish copying' became less necessary, while inconsistencies and anomalies became more apparent after printed materials began to be produced, a distrust of received opinion and a fresh look at the evidence recommended itself to all manner of curious men.

The difference between my philosophising and that of Pico is this: I learn more from the anatomy of an ant or a blade of grass...than from all the books which have been written since the beginnings of time. This is so, since I have begun...to read the book of God...the model according to which I correct the human books which have been copied badly and arbitrarily and without attention to the things that are written in the original book of the Universe...[69]

The idea of observing natural phenomena directly and carefully was as old as Aristotle or Galen. The phrase 'ego vidi' was not lacking in many scholastic commentaries.[70] Manuscript margins show skillful renderings of species of recognizable insects and birds. But the chance

---

[67] On Paracelsus see chap. 3, n. 337, volume 1 above. On Aretino's followers, see Grendler's *Critics of the Italian World*, chap. 1.

[68] See especially chap. 4 in Haydn, *Counter Renaissance*.

[69] Tommaso Campanella, Letter of 1607, cited by Garin, *Italian Humanism*, p. 215.

[70] The phrase 'ego vidi' is cited as 'Buridan's motto' and the frequency of its use in the fourteenth century is noted by Gabriel, *The College System*, p. 18.

to discard inherited schemes, collect fresh data and build improved models on them came only after print. In view of the output of corrupted data ('of human books copied badly') during the first century of printing and in view of the new possibility of duplicating fresh records, a reaction of some new kind against accepted texts, fixed lectures and received opinion was almost inevitable. But it would be wrong to assume that a rejection of technical literature paved the way for the rise of modern science. It was not the burning of books but the printing of them that provided the indispensable step.

In view of the errors inherited from scribal records and the way habits of 'slavish copying' persisted after they were no longer required, the empiricist reaction is understandable. It is easy to sympathize with those who placed more reliance on fresh observations than rote learning. Nevertheless insistence on going directly to the 'book of nature' soon took on the very attributes it was intended to repel. It became a ritualistic literary formula, devoid of real meaning.[71] 'As Olschki says of the natural philosophers: All of these thinkers who begin with the motto: "Away from books!"...know natural phenomena only from books! What they offer as observational material is merely anecdotes based on their own experience or known from hearsay...'[72] The unending stream of publications issued by exponents of the 'new philosophy' suggests that the virtuosi were not entirely consistent in attacking the written word.

When the Royal Society published a volume of 'Directions for Seamen, Bound for Far Voyages' in 1665, it defined its aim 'to study Nature rather than Books' but it also noted its intention 'from the Observations...to compose such a History of Her [i.e. Nature] as may hereafter serve to build a solid and useful Philosophy upon.'[73] Presumably Royal Society publications were designed to be read. Did not the Society actually aim at getting more of nature *into* books? However much they valued knowledge acquired through direct experience, members of the new scientific academies were still engaged in processing data and purveying it at second hand. Unlike shepherds or huntsmen, astronomers and anatomists could not really dispense with access to

---

[71] See e.g. Descartes' account of his decision to abandon 'the study of letters' and set out to study the 'great book of the world,' *A Discourse on Method*, part 1, pp. 6–7.

[72] Adelmann, Introduction to *The Embryological Treatises of Hieronymus Fabricius of Aquapendente*, p. 54.

[73] Notice appearing in the *Philosophical Transactions*, Jan. 8, 1665/6 cited by Bernard Smith, 'European Vision,' p. 65.

treatises and records. Insofar as they were involved in actual investigations, rather than philosophizing or propagandizing, they also had to master the technical literature available in their day. Indeed all work in science is incomplete until the report has been written *and* presented in published form. The irreducible 'fact,' the direct observation and any kind of raw data must be processed by being written down and made available for checking and confirmation by other eyes.

To most twentieth-century observers, it seems quite obvious that scientists must do more than make careful observations and show proper respect for 'stubborn facts.' When this point is made, however, it is usually to suggest that something more than induction is entailed in scientific activity. It is necessary, most authorities agree, to couple empiricism with rationalism and to develop theoretical frameworks for ordering collected facts. Both data collection and laboratory tests are often assigned a secondary role to the use of mathematical logic and resort to thought experiments. But there is yet another task that must be undertaken. It is too obvious, perhaps, ever to be spelled out. Before a scientist embarks on mental voyages or real ones, written records of previous undertakings have to be surveyed. A 'search of the literature' is so indispensable that an illiterate scientist is close to being a contradiction in terms. John Hale has suggested that the explorer may be distinguished from other voyagers because he works 'in the service of an organised vision of what might be found' and seeks 'to relate it to what is known. Unlike the wanderer...the explorer sees himself as contributing to a sum of knowledge he has assessed beforehand.'[74]

The point is relevant to the scientist as well. It is not only his command of technical literature – but also his capacity to put his findings in a form where they can be correlated with prior work – where they can be accepted or rejected by consensual validation – that helps to distinguish the scientist from the shrewd observer or from the speculative 'crank' and the ingenious gadgeteer.

the report of an experiment is a very long way...from that direct... wrestling with...Nature that the individual research worker experiences in his own laboratory.

When we say that scientific knowledge is...firmly based on empirical

[74] Hale, *Renaissance Exploration*, p. 9.

evidence, we do not mean that each scientist has seen with his own eyes all the wonders in which he believes. We mean that there exists a collection of reports of observations made by reliable witnesses and set out according to certain conventions...These reports...give...a carefully edited version of...events...by becoming part of the stock of public knowledge they have become...second-hand information, far removed from the direct experience of any one of us.[75]

This citation comes from an English physicist who agrees with Robert Merton that science is public rather than private knowledge and who also stresses the role of the printing press in making this form of knowledge possible. 'Modern science arose shortly after...printing ...this may have been no accident...the communications system needed in the scientific community could not have been provided by a less powerful technique.'[76]

After reading Professor Ziman's analysis, the paradox implicit in Browne's 'book of nature' becomes clear. The notion of a 'universal publick manuscript' may tickle our fancy as a Baroque conceit. But it is important to remember that there is no way of making fresh observations 'universal' and 'public' as long as they can be recorded only in manuscript form.

It is surprisingly easy to be absent-minded on this point. Most authorities either seem to forget that all records had to remain in manuscript form until the fifteenth century, or else they discount the importance of this fact. More often than not it seems sufficient to note that a 'collective memory' was transmitted first by word of mouth and then by writing without paying attention to the incapacity of scribal culture to make detailed records 'public' and at the same time preserve them intact. When Kenneth Boulding describes the emergence of a 'public image,' for example, he mistakenly assigns to manuscript maps the capacity to convey a uniform spatial reference frame. Although world maps before print actually came in oddly assorted shapes and sizes, Boulding seems to imagine them as being slightly fuzzier versions of our modern uniform outline maps. They were blurred around the edges, he suggests, until the voyages of discovery led to a 'closure of geographic space...looking over the long course of recorded history there is an orderly development in the...spatial image...early images

[75] Ziman, *Public Knowledge*, p. 35.
[76] Ziman, *Public Knowledge*, p. 45. For definition of science as 'public and not private knowledge,' see Merton, *Science, Technology*, p. 219.

can always be seen as partial unclear expressions of later more exact images...'[77]

When one places a reconstruction of a Ptolemaic world map derived from the second century A.D. beside mappaemundi designed later on, it becomes clear that this statement needs qualification. Instead of demonstrating 'orderly development' a sequence of hand-copied images will usually reveal degradation and decay. A survey of maps issued during a millennium or more shows how the 'course of recorded history' produced 'spatial images' that cannot be ordered even by taking full advantage of hindsight and present techniques of placing and dating past records.

More than 600 maps and sketches made between 300 and 1300 have survived the ravages of time...regardless of size and the quality of workmanship, it is impossible to trace in them a developmental process, a progression of thought...It is also impossible to grade them in terms of accuracy and utility.[78]

The 'disassociated transcript' that Boulding describes could emerge only after the shift from script to print. To confuse our modern uniform reference frame with the multiform 'world pictures' that hand-copying produced is to lose sight of the obstacles to systematic data collection in the past and to misconstrue what happened when such obstacles were removed.

We learn our geography mostly in school, not through our own personal experience. I have never been to Australia. In my image...however it exists with 100 percent certainty. If I sailed to the place where the map makers tell me it is and found nothing there but the ocean, I would be the most surprised man in the world. I hold to this part of my image...however purely on authority...what gives the map this extraordinary authority, an authority greater than that of the sacred books of all religions...is a process of feedback from the users of maps to the map maker. A map maker who puts out an inaccurate map will soon have this fact called to his attention by people...who find that it violates their...personal experience.[79]

The 'process of feedback' described in this passage was one of the more important consequences of printed editions. We have already noted how Ortelius' atlas was expanded and how the map-publisher

---

[77] Boulding, *The Image*, p. 77. This comment is cited with approval by Shera, 'An Epistemological Foundation for Library Science,' p. 23.
[78] Lloyd Brown, *The Story of Maps*, p. 94.
[79] Boulding, *The Image*, p. 66.

solicited data from informed readers throughout Europe.[80] The generation that followed Ortelius and Mercator saw further developments. After the 'golden age of Antwerp' had faded, new firms founded by Dutch map-publishers and globe-makers such as W. J. Blaeu and J. Hondius turned Amsterdam into the central city for data collection on a truly worldwide scale – a process which culminated in the twelve volume *Grand Atlas* of Joan Blaeu. Joan's father, Willem Janszoon, who founded the firm, is worth singling out for attention for his many contributions to the process described by Boulding, and for the way he exploited diverse advantages inherent in the new medium.

W. J. Blaeu started out as a clerk in the herring trade, then worked on Hven as one of Tycho Brahe's assistants in 1595–6, and finally established a thriving business in Amsterdam, making and selling astronomical and navigational instruments, sea charts and guidebooks from his shop on the waterfront. By 1637 his firm, with its sign of a golden sundial, was established in new premises (almost as elaborate as those of Plantin's 'Golden Compasses' in Antwerp) with nine presses for letterpress printing, six presses for copperplate work, a typefoundry, and rooms set aside for engravers. The bookshop, however, was left in the old store 'on the water near the old bridge.' Although he died (in 1638) before his son's grand atlas was published, he had lived to see the announcement of the forthcoming work appear in an Amsterdam newspaper of February 11, 1634.[81]

Blaeu's activities as instrument-maker ranged from designing an improved press (the first to improve on Gutenberg's design) to producing a huge quadrant, which spurred the building of the 'famous Observatory at Leiden.' As a publisher he preceded the Elseviers in issuing editions of contemporary heterodox authors, such as Grotius, in convenient small formats. His edition of Copernicus' *De Revolutionibus* was neatly timed to appear after the condemnation of 1616 had publicized the newly forbidden astronomical theory. At the same time that he served the Latin-reading Commonwealth of Learning he also furnished simplified latitude tables, vernacular pilot guides and printed sea charts to sailors – in the latter case offering the equivalent of a money-back guarantee that his printed cards were better than any

---

[80] See pp. 109–10, volume 1 above.

[81] For data see Keuning, *Willem Jansz. Blaeu*; Koeman, *Joan Blaeu and His Grand Atlas*. A special issue of *Quaerendo* (1973) III, 2 is devoted to W. J. Blaeu and contains useful articles by Wytze Hellinga, Ernst Crone, de la Fontaine Verwey *et al.*

hand-copied ones.[82] His role in publicizing 'Tycho's star' and in competing with his rival Hondius for the latest information about unchartered heavens belongs in a later chapter of this book. Here let me just underline the significance of finding Blaeu and his rivals jostling each other at the docks of Amsterdam while waiting for the return of an expedition, and plotting to secure the ship's log or its pilot or captain in order to place new data on their maps and globes.[83] We are thus provided with a glimpse of how the process of 'feedback' that Boulding seems to take for granted had begun to accelerate in the early seventeenth century.

This process has, indeed, never ceased; increments of information are still being added to geodetic surveys, and map-makers (as Boulding notes) are still being 'checked by the fact that it is possible to travel through space.' But this kind of checking could not occur until voyagers were provided with uniform maps and encouraged to exchange information with map-publishers. Even then it took many centuries and cost many lives to achieve the absolute confidence a modern atlas conveys.[84] The story of the prolonged impossible quest for a northwest passage indicates how difficult it was to achieve a final closure of geographic space and how important was the role played by communications in the process.

in spite of one fruitless or fatal voyage after another the expeditions still sailed on their impossible missions. The difficulties were not only physical... but also sprang from the inability of one explorer to pass on his knowledge to another...The outlines traced on a chart might be clear enough, but when this information came to be incorporated in a map covering a larger area, it might well be fitted into the wrong place in the jigsaw of straits, fjords and islands. Time after time the same mistakes were made, the same opportunities missed...[85]

---

[82] Blaeu discusses the advantages of his newly printed 'Sea-Cardes' in the 1612 edition of the *Light of Navigation* (the English translation of his popular pilot guide: *Het Licht.*) He notes that some pilots prefer the written ones 'dayly made and everie day corrected' but argues 'they cannot be made so sound nor with such speed' as printed ones and being often 'copied by the ignorant' are also more liable to error. He assures the reader that printed cards are 'as easie to correct.' Furthermore 'if any man can show us' an error to be corrected, it will be done 'at our charge.' W. J. Blaeu, *The Light of Navigation: Facsimile of 1612 Edition.* (Thanks are due to Rachel Doggett, of the Folger Library staff, for bringing this information to my attention.)

[83] In addition to discussion on p. 600 below, see Verwey, 'Willem Jansz. Blaeu,' pp. 87–105 for relevant material.

[84] How Kepler was misled by his favorite geographers Ortelius and Mercator is noted by Rosen, *Kepler's Somnium*, appendix 224–5.

[85] Hale, *Renaissance Exploration*, p. 75.

The recurrence of mistakes and missed opportunities was much more prevalent before the advent of printing. That many surprises were encountered by mariners in the fifteenth and sixteenth centuries is something even American schoolchildren are taught. The maps consulted in the 'age of discovery' entirely lacked the 'extraordinary authority greater than that of the sacred books of all religions,' which Boulding now consigns to his modern maps. This point is worth keeping in mind when considering changed attitudes toward divine revelation. Confidence in the sacred word was affected by the new authority assigned to literature which described the mundane.

Some of the greatest obstacles holding back the exploration of the globe... are psychological not technical. It was not so much men's inability to overcome natural barriers which prevented them from extending the range of their knowledge by new discoveries as the notions they had of the world around them.[86]

The statement goes on to note that Phoenicians and Vikings were not held back by the lack of technical equipment available to later mariners. Whatever landfalls were made, however, the goal of extending the range of knowledge by new discoveries was still technically as well as psychologically blocked throughout the age of scribes.

From 300 until 1300 there were many merchant adventurers, pious pilgrims, and fierce Norsemen who set out to sea or travelled overland. From evidence gathered after the thirteenth century, we know that trained cartographers took advantage of reports sent back to charthouses and merchant companies in the later middle ages. A special atlas once completed could not be 'published,' however. A fifteenth-century monastery near the University of Vienna served as a major center for the collection of geographic information and advanced cartography. Maps drawn in Klosterneuberg could be seen by visiting scholars and astronomers.[87] But however such exceptional manuscript maps were handled, they were unavailable to scattered readers for guidance, for checking and for feedback. The best maps, indeed, were

[86] Issawi, 'Arab Geography,' p. 117.
[87] Durand, The Vienna-Klosterneuberg Map-Corpus, passim. The scholarly circle at Klosterneuberg, where Augustinian friars, collaborating with scholars from Padua and Vienna imported manuscripts containing astronomic, geographic and mathematical data and had them copied by professional scribes, seems to represent a unique enterprise in the fifteenth century – unlike the competing map-publishing firms later on. By the seventeenth century there were no less than eighteen chief map-making centers in Europe according to Brown, Story of Maps, pp. 156–7.

often carefully hidden from view – like the map made for a fourteenth-century Florentine merchant which was placed in a warehouse 'secretly and well wrapped so that no man could see it.'[88] To make multiple copies would not lead to improvement but to corruption of data; all fresh increments of information when copied were subject to distortion and decay.

This same point also applies to numbers and figures, words and names. Observational science throughout the age of scribes was perpetually enfeebled by the way words drifted apart from pictures, and labels became detached from things. Uncertainty as to which star, plant, or human organ was being designated by a given diagram or treatise – like the question of which coastline was being sighted from a vessel at sea – plagued investigators throughout the age of scribes. No wonder it was believed that one of the greatest secrets God entrusted to Adam was how to go about naming all things!

Writing of Conrad Gesner's *History of Animals* Professor Thorndike makes the simple but fundamental observation that even it is primarily concerned with names and words and with information and allusions for the use and enjoyment of the scholar and literary reader rather than with the collection and presentation of facts for scientific purposes.[89]

In my opinion, this observation is *too* simple. Gesner and his contemporaries lived in an era when science and scholarship were necessarily interdependent. To collect and present 'facts' required mastery of records made by observers in the past. Sixteenth-century investigators had to be concerned with ancient languages and inscriptions, with 'names and words,' whether their interests were 'literary' or not. To classify flora and fauna or place them on maps meant sorting out the records left by previous observers as well as observing freshly for oneself. 'Historical' research and 'scientific' data collection were close to being identical enterprises. Thus, geographers, such as Ortelius, had to engage in research on old place-names and often inspired major studies in philology as well as topography. An astronomer such as Copernicus had to steep himself in ancient chronologies and master

---

[88] See reference in Datini's journal to a Florentine jewel merchant cited by Origo, *The Merchant of Prato*, p. 99. According to Penrose, *Travel and Discovery*, p. 25, the data contained in the now famous Catalan Atlas of 1375 would have 'surprised' Chaucer and Petrarch. See also reference to Dante's ideas of world maps gleaned from looking at monastery walls. Orr, *Dante and the Early Astronomers*, pp. 224–5. The crude pictogram available to readers of manuscript copies of Marco Polo's *Travels* is illustrated in Skelton's useful *Explorer's Maps*, fig. 3.

[89] Endicott, introduction, *Prose of Browne*, p. xv.

inscriptions on coins. As a celestial globe-maker, W. J. Blaeu learned Latin, Greek and even Arabic terms. Not even mythology could be ignored by astronomers trying to match Greek constellations with Arabic ones. If anatomists were not well trained in language studies, and lacked the experience of editing ancient texts, they were likely to have the sort of difficulty that Leonardo had, when he became puzzled as to just which organs Galen was describing. Even while noting how geography tended to become a branch of philology and how Boccaccio had devoted a treatise to diverse names assigned to bodies of water, George Sarton seems surprised at the way 'curiosity about natural phenomena' was combined with 'literary' and 'historical' research.[90]

The combination is no way surprising. Indeed many early scientific field trips were launched by publishers, editors and translators who were producing books for new markets and thus had strong 'literary' interests from the first.[91] The work of a 'naturalist' such as Pierre Belon, as presented by Sarton himself, provides a good case in point. Belon

who was planning to translate Dioscorides and Theophrastus into French, was inhibited at every step by the difficulty of identifying the plants and animals which were dealt with in the ancient books. He realized...the need of going to the East and seeing with his own eyes the...creatures which the Greek naturalists had described.[92]

He secured royal patronage for an expedition to the Near East and returned with an account of the plants and animals he had observed. His book became a landmark in natural history and was published in many editions and translations, after first being printed in Paris in 1553. Sarton's discussion seems unexceptionable up to this point, but then he comments:

As distinguished from the majority of his learned contemporaries Belon was primarily a naturalist, not a humanist...real naturalists caring for the objects of nature rather than for literal descriptions were very rare. It is passing strange that it took so long for intelligent men writing about nature to discover their opportunities.[93]

[90] Sarton, *Six Wings*, p. 6.
[91] The first example of such a 'field trip' known to me is the one so described by William Ivins which was sponsored in the 1480s by Gutenberg's erstwhile assistant Peter Schoeffer in connection with his herbal *Gart der Gesundheit*. See p. 266, volume 1 above.
[92] Sarton, *Appreciation*, p. 57.   [93] Sarton, *Appreciation*, p. 60.

To oppose the 'objects of nature' to 'literal descriptions' of them is to adopt an approach that itself seems somewhat strange. Belon's point of departure, after all, was an effort to translate 'literal descriptions.' Had he not been trying to identify objects described by the ancients, his approach to natural phenomena would have taken a different form. Far from being indifferent to literal description he was frustrated precisely because he could not get it right.

The early editors of Theophrastus, Dioscorides, Pliny and Galen faced the usual problems of editing any classical work during the Renaissance. They had to work from manuscripts which were usually poor copies of earlier copies. The ravages of neglect and the ignorant mistakes of scribes turned every text into a series of puzzles for the diligent editor to solve by ingenious emendations. While Renaissance philologists generally had to rely on their knowledge of ancient languages...to make their textual corrections, with the botanical treatises they could make sense out of corrupt passages by inspecting the living plants in question.

The labor of collating classical botanical texts with nature flourished in the sixteenth century...The ancient authors provided a model through their accounts of the long journeys they had undertaken...

The lack of a technical descriptive vocabulary though made it very hard to identify the plants named...with living plants in the field. If living plants alone could not communicate...then the obvious alternative was to rely on pictures...[94]

The labor of collating 'classical texts with nature' thus led to departing from classical precedent by resorting to woodblocks and engravings. The decision to 'rely on pictures' was a radical departure in more than one respect. 'The weight of ancient opinion discouraged the use of illustrations to record and convey botanical knowledge.'[95] Ironically the slogan of the empiricists – that one should use one's own eyes and trust nature not books – derived from an experience which printing outmoded. Classical authorities had warned against trusting hand-copied pictures for the excellent reason that they degenerated over time.[96] When Galen said that 'the sick should be the doctor's books' he was justified by the circumstances of scribal culture. Paracelsians

[94] Reeds, 'Renaissance Humanism and Botany,' pp. 27–9.
[95] Reeds, 'Renaissance Humanism,' pp. 27–9.
[96] See William Ivins, *Three Vesalian Essays*, pp. 50–1 where relevant remarks from Pliny are cited and pertinent issues discussed. On botanical illustration, in addition to standard accounts by Singer, Nissen, Arber, Blunt *et al.* see Stannard, 'The Herbal as a Medical Document,' pp. 212 ff, where the medieval separation of textual and illustrative materials associated with the Dioscoridean herbal is described in interesting detail (p. 217).

who repeated the phrase were actually being less responsive to changed circumstances than Latin-writing professors such as Fuchs and Vesalius who had freshly rendered drawings transferred for duplication on durable woodblocks. Since the 'living plant alone could not communicate' as well as the repeatable image could, only a small fraction of the world's plants had been known to the ancients. After the talents of painters and woodcarvers were tapped, fresh information that lacked respectable classical ancestry began to make its way into scientific texts.

Elsewhere, Sarton again reproaches early-modern investigators for excessive concern 'with words rather than facts.' The editors of early printed editions of scientific treatises, he complains,

illustrate the relative weakness of the typical Renaissance approach...It was literary and wordy instead of being experimental and matter of fact. It took scholars an astonishing long time to discover that science could not be investigated profitably in any book except the Great Book of Nature. The few who realized this were more likely to be rebels like Bernard Palissy...[97]

Insofar as Bernard Palissy was a rebel, it was surely not as a potter trying out a new glaze; it was rather as a craftsman trying his hand at writing books. Generations of potters had been observed at their kilns, but none had contributed to French literature before. It was as an artisan author that Palissy was a pioneer. Partly because more men could serve in this capacity from the sixteenth century on, more of nature could be placed in books. Printing made it possible not only to sort out old records but also to secure fresh records and drawings made by careful observers in an easily portable form.

Well before printing, observations drawn from nature had been made by painters and woodworkers, goldsmiths and stone carvers who were unfamiliar with scribal conventions. Even in the sixteenth century, few had their eyes trained on books; before the advent of printing, most were entirely unlettered. Thereafter they rarely mastered the language which was used in the schools. They had not received university degrees after committing to memory the words of professors reciting from Galen while peering vaguely at the cadaver on the dissecting table. They did not know that only plants bearing Latin names were deemed worthy of inclusion in learned treatises. They carried out the instructions of editors and authors as carefully as they could, but, on occasion, they erred by turning out pictures that were 'truer to life' than the

[97] Sarton, *Appreciation*, p. 5.

texts they were intended to illustrate.[98] Field trips to distant regions and specimens sent in from scattered readers, thus were supplemented by a new look at ordinary garden variety plants grown for centuries at home.

As Karen Reeds points out, anatomists and botanists experienced the effect of the challenge to received opinion somewhat differently – the latter in a more gradual manner than the former. 'No botanist had to challenge the authority of Dioscorides in the way that Vesalius had to oppose Galen.' Nevertheless the limitations of the ancient authority who had described some 600 plants became increasingly apparent as the new process of data collection gathered momentum. By 1623, the number had grown from 600 to 6,000.

As botanists perfected their techniques for collecting and sharing their data and increased the geographical range of their botanical explorations they gradually realized that the ancients, far from being omniscient in botany, had named but a small fraction of the plants in the world...every day seemed to bring forth 'new founde Herbes wherof is no mention in any olde auncient writer.'[99]

As we noted in an earlier chapter, once fresh observations drawn from nature could be duplicated in printed books, they became available to scattered readers who could, at long last, check books against nature and feed back corrections with new observations to be incorporated into later editions. The 'information explosion in botany and zoology' that occurred during Captain Cook's voyages and the receipt of packages of seeds by Linnaeus from scattered members of the reading public (who hoped they might be immortalized in his next volume), represent later phases of a process that was already under way in the mid-sixteenth century.[100]

Indeed, plant observation from the mid-sixteenth century onward acquired much the same character as bird-watching does today and depended in somewhat the same way on visual aids in pocket-sized reference guides.[101] Botanical publication also began to take a serial form.

[98] Arber, 'From Medieval Herbalism,' pp. 322–3 describes how Weiditz drew plants, excluded from Brunfels' conventional scheme, for the celebrated herbal of 1530 which turned out to be landmarks in the history of plant delineation. A. R. Hall, *Scientific Revolution*, pp. 43, 47 notes that the cuts for Vesalius' *De Fabrica* were occasionally more accurate and less traditional than the text they illustrated.   [99] Reeds, 'Renaissance Humanism,' p. 540.

[100] On public response to Linnaeus, see Eisley, *Darwin's Century*, p. 17. The process of feedback initiated in both botany and zoology is discussed in section 4, chap. 2, volume I above.

[101] See reference to pocket-sized edition of Fuchs' herbal in chap. 2, n. 308, volume I above.

Mattioli won fame for his commentaries on Dioscorides, first published in 1554 and reprinted in many editions, periodically revised and corrected, not only in Latin but in many vernaculars. Mattioli's commentary on Dioscorides became a treatise on botany just as a 'Ptolemy' was actually a new treatise on geography. His publications were immensely popular; some 32,000 copies of them were sold. His authority was so great that discoverers of new plants ...communicated their information to Mattioli to be included in his next edition.[102]

Mattioli's successive editions, which were periodically revised and corrected to take into account this feedback from readers, acted very much like later scientific periodicals. This sort of collaborative publication suggests why it is a mistake to delay the effects of printing until the late seventeenth century and learned periodicals such as the *Transactions* of the Royal Society.

In later sections, I hope to elaborate on some of these points. The main purpose of this introductory section has been to suggest that the views of natural philosophers were transformed by print in ways that have yet to be taken into account. The same point applies to activities pursued by late medieval craftsmen. The new technology equipped both groups to reach for old goals by new means. When considering the scientific revolutions of early-modern times, changes wrought by the new presses ought to receive higher priority. Insofar as a major turning point occurred in the late fifteenth century, I contend, it was not that men turned from books to nature, but rather that books went from script to print.

2. PROBLEMS OF PERIODIZATION REVISITED

(a) *Burckhardtians versus Medievalists*

At present this thesis is unconventional. Most historians who deal with the rise of modern science have to confront the issue of periodization, and at some point must pause to balance evidence of continuity against indications of change. The 'problem of the Renaissance' will loom large at such points for Burckhardt's claim that the Italians were the first-born sons of modern Europe explicitly encompassed the 'sphere of the natural sciences.'[103] In discussing the study of nature, Burckhardt

---

[102] Sarton, *Six Wings*, pp. 138–9. See also 144–6 concerning relevant role played by Plantin's firm in sponsoring botanical publication.

[103] See Burckhardt, *The Civilization of the Renaissance* II, part IV, 'The Discovery of the World and of Man,' especially chaps. 1 and 2. The view of Durand, 'Tradition and Innovation in 15th

distinguished sharply between the occasional medieval schoolman who managed to free himself from 'slavery to books and tradition' and the collective emancipation of a 'whole people' which occurred on the Italian peninsula. He also made an invidious comparison between the widespread delight taken by Italians in investigating nature and the indifference exhibited by other nations.[104] However defended or attacked, extended or delimited, the thesis has loomed large in subsequent treatments of Renaissance science. Indeed the 'primacy of Italy' has been assigned more attention when setting the stage for the 'rise of modern science' than the effects of the shift from script to print. Here, as elsewhere, when dealing with problems of 'modernization,' I think scholarly priorities ought to be revised.

Let me forestall misunderstanding: I am not denying that certain Italian developments ought to be singled out for special emphasis. When observing the sculpture and paintings that were produced by the Italians during the Renaissance, it seems quite legitimate to refer to a native genius. The nude figures rendered by Italian artists such as Mantegna or Pollaiuolo moreover were more important than those of other regions in shaping the new visual aids which were significant for the 'new' anatomy.[105] Similarly, when dealing with medical studies during the early-modern era, certain Italian universities have to be singled out for special notice. Given the sequence that runs from Vesalius to Harvey, one can scarcely avoid assigning a very special role to the University of Padua. Nevertheless the national pride of Flemings and Englishmen is needlessly offended when innovations associated with either of these celebrated figures are attributed to the native genius of Italians. It also becomes difficult to discern some of the significant new elements that characterized De Fabrica or De Motu when the Italianate theme is overplayed.

When Vesalius is portrayed as working near 'the countryside of Petrarch' and in Titian's Venetian studio and there is nothing said about the long line of Flemish physicians from whom he was descended, or about his studies at Louvain and Paris or his editing of medical texts, one senses that the theme is being overstressed. The suspicion deepens

century Italy,' p. 25, that Burckhardt ignored science 'almost completely in his periodization scheme' needs qualifying. Although Burckhardt treated science in a very cursory way, it was important 'in his periodization scheme,' as later debates suggest.
104 Burckhardt, *Civilization of the Renaissance* II, 283.
105 For relevant illustrations of engravings by Pollaiuolo and Mantegna, see Mayor, *Prints and People*, figures nos. 184–91.

when told that a reader of *De Fabrica*, unlike *De Revolutionibus* 'is not repelled by the crabbed Gothic lettering of the North but is invited by the bold clear typeface of Italian printing.'[106] After all, *De Fabrica* was actually printed under German Swiss auspices by the son of a Northern painter named Herbst. Vesalius went to much trouble to get heavy blocks carried out of Italy, over the Alps to Oporinus' famous workshop in Basel. The cóntrast with Copernicus' Northern 'Gothic' work also suggests how arbitrary this kind of pattern weaving can be, not only because the types used in *De Revolutionibus* do not fit the description, but also because Copernicus visited Italy and there are reasons for believing that he was influenced by the teacher he encountered there.

Especially when dealing with advances in astronomy, I think, insistence on Italian initiative comes close to being a distracting nuisance. The cosmopolitan Latin-writing élite to which professional astronomers belonged does not lend itself to efforts at separating out 'Italianate' elements from the rest. In extending his claims for 'the countrymen of Columbus'[107] Burckhardt unwittingly provoked an unending series of embittered 'Columbus Day' disputes with Germans, Danes and Poles. One reads: 'it was in Italy not Nürnberg that Copernicus' thoughts turned to astronomy'[108] and one finds it hard not to be distracted by thinking of the deluge of articles in Polish about the university of Cracow such a statement is likely to provoke. A Heilbronn printer of 1492 proudly claimed Regiomontanus for the Germans[109] whereas Burckhardt placed him alongside Copernicus and other learned men who confessed themselves 'to be Italy's pupils.'[110] Both views can be justified, but efforts to do so seem destined to generate more heat than light.

As these comments may suggest, exclusive emphasis on the genius of any one people or nation (however welcome to patriotic Italian scholars) can easily exacerbate national rivalries and rarely yields useful results. Furthermore, in the course of claiming that Italians took the lead in

---

[106] Gillispie, *The Edge of Objectivity*, p. 57. Later on (p. 60) Brussels, Louvain and Paris are mentioned with a comment that Vesalius 'hated his teachers' but without noting how much he learned from their lectures or from helping them edit Galenic texts. That 'crabbed Gothic' was often easier to read than 'Italic' is also overlooked.

[107] Burckhardt, *Civilization of the Renaissance* II, 281–2.

[108] Wightman, *Science and the Renaissance* I, 111.

[109] See discussion of Santritter of Heilbronn and other relevant material in Thorndike, *A History of Magic and Experimental Science*, pp. 332–7.

[110] Burckhardt, *Civilization of the Renaissance* II, 286.

scientific pursuits, Burckhardt also stressed their empiricism and their collective commitment to investigation and exploration. The entire nation, he suggested 'took a natural delight in the study...of nature at a time when other nations were indifferent.' Here again I think he helped to sidetrack later studies. By setting the venturesome nature-lovers of Renaissance Italy against the sedentary schoolmen of medieval Europe, he incorporated the false dichotomy of books versus nature into his periodization scheme. Medieval man was, accordingly, portrayed as enslaved by 'books and tradition' and emancipation attributed to the 'nautical' nature-loving Renaissance Italians. To make a convincing case, however, the otherwise conspicuous role played by 'books and tradition' in quattrocento Italy had to be glossed over. Even latter-day Burckhardtians found this difficult. As one has confessed: although 'the Renaissance...brought a refreshing breeze into Christendom through contact with naturalistic paganism...it was more concerned with book-learning than with the first-hand study of nature...'[111] By emphasizing pagan and naturalistic elements in antiquity and by pitting them against Christian dogma, the classical revival could be partly modernized – a tactic Burckhardt's followers exploited to the hilt: 'Into this oppressive atmosphere, the recovered classics of Greece and Rome came like a refreshing sea breeze. Poets and painters...were inspired with a new interest in natural phenomena...In these respects modernism was essentially a revival of antiquity brought about with the aid of the literature of antiquity.'[112] Even when presented as an anti-clerical device, however, the cult of antiquity retained certain imitative and bookish tendencies. Burckhardt was never entirely able to reconcile the backward-looking veneration of the ancients with the forward-looking 'genius of the Italian people' and he argued against assigning too much significance to the classical revival while deliberately relegating the topic to a subordinate position in his book.[113]

Quattrocento bookworms were embarrassing to Burckhardt, and he was not entirely successful in fitting them into his scheme. By calling into question their contribution to early-modern science, he set the terms for future debate. However much one might stress the achieve-

111 Wolf, *A History of Science, Technology* I, 8.
112 Wolf, *A History of Science, Technology* I, 2. This view of 'modernism' is essentially the same as that of Gay – as is suggested by the subtitle of the first volume of the two-volume work: *The Enlightenment: An Interpretation I – The Rise of Modern Paganism.*
113 See Burckhardt, *Civilization of the Renaissance* I, part III, 175 ff.

ments of Renaissance artists and engineers, explorers and algorists, the fact remained that dusty parchments and ancient authors were no less highly valued in Medicean Florence and Rome than they had been in medieval Oxford or Paris. Indeed there were fewer books to be 'enslaved' by in the earlier era and less strict observance of ancient grammatical rules. Before Gutenberg also, there were more keen-eyed observers and intrepid voyagers who never consulted any books at all.

The dichotomy 'books versus nature' could thus be turned against the Burckhardt thesis by medievalists – as much of Lynn Thorndike's work shows. Thorndike was just as fond of denouncing bondage to old books as Burckhardt had been. He was much less ambivalent than the Burckhardtians about the role played by humanism. He went so far in derogating Renaissance book-hunters that he described the recovery of Ptolemy's treatise on geography as a setback while noting that medieval explorers had already ventured well beyond the Greek oecumene. Ignoring the problem of distinguishing 'Cathay' from 'China' or of locating either on oddly assorted scribal maps, he even claimed that 'the thirteenth century knew China better than we knew it in the nineteenth century.'[114] On such points one might object that enthusiasm for medieval accomplishments was pressed too far.[115] But it was difficult to find fault with the contention that medieval mariners and merchants were just as observant and venturesome, often better travelled, and certainly less bookish than were the contemporaries of Petrarch and his successors. Similar arguments were framed by others who learned, from studying art history, that medieval craftsmen had often taken nature as their guide. The 'astonishingly life-like' renderings of plants and animals in the sketchbooks of artists serving Hohenzollern emperors or Dukes of Milan were not completely incompatible with Burckhardt's very elastic periodization scheme. However, images found in more distant places and times (such as the famous 'leaves of Southwell' or the Bury Saint Edmunds herbal) suggested that careful observation and recording of natural forms simply did not originate with the Italians of the Renaissance.[116]

---

114 Thorndike, *Science and Thought*, pp. 19–20.
115 On confusion as to whether China and Cathay were the same and on earlier difficulties regarding 'Sina and the Seres,' see Needham, *Science and Civilisation in China* I, chap. 7, (d) (2), pp. 168–70.
116 Pächt, 'Early Italian Nature Studies.' On Southwell carvings and the twelfth-century herbal, see especially pp. 29–30.

Accordingly, when Whitehead came to the point of discussing the 'final ingredient necessary for the rise of modern science,' he moved into territory that was entirely foreign to Burckhardt's scheme since it was first occupied by Benedictines and then by stonecutters who worked outside Italy before Giotto's day.

Gregory and Benedict were practical men with an eye for the importance of ordinary things...The alliance of science and technology by which learning is kept in contact with irreducible and stubborn facts owes much to the practical bent of early Benedictines...

The influence of this contact between the monasteries and the facts of nature showed itself first in art. The rise of Naturalism in the later Middle Ages was the entry into the European mind of the final ingredient necessary for the rise of science. It was the rise of interest in natural objects and natural occurrences for their own sake. The natural foliage of a district was sculptured in out of-the-way spots...every art exhibited a direct joy in the apprehension of the things which lie around us. The craftsmen who executed the late medieval sculpture, Giotto, Chaucer, Wordsworth, Walt Whitman... Robert Frost are all akin to each other in this respect. The simple immediate facts are the topics of interest, and these reappear in the thought of science as the irreducible stubborn facts...[117]

It is noteworthy that nothing is said, in this famous passage, about how the craftsman's keen interest in natural forms came to be shared by philosophers to the point of checking their propensity for logic-chopping. Not only is the gap between craftsmen and schoolmen left open; the distance that separated the views of medieval artisans from those of nineteenth-century romantic poets has been incautiously closed. An introduction to a recent survey suggests how this sets perspectives askew: 'Medieval artists and craftsmen who turned from books to nature are sometimes credited with being initiators of the scientific revolution.'[118] Wordsworth, Goethe and other literati did, indeed, turn 'from books to nature,' from 'gray' theories to 'green' leaves. But 'medieval artists and craftsmen' were not well equipped to do this. Few possessed books from which to turn; many had not learned how to read.

Be that as it may, Whitehead's much quoted passage does serve to demonstrate how keen-eyed observers who took 'nature as a guide' could be seen at work in Europe outside Italy and before the Renais-

[117] Whitehead, *Science and the Modern World*, p. 27.
[118] Marsak (ed.) *The Rise of Science in Relation to Society*, introduction, p. 1.

sance. With much of Burckhardt's initial argument taken over by the enemy camp, his latter-day defenders often turn his thesis upside down. They thus stress the difference between framing a scientific theory and simply experiencing nature in the raw. They downplay naive empiricism while stressing the retrieval of Alexandrian texts. Against the medievalists who now echo the master's first verdict that humanism did 'injury to the inductive investigation of nature,'[119] they assign positive value to a classical revival which enriched scientific literature as well as belles lettres. By emphasizing the advantages of studying Euclid and Archimedes (rather than the negative effect of repeating errors drawn from Pliny or Galen) and by stressing 'Pythagorean' or 'neo-Platonic' concern with mathematics, book-hunting and Greek studies could be seen as helpful. 'In the realm of science, the outcome of this looking backward was a big leap forward...'[120] Or, as another authority put it: 'Il faut reculer pour mieux sauter.'[121]

In celebrating the rebirth of Alexandrian science under the aegis of Renaissance editors, the latter-day Burckhardtians were themselves reviving doctrines held by an earlier school. For much the same emphasis on the Alexandrian revival had been characteristic of those Victorians who had pioneered in the history of science.[122] In the days of William Whewell, however, it was commonly assumed that the middle ages were dark as far as the 'exact sciences' were concerned.[123] Poets and artists might find the Gothic revival congenial; but nineteenth-century historians of science, still under the spell of the Royal Society, believed the cause of science was bound to languish whenever belief in ghosts and spirits was sustained.[124] They saw no reason to question the claims that were made in the prefaces of early printed editions where editors and publishers congratulated themselves on

119 Burckhardt, Civilization of the Renaissance II, 286. This somewhat grudging concession to Libri's Histoire des Sciences Mathématiques en Italie (1838) is frequently repeated.
120 Rosen, 'Renaissance Science as Seen by Burckhardt and his Successors,' p. 79.
121 Boas, Scientific Renaissance, p. 27.
122 Whewell's description of the dark and barren 'Stationary Period of Science' between ancient Greece and modern Europe, is noted by Wightman, Science and the Renaissance I, 5. See also A. R. Hall, 'On the Historical Singularity,' p. 203.
123 This view is still reasserted by some historians of mathematics in the present century. See e.g. reference to 'thousand-year stupor' by Dantzig, Number, p. 129, and Unguru, 'Witelo and Thirteenth century Mathematics.'
124 Of course this view has also retained supporters down to the present. That the medieval Christian Church was a 'chief obstacle' to science is asserted by Wolf, History of Science, Technology, I, 8 among others. As is noted below, despite his viewing humanism as a curse, Randall, 'Scientific Method in the School of Padua,' departs from medievalists such as Duhem because he stresses lay, anticlerical elements.

restoring noble disciplines after centuries of neglect. That nothing of consequence had occurred in the exact sciences between the days of Ptolemy and those of Regiomontanus could be taken for granted. Needless to say this is no longer the case. A respected authority can state quite flatly 'It can no longer be held that the Middle Ages was a period of scientific stagnation...'[125] Indeed Whewell's view has been vigorously assailed since the beginning of this century as a 'strange delusion.' 'The physicists of the sixteenth century were hailed as creators to whom the world owed the renaissance of the sciences. Very often they were only continuators and sometimes plagiarists.'[126]

Ever since Pierre Duhem's first volume appeared, more and more medieval commentaries and treatises have been uncovered showing that problems in 'exact sciences' were being tackled by medieval schoolmen by methods that came close to anticipating later innovations. In the eyes of Duhem and his successors, the Alexandrians had little need of being reborn. By encouraging continuous examination of Aristotle's physics, scholasticism had sown the seeds that were to flower in Western science, and the humanists did little save postpone fruitful results. Not only did their bookish revival point away from craft empiricism. Not only was it imbued with an élitist intellectual contempt for mechanical and manual work. It was also strongly biased against the exact sciences.

Many scholars now agree that 15th-century humanism...was an interruption in the development of science. The so-called 'revival of letters' deflected interest from matter to literary style and in turning back to Classical Antiquity, its devotees affected to ignore the scientific progress of the previous three centuries. The same absurd conceit that led the humanists to abuse... their immediate predecessors...also allowed them to borrow from the scholastics without acknowledgement...[127]

In hailing medieval contributions to the exact sciences, some authorities stress the condemnation of Aristotle on theological grounds, the role played by friars at Oxford and Paris and the diffusion of major scholastic commentaries to other centers of Dominican and Franciscan learning until finally, the long ripening seeds flowered in Galileo's physics. Others (notably Randall) stay closer to anti-clerical Italianate

---

125 Schmitt, 'Essay Review: A Fresh Look at Mechanics' I, 161.
126 Pierre Duhem, cited and tr. by Rosen, 'Renaissance Science,' p. 94, from Duhem's *Système* VII, 3–4. Similar views attacking the sixteenth-century editors' prefaces are in Thorndike, *Magic and Experimental Science*, pp. 332–4.   127 Crombie, *Augustine to Galileo*, pp. 268–9.

themes by stressing the role played by lay faculties of medicine and the movement of dissident Averroists to Padua. Whether they stress theologians or lay faculties, the anti-humanists agree that attacks on scholasticism and the graduate faculties at the universities rendered a serious disservice to science by deprecating the very groups who were developing the most promising lines of inquiry. Thus the debate over the rise of modern science has become a vehicle for propelling old battles between scholastics and humanists, graduate studies and under-graduate 'liberal arts.' Instead of helping to bridge the gap between our so-called 'two cultures,' historical scholarship in this field has done much to perpetuate old feuds.

Mathematics and astronomy were assiduously cultivated...and great things were being done when humanism ushered in the anthropocentric Renaissance and bid fair to crush all scientific interest in the world of nature.

Despite the popular legend to the contrary, for natural science, humanism was and has remained an almost unmitigated curse. Had it not centered the interests and energies of the best intellects upon the essentially unscientific... narrowly ethical classic Greeks and Romans, there is every possibility that a Galileo might have lived in the fourteenth century instead of the seventeenth, and that scientific investigation and discovery might have been three hundred years further advanced than they are now.[128]

Humanism was *almost* an unmitigated curse because there was one alleviating factor, namely the 'revival of Alexandrian mathematical science.' By acquainting investigators with the 'methods of mathematical analysis and synthesis of Archimedes,' Randall admitted, quattrocento Greek studies did supply a missing ingredient.[129] Yet later research showed that even this ingredient was not completely lacking before the Renaissance. As Marshall Clagett has made clear, Archimedes was not unknown to the schoolmen and was, indeed, translated into Latin by the very same Fleming who also made Aristotle available to Aquinas. According to Clagett, Archimedes played a 'modest but nevertheless important part in that thin tradition of Greek mathematics and physics that trickled down through the Middle Ages

---

[128] Randall, *The Making of the Modern Mind*, p. 212. See also passage in later rev. ed. (New York, 1940), 'by 1375 the genius of Descartes, Galileo and Copernicus had been anticipated' (p. 212).

[129] Randall, *Modern Mind* (rev. ed.), pp. 215; 217. See also Randall, 'Scientific Method in the School of Padua,' p. 179. According to Butterfield, *The Origins of Modern Science*, p. 58, 'the last pocket of the science of antiquity...recovered in time to be...a factor in the formation of our modern science' was 'the works of Archimedes, made generally available in translation in 1543.' Here, as elsewhere, a key issue is how to define 'generally available.'

into modern times.'[130] A difference remained, nevertheless, between a thin trickle and a full-blown revival. The most 'advanced' work on statics in the middle ages for example was composed without Archimedes' help.[131] Although William of Moerbeke's late thirteenth-century translations made most of the corpus available (in the very form that was printed later on),[132] the more sophisticated texts tended to go unread. They could not be exploited by 'medieval mathematicians who had a rather elementary knowledge of geometry.'[133] Mastery of 'the *more advanced elements* of Archimedes', as Duhem himself noted, continued to elude the grasp of the schoolmen. Until this mastery was achieved, the 'doctrines whose seeds had been planted by Oresme and Buridan' could not 'flower or bear fruit.'[134] In addition to mathematical tools, moreover, Duhem noted that observational instruments were also lacking.

Duhem's efforts to explain why 'scholastic physics could not pass beyond the boundary to which fourteenth century Parisians had brought it' suggested that other factors than the 'curse' of humanism might have been at work. The existence of this boundary, and the incapacity of the schoolmen to traverse it, has been acknowledged by many medievalists. 'After the great beginnings in the fourteenth century' Clagett comments 'one might expect a further development at Paris in the fifteenth century. Such does not appear to be the case... Thomas Bricot's discussion suffers in comparison with the pristine account of Buridan.'[135] Similarly Moody notes that the fourteenth-century scholastics had not used 'the new ideas they had worked out

---

130 Clagett, *Archimedes* I, 14.

131 Clagett and Moody (ed.) *The Medieval Science of Weights* refer to the failure of Jordanus to use Moerbeke's translation in their introduction (p. 10). They also note that sixteenth-century authors such as Cardano, Tartaglia, and Benedetti, seem to borrow theorems from Jordanus without acknowledging their debt and even while criticizing his work (p. 20).

132 According to Durand, 'Tradition and Innovation,' p. 45, the first printed editions (in 1503 and again in 1543) of Archimedes' work 'brazenly plagiarized' William of Moerbeke's text. Although accusations of plagiarism are common for the period, one may question its use before literary property rights were clearly fixed. At all events, Durand holds that Archimedes 'remained dormant' from Moerbeke's day until the sixteenth century.

133 Clagett, *Archimedes*, p. ix. It should be noted that their 'elementary knowledge of geometry' still put the thirteenth-century schoolmen well ahead of those of the eleventh century who had no knowledge of Euclid and could not figure out what Boethius meant when he referred to the interior angles of a triangle, and – after consulting Fulbert at Chartres – were still none the wiser. See Southern, *Making of the Middle Ages*, pp. 201–2.

134 Duhem, cited and tr. by Rosen, 'Renaissance Science,' p. 96 (from *Système* X, 45).

135 Clagett, *The Science of Mechanics in the Middle Ages*, p. 638. See also similar comments on 'decline 'and 'stagnation' reflected in a treatise by Blasius of Parma written around 1400 in Clagett and Moody, *Medieval Science of Weights*, p. 20.

for special cases' to 'build a new science that would replace Aristotelian physics and cosmology...'[136] Even Crombie observes that 'there was no continuous mathematical tradition comparable with that in logic.'[137] Such admissions offered the latter-day Burckhardtians at least one issue they could still exploit with some success.

(b) The shortcomings of medieval science – suggestions for a new approach

Much as the difference between transitory, limited revivals and a permanent total Renaissance was stressed by Panofsky, so too the difference between partial anticipations and actual breakthrough is underlined by those who regard Burckhardt's scheme as useful for the history of science.

Who extended the use of alphabetic letters after Jordanus Nemorarius introduced them to replace numbers in arithmetical calculations? Who developed Oresme's graphs? Why did the magnificent work of Frederick II on ornithology or of Peter the Stranger on the magnet, or of Theodore of Freiburg on the rainbow, find no worthy successor?[138]

In trying to explain why so many promising starts petered out, Rosen agrees with Duhem that medieval investigators were handicapped by the absence of certain essential pieces of equipment – such as mathematical skills and observational instruments. He also approves of Duhem's pointing to a craze for the dialectic as a major pitfall. Being trained to win 'victory in debate' rather than to 'search for the truth' deflected the talents of the schoolmen even before humanists had aroused interest in belles lettres.[139] Perhaps the most important obstacle of all, in Rosen's view, was the failure to distinguish between problems posed by falling angels and those posed by falling stones. Here the diagnosis departs sharply from that of Duhem's school by suggesting that theological concerns sidetracked medieval science from the start.[140]

---

136 Moody, 'Galileo and his Precursors,' p. 42.
137 Crombie, *Augustine to Galileo*, p. 269.
138 Rosen, 'Renaissance Science,' p. 95.
139 Rosen, 'Renaissance Science,' pp. 94–7. Duhem's objection to oral disputation (cited by Rosen from *Système* VII, 621–2) has been repeated by Dijksterhuis. See discussion, p. 506, below.
140 Rosen, 'Renaissance Science,' pp. 94–5. The extent to which mental energy was expended on describing the movements made by angels or the increase and decrease in the intensity of love seems to be brought out more clearly by Rosen than by other authorities, who often leave the supernatural context of much medieval speculation out of their accounts.

When confronted by the extreme verdict that 'humanism' was an 'unmitigated curse' for Western science, it is perhaps necessary to redress the balance by suggesting that the enthronement of theology was not an unmixed blessing. But it also seems that this particular debate has been conducted in a way that brings all kinds of prejudice into play. As long as the limitations imposed by the conditions of scribal culture go unnoted, less neutral agencies will go on being blamed. Efforts to account for the gap between medieval anticipations and seventeenth-century fulfillment seem to have reached the point where old debates are being perpetuated with diminishing returns.

The humanists turned the much praised subtle doctor of the late thirteenth century (Duns Scotus) into the nursery Dunce of the sixteenth. Modern historians, admiring the ingenuity of fourteenth-century mathematics and physics, deplore this antipathy and regard humanist worship of antiquity as having been harmful to the smooth advance of science. But however high the achievements of the fourteenth-century philosophers in certain directions, some other ingredient was needed to stimulate the development of modern science...the medieval inspiration was at a low ebb by the beginning of the fifteenth century and the Greek inspiration had, at the moment more to offer.[141]

If one is persuaded that a 'smooth advance of science' had not been possible before the advent of printing, then one may avoid assigning humanism too much credit as well as too much blame. To skip over the Latin–Arabic tradition and go more directly to the Greek sources probably did prove helpful for students of Euclid, Archimedes or Appollonius.[142] But the 'Greek inspiration' although important, was by no means the only significant ingredient that early printers supplied. The Greeks, for example, had no words for the ciphers and zeros that came via Moslem routes. The discarding of Roman numerals was an anti-classical act. The mixture of many ingredients was in itself a new source of inspiration and there were also significant changes in the way the mixture could be imbibed. By paying more attention to the en-richment of technical literature that came after printing, and by appreciating the widened range of materials that could be surveyed at one time, it might be possible to accommodate conflicting claims made

---

[141] Boas, *Scientific Renaissance*, p. 27.

[142] For a detailed, thoroughly documented discussion of the humanist retrieval of Greek mathe-matical texts in Italy see Rose, 'Humanist Culture and Renaissance Mathematics.' (A useful bibliography bearing on the debate is given in footnotes 2 and 3, pp. 46–7.)

for rival schools and to view the shortcomings of earlier scholars in a more sympathetic light.

'It was not medieval mathematicians who became oblivious of Archimedes' rule, but it was modern historians who became oblivious of medieval mathematicians' remarks a scholar who has uncovered evidence that a sophisticated mathematical tool (in the form of a theory of decimal fractions) was developed by Bonfils in the fourteenth century.[143] In fact, this tool, although invented, was never given to anyone to use. 'The theory was jotted down on a piece of paper in Hebrew, and put away. There it remained buried, for about six centuries. The old Hebrew copyist failed to grasp its meaning...Bonfils' invention exercised no influence on his contemporaries or successors...'[144] If we are trying to understand 'the rise of modern science' should we begin with Bonfils' well-kept fourteenth-century secret or Simon Stevin's well-advertised sixteenth-century work? Both started from more or less the same position – with a retrieval of Alexandrian texts. Bonfils passed nothing on to Stevin. Stevin, however, passed a great deal on to us.[145] Much the same problem is posed by Thorndike when he chides Dreyer and others for cutting Copernicus and Tycho off from their 'medieval background.' He points to a thirteenth-century treatise by Campanus of Novara arguing in favor of reducing the number of 'spheres' – a treatise that Dreyer failed to mention. Neither Copernicus nor Tycho knew of this treatise, but Thorndike believes that Dreyer, as a modern historian, ought to take 'a broader view.'[146]

Doubtless, it is useful to note that Copernicus was not the first Christian astronomer who sought to simplify the Ptolemaic scheme and that parsimony was valued by mathematical astronomers even before 'Occam's razor' had been described.[147] Nevertheless, Thorn-

---

[143] Gandz, 'The Invention of the Decimal Fractions,' p. 25. (Bonfils is better known for contributing a set of astronomical tables in his effort to help determine the Jewish calendar.)

[144] Gandz, 'The Invention of the Decimal Fractions,' p. 31.

[145] On Stevin's work, see Sarton, 'Simon Stevin of Bruges (1548–1620)'; and 'The First Explanation of Decimal Fractions and Measures (1585).' Also Dijksterhuis, *Simon Stevin*, and Struik, 'Mathematics in the Netherlands.'

[146] Thorndike, *Magic and Experimental Science*, pp. 407–8.

[147] That Copernicus' desire for simplicity is often overplayed to the point of falsifying the number of epicycles required by Ptolemaic astronomers is persuasively argued by Robert Palter, 'An Approach to the History of Early Astronomy.' When discussing the issue, the outlook of professional astronomers needs to be distinguished from that of the layman baffled by *any* sophisticated reckoning scheme as reflected in the oft-cited remark of the medieval king: When the complexity of drawing up tables was explained to King Alfonso, 'he remarked that it was too bad, God had failed to consult him when creating the universe.' (See Toulmin and Goodfield, *The Fabric of the Heavens*, p. 179; Thomas Kuhn, *Structure*, p. 69.)

dike's 'broader view' is too often ungenerous to sixteenth-century scientists who are seen as 'strangely deluded' because they failed to acknowledge medieval precursors whose treatises are now accessible to us but were not to them. Any adequate account of Copernicus' or Tycho's 'medieval background' must take into consideration that we now see more of the 'thin trickle' from Alexandria than did the generations before us. Sixteenth-century investigators did not have our capacity to 'search the literature.' They lacked the resources of a knowledge industry developed after four or more centuries of print. When they claimed to be 'restoring an art' or 'reviving a discipline' buried since Alexandrian days, they were not necessarily indulging an 'absurd conceit.'[148] They were often telling the truth as they saw it. The point is that they were bound to see things differently from us. To take a really 'broad view' one has to keep this difference in viewpoints constantly in mind. The technical literature inherited by sixteenth-century virtuosi was subject to discontinuities which have now been filled in. Insofar as modern historians are absent-minded on this point, they are 'strangely deluded' themselves.

In calling for more caution when extrapolating continuous lines between medieval 'precursors' and early-modern pioneers, I may seem to be simply repeating what others have already said. The fallacy of overestimating early-modern erudition has often been underscored. For example, Rosen questions the 'allegedly continuous development of modern mechanics from the thirteenth century on' on the grounds that many medieval solutions which are now seen as anticipations of Galileo's work were probably unknown to Galileo.

Galileo did not possess Duhem's enormous erudition. He was not an assiduous reader, preferring to consult what he liked to call the book of Nature ...he felt little sympathy for the long-winded theological speculations, mythological allusions and autobiographical meanderings in which Kepler concealed his genuine achievement.[149]

As this citation shows, although others also object to tracing continuous lines, they usually do so without reference to the state of communications, and with the dichotomy 'books versus nature' featured prominently instead. Admittedly this dichotomy did loom large in Galileo's writings. He repeatedly urged that the book of nature was more

[148] Crombie, *Augustine to Galileo*, p. 269.
[149] Rosen, 'Renaissance Science,' p. 88.

trustworthy than the books of Aristotle and told his readers to turn their gaze away from pictures printed on paper to look at the real world instead.[150] With the advantage of hindsight, it is easy to understand his position and hard not to share it as well. Now that we know they were wrong, it is difficult to sympathize with those stubborn professors who seemed to trust Aristotle and Galen more than their own eyes. We are more likely to cheer on those bolder spirits who behaved like Paracelsus when he denounced Galen, burned Avicenna, and described the human body as the only trustworthy book.

Nevertheless, one must also consider that the destruction of ancient Greek and Arabic medical texts would have meant the onset of a new dark age for medieval faculties of medicine. It was not until after Avicenna's *Canon* had been secured by print that the act of discarding it could be taken as an advance. The publication of certain texts by Galen, far from perpetuating conventional views, broke new ground in the early sixteenth century. When a sixteenth-century anatomist stated that 'one ought to trust one's own eyes rather than anatomical books,' he may have been dutifully quoting from Galen himself.[151] To have burned any of Archimedes' texts, moreover, would at no point have been helpful to the budding science of mechanics. With his access to Archimedes safely secured, Galileo may have saved time by ignoring solutions buried amid 'errors and obscurities' in medieval Latin texts. But the case of Archimedes shows that reading the book of nature and studying ancient texts were by no means incompatible. And, of course, the same point applies to reading Apollonius' work on conic sections or plowing through Kepler's turgid prose. When it came to planetary astronomy, had he been as assiduous about studying certain texts as he was in training his telescope on the night skies, Galileo might have been spared some frustrating struggles with

[150] See e.g. citation in Garin, *Science and Civic Life*, p. 127. Galileo's instructions recall ancient warnings based on the corruption of hand-copied images. See pp. 485–6 above.

[151] The new awareness Vesalius achieved by careful study of each of Galen's works is stressed by Edwin Clarke, review, *Medical History* (1964), pp. 380–3. That a sixteenth-century anatomist was often merely repeating Galen's dictum when writing that 'he intended to trust his own eyes rather than books' is noted by Gernot Rath, 'Charles Estienne,' pp. 354–9. Rath also notes the fascinating problem presented by the 'rete mirabile' – a network of vessels at the base of the brain (actually found in cattle but not in man) which was described by Galen. Many Renaissance anatomists saw this 'rete' with their own eyes after dissecting human cadavers or so they said. The habit of keeping a head of an ox or lamb on hand when human dissection occurred in order to demonstrate certain arteries more clearly, helped to confuse matters. (See Boas, *Scientific Renaissance*, pp. 142–3 n.) At all events, the example shows why seeing 'with one's own eyes' is not sufficient to establish a scientific theory.

celestial mechanics.[152] Moreover, any seventeenth-century reader who took his advice too much to heart and turned away from all 'pictures printed on paper' would have lost track of all the new findings that were set forth on the sky maps, sea charts and great atlases of the day.[153]

As these comments suggest, when too much weight is placed on the antinomy: books versus nature, the crucial issue of access to technical literature is likely to be concealed. The importance of the issue is suggested by the fact that most of the great scientists of antiquity had access to the greatest libraries of antiquity. Galen of Pergamum was the foremost teacher of Vesalius, as Ptolemy of Alexandria was of Copernicus. Alexandrian achievements did not get surpassed until printing made it possible to put the 'world on paper' for all armchair travellers to see. Until the advent of printing, recovering and preserving what had been known to the ancients had to take precedence over any other task, and the chief function of a given graduate faculty was to serve as the custodian of a particular corpus of inherited texts.

Why these fourteenth-century scholastics did not exploit the new ideas they had worked out for special cases and build a new science that would replace Aristotelian physics and cosmology may well be asked. I would suggest that, as teachers in universities whose philosophical curriculum was built out of the books of Aristotle, they had neither opportunity nor motivation to overhaul; their job was to make the best sense they could out of their textbooks, not to abolish them.[154]

Insofar as they were chiefly responsible for preserving and transmitting inherited texts, natural philosophers were in much the same position as professors of the law faculties during the middle ages. As Butterfield puts it, they were 'for the most part...only playing on the margins' of Aristotle's system.[155] Much as generations of glossators and post-glossators played variations on themes set forth in the *Corpus Juris*, so too did commentators on Aristotle's physics spin off in certain new directions. In both instances, texts were reinterpreted under the

---

152 That Galileo was alerted to Kepler's theory of elliptical orbits as early as 1612 but that he probably found Kepler's unsystematic clumsy presentation posed unsurmountable difficulties, is suggested by Father Russell. See Russell, 'Kepler's Laws of Planetary Motion, 1609-1666,' p. 6.
153 Two recent publications issued by the Theatrum Orbis Terrarum in Amsterdam have cogent titles: de Vrij, *The World on Paper* (a descriptive catalogue of cartographical material published in seventeenth-century Amsterdam) and Koeman, *The Sea on Paper*.
154 Moody, 'Galileo and his Precursors,' p. 42.
155 Butterfield, *Origins of Modern Science*, p. 58.

THE BOOK OF NATURE TRANSFORMED

impact of new circumstances and currents of thought. Whatever new paths were opened up in natural philosophy (as in law), however, the professors were at no time placed in a position where it would be feasible to discard rather than to explicate the corpus of inherited texts.

contrary to widely accepted opinion, there was no such thing as a fourteenth-century science of mechanics in the sense of a general theory of local motion applicable throughout nature and based on a few unified principles. By searching the literature of late medieval physics for just those ideas...that turned out, three centuries later, to be important...one can construct... a medieval science of mechanics that *appears* to form a coherent whole and to be built on new foundations replacing those of Aristotle's physics. But this is an illusion, and an anachronistic fiction, which we are able to construct only because Galileo and Newton gave us the pattern by which to select the right pieces and put them together...[156]

To imply, as does Randall, that fourteenth-century graduate faculties were on the verge of a 'breakthrough' such as the one which occurred in Galileo's day is to ignore all the limits imposed on the circulation of technical literature as long as hand-copying prevailed. If promising beginnings traced in manuscripts seemed to peter out with negligible results, if significant ancient work 'lay dormant' as did Archimedes' more difficult treatises, the conditions of scribal culture ought to receive at least some share of the blame. The many defects that plagued medieval investigations: a low level of mathematical skills, an absence of observational instruments, a tendency toward 'unbridled speculation' and so forth – may also be partly attributed to the state of communications.

It seems significant that Crombie refers to 'the medieval predicament of intellectual aspiration failing to get into communication with practical demand' and to 'an incomplete dialogue between theoretical concepts and practical quantifying procedures.'[157] Until print transformed conditions governing communication and dialogue, this kind of predicament was likely to persist. Thus 'theoretical concepts' could not make 'contact with the data of observation' until it became possible to publish 'open letters' and take full advantage of reports sent from field trips by incorporating new data in updated editions of charts, maps and texts. Similarly instrument-makers had few incentives

[156] Moody, 'Galileo and his Precursors,' pp. 42–3.
[157] Crombie, 'Quantification in Medieval Physics,' pp. 158–9.

to make inventions known until new forms of publicity brought patronage and profits to their door.[158]

Dr. Crombie notes that the men he is considering made little contribution to the permanent body of scientific knowledge and that their actual researches are absurdly inadequate to the notions of scientific method they ostensibly entertained.

Now I find this discrepancy between alleged conception and actual performance puzzling...Dr. Crombie's only explanation...is that 'something seems to have kept the gaze [of the medieval thinkers] turned in a direction different from that which seventeenth-century science has taught us to seem obvious...'[159]

Given the difference between a sequence of corrupted copies and a sequence of improved editions of a given reference work, one might expect that scribal scholars would look in a 'different direction' from virtuosi who lived after printing. As long as energies were bent toward retrieval and preservation, little could be spared for moving ahead with new research. Careful observations once set down in writing were subject to loss or erosion over time. The feats of data-collection achieved at Alexandria represented the outermost limits of what successive generations could achieve. The recovery of Ptolemy's astronomy and later, of his geography, were naturally regarded as constituting significant advance.

Untenable and long refuted theories were revived time after time, to be refuted and rejected once again; in general this tended to foster a mental attitude which looked to the past rather than to the future and which, on the grounds that scientific truths had all been known in the past and that the only problem was to rediscover them, led investigators in precisely the wrong direction. They did not realize that science is always a thing of the future.[160]

But science was not 'always a thing of the future.' To scholars struggling over the meaning of Euclid's theorems or receiving Latin translations of the *Almagest* with gratitude, science was very much a thing of the past. Even a century-old treatise might be better than one newly composed, as an historian of medieval optics suggests.

The main optical activity of the fourteenth century was copying Pecham's

---

[158] For further discussion and examples, see p. 241, volume I above and pp. 556 ff. below.
[159] Nagel, comment in *Critical Problems* (ed. Clagett), pp. 153–4.
[160] Dijksterhuis, *The Mechanization of the World Picture*, p. 167, section II, no. 98.

Perspectiva Communis...We are no closer to the proper theory of pinhole images at the end of the fourteenth century; indeed we are possibly farther away...the thirteenth was not only clearer than the fourteenth on the problem to be solved, it was also clearer on the proper terms of the solution.[161]

In the same vein it seems unfair to complain of 'unbridled speculation' without pausing longer over the difficulty of preserving precise data against which theorizing could be checked. Similarly, the 'prominent place which oral disputation occupied in...teaching' needs to be related to the problems of providing students with books. Among other 'obstacles in the way of an unprejudiced study of nature,' Dijksterhuis singles out 'the immoderate application of an idea sound in itself, namely the stimulating and clarifying effect of an oral exchange of views.' Unfortunately, he says, echoing Duhem, oral exchange was overdone and thus

produced the reverse of the effect aimed at. The numerous disputes...on the success of which the student's career depended, inevitably resulted in arguments being conducted for the sake...of defeating one's opponents...the inquiry after truth becoming of secondary importance. In general the medieval method of university teaching had the serious disadvantage of appealing too much to human vanity...young scholars who wished for promotion had to shine in debate...[162]

It is difficult to ascertain when, if ever, scientists or academics generally ceased to engage in competitive displays of virtuosity, lost their propensity for polemics and became pure and disinterested seekers after truth. It is easier to determine when heavy reliance on verbal argument, unwritten recipes and mnemonic aids were reduced, and young scholars who were not gifted in verbal disputation could still 'shine' as authors of treatises. After the advent of printing, priority struggles could replace 'dialectical orgies' as the chief outlet for competitive drives.[163] The cause of science gained by this substitution, even if appeals to human vanity were not diminished. At all events, dependence on oral exchange was not an 'effect that anyone aimed at' during the fourteenth century nor was it peculiar to the schoolmen. It was shaped by material conditions that no one group of scholars controlled. By making the thin and unreliable flow of technical literature

---

161 Lindberg, 'The Theory of Pinhole Images in the 14th Century,' pp. 299; 323.
162 Dijksterhuis, *Mechanization of the World Picture*, pp. 167–8, section II, no. 99.
163 On priority struggles, see pioneering studies by Merton, collected in *The Sociology of Science*.

more responsible for the frail and often stunted character of medieval science, one might be less inclined to blame other scapegoats. Mixed motives could be more evenly distributed. The role played by theology on one hand and humanism on the other could be viewed with more equanimity and perhaps one could obtain agreement that neither served Western science as an unmixed blessing or as an unmitigated curse.

In suggesting that the advent of printing ought to figure much more prominently when setting the stage for the scientific revolutions of the early-modern era, I am not being entirely unconventional. Similar views have been set forth before – emphatically and repeatedly by the late George Sarton.

The discovery of printing was one of the great turning-points in the history of mankind, and it was of special importance for the history of science. It changed the very warp and woof of history, for it replaced precarious forms of tradition (oral and manuscript) by one that was stable, secure, and lasting; it is as if mankind had suddenly obtained a trustworthy memory instead of one that was fickle and deceitful.[164]

Although often overlooked by other authorities, Sarton's later writings convey a sense of full awareness of the importance of printing for the history of science. Unlike either medievalists or Burckhardtians, Sarton firmly seized on the 'double invention of printing from movable type and engraving from copper plates' as an epoch-making event.[165] He pointed to the 'transmutation of values' the new technology entailed, and even went so far (too far in my opinion) as to state that 'the main event separating the period we call Renaissance from the Middle Ages was the invention of printing.'[166]

These bold assertions appear in at least three works by Sarton, and he is a founding father of the history of science. Yet they have not been taken up by others nor provoked sufficient controversy to attract attention in review articles. This may be partly because they take the form of scattered aperçus and glancing references which stop short of sustained discussion. More important, Sarton's strong positive assertions are counterbalanced by equally strong negative ones expressed in passages which underline 'the extraordinary incuriosity or inertia' of

[164] Sarton, Six Wings, p. 3.
[165] Sarton, Six Wings, pp. 116; 119.
[166] Sarton, Appreciation, p. xi; see also on p. 89; 'The age of incunabula was the infancy of the Renaissance itself.' As noted above (p. 171, volume 1), to follow this suggestion would simply compound the confusion that has already surrounded the much used term.

early printers and the 'retrogressive' character of incunabula.[167] These passages reflect Sarton's repeated surprise at the way early printers perpetuated literary trends followed by copyists and overlooked new discoveries made by the *avant-garde* of the day. At one point, he refers to the 'ambivalent' effects of typography, which 'helped the birth and diffusion of new ideas but also gave a new lease on life to the old ones.'[168] His own ambivalence about the 'great turning point' was pronounced. One gains the impression of too high expectations being deflated over and over again.

One would have thought the breath-taking discoveries of the navigators... would have turned attention from the little books of men to the great book of Nature but this happened much less often than one might expect. More weight was given to Strabon's words than to those of Columbus...and the expedition of the Argonauts was considered more interesting than Magellan's.[169]

Such passages show that Sarton also undermined his positive thesis by endorsing the views of the extreme empiricist and thus discounting the significance of technical literature.[170] If science could advance only when the 'little books of men' were set aside; if 'science could not be investigated properly in any book' except the metaphorical 'great book of Nature,'[171] then shifts affecting real quartos and octavos could not be made to seem significant. In his earlier writings, at all events, the negative thesis that printing contributed to cultural inertia is so prominent, it is often (erroneously) cited as the only view of the impact of print Sarton had.

(c) *Corrupted materials duplicated: the illusion of cultural lag*

As Sarton's mixed verdict on the 'ambivalent' effects of typography may suggest, the distracting effect of debates over Burckhardt is not the only reason why the importance of printing is discounted by historians of science. The inferior quality of the materials that were duplicated by

---

[167] Sarton, *Appreciation*, p. 92; *Six Wings*, pp. 27; 246, n. 14. As noted above (n. 2) the 'retrogressive character' of incunabula was first set forth by Sarton in his 1938 *Osiris* article on 'Scientific Literature' which was, in turn, inspired by the pioneering study by Klebs, 'Incunabula Scientifica et Medica.' The same view was again asserted in a 1943 article: 'The Study of Early Scientific Textbooks.'   [168] Sarton, *Appreciation*, p. 168.

[169] Sarton, *Six Wings*, p. 6.

[170] See reference in *Appreciation*, p. 27, to physicians in Ferrara whose 'eyes were open' not just to 'Greek and Latin books in the library' but to 'the book of nature.' This passage also includes admiring references to the views of Paracelsus.   [171] Sarton, *Appreciation*, p. 5.

many early printers also has to be considered. It is true that a few scholar–printers (such as Oporinus) worked closely with experts in several fields and there were some scientist–printers (such as Regiomontanus or Charles Estienne) who published innovative works themselves. In such cases, publication programs could and did take advantage of special technical expertise and thus contributed directly, as Sarton suggested, to 'the birth and diffusion of new ideas.' But most early printers and publishers simply duplicated somewhat indiscriminately whatever manuscript materials were already being circulated by stationers and scribes. They also began to put together their own collections of prophecies and prognostications and sought to exploit the appeal of the most sensational 'pseudo-science' – much as do tabloid journals even now. Thus a great deal of scientifically 'worthless' material was duplicated and gained a wide circulation during the first century of print. Even while much 'useless' stuff got printed in numerous editions; many treatises, now judged to be of unusual scientific value, suffered a fate similar to Leonardo's notebooks and 'circulated or remained stagnant' in manuscript form.[172] Because of his early death, some of Regiomontanus' work may have reached Copernicus in this form;[173] while Copernicus' own delayed appearance in print is often cited by those who caution us against exaggerating the positive function performed by the new medium. 'Scientific advance was not dependent on the printed word, indeed many scientists like Copernicus withheld their work from the press for many years...'[174]

Once his work did get printed, moreover, Copernicus' views were still slow to spread. Arthur Koestler has described *De Revolutionibus* as 'an all-time worst-seller' and scolds its author for failing to exploit publicity techniques.[175] One need not agree with Koestler in order to

[172] See Thorndike, *Magic and Experimental Science*, p. 6. In my view the 'stagnation' of innovative works in manuscript form during the sixteenth century is overplayed by Thorndike. The intervals between death and posthumous publication that he cites are not long – at least compared to those experienced by the Alexandrians. The terms 'worthless' and 'useless' have been put in quotes to convey the opinion of authorities, such as Thorndike. In my view the so-called 'rubbish' ought to be re-evaluated along the lines of analysis that anthropologists have developed.

[173] This possibility should not be exaggerated. Copernicus did *not* see a most important treatise by Regiomontanus until 1539, precisely because it remained in manuscript form, from the 1470s to the 1530s. (See p. 591 below.)

[174] Boas, *Scientific Renaissance*, p. 30. In a previous paragraph on 'printing and science' (pp. 29–30), Boas raises several pertinent issues.

[175] Koestler, *The Sleepwalkers*, p. 191. For sharp criticism of Koestler's ill-founded judgment, see Rosen, 'Biography of Copernicus,' *Three Copernican Treatises*, pp. 406–7. See also discussion in chap. 7, below.

acknowledge that printers were not mobilized by Latin-writing professional astronomers as they were by religious reformers. Evangelism came more naturally to clerics who inherited an apostolic tradition than to mathematicians who harked back to Pythagoras and temple scribes.[176] As agents of diffusion, at all events, printers snarled the periodization schemes of modern historians. For they did much in the second half of the sixteenth century to familiarize readers with the world-picture that emerged in Dante's era. It is the medieval 'Sphaera' of 'Sacrobosco' and not the *De Revolutionibus* (or the *Almagest*, for that matter) that proved 'supremely popular' and ran through hundreds of editions down to 1600 and beyond.[177]

As noted earlier, it is a mistake to imagine that 'medieval world pictures' merely 'survived' in Elizabethan times. Thanks to printers and engravers, Ptolemaic models of the movement of planets and distribution of land masses, along with Aristotle's cosmological schemes, were more often graphically conveyed and were much more widely distributed to sixteenth-century poets and playwrights than they had been to minstrels and mummers of Dante's own day. Insofar as we are likely when using the term to envisage the 'exactly repeatable' image that our textbooks contain, 'medieval' is a misleading adjective. Even the familiar geocentric diagram with its concentric circles representing celestial and infernal regions – although it had been sketched in medieval manuscripts – was not really fixed as a uniform world picture until post-medieval times.[178] Be that as it may, the reproduction of pre-Columbian maps beyond the completion of Magellan's voyages, and the duplication of pre-Copernican schemes down to Newton's day casts doubt on the proposition that printing 'hastened the trans-

---

[176] A contrast between the publicity assigned Christian themes and the secrecy that surrounded techniques and craft 'mysteries' is discussed in chap. 3, volume I, above. See pp. 270.

[177] On the *Sphaera Mundi* by 'Sacrobosco' (sometimes called John of Holywood), see Thorndike (ed. and tr.), *The Sphere of Sacrobosco and Its Commentators*, introduction. Rosen, review of Thorndike's edition, *Isis* (1949), pp. 257–64, and entry no. 70 in Stillwell, *Awakening Interest*, p. 22. According to Johnson, 'Astronomical Textbooks in the Sixteenth Century,' pp. 293–4, 'There can be no complete census of editions of this supremely popular manual' because new versions 'are constantly turning up.' First printed in Venice in 1472, at least thirty editions were turned out before 1501 and at least 200 by 1600. As is noted below (p. 517) the 'Sphaera' like 'Ptolemy' became a vehicle for new commentaries and new data often carried in the form of appendices, supplements, etc.

[178] See reference to Tillyard, p. 79, volume I, above. The misleading character of most modern diagrams depicting the so-called 'Ptolemaic system' is stressed by Hanson, 'The Copernican Disturbance and the Keplerian Revolution.' For description of degeneration of scribal diagrams see Van der Tak, 'Calcidius' Illustration of the Astronomy of Heracleides of Pontus,' *Mnemosyne* (1972).

mission of the new discoveries,' and leads most authorities to argue that the contrary was the case.[179] Some even argue that early printers initially limited, rather than extended, literary resources available to professional élites, because they duplicated such a small and inferior sample of extant fifteenth-century manuscripts.

Printing did not...in the first instance alter the cultural background of Europe. In fact...it may have initially limited it. Febvre and Martin have pointed out that the expense involved...made selection inevitable, so that although more copies of a given text were available, the range of texts was narrower and reflected the judgement of the printer-publisher.[180]

But manuscript books did not become less available simply because not all of them got into print at once. 'The printed book-trade did not immediately displace the ms. trade, but was simply added to it... The average library, whether public or private, contained mss. as well as printed books...a doctor might have one treatise of Aristotle in printed form and another in ms. form.'[181] However undiscriminating early printers may have been, they did not subtract from existing book supplies. They never narrowed, but continuously enlarged, the range of titles available in a given library.[182]

Perhaps printing failed to 'speed up' the adoption of 'new' theories, as Febvre and Martin assert. It is certainly difficult to measure acceleration (or even determine novelty), as one must do in order to test any proposition relating to relative speeds before and after print. (How 'rapidly' did manuscripts transmit news of Viking landfalls or theories of pinhole images? Should Ptolemy's geography be considered new or old in the 1420s?) It may be less troublesome to consider the rejection of old theories than the adoption of new ones. Perhaps we may agree that printing did 'speed up' the downfall of Ptolemaic astronomy, Galenic anatomy and Aristotelian physics. Given the authority exerted by Ptolemy's 'Great Composition' for more than a thousand years, surely the vitality of the *Almagest* in printed form is relatively short-lived. Much the same thing could be said of Galen's work on anatomy and embryology or of Aristotle's natural philosophy. The habit of citing medieval recensions and commentaries such as Sacrobosco's

---

[179] Hellman, 'Science in the Renaissance', p. 186; Wightman, *Science and the Renaissance* I, 70; and Febvre and Martin, *L'Apparition*, p. 148.

[180] McLean, *Humanism and the Rise of Science*, p. 22.   [181] Sarton, *Appreciation*, p. 4.

[182] Stillwell, *Awakening Interest in Science*, pp. ix–x comments on vast backlog made available by early printers.

Sphaera or Mondino's *Anatomia* as if they were independent compositions, ought not to be taken as a sign that Alexandrian works were at any time outmoded or surpassed. Although much of the *Sphaera* was not based directly on Ptolemy, for example, most of it did derive from Arabic recensions of Ptolemy's great work. It is not entirely correct to say its author 'slavishly copied an elementary Arabic treatise' since he did draw on more than one Arab treatise and even drew on Martianus Capella as well. Nevertheless, where the author departed from copying others, it was usually to fall into error on his own (often by revealing his 'pitiful ignorance of Greek').[183] Oddly enough, the same authority who describes early printed maps as retrogressive because bound by Ptolemaic conventions also describes this inferior medieval recension as one of the 'most useful books of all time'.[184] The *Sphaera* may offer valid evidence that the sphericity of the earth was known to the schoolmen well before the age of Columbus. But the superior technical expertise of the Alexandrians, who were ultimately responsible for this knowledge, must be kept in mind.

It is also important to note that during the later middle ages, the effect of an astronomical text teaching that the world was round was *not* reinforced by various scribal mappae mundi and crude, stylized pictograms, which probably conveyed to 'the average uncritical copyist or student' 'a flat disk-shaped' image of the earth.[185] According to Bagrow, printing extended the life of the T-O diagram well into the sixteenth century.[186] In the hands of copyists, however, this diagram seemed to have an indefinitely long lease on life. How many armchair travellers (before the sixteenth century) had a chance to see anything else?

The mappae mundi survived for longer than might have been expected. Competent portolani or coastal charts exist from the end of the thirteenth century and probably existed even earlier, but though these might have

183 See comment on John of Holywood who 'slavishly copied an elementary Arabic treatise,' in Thomas Kuhn, *Copernican Revolution*, p. 123. Comment on ignorance of Greek comes from Rosen's review of Thorndike's edition of Sacrobosco's work, p. 259. See also remarks on Campanus of Novara's *Theorica Planetarum*: 'When Campanus does produce an original argument, it can be a singularly poor one,' Benjamin and Toomer, *Campanus of Novara*, p. 25.
184 Penrose, *Travel and Discovery*, p. 12.
185 Durand, *Vienna-Klosterneuberg Map-Corpus*, p. 18. See also, Oakeshott, 'Some Classical and Medieval Ideas in Renaissance Cosmography,' p. 248 where ignorance of spherical theories among late medieval literati and many scribal illuminators is noted. Additional data is offered in Penrose, *Travel and Discovery*, p. 25; Orr, *Dante and the Early Astronomers*, pp. 224-5 and Skelton, *Explorer's Maps*, fig. 3.   186 Bagrow, *History of Cartography* p. 91.

been useful to mariners, it did not follow that the learned would consent to take notice of them.[187]

How could the learned 'consent to take notice' of works that were forever kept out of their sight? Freshly drawn charts were no more immune to degradation by copying than any other scribal work. To be useful to a large number of scattered armchair travellers, maps had to be copied many times. Even portolani became stereotyped and increasingly less useful when subjected to repeated duplication.

As these remarks suggest, the average output of early printers can be described as retrogressive only when the materials they inherited from copyists are ignored. The output of copyists *is* usually ignored when developments are traced from the early middle ages onward. We are encouraged to move from one fresh composition to another – from one newly retrieved ancient masterpiece to another – until the age of Gutenberg arrives. The printer is expected to take over where culture heroes selected by hindsight – the most innovative thinker, learned scholar, or sophisticated draughtsman (as presently defined) – left off. Not surprisingly he falls short of these high expectations. In most cases he took over from the stationer and the 'slavish copyist' who handled materials which were in steady demand. The most useful and much used reference works were not only likely to be corrupted, but were also conveyed without title pages to help place or date them. They came to early printers in a state of disarray.

The Middle Ages is supposed to be a period of more or less complete stagnation. 'Progress' is thought to be solely a modern achievement. But could anyone put Isidore of Seville's *Etymologies* beside the great *Summa* of Thomas Aquinas and say there was no intellectual progress between the seventh century and the thirteenth?[188]

When instructed to think of medieval intellectual trends in this way, the late fifteenth-century printers who turned out editions of the seventh-century *Etymologies* will appear to be setting things back. In fact, they were merely continuing the work of previous copyists. They were duplicating a useful reference work that the *Summa* had not outmoded and that went on being used beyond Aquinas' day. The *Specu-*

---

[187] Hunter, 'Elizabethans and Foreigners,' p. 39.
[188] McIlwain, 'Medieval Institutions in the Modern World,' p. 73. A similar comment, contrasting Isidore's *Etymologies* with a late thirteenth-century *Compendium Philosophae* by a student of Albertus Magnus is made by Boüard, 'Encyclopédies Mediévales, Sur la 'Connaissance de la Nature et du Monde' au Moyen Age,' p. 301.

lum of Vincent of Beauvais and other later medieval 'encyclopedias' may 'replace' Isidore's work in modern surveys and texts. But in the late fifteenth century, habits of dating texts and arraying them in chronological sequence were just beginning to be formed. The late fifteenth-century Venetian bookseller who kept eighty copies of the *Etymologies* in stock[189] was not introducing a bizarre or anachronistic element into the bookish culture of the quattrocento. He was merely trying to continue, as earlier stationers had done, to serve a reading public that was oblivious to the kind of 'intellectual progress' modern scholars regard as obvious now.

The same point applies to the crude mappa mundi which illustrated the first edition of the *Etymologies* (printed in Augsburg in 1472) and is now registered in history books as the first world map to appear in print.[190] Although this woodcut simply duplicated the work-in-progress of contemporary copyists, it appears to be out of keeping with what we have come to expect of fifteenth-century cartography. In view of a 'continuous development' which modern scholars find 'conspicuous on manuscript maps' (after they have lined up a sequence of freshly drawn work) printed maps will seem to be regressive. This is especially true for the fifteenth and sixteenth centuries when hand-drawn mariners' charts were registering coastlines unknown to the ancient world and printed maps were just beginning to introduce Ptolemy's world to armchair travellers. When one surveys the first century of printed cartography, we are told, 'one is struck by the lack of continuous development so conspicuous in manuscript maps.'[191]

The epic discoveries of the Portuguese and Spaniards were recorded more quickly and more accurately in manuscript maps than they were in early printed maps, which were still bound by Ptolemaic conventions as well as even by those of the unrealistic mappae mundi.[192]

The advent of printing ushered in a century of cartographic retrogression marked by 'constant backslidings and bizarre anachronisms.'[193] It was not until the late sixteenth century that the work of Ortelius, Mercator and a new school of Dutch geographers finally emancipated printed cartography from archaic conventions.

[189] R. E. Taylor, *No Ryoal Road*, p. 200.   [190] Bagrow, *History of Cartography*, p. 91.
[191] Penrose, *Travel and Discovery*, p. 318. There is a basic paradox here for scribal cartographers were freer to make fresh maps and spend less time copying older ones after printed cartography got under way.   [192] Penrose, *Travel and Discovery*, p. 299.
[193] Penrose *Travel and Discovery*, p. 318.

The period of cartographic incunabula, characterized by a slavish following of old doctrines and strongly influenced by Ptolemy, was closed – to be succeeded by a new period, distinguished by an effort to found the knowledge of the earth not on the writings of the ancients but on first hand information and scientific investigation. Manuscript cartography had, as we have seen, freed itself long before...[194]

Insofar as printing affected developments in cartography one might conclude from Penrose's account that it introduced backslidings and anachronisms into a discipline previously subject to 'continuous development.' Yet the very fact that early printed maps were bound not only by recently recovered Ptolemaic conventions but also by those of the 'unrealistic mappae mundi' should serve as a reminder that not all of 'manuscript cartography' registered 'continuous development' in the age of Henry the Navigator.

Even when the world maps of the later Middle Ages, drawn for the most part in the scriptoria of monasteries, attempted a faithful delineation of known geographic facts...they still respected the conventional pattern [of] Christian cosmography... *Until the second half of the fifteenth century* the habitable world continued to be represented as a circular disc surrounded by the ocean sea, with Jerusalem at the center and east (with the Earthly Paradise) to the top; and the symmetrical pattern of the T-O diagrams was still reflected in the more elaborate mappae mundi...

Variations of this basic pattern were introduced to admit new geographical information or ideas or new cartographic concepts.[195]

The 'slavish following of old doctrines' registered on early printed maps reflected the prolongation of scribal conventions. Isolated portions of scribal culture had never been dominated by these conventions but, by the same token, these portions were isolated, fragmentary – largely composed of coastlines enclosing dark interiors – and destined to be garbled when assimilated into more comprehensive world pictures.

Cartographic incunabula appear bizarre because certain portions of scribal output, the very portions that were most accessible to fifteenth-century scholars, and to the printers who served them, have now slipped out of view. Once having been duplicated, diverse assorted and oddly-shaped images were later outmoded and are now concealed by print-made schemes. These schemes do not allow for localized methods of record keeping. Hence they overlook the coexistence of incongruous

[194] Penrose, *Travel and Discovery*, p. 325.
[195] Skelton, 'The Vinland Map,' p. 111. (Italics mine.)

images of the world and the prolonged absence of uniform conventions as to how to depict it. Continuous development appears conspicuous on late manuscript maps because the discontinuities that characterized scribal culture are left out of account. Hand-drawn charts accurately depicting new voyages are neither left in coastal charthouses nor transferred in garbled form onto mappae mundi nor even duplicated by early printers as up-to-date supplements to Ptolemies. Instead they are mentally transferred onto modern outline maps to mark steady advances in the age of discovery.[196] When the outlines of 'archaic' pictures are prematurely erased, the fifteenth-century vogue for Hellenistic geography is seen to be regressive. 'In the history of human knowledge there are few stranger chapters than that which records the influence of the Ptolemaic revival in delaying the formation of an accurate world map in the 15th, 16th and 17th centuries.'[197] This chapter seems strange because expectations formed by a print culture have been projected back into early-modern times. Just as Copernicus began where the *Almagest* left off, so too did Ortelius and Mercator find in the ancient *Geographia* a point of departure for their mid-sixteenth-century work. Before an 'accurate world map' could register new voyages, old rules governing the construction of world maps had to be studied and absorbed.

The Geographia is a complete cartographer's handbook. It states clearly the fundamental distinction between chorography and geography; it specifies the need of precise astronomical measurement and correct mathematical contraction, describes the method of making terrestrial globes and of projecting maps on a plane surface.[198]

The Ptolemaic revival was just as indispensable for Mercator and Ortelius as it was for Copernicus. The major achievements of the 'golden age' of map-publishing were predicated on thorough mastery of the Alexandrian heritage, which had to be assimilated before it could be surpassed. Moreover, successive editions of a 'Ptolemy' often contained surprising 'news' in the form of a preface, an extra supplement or appendix. Whereas modern publishers try to boost sales by

196 See e.g. Stavrianos, *The World Since 1500*, where 'Western Man's Knowledge of the Globe' is graphically conveyed by an array of identical outline world maps with expanding knowledge indicated by spotlighting a small portion for the first century, a larger one for the fifteenth century and a still larger one for the sixteenth century. Actually no one saw any portion of the world represented in this way during the centuries indicated.

197 C. R. Beazley, *The Dawn of Modern Geography* III, 517.

198 Durand, *Vienna-Klosterneuberg Map-Corpus*, pp. 12–13.

tacking new titles on old textbooks, early printers served academic markets which valued ancient wisdom. New contents were often concealed in old wrappings. Counting the frequency with which old titles crop up on sixteenth-century book lists, although often taken as hard evidence of cultural lag, provides nothing of the kind. Even the much published *Sphaera* of Sacrobosco might be filled with fresh data before being issued by the early printers.[199]

Thus the duplication in print of extant scribal maps and ancient geographical treatises, even while seeming to provide evidence of 'backsliding,' also provided a basis for unprecedented advance. To found knowledge of the whole world 'on first-hand information' is, literally speaking, quite impossible. Access to a wide variety of second-hand information furnished by reports, ship's logs, charts, over the course of many generations is required. Above all, a uniform grid is needed for assimilating all the assorted information that may be supplied. Before the outlines of a comprehensive and uniform world picture could emerge, incongruous images had to be duplicated in sufficient quantities to be brought into contact, compared and contrasted.[200]

The production of an atlas such as the *Theatrum* with its alphabetical index, list of authors consulted, and orderly progression of maps which expanded in number over time, entailed an enterprise whose novelty needs underscoring. Collaborative ventures in large-scale data collection, which had been intermittent and limited to the facilities provided by one charthouse or manuscript library became continuous and ever-expanding. Here in particular it would be helpful to elaborate on comments made in passing, about the way new presses increased scholarly access to texts. 'The tyranny of major authorities inherent in small libraries was broken. The scholar could indulge in an ease of computation and cross-referencing formerly unthinkable.'[201]

Limits set by the very largest manuscript libraries were also broken. Even the exceptional resources which were available to ancient Alexandrians stopped short of those that were opened up after the shift from script to print. The new open-ended information-flow that

---

[199] Thus the second chapter of sixteenth-century editions of the *Sphaera* is a good place to look for early references to the 'new world' according to Goldschmidt, 'Not in Harrisse.' See also examples of new data given on p. 590, below.

[200] Brown, *Story of Maps*, pp. 160-1 discusses some of the problems entailed in the ten years spent by Ortelius and his collaborators planning and designing the novel publication.

[201] A. R. Hall, *Scientific Revolution*, p. 10.

commenced in the fifteenth century made it possible for fresh finding to accumulate at ever-accelerated pace. It extended the number of skilled investigators who could collaborate on large projects, such as mapping the earth and locating all the creatures, plants and rocks that could be found upon it. In this regard, the walled libraries of the age of scribes may be related to the closed cosmos envisaged by generations of philosophers. Limits had been set to the data that could be collected, preserved, and transmitted about distant landmasses and oceans, exotic flora and fauna, or constellations seen in Southern skies. Just as geographic space stopped short at the Pillars of Hercules, so too did human knowledge itself appear to stop short at fixed limits set by scribal data pools.

Note how frequently the Pillars of Hercules, with their supposed inscription 'ne plus ultra' are used to indicate the closed circle of ancient knowledge... the vast increase in geographical knowledge over that of the ancients operated consciously and unconsciously in undermining the supposed superiority of the classical writers, a fact later conspicuously revealed in various geographical figures of speech used to express modern progress in knowledge.[202]

With the shift from script to print, the closed circle was broken. Just as the number of known plants, having increased from 600 to 6,000, multiplied ever more rapidly thereafter, so too many other forms of data collection – entailing feedback from reader to publisher – pointed to an indefinite expansion. Concepts of limitlessness and infinity were not unfamiliar among Christian scribal scholars, to be sure, but such concepts were employed to contrast the limitations of human cognition with the ineffable, unknowable divine mysteries of the Godhead. When seventeenth-century natural philosophers titled their treatises 'Plus Ultra,' they were expressing something more than traditional Christian doctrines pertaining to Adam's dominion over nature. They were suggesting that limits previously set to human knowledge were illusory. They were laying claim in the name of future generations to all the unfathomed depths and celestial regions that had always before been reserved for God alone.

When engaged in comparing the limited Greek oecumene with the ever-widening horizons of the age of reconnaissance or when tracing the cosmological movement from 'a closed world to an infinite

[202] R. F. Jones, *Ancients and Moderns*, p. 290, n. 25.

universe,' it is worth devoting more thought to the appearance of a 'library without walls.' The large library, as Sarton noted, is just as much a scientific instrument as is the telescope or cyclotron.[203] Laboratory facilities were lacking to sixteenth-century observers. Star-gazers still had to rely only on their 'naked' eyes. But the flow of information had been re-oriented, and this had an effect on natural philosophy that should not go ignored.

[203] Sarton, 'A Summing Up,' p. 370.

6

TECHNICAL LITERATURE GOES
TO PRESS:
SOME NEW TRENDS IN SCIENTIFIC
WRITING AND RESEARCH

1. BRIDGING THE GAP BETWEEN TOWN AND GOWN

It is worth pausing over the fact that a new kind of collaborative
venture in data collection had been set in motion even before laboratory facilities were built or new observational instruments had been
invented. The shift from script to print helps to explain why old theories
were found wanting and new ones devised even before telescopes,
microscopes, and scientific societies had appeared. Gutenberg's invention
not only preceded Galileo's tube; it was a more versatile aid and
affected a wider range of data. Some professors shunned controversy
and withheld treatises from the press just as some refused at first to
look through the telescope. But none failed to consult printed reference
guides or preferred to have to copy out tables by hand. Whatever views
were held concerning Aristotle, Ptolemy or Galen, whatever objections
were posed against using vernaculars or courting publicity; printed
maps, charts, and diagrams found rapid acceptance from all. Indeed
Latin-reading professional groups profited from new kinds of book
learning just as much as did untutored artisans. In view of the many
new printed treatises that William Gilbert consulted, for example, it
is somewhat misleading to describe *De Magnete* as being based 'only
on observations and experiment.'[1] Gilbert probably gleaned as much
useful data from reading technical works composed by others as from
observing and experimenting on his own. That Tycho Brahe and Isaac
Newton could learn so much by reading on their own also had significant consequences for their work. Logarithms and slide-rules,
moreover, served Latin-reading astronomers as well as vernacular-

[1] Zilsel, 'The Origins of William Gilbert's Scientific Method,' p. 17.

reading artisan-engineers. Charts and diagrams helped professors as well as surgeons, surveyors and merchant adventurers. Increased freedom from 'slavish copying' and fruitless book-hunting was particularly helpful to teachers and students. Until the recent advent of computers, has there been any other invention which saved so many man-hours for learned men?

It is also worth noting that professors were encouraged to spend more time in urban workshops with mechanics and merchants after bookhands were replaced by typefonts and master printers took over from university stationers and scribes. Professors and printers began to engage in fruitful collaboration almost as soon as the new presses were installed. The former were often hired by the latter to serve as editors, translators or correctors. They sometimes helped to finance and often supervised the output of medical and astronomical texts. As a young professor of mathematics at Ingolstadt, Apianus (Peter Bienewitz) also ran his own press. As royal professor of mathematics, Oronce Finé worked in several Paris print shops. New careers as science writers were opened to professors no less than to artisans, while the scientist–printer deserves to be placed alongside the scholar–printer as a new kind of protean, Renaissance man.

It seems necessary to pause over interchanges between printers and professors because current interpretations tend to keep them apart – even while conveying the impression that changes wrought by printing left academic science undisturbed. In this regard two opposite schools reinforce each other. On the one hand, those who stress problem-solving and the life of the mind when considering scientific change, are likely to exclude early printers and their presses along with other 'external' or 'socio-economic' factors. Even if they do not go as far as a review article suggests, by lumping the printing press with 'witchcraft and patent law' as 'alien to intellectual history,'[2] they are not likely to regard the establishment of printers' workshops as having a direct bearing on the technical and cerebral activities with which they are concerned.

On the other hand, those who stress the 'sociological roots' of early-modern science and try to integrate star-gazing with more mundane activities also drive a wedge between new workshops and old lecture halls.[3] Artist–engineers, merchants, mechanics, and other lay urban

[2] 'Toward a New History of the New Science,' *Times Literary Supplement* (Sept. 15, 1972).
[3] See e.g. Zilsel, 'The Sociological Roots'; Struik, 'Mathematics in the Netherlands'; Baron, 'Toward a More Positive Evaluation.'

groups are thus set against clerical Latin-reading élites. Insofar as a 'progressive' alliance of capitalists and artisans is arrayed against tradition-bound clerical–feudal ideologues, this alignment seems to owe something to Marxist schemes. It also fits well with the older polemic of lay humanists against scholastics and of artisan-authors against Sorbonnistes. It owes a special debt to attacks on Oxford and Cambridge by seventeenth-century Puritan pamphleteers. Whatever its sources, the dichotomized scheme often does more to hinder than to help us to see how social factors may be related to scientific change. 'Sociological roots' are artificially prevented from ever bearing anything but bitter fruit for Latin-reading learned men. The fact that early printers were close to merchants and mechanics is mistakenly taken to indicate that they were distant from professors and professional élites. When new contributions from non-academic milieux are stressed by historians of science, the importance of Gutenberg's invention is often acknowledged. But when dealing with theories that were developed or recast within libraries and lecture halls, the impact of printing is usually left out of account.

The misleading impression conveyed by this lopsided approach is akin to that developed in Reformation studies, where the impact of print on heresy is stressed while its impact on orthodoxy is ignored. As was the case with Thomist theology or Jerome's translation of Scripture, so too it seems likely that late medieval natural philosophy did not continue unchanged.[4] Much as theologians were divided over new issues posed when Bible study went from script to print, so too were other university faculties affected by new methods of processing Aristotelian and Alexandrian texts.

In the late fifteenth and sixteenth centuries various forces combined to undermine scholastic Aristotelianism as a dominant philosophy...

Mental horizons were extended...by the humanists who recovered a whole world of classical thought which however was now seen to exhibit far greater conflict and diversity than had been evident from the few ancients who dominated scholastic thinking...

[4] For excellent summary of pertinent issues and suggestions for further research on Renaissance Aristotelianism, see monograph and article by Schmitt, *A Critical Survey and Bibliography*; 'Toward a Reassessment of Renaissance Aristotelianism.' How the Aristotelian tradition was affected by the shift from script to print seems to me to be worth further investigation. That many important scholastic scientific treatises by fourteenth-century Paris and Oxford masters were printed between 1470 and 1520 is documented by Clagett, *Science of Mechanics*, pp. 652–3 and by Schmitt, 'Essay Review,' p. 173, n. 10.

There was...a re-structuring of scholastic Aristotelianism to meet the new challenges...Protestant neoscholasticism borrowed...from learned Jesuit commentators of the Iberian peninsula. At some of the Italian universities notably Padua, a 'purified' Aristotelianism provided the background for important advances in the life sciences...[5]

Heightened awareness of 'conflict and diversity' in the classical tradition, surely owed something to the enrichment of literary diets that came with increased book production. The same point applies to clashes between 'Greeks' and 'Arabs.' Advanced instruction in Aristotle's physics was less likely to clash with Ptolemaic computations when complete manuscript copies of the *Almagest* were circulated among a small circle of professional astronomers and rarely seen by commentators on Aristotle.[6] Similarly, differences between Arabic and Galenic doctrines were less troublesome when the full Galenic corpus had not been retrieved. Once printed editions of Averroes and Ptolemy, Avicenna and Galen could be studied in the same place at the same time, contradictions previously concealed by glosses and commentaries and compilations were laid bare.[7] As was the case with the Scriptures, the process of copy-editing in the printers' workshops also encouraged a new awareness of internal inconsistency in a given textual tradition, forcing literalists and modernists apart.

Recent investigations would...tend to make one hesitant in concluding that the innovations and criticisms in the academic sciences – astronomy, physics, anatomy – which we call the scientific revolution, were the product solely or even chiefly of forces and changes operating outside the universities. Rather it would seem that in relation to these subjects it was a case of internal strife, one party of academic innovators trying to wrest the field from a more numerous one of academic conservationists. Certainly this was the case with Vesalius and his fellow anatomists, with Copernicus, with Galileo. It was the academic and professional world that was passionately divided on the question of the inviolability of the Galenic, Aristotelian or Ptolemaic doctrines; these quarrels of learned men had as little to do with capitalism as with the Protestant ethic.[8]

---

5 Rattansi, 'The Social Interpretation of Science,' pp. 7–8.
6 For data on Averroist critique of Ptolemy, printed in Padua in 1473, and Rheticus' plea for Ptolemy's return to his ancient place of honor after long exile from the schools, see Rosen, *Three Copernican Treatises*, pp. 132, 141, 195n, 251. See also chap. 7, n. 15, below.
7 See e.g. discussion of 'gulf' between Arab commentators and texts of Galen and Hippocrates disclosed by Symphorien Champier in published texts of 1507–33. Holmes, 'A Brief Survey of the Use of Renaissance Themes,' pp. 38–9. See also Temkin, *Galenism*, pp. 126–9.
8 A. R. Hall, 'The Scholar and the Craftsman,' p. 7.

If the effects of printing were more completely described, 'forces and changes operating outside the universities' could probably be more clearly related to the 'quarrels of learned men.' At the same time the position of 'academic innovators' and the disputes they provoked also might be clarified. Regulations fining professors for departing from a given text, for example, had served a useful purpose when lecturing was linked to dictating and students served as scribes; for the transmission of precise information was imperilled whenever a professor altered a passage or interpolated a comment. After the advent of printing, such rules lost much of their reason for being. Yet even as their vital functions ebbed, they were harder to evade and could be enforced more rigorously. The petrification of rules holding teachers to certain texts did not mean that universities were impervious to forces or changes operating outside. On the contrary! Petrification was itself a form of change and precipitated academic divisions of a new kind. Ciceronians, Bartholists, Peripatetics, and Galenists were placed in much the same position as orthodox churchmen who objected to revision of the Vulgate text when scholar–printers set to work.

But sixteenth–century universities also sponsored trilingual studies and produced polyglot scholars who edited and translated Bibles. It would be misguided to take official statements objecting to any tampering with the Vulgate as representing all biblical scholarship in the sixteenth century. To take regulations fining professors who departed from Galen as representing all academic science during the early-modern era seems no less unwarranted. At present, however, historians of science who deal with the effects of printing do seem to depict academic science as inflexibly set against innovation. A case in point is provided by Stillman Drake's pioneering essay on printing and the rise of early-modern science.[9] As a suggestive discussion of a much neglected topic, Drake's treatment is illuminating. Nevertheless, it discounts the impact of print on Latin-writing professional élites and conveys the impression that the 'spread of science beyond the Universities' left academic institutions untouched. An innovative 'non-U' science, spearheaded by early printers, is thus sharply contrasted with an older 'academic' science that resisted the winds of change and remained 'Aristotelian to the core.' 'Official science,' we are told, 'continued after the invention of printing much as it had before.'

9 Drake, 'Early Science,' *passim*.

Without pausing over the question whether academic Aristotelianism itself did not undergo change and without taking up other criticisms that have been directed at Drake's views,[10] it must be noted that he deals with the effects of print on a limited portion of early-modern science. Developments in mechanics pointing to the downfall of Aristotelian physics are stressed. Vernacular translation by self-taught artisan-authors, such as Tartaglia, loom large. But innovations in such fields as astronomy and anatomy, which were of equal significance in the so-called 'rise of modern science,' are set aside. Thus, although the resistance of Paduan professors to Galileo's views is stressed, the repudiation of Ptolemaic theories by Copernicus, Rheticus, Maestlin, Kepler *et al.* is passed over. The same point may be applied to the repudiation of Galenic theories by Latin-writing professors of anatomy, from Vesalius to Harvey. As these cases suggest, the portrayal of 'official science' as tradition-bound and impervious to print culture, which some authorities may find plausible when Galileo's assault on Aristotelian physics is stressed, becomes more implausible when the downfall of Ptolemy and Galen is also brought into view.

Even when discussion is restricted to Galileo's career, moreover, it seems unwise to place professors at too great a distance from printers. After all, Galileo was himself a Paduan professor when his first vernacular publication appeared.[11] His exploitation of publicity as a self-proclaimed inventor of the telescope also occurred while he was still holding an academic chair. His lectures at the university had to conform to fixed texts, but his freedom to publish was not thereby restrained. Interpretations based on the old polarities which set the lay humanists of Florence against the Aristotelian faculties of Padua are misleading in this regard. A recent article goes so far as to credit Florentine humanism with the capacity to have created a general reading public, to have provided Galileo with his audience and to have rendered

10 See Schmitt's 'Essay Review' for pertinent criticisms of Drake's general approach. Although issues pertaining to printing are not raised, Schmitt poses several objections that concur with views expressed here. See especially treatment of Latin versus vernaculars (p. 167) and of exclusive focus on mechanics (p. 175, n. 41 and 42).

11 This was a vernacular pamphlet 'Le Operazioni del compasso geometrico et militare' printed in 1606, on a press in Galileo's 'own house' and dedicated to Cosimo II. It described a 'proportional compass' or 'sector,' presumably 'invented in 1597' and gave rise to a priority dispute between Galileo and a rival claimant that was decided in favor of Galileo by the university officials. Galileo's printed defense against the 'calumnies and impostures' of his rival, in 1607, marks his debut as a formidable polemicist. See Drake, *Discoveries and Opinions of Galileo*, p. 16, and two essays in *Galileo, Man of Science*, (ed. McMullin): Bedini, 'The Instruments of Galileo,' pp. 256-92; Boyer, 'Galileo's Place in the History of Mathematics,' p. 237.

him independent of established authority. 'The public to which Galileo turned for support after 1610 was composed not of university professors but of ordinary citizens like Michelangelo Buonarroti Jr, Jacopo Nardi, Cosimo di' Bardi and, of course, Cosimo de Medici and Cristina of Lorraine.'[12] The names cited are not those of 'ordinary citizens' in most senses of the word. If a grand duke and a grand duchess are to be viewed as forming a 'general reading public,' then humanism may well deserve credit for this category. But Florentine princes and patricians (who did, after all, represent 'established authority' of a kind and who had supplied patronage to scribal scholars for centuries) probably ought to be distinguished from the even more 'general' reading public who purchased both the Latin version and the vernacular translations of the *Starry Messenger* in the early seventeenth century. At all events, Galileo was in some ways more independent of 'established authority' and more certain of reaching the 'general reading public' while he remained a Paduan professor than after he was assured of a living by the Grand Duke of Tuscany.

As a professor at Padua, Galileo had not been kept from association with Venetian merchants, mechanics, or men-of-affairs. Even while holding a university chair, he had been able to lay claim to new intellectual property-rights as an inventor and instrument-maker. He expressed a wish to devote himself more exclusively to writing books, in his letter requesting Medici patronage. Nevertheless he had managed quite well as a Paduan professor to get several works into print. News of Galileo's tube had travelled fast and far. When considering quattrocento trends, one may perhaps contrast the 'clerical atmosphere of medieval...universities' with the 'symbiosis of thought and action' in Florentine workshops. As an 'heir' of Florentine humanism, Galileo probably had such contrasts in mind.[13] Yet it seems doubtful that moving to Florence enabled Galileo to link 'the world of scientific research' with 'that of technology.'[14] The move brought him aristocratic

12 Cochrane, 'Science and Humanism,' p. 1057. Since Galileo had already dedicated his 1606 pamphlet to Cosimo II, he was not really 'turning' to his former pupil, the Grand Duke of Tuscany, *after* 1610 'for support' but rather continuing to cultivate a potential patron whose favor he had long sought. For biographical data see Geymonat, *Galileo Galilei*.

13 Baron, 'Toward a more Positive Evaluation,' stresses the university-workshop opposition and Eugenio Garin's two essays, 'Galileo and the Culture of His Age,' and 'Galileo the Philosopher,' in his *Science and Civil Life*, persuasively depict Galileo as an heir of the Florentine humanist tradition.

14 Drake, introduction to 'Letters on Sunspots,' *Discoveries and Opinions*, p. 78. Drake's suggestion that men-of-affairs at the Florentine court made more suitable companions than Galileo's

patronage but took him away from easy access to Venetian presses –
to the very workshops where the two worlds had already become one.
When he left the university, he not only left Latin lectures, Aristotelian
curricula and hostile colleagues behind; he also placed himself in a
position that resulted in his house arrest. He moved to Florence partly,
perhaps, because he was nostalgic about his native region; more certainly because he had finally secured Medici patronage. His preference
for the vernacular was not accompanied by any democratic distaste
for currying the favor of élites. When discussing mathematics, astronomy, or anatomy, Galileo could be quite contemptuous of the common man who relied on 'common sense' or sense impressions. In his
insistence on the superiority of the trained investigator to the ordinary
observer he often seems to be more of an élitist than some of
his interpreters suggest.[15] His move to Florence won him princely
patrons and audiences with popes. He also achieved membership
in an early scientific society. But he lost immunity from the
Inquisition and had to bow, in the end, to non-academic thought-
control.

In Galileo's case, scientific innovation went together with a flair for
publicity, a resort to vernacular pamphleteering, and attacks on
Aristotelian professors. Yet others who contributed to the downfall of
Ptolemy and Galen often shied away from publicity and wrote for
Latin-reading peers. Galileo created the greatest stir, and his trial had
spectacular historical consequences. Thereafter the 'quiet' rise of
modern science was caught up in the 'noisy' clash of rival faiths.
Galileo's case was exceptional, and exceptions – however spectacular –
ought not to be taken as rules. This is especially true of efforts to relate
print culture to early-modern science.

Reverberations from the seventeenth-century trial are likely to lead
us astray when dealing with earlier developments. Even when dealing
with the century of genius, a distorted view may result. In his persua-

'former professorial colleagues' also seems to me to overlook the diverse opportunities
extended by the Venetian milieu. On pp. 70-1 Drake cites a passage from Doni's *I Marmi*
contrasting the lively stimulating Florentine atmosphere with the 'dreamy' Venetian one.
Yet Doni himself was better supported by Venetian presses than Florentine ones. Contrasts
between the two city-states ought to allow for the changing position of printers and censors
within them, especially when dealing with early-modern science.

15 See passages in 'Letter to the Grand Duchess Christina,' where he indicates the shortcomings
of 'vulgar' and 'brutish views' (Drake, *Discoveries and Opinions*, pp. 196-7). See also comment
by Shea, *Galileo's Intellectual Revolution*, p. 47, n. 36 questioning conventional view of Galileo
appealing 'over the heads' of professors to 'ordinary' laymen.

sive account of 'Galileo and the Culture of His Age' for example, Eugenio Garin describes how the Italian universities, after welcoming censorship to crush anti-Aristotelians, taught 'a tired, used-up knowledge that found no echo anywhere.' At an earlier time, Garin suggests, a curriculum reform had seemed possible. 'The introduction of new texts' by Platonists and other innovators had begun to undermine ancient authorities and created a 'tension between the universities and the mental climate outside them.' But the invaders were repelled. Pisa and Padua became strongholds of reaction. A prolonged battle of books between the lay humanists of Florence and the scholastic professors of Padua ended in a defeat of the former. In Garin's version, which resembles that of Drake, the universities were left 'to propagate nothing but an utterly exhausted tradition.'[16]

When Galileo is made to share 'the culture of his age' with other contemporary scientists, the Italian academic climate appears in a somewhat different light. William Harvey was at Padua between 1592 and 1610, and studied under a professor who served as Galileo's doctor there. Harvey went to Padua on the advice of his mentors at Cambridge to take advantage of the superior training that was available on the continent. To the erstwhile Cambridge undergraduate, Paduan studies were notably innovative and experimental. Aristotle loomed in certain courses, to be sure. But this was probably more of a help than a hindrance in Harvey's work.[17]

A rigorous training in logical argument as well as in techniques of dissection were fruitfully combined in De Motu. It could be argued that required courses in logic actually sharpened Harvey's perception of contradiction. It is clear, at all events, that he did pay close attention to shaky arguments in newly printed anatomy texts (even pausing to correct an important misprint) and that the much abused universities

16 Garin, *Science and Civil Life*, pp. 94–7, 101. In previous passages, pp. 80–9, Garin makes indirect references to the impact of print by bringing in the repressive effects of the Index on Italian cultural life. His condemnation of Paduan Aristotelianism is linked to his belief that the Paduan philosophers were spurious 'freethinkers' who took advantage of the Index to censor anti-Aristotelian opponents and thus stifle scientific advance. For different view of the University of Padua, see Randall's article, 'Scientific Method' and many later references cited by Schmitt, 'The Faculty of Arts at Pisa.' On p. 250, n. 24 Schmitt dismisses the notion of a university as 'a center of free inquiry' as a 'romantic ideal' rather than an historical reality.

17 See Whitteridge, *William Harvey*, pp. 3–4. Whitteridge notes that the founder of Harvey's College at Cambridge, John Caius, had been friendly with Vesalius at Padua and had later attended dissections by the barber–surgeons of London even while serving as a fellow of the Royal College of Physicians, thereby bridging town–gown divisions. Harvey's use of Aristotle has been underlined in many studies by Walter Pagel. See e.g. 'William Harvey.'

had prepared him rather well for this task.[18] 'The doors of sixteenth century universities were closed to new scientific ideas from the outside,' according to one of Galileo's biographers.[19] Harvey's model of the circulation of the blood was a new scientific idea that came from the inside – after more than a half-century of almost exclusively academic debate. Harvey was not a proponent of vernacular science-writing, nor did he share Galileo's flair for publicity and distaste for academic life. On the contrary, he wrote in Latin for specialists and procrastinated about attacking Galen in print.[20]

To make too much of Harvey's Aristotelian Latin learning, however, would be just as misguided as to overplay Galileo's occasional use of the vernacular. Although Drake's discussion of printing seems to me to be one-sided it does nevertheless offer a necessary corrective to the disdainful treatment of the output of early printers by medievalists such as Lynn Thorndike. Thorndike briskly dismissed the 'bungling' of amateurs and the 'billingsgate' of Paracelsus. In his view, the new presses served only to spread a 'little learning' 'more thinly over a greater population.' They augmented superstition while obscuring genuine scientific work.[21] Contributions to the 'exact' sciences made by Northerners, such as Gemma Frisius or Simon Stevin and by the numerous Italians who are discussed by Drake – all of whom wrote in the vernacular for literate laymen – are simply left out of Thorndike's account. Yet these vernacular science-writers did more than spread a smattering of old learning thin. Granted that Latin remained the language of the cosmopolitan Commonwealth of Learning; vernacular science-writing aimed at non-academic readers (including prospective patrons and purchasers of instruments) probably did help to transform some older fields of learning. It attracted amateur interest in new discoveries while creating new disciplines, such as applied mathematics and mechanics, at the same time.

[18] Harvey's close study of the 1593 edition of Realdus Columbus' *De Re Anatomica* and his picking out an important misprint (of *systole* for *diastole*) is described by Whitteridge, pp. 49, 70–2, 92.
[19] Drake, 'Early Science,' p. 49. Here, as elsewhere, Drake agrees with Garin.
[20] Whitteridge, *William Harvey*, pp. 105–6. Harvey's choice of a relatively unknown foreign firm (run by an English relative of the de Bry family in Frankfurt) for the first edition of *De Motu* is attributed to persuasion exerted by Robert Fludd. Weil, 'William Fitzer,' pp. 142–3. Harvey's friendship with Fludd links him to heterodox Rosicrucian currents which seem to be excluded from Whitteridge's account. The first favorable notice of Harvey in print came from Fludd in a Frankfurt publication of 1629. The major boost came from Descartes in *Discours sur la Méthode* (1637). See Whitteridge, *William Harvey*, pp. 150–3.
[21] Thorndike, *History of Magic and Experimental Science*, pp. 5 ff.

The applied mathematicians of the sixteenth century, for example, helped to transform the language of numbers in a way that laid the basis for later innovations by virtuosi such as Fermat and Descartes. Members of this new occupational group, although eager to profit from publicity, ought not to be categorized as mere popularizers or publicists.[22] Nor does this point apply only to the new mathematical practitioners described by Dirk Struik or E. G. R. Taylor. It applies just as well to the 'chemical teachers' described by Owen Hannaway and Marie Boas. The latter points to 'simple, precise and detailed' works of instruction such as 'Chemistry for Beginners' which left 'no room for alchemical secretiveness' and won acceptance for a new field of study in the schools.[23] Similar developments affected other life-sciences, as numerous medical treatises and botany books attest. In all these fields, a new style of exposition, 'simple, precise and detailed' affected interpretations of natural phenomena and encouraged a deflation of overblown theories which Latin verbiage had previously concealed.

One may agree with Thorndike that printing opened up new opportunities for bunglers and braggarts to set forth absurd claims and for charlatans to profit from mass credulity. But one also ought to note that verbal confidence games had not been unknown in medieval lecture halls. Certain kinds of academic trickery became less feasible. Arguments aimed at intelligent practitioners, at architects, surveyors, surgeons, apothecaries, navigators and the like, were bound to be different from those which were designed to impress academic colleagues or to win a rhetorical contest held at papal and princely courts. The increased use of vernaculars sometimes did a disservice to the cosmopolitan Commonwealth of Learning.[24] It often owed much to an

---

22 On important contributions made by mathematical practitioners and instrument-makers in paving the way for later departures from 'traditional methods and standards of solution' associated with the work of Fermat and Descartes see Mahoney, *The Mathematical Career*, pp. 8–10; Struik, 'Mathematics in the Netherlands'; and E. G. R. Taylor, *The Mathematical Practitioners of Tudor and Stuart England*.

23 Boas, *Scientific Renaissance*, pp. 164–5; see also Hannaway's discussion of Libavius and his confrères.

24 In a letter to a Paduan friend about his *Letters on Sunspots*, Galileo shows the impossibility of writing for the vernacular-reading 'everyman' without excluding foreign scientists – such as his German Jesuit rival, Scheiner, who could not read Italian. See citation in Drake, introduction to *Letters on Sunspots*, in *Discoveries and Opinions*, p. 84. In the *Sidereus Nuncius*, where he wanted his message to reach beyond compatriots to 'astronomers and philosophers all over Europe as quickly as possible' (Drake, introduction to *The Starry Messenger*, p. 19) Galileo wrote in Latin. In either language, however, he employed a clear plain prose style, aimed at

insular, patriotic outlook that worked at odds with the authors' professed desire to serve humanity. It was partly propelled by the desire to profit from an invention or an instrument that could be bought at a given author's home. Nevertheless vernacular science-writing enlarged and democratized the Commonwealth of Learning. It extended the range of talents that were tapped, linked instrument-making with mathematical theorizing and helped to propel data collection in many new directions.

Yet although the increased use of vernaculars was a significant development, it was by no means the most important of the many changes undergone by scientific communications. For one thing, many of the new 'simple, precise and detailed' texts were first written in Latin and translated thereafter. For the most part, scientific textbook writing was done by authors (Agrippa, Robert Recorde, Pacioli *et al.*) who had command of both ancient and modern tongues. For another thing, the chief language of science (as Galileo pointed out) was neither Latin nor the 'Volgare,' but numbers and figures, circles, triangles, and squares. The discarding of Roman numerals or rhymed verses in old French represented changes that cut across town–gown divisions and penetrated college halls. These changes are well reflected in the new printed materials turned out by applied mathematicians, whose books often served to advertise their instruments. Thus diverse textual traditions, previously transmitted by separate channels, were freely combined. 'With the Greek rudiments, they freely mixed material taken from arabic texts and applied algebra.' The new possibility of printing tables and maps led to practical compromises that violated philosophical dogma but produced genuinely useful paper tools.

trigonometric theorems...meant little to the navigator until translated into computational techniques...the preparation of...tables in turn required that one surrender geometrical exactitude for accurate arithmetical approximation and interpolation...in contrast to the canons...the navigator, the map maker, the engineer...treated arithmetic and geometry as realms with a common open border...Stevin...honored Archimedes' geometry, devised...decimal place-value fraction...and did research in algebra... Napier...conceived of logarithms in terms of motions of points along a line but Euclid was ignored as ratios of these motions were computed in numbers

clarification rather than mystification. For discussion of his literary styles see D. Della Terza, 'Galileo, Man of Letters,' pp. 1–23.

and rounded off...The goal was not theoretical rigor but a sufficiently accurate technique for manipulating large numbers and trigonometrical functions.

The same practical spirit overrode the classical...distinction between the mathematical and mechanical and fostered increasing research on mathematical instruments...Within six years of the publication of Napier's... *Logarithms* and within three years of Briggs'...Richard Gunter and Edmund Wingate had reduced logarithmic computation to a small instrument, the first slide rule.[25]

Uniform mathematical symbols brought professors closer to reckonmasters. They did not separate academicians from artisans, although they did move scientists away from poets. To the warfare between scholastics and humanists was added a new schism, between the party of number and the party of words. Print insured a victory of the 'algorists' over the 'abacists.' It saw new arithmetic texts displace Boethius in the schools. Other branches of the *quadrivium* and more advanced mathematics were also transformed. The achievements of a sixteenth-century virtuoso such as Viète were not based on a critique of Aristotle's physics, but on manipulating Indo–Arabic symbols to solve problems that Aristotle had not posed. Higher mathematics was detached from the concerns of medieval natural philosophers, much as business arithmetic was taught without reference to moral or theological concerns. Both developments reflected the rapid expansion of a new knowledge industry after print. As was the case with classical archeology or locating plants, the language of number was propelled as an autonomous discipline and the solution of problems became subject to incremental change.

Let me note in passing that the way letters, numbers, and figures were pulled and pushed into new alignments by early printers and engravers is worth further thought. Human proportions were made to conform with letters once inscribed on ancient Roman arches, even while Roman numerals were being replaced by Arabic ones.[26] Solid geometrical forms were presented on two-dimensional planes and heavy wooden tables gave way to paper ones. In short, the basic 'building blocks' of the *quadrivium*: words and letters, numbers and figures,

25 Mahoney, *The Mathematical Career*, pp. 9–10. How Latin-writing astronomers must have welcomed these 'practical' inventions is suggested by the enormous effort it cost Rheticus and his successors to compile tables of functions before Napier. See chap. 7, n. 162 below.
26 For pertinent references, see later discussion of Luca Pacioli's work in this chapter, pp. 548–9 below.

even notes of music and lyrics for songs were rearranged, recast and almost literally thrown into a melting pot from whence they emerged in altered guise. To investigate how different branches of the *quadrivium* were affected by such changes is too formidable a task to be undertaken here. Let me merely suggest that each of the four disciplines underwent a complex metamorphosis after printing and their relationship to each other was also changed in various ways. Thus algebra moved closer to plane geometry; while the conic sections of solid geometry reshaped the music of the spheres.

Changes affecting different branches of the *quadrivium* could scarcely fail to penetrate Latin schools and college halls. The mistaken view that academic science was impervious to innovative trends has been traced, in a recent study of medical faculties in England, to false impressions left by statutory regulations that concealed the new content which was poured into old forms. 'Again and again, from the late Elizabethan period on, one finds countless examples of changeless academic...regulations and transformed subject matter.'[27] The same point applies to the contents of arithmetics, grammars, and other textbooks which often varied, after printing, from one edition to another.[28] 'A survey of works...published for academic use shows an overwhelming predominance of texts over a hundred years old... nothing could better illustrate the stagnation of scientific advance in the fifteenth century.'[29] Yet the stagnation may be illusory – based on failure to appreciate how often new contents were concealed by old labels.[30] At Copenhagen when the young Tycho Brahe was there, for example, students were presumably studying a traditional 'Aristotelian and conservative' curriculum.[31] Yet they were also furnished with new Greek and Hebrew grammars in accordance with Melanchthon's program of reform. Like earlier medieval students, they were being given Sacrobosco's *Sphaera* but in place of a medieval commentary

---

[27] R. G. Frank, 'Science, Medicine,' p. 200. This point needs to be balanced against the undeniable conservatism of statutory regulations which were not entirely without significance. See argument of Charles Webster, *The Great Instauration*, p. 199, defending the condemnation, by Puritan zealots, of 'scholastic' education.

[28] For a study of successive editions of Recorde's *Ground of Artes* see Easton, 'The Early Editions.'

[29] Goldschmidt, *Medieval Texts*, p. 23.

[30] See e.g. contrast drawn between the many early editions of Sacrobosco's *Sphaera* and the neglect of more noteworthy medieval scientific treatises by early printers serving academic markets in Wightman, *Science in a Renaissance Society*, p. 60. Actually editions of Sacrobosco could serve as vehicles for new information. See chap. 5, n. 199 above; p. 590 below.

[31] Christianson, 'Tycho Brahe.'

THE BOOK OF NATURE TRANSFORMED

there was Regiomontanus' more sophisticated critique. Similarly a seemingly 'conservative' Ptolemaic text such as Apianus' *Cosmography* contained a new and useful supplement on triangulation supplied by Gemma Frisius.[32] Even while taking the traditional cycle of studies associated with the *trivium* and *quadrivium*, Tycho as a teenage student was mastering new mathematical and linguistic skills and being exposed to new data – albeit often in concealed form.

Although Struik suggests that 'the universities and the Latin schools were not the carriers of life in the exact sciences,' he also notes that the *Arithmetica* of Gemma Frisius found its way into almost every Latin school, while Gemma Frisius himself taught geography and mathematics at Louvain, the 'bulwark of theology and scholastic learning.'[33] Napier's work on logarithms was perfected and printed under the guidance of an eminent professor: Sir Henry Briggs. The academic posts held by men like Frisius and Briggs and the uses to which decimals and logarithms were put, point to the fallacy of over-playing the gap between 'the latinized university doctors' and the 'uncouth technicians and bookkeepers of the commercial cities.'[34]

The *Ground of Artes* by Robert Recorde known in twenty-eight editions... must have been 'read to pieces.'...Recorde was no 'rude mechanical' but a Fellow of All Souls, Oxford (1531) and a Doctor of Medicine, Cambridge (1545)...involved also in the 'modern' enterprise of mining and employed at the Bristol mint.[35]

[32] Christianson, 'Tycho Brahe' notes that Tycho had a 1558 Wittenberg edition of Sacrobosco's *Sphaera* and Gemma Frisius' edition of Apianus' *Cosmography*. Struik notes that Gemma's new prescription for triangulation was attached to Apianus' text.

[33] Struik, 'Mathematics in the Netherlands,' pp. 48–9. It was at Louvain, incidentally that Gemma Frisius and Vesalius met, thus suggesting how some 'scholastic' strongholds housed pioneers of early-modern science. In view of its trilingual curriculum, Louvain was also more unconventional than Struik's characterization suggests.

[34] Struik, 'Mathematics in the Netherlands.' The versatile role played by Briggs, interchanges between Oxford and London, and the fallacy of portraying English universities as resistant to new philosophy are brought out by Shapiro, *John Wilkins*, p. 15 and *passim*. See also R. G. Frank's two-part article: 'Science, Medecine'.

[35] Wightman, *Science in a Renaissance Society*, p. 101. On Recorde, see E. G. R. Taylor, *Mathematical Practitioners*, pp. 50–3. The successive editions of Recorde's first vernacular textbook, which are studied by Easton, culminate in an advertisement for *Decimals Made Easy* in 1699. Recorde's titles for his series of textbooks, beginning with *The Pathway to Knowledge* (1551) going on to *The Gate of Knowledge* and *The Castle of Knowledge* and ending with the uncompleted *Treasure of Knowledge*, suggest a kind of educational 'pilgrim's progress' – moving from 'ground' to 'pathway' to 'gate' to 'castle' (where Copernican doctrines are explained) to ultimate 'treasure' (along lines that point to the later 'Rosicrucian Enlightenment' as described by Frances Yates). Recorde and John Dee were fellow students at Cambridge and shared similar pedagogical concerns. Later editions of *The Ground of Artes* carried advertisements for Billingsley's English *Euclid* containing Dee's celebrated introduction.

The 'carriers of life in the exact sciences' consisted more and more of equations, diagrams, tables, maps and charts that could not be conveyed by lecture or disputation and that required silent scanning to be comprehended and absorbed. Instead of taking dictation from masters, college students became increasingly able to learn mathematics by teaching themselves. After 'silent instructors' had been produced in urban workshops, new lectureships in mathematics were introduced into the schools. Simon Stevin not only matriculated at Leiden, he ended by taking on a teaching post there. Stevin's appointment at Leiden was not the only sign that this famous Northern university was receptive to change. 'Universities in those days followed a traditional scheme of four faculties: law, medicine, theology, philosophy; but Leiden was not long in adding to these such appendages of modern universities as an engineering school, botanic garden, observatory and university press.'[36]

These signs of modernization were by no means peculiar to Leiden at the end of the sixteenth century. Earlier decades had seen the study of mathematics and botany flourish at new universities such as Wittenberg, while old university centers such as Paris and Padua acquired new facilities and faculty chairs. 'The Paduan school of anatomy owed its initial renown to Vesalius.'[37] His experiences at Paris and Louvain also placed Vesalius well within those academic circles, which are usually deemed tradition-bound. Yet the sixteenth-century Fleming also spent much time in the company of engravers and printers – where outsiders and mavericks, such as Paracelsus and Servetus, also could be found. For Vesalius, as for his printer Oporinus, there seems to be no clear division of work between academic circles and a reading public composed of surgeons, city physicians, artists, and literati. One of his earliest publications (in 1538) suggested how he helped to break down such divisions. Large placards or charts designed to be held up for audiences at his lectures were published as prints and were made available to interested observers in many towns.[38] Much as preachers extended their range by using presses as well as pulpits, so too did professors such as Vesalius reach a larger public outside college halls. As was the

---

[36] D. W. Davies, *The World of the Elseviers*, p. 12.
[37] Whitteridge, *William Harvey*, p. 15. On the University of Wittenberg see Dannenfeldt, 'Wittenberg Botanists' and Westman: 'The Melanchthon Circle,' 'Three Responses.'
[38] Saunders and O'Malley, *The Illustrations*, p. 16. The importance of anatomical prints such as these for the work of Rabelais is noted by Kline, 'Rabelais and Printing,' p. 50.

case with preachers also, the new publicity often generated new interest in watching celebrated authors perform. As Vesalius became something of a celebrity, anatomy lessons generated the same kind of excitement as other Baroque spectacles or theatrical events.[39]

When the discussion is broadened to include other figures than Galileo and other fields than mechanics and physics, moreover, clear-cut distinctions between academic and non-academic science become ever more blurred. The most advanced work in physics had taken the form of Latin commentaries on Aristotle's works and stemmed from courses in Natural Philosophy given by schoolmen. But advanced work in other fields often occurred outside lecture halls. The full text of Ptolemy's *Almagest* was probably harder for college students to obtain than Aristotle's *Physics*, for graduate faculties did not offer advanced instruction in astronomy.[40] Throughout the middle ages, most professional astronomers themselves were likely to be found outside college halls. They frequented courts, town halls, and charthouses. They cast horoscopes for princes or helped navigators and cartographers; advised on coinage or weights and measures; and worked with churchmen on calendrical problems. Town–gown divisions continue to seem irrelevant, and patronage by prelates and princes continues to dominate the scene after the end of the middle ages – from the days of Regiomontanus (who served a King of Hungary before obtaining a patron who financed his Nuremberg press) to those of Copernicus, Tycho, Kepler, and beyond. Whatever the impact of print on astronomy (and I believe it was considerable) it could not do very much to encourage professional astronomers to work on practical problems outside universities. Few astronomers had worked for long inside universities before.[41]

Much the same point may be made about developments in higher

---

39 Cohen, 'Diagrams and Illustrations,' offered a graphic demonstration of new public interest in Vesalius' demonstrations as opposed to the bored and indifferent spectators at earlier anatomy lessons by contrasting the illustration in Ketham's *Fasciculus Medicinae* (Venice: Gregoriis, 1493/4) with the frontispiece of *De Fabrica*. Perhaps these renderings should be regarded less as accurate reports than as two artists' conceptions of how the scene *ought* to be represented. In either case, the contrast is worth noting.

40 Crombie, *Augustine to Galileo*, p. 149, mentions Ptolemy's *Almagest* among 'texts prescribed' at medieval Oxford but other studies of medieval curricula seem to confirm above remarks. See e.g. Weisheipl, 'Curriculum at the Faculty of Arts,' pp. 142; 170; 172. Also Gabriel, *The College System*, pp. 19, 41 n, 140.

41 Thus it is not clear whether Campanus of Novara ever did serve as a professor, while his services at the papal court are well documented. See Benjamin and Toomer, *Campanus of Novara*, p. 11.

mathematics. It is not at all surprising that Leonardo Fibonacci, the most accomplished Western mathematician of the thirteenth century, was linked with the astronomer Michael Scott through Frederick II's court rather than through university affiliations. Fibonacci's *Liber Abaci* seems to have been as little studied in the schools as was Ptolemy's full *Almagest*.[42] Simplified recensions by Sacrobosco served for teaching the rudiments of astronomy and arithmetic alike. Despite the brilliant work done on the margins of Aristotle's *Physics*, higher mathematics was assigned an extracurricular role in most medieval universities.[43] Formal instruction was limited to a cursory undergraduate 'eight-day' lecture course. While holding his 'chair' as a professor of mathematics, Galileo himself also gave private instruction at home.

It would be a mistake therefore to imagine that some sort of medieval academic monopoly had to be broken in order to release the talents of mathematical virtuosi such as Tartaglia, Cardano, Viète, Fermat, Pascal, Descartes, Leibniz *et al*. Before concluding that the 'new philosophy and science were forced to take root outside the academic garden where they should have found most fertile soil,'[44] it is worth noting that some hardy perennials had flourished for centuries outside university walls. The mathematical wizards of medieval and early-modern times had varied careers – ranging from merchant apprentices and self-taught reckon-masters to college professors and closet philosophers. They included doctors, lawyers, and clergymen who played with numbers in their spare time. However one may classify this variegated group, their academic affiliations (like their preference for Latin or vernaculars) often seem to be beside the point.[45]

The situation is somewhat different with regard to the life sciences, for medicine – unlike astronomy or mathematics – *was* taught by graduate faculties. Indeed, instruction in the *quadrivium* was mainly designed for undergraduates planning to take a medical degree. Advanced work in

[42] The composition and limited circulation of Fibonacci's treatises are covered by Rose, *The Italian Renaissance of Mathematics*, pp. 82–3. For interesting speculation on the circulation of his treatise on 'practical geometry' see Shelby, 'The Geometrical Knowledge,' p. 404. On Frederick II's court, see Haskins, *Studies*, p. 249.

[43] On private classes held for teaching mathematics and uncertainty about the academic status of Jordanus, Gerard of Brussels, etc. see Beaujouan, 'Motives and Opportunities' in Crombie (ed.) *Scientific Change*, p. 235. That mathematics was outside the regular university courses when Vittorino da Feltre was at Padua in the 1400s is noted by Woodward, *Vittorino da Feltre*, p. 7.

[44] A. R. Hall, 'The Scholar and the Craftsman,' p. 9.

[45] On the 'hodge-podge of varied activities' entailed in early-modern mathematics and absence of any term to cover them, see Mahoney, *The Mathematical Career*, p. 14.

medicine, as in law, was thus handled under academic auspices. Professors of medicine, however, also served as physicians and gained clinical experience at courts and in towns. Throughout the middle ages, moreover, there were branches of medicine practiced by surgeons and apothecaries that were excluded from the curriculum and had tenuous academic affiliations or none at all. It has been said, of medical studies during the later middle ages, that a 'tide of ink and parchment separated brain from hand.'[46] The influx of ancient texts in Latin translation probably increased divisions between professors and practitioners. Classical objections to scholars dirtying their hands were revived. Professors of medicine increasingly devoted themselves to study of Latin, Greek, and Arabic texts; surgeons and apothecaries were without Latin learning and worked outside the schools. As we have noted when discussing the problems of the Renaissance, the advent of printing helped to reverse these trends. Collaboration between the painter who belonged to the apothecary's guild and the learned physician was thus an important feature of early printed herbals. The output of vernacular texts for surgeons and the provision of anatomical illustrations for medical texts also brought 'hand and brain' together in new ways. Above all, the cause of literate surgery, which had received repeated setbacks during the middle ages, was finally secured.

In the later middle ages, Mondino's *Anatomia* had found a place in the schools, but Gui de Chauliac's *Chirurgia* had not. Gui himself was an academically trained man who studied at Bologna and Montpellier before serving the townsmen of Lyons and the Avignon Popes. He urged surgeons to master letters and study anatomy before setting out to practice their craft. Under the aegis of the Avignon Papacy, Gui collected a fine library and temporarily broke the monopoly of the Italians at Bologna where surgical texts were jealously guarded. But with the end of the Avignon Popes and the outbreak of the Hundred Years War, the library was dispersed, and the cause of literate surgery beyond the Alps received a setback again.[47] Gui's program was not implemented until the sixteenth century when the 'new anatomy'

[46] Lynn White, 'Pumps and Pendula,' p. 102. See also Singer, 'The Confluence,' p. 263.
[47] The difficulty of sustaining the cause of literacy for surgeons before printing is noted by Malgaigne, *Surgery and Ambroise Paré*, pp. 33; 63. See also Talbott and Hammond, *The Medical Practitioners*, pp. viii–lx. Many editions of Gui's work were printed before 1501 in French, Latin, Dutch, and German. See Sarton, *Six Wings*, p. 300, n. 71.

became an accepted part of the curriculum at universities. In the 1550s, a new course in anatomy given at Paris signalled the acceptance of Gui in French medical schools. Later in the century a Montpellier professor edited a new French edition of the *Chirurgia* so that 'those who have a natural bent for the surgeon's calling' could take advantage of 'books which are silent instructors' and 'nowadays carry farther than public lectures.'[48]

In the case of anatomy, one may see how courses and texts worked together and varied talents were pooled in new ways. But even while new forms of collaboration were encouraged, old rivalries were also exacerbated. Divisions of labor between surgeons, physicians, and apothecaries varied so greatly from region to region that few generalizations hold true. Still, it seems safe to suggest that changes wrought by print intensified wrangling between diverse groups almost everywhere. In England, for example, the seventeenth-century publication of the London *Pharmacopoeia*, even while dignifying the apothecary's craft, also precipitated vigorous attacks on the *status quo* by disclosing how many impossibly complicated, absurd and extravagant remedies had been passed down for centuries by 'slavish copyists' in the schools.[49] Attacks on money-grubbing physicians and claims made for cheap, sure-fire home remedies in some of the literature provoked by the *Pharmacopoeia* have a remarkably modern ring. So too does the promotional literature, issued outside the medical establishment, advertising pills and panaceas for sale. In a modern vein also, academic medicine proved sensitive to commercial pressures associated with new forms of publicity. Paracelsus' plans for an elaborate publication proving guaiac useless for treating syphilis led to trouble with the Leipzig medical faculty who feared loss of Fugger patronage if Fugger revenues from guaiac were imperilled.[50] Quarrels between physicians and surgeons seem to have been especially bitter and prolonged in France, where intermittent hostilities continued for three centuries or more.[51]

---

[48] Sherrington, *The Endeavour*, p. 111. The citation comes from Isaac Joubert who, along with his father, Laurent Joubert (Dean and Chancellor of the University) was on the Montpellier medical faculty. How these Protestant professors of medicine contributed to the vernacular translation movement (discussed in chap. 4, volume 1 above) is described by Sherrington, pp. 108–14.   [49] Brockbank, 'Sovereign Remedies,' 1–13.

[50] Pagel, *Paracelsus*, pp. 24–5.

[51] Hostilities between French physicians and surgeons during the seventeenth and eighteenth centuries are noted in many studies. See e.g. Sherrington, *The Endeavour*, pp. 104–6; Solomon, *Public Welfare*, chapter 5; and Barber, *The Bourgeoisie*, p. 24. On appointment of Paré in sixteenth century Paris, see n. 58, below.

Prolonged struggles over status and role among members of the medical profession show, once again, that university faculties were not insulated from the winds of change. The University of Paris which had been the main center of the university book-trade in the age of scribes was particularly vulnerable to the new currents. The very closeness of print shops to colleges in Paris encouraged friction as well as new forms of interchange. In this regard the active role performed by Parisian printers needs to be contrasted with the more passive role previously performed by stationers and scribes. Here again too much emphasis on trends traced in Galileo studies are likely to lead us astray.

In France no second stream of science outside the universities seems to have flourished, perhaps because the University of Paris continued much longer than other universities to pursue the medieval tradition that linked mathematics to physics. Perhaps there is also a connection with the fact that printing in Paris was much more closely linked to the University than in any other city.[52]

In the age of the scribe, Parisian stationers, who handled the university book-trade, tended to play a subservient role. In the age of the printer, however, book provisions for faculties at the unversity were handled by more independent entrepreneurs. As is suggested by the case of Robert Estienne, Parisian printers did not necessarily pursue the same policy as Sorbonne theologians. On more than one occasion, the two groups sharply clashed. Paris printers were also more sensitive than earlier stationers had been to the demands of kings and parlements. The printed book-trade was too large and varied to be controlled by old university regulations. Although some Paris printers might still serve, as had the stationers, in the role of college officials, they were often linked with branches elsewhere in France and with foreign firms as well.[53] Their multifarious connections have to be examined before the strength of any one link can be made clear.

It is quite true that French printers sometimes served the University of Paris in official capacities.[54] It is also clear that certain Parisian colleges

52 Drake, 'Early Science,' p. 52. It seems doubtful that links were closer in Paris than in other university towns such as Wittenberg, Tübingen, Leiden or Cologne.

53 Bietenholz, *Basle and France* offers data on networks linking Paris firms to outside ones. Parent, *Les Métiers*, pp. 51, 124–5, 168 discusses the activities of some five hundred bookmen who inhabited university *quartiers* and notes the shift from the Sorbonne to royal regulatory power.

54 Sherrington, *The Endeavour*, pp. 3–4 describes services rendered to out-of-town students by de Colines and the Estiennes. The end papers of Sherrington's biography provide useful maps, pinpointing the numerous celebrated sixteenth-century print shops that clustered around the University of Paris.

held scholastic physics in high esteem – to the point of arranging for the early printing of treatises by Oxford and Paris schoolmen.[55] But although late medieval academic markets were important to early printers, tapping new markets was also profitable and was vigorously pursued. A so-called 'second stream' of non-academic publication may be found near the Seine (and the Rhône) throughout the first century of printing. Treatises by a new breed of vernacular science-writers came off French presses no less frequently than did Rabelaisian satires on pedants, priests, and Sorbonnistes. In Lyons, no less than London, practicing apothecaries broke into print by attacking 'The Abuses and Ignorance of Physicians.'[56] In Paris, no less than Nuremberg, engravers (such as Geoffroy Tory) also wrote treatises on geometry. As is noted below, French presses sponsored the debut of an anatomist–printer, Charles Estienne. They made it possible for artisans such as the potter Bernard Palissy to gain access to writings by Paracelsus and Cardano and to turn out popular attacks on the Sorbonne. Palissy's *Discours Admirables*, containing his lectures to Parisian 'physicians, dilettanti, and *gens du monde*' and inviting his readers to come to his shop for demonstrations of his work, epitomized the new genre of vernacular science-writing that was ushered in by printing.[57] So too did the works of the self-proclaimed barber–surgeon, Ambroise Paré. That Paré, who knew no Latin, was elevated to the rank of college professor (albeit at a college for surgeons, not physicians) suggests how some academic conventions were broken (to the consternation of some Paris professors) rather than inertly sustained.[58]

Moreover these trends encompassed mathematics as well as medicine. French engravers, no less than French barbers, became authors and professors. Euclid and Archimedes were translated into French as into other tongues. French tutors and reckon-masters were just as eager as their counterparts elsewhere to attract wealthy pupils and patrons while

---

55 Clagett, *Science of Mechanics*, pp. 652–3 lists pertinent titles printed under the auspices of the College of Montaigu. The anti-humanist, Gallican and Ockhamist views of Montaigu's faculty are described by Renaudet, *Préreforme*, pp. 463 ff.

56 On this Lyons publication by Pierre Braillier, an apothecary, see N. Z. Davis, 'Printing and the People,' p. 215.

57 Rossi, *Philosophy Technology*, pp. 1–4 reviews recent literature on Palissy and discusses his possible influence on the young Francis Bacon. See also Sarton, *Six Wings*, pp. 164–71.

58 Distinctions between Latin-reading, learned 'surgeons of the long-robe' at the Collège de Saint Côme and barber–surgeons are covered by Sarton, *Six Wings*, p. 197. Paré created a stir by being admitted to the St Côme faculty without Latin learning. For further references, see *Six Wings*, pp. 300–1, n. 75; n. 76.

achieving the more elevated status conferred by literary fame. There was no dearth of new arithmetic books in sixteenth-century France. The 'medieval tradition that linked mathematics to physics' and both to glosses on Aristotle's books was not a prominent feature in most of the texts, although many of them did attempt to dignify and elevate tricks of the reckon-master's trade. The same literary devices that had earlier adorned anthologies of devotional literature began to appear in arithmetic books which dealt with tables of interest and accounting. The importance of cultivating business arts by financiers and statesmen was stressed by authors with aspirations toward upward mobility who added particles to their own names while aiming their books at officials and governors. The same authors also found ways of dignifying applied or practical geometry. Its usefulness to gentry with landed estates and to nobles entrusted with military command could be underlined.[59]

As these comments suggest, the shadow of the Sorbonne did not prevent French publishers from issuing numerous texts that placed a new language of numbers at the disposal of merchants, surveyors, and military men. Nor did sixteenth-century French academies, which were affiliated with scholar–printers and editors, seem unwilling to press for curriculum reform. On the contrary, projects for reforming the teaching of mathematics went together with plans to reform orthography and grammar and with a celebration of the elegance of the French language itself. In this regard it may be a mistake to dismiss all the 'critiques of method' by 'anti-Aristotelian philosophers,' such as Francis Bacon and Peter Ramus as having little or no effect on university science.[60] Although Ramus contributed nothing to the 'new mechanics,' he did help to propel mathematics as a separate discipline. He also issued a challenge that captured the imagination of the young Kepler.[61] In his *Scholae Mathematicae*, published at Basel in 1569, he served mathematicians and atronomers – much as Vasari served painters and sculptors – thus elevating calculators to the dignity achieved by inspired poets and artists.[62] In developing new terms such

59 For data see two articles by N. Z. Davis, 'Sixteenth-Century French Arithmetics'; and 'Mathematicians in the Sixteenth-Century French Academies.' The possible relevance of these texts to the 'spirit of capitalism' is noted on p. 384, volume 1 above.
60 Drake, 'Early Science,' pp. 49–50.
61 See p. 651 below.
62 Rose, *Italian Renaissance of Mathematics*, p. 259, notes that Ramus was preparing an enlarged second edition when killed during the Massacre of St Bartholomew's eve and that his first edition was used by Bernardino Baldi for his large-scale *Lives of Mathematicians* (which covered some two hundred biographies but was never published).

as 'negative number' he could perhaps be said to have contributed something to the 'new math' of his day. Unlike Francis Bacon, at all events, Ramus was keenly aware of the significance of the language of numbers. He worked zealously to reform the French university curriculum, pointing to German achievements (especially to Melanchthon's reforms) as a spur to patriotic Valois kings.[63] At least one of his projects was crowned with some success, when new chairs in pure and applied mathematics were established at Paris. The French example in turn was used to prod English authorities by curriculum reformers there.

2. PUBLICIZING SCIENCE: NEW CAREERS OPEN TO VARIED TALENTS

In both medicine and mathematics, expanding academic opportunities went hand in hand with the chance to achieve literary fame. The new forms of authorship and intellectual property rights created by print proved no less attractive to would-be professors than to artisans and other groups. The chance to serve expanding book markets encouraged the adoption of new attitudes on the part of professors, tutors, and clerks. Literate élites underwent internal transformations as old pedagogical impulses were drawn into new channels. Science-writing provided sixteenth-century teachers with alternative ways of exerting their talents. They were confronted by a variety of conflicts and choices that had not confronted many clerks before.

The career of Jacques Peletier du Mans (as has been demonstrated by Professor Davis) offers a good illustration of this point.[64] Peletier moved in and out of teaching posts at Bayeux, Poitiers, and Bordeaux while turning out books on diverse branches of the *quadrivium* and collaborating with other members of the Pléiade in their projects for purifying and glorifying French. Intervals spent between teaching posts found him lodging with printers in Paris and Lyons while preparing treatises for

---

[63] Hooykaas, *Humanisme, Science et Réforme*, chap. x, discusses Ramus' role as proselytizer for mathematical studies and his survey of the state of mathematics in sixteenth-century Europe. Ramus was especially impressed by developments in German cities and helped to propel the claim that Melanchthon was 'the preceptor of Europe' and that Wittenberg was the nursery of science. See also the facsimile of the 1569 Basel publication: Petrus Ramus, *Scholae in Liberales Artes*.

[64] See N. Z. Davis, 'Peletier and Beza Part Company,' for above account.

their presses. In the winter of 1547-8, Vascosan's shop in the Rue Saint Jacques[65] was the scene of daily discussion and argument between Peletier and his learned friends (such as Theodore Beza) on the kind of problems that ought to go into arithmetic books, on using Latin as against French, and on the usefulness of devising a uniform orthography. In Lyons during most of the period from 1553 through 1555, Peletier made his headquarters at 'the atelier of Jean I de Tournes.' He tutored young Jean II in mathematics and saw some of his views on orthography incorporated into the handsome French Protestant Bible that de Tournes printed in 1554. Troubled by the outbreak of religious warfare, and determined to remain in the Catholic fold, Peletier later withdrew from association with Protestants, renounced vernacular science-writing and his projects for reform. But his experiences at Paris and Lyons suggest that printers played a larger role in shaping sixteenth-century academic careers than is noted in many accounts.

This point may be reinforced by taking as a second example the career of Oronce Finé, royal lecturer at the University of Paris in the 1530s. Although he has been described as the 'most lustrous mathematician of his day,'[66] Finé's work as an astronomer was technically inferior to that of many of his contemporaries. His skills seem to have been displayed to better advantage as a teacher, technician, and book illustrator. He was fond of parading his considerable fund of Latin learning and wrote several treatises against contaminating 'higher' mathematics with the vulgar problems posed in commercial arithmetics. Yet he also contributed to vernacular science-writing (probably with 'vulgar' commercial motives in mind) and expounded diverse branches of the *quadrivium* for early sixteenth-century laymen. His defense of the vernacular was characteristically élitist: 'because many noble and fine minds among the gentry and bourgeois no less than mechanics lack knowledge of Latin.' But he still made use of new presses to teach a wider public than could be taught in college halls. Moreover, he proved just as versatile as any other 'Renaissance man'

---

65 In providing hospitality for Peletier, Vascosan was carrying on a family tradition. His father-in-law, Josse Bade (Badius) had been equally hospitable. See Parent, *Les Métiers*, p. 170.
66 N. Z. Davis, 'Sixteenth Century French Arithmetics,' pp. 30–1. Finé's technical inferiority was pointed out to me by Owen Gingerich. For basic study of his work see Ross, 'Studies on Oronce Finé' and also by the same author, 'Oronce Finé's De Sinibus Libri II,' pp. 379 ff. Other useful references are offered by Hilliard and Poulle, 'Oronce Finé et L'Horloge Planétaire,' pp. 320–1; Brun, *Le Livre Français*, p. 43.

when advising François I on fortifications during the Italian campaign or when developing new techniques for cartographers and surveyors. Like most medieval mathematicians and astronomers, Finé was both willing and able to work with his hands, designing instruments and maps to rival those produced by other skilled craftsmen and even serving the Paris printer, Simon de Colines, as a designer of title borders in his spare time.

As these two examples may suggest, pedagogues were perhaps more likely than were craftsmen to take advantage of new careers opened by print and to contribute to the enrichment of technical literature. 'It is paradoxical that the first treatise on mining and metallurgy next to Biringuccio's in date but wider in scope was composed by a man who was neither a miner nor a metal worker but a physician and burgomaster; Agricola had been a teacher of Greek and Latin.'[67] What seems paradoxical is the assumption that teachers of Greek and Latin, who were friends of scholar–printers, were *not* going to be involved in a literary translation movement. Surely there were very few merchants, miners, or metal workers who might have had the leisure and requisite literary skills. Knowledge of Greek and Latin was obviously helpful for translating Greek and Latin technical texts. A town physician and schoolmaster like Erasmus' friend Georg Bauer seems to me to have just the right mix of talents to produce the famous handbook. Much as medieval kings had called on professors to convert certain texts into mother tongues, so too did printers have to turn to Latin scholars when making ancient treatises on arts and crafts available to lay readers. Artisan-authors were often encouraged by printers to write new texts in their own tongue, but a vernacular translator required some command of Latin in order to function at all. Moreover, vernacular translation was not always the best way to achieve widespread use. An English alchemist asserted he was employing 'blunt and rude English' in order 'to please ten thousand laymen' instead of 'ten able clerks.'[68] Yet Dutch and Flemish treatises on mathematics and on botany had to be

[67] Sarton, *Six Wings*, p. 125. In view of the tendency to underrate the extent to which the cult of antiquity was compatible with curiosity about metallurgy and mechanics it is worth noting that study of classical technical literature 'awakened and fortified' Agricola's 'scientific curiosity' according to Sarton, *ibid*. A recent detailed study of Renaissance editions of the pseudo-Aristotelian *Mechanica* offers useful evidence of the initiative supplied for these publications by classical scholars, literati, and printers (beginning with Cardinal Bessarion and Aldus Manutius). Rose and Drake, 'The Pseudo-Aristotelian "Questions."'

[68] Thomas Norton, *The Ordinall of Alchemy* (1477) cited by Jones, *Triumph*, p. 5, n. 8.

converted from a little-known vernacular into Latin in order to reach wider markets abroad.[69]

Furthermore, the use of vernaculars for the purpose of popularization had been a familiar resort of teachers and preachers before printing. Vernacular preaching had become an important branch of pulpit oratory in the age of scribes. A lively anecdotal style was increasingly cultivated when composing sermons designed to keep congregations awake.[70] That freshness and novelty were also prized is suggested by prefaces to preachers' anthologies.[71] Moreover, medieval texts for beginners in such fields as astronomy or optics had been written for the benefit of students attending the papal college and cathedral schools.[72] Private tutors and teachers trying to impart learning to young pupils had also anticipated later trends. Those who served in princely households or who taught in court schools also tried to simplify and enliven inherited materials as well as translate important works into vernacular tongues.

This is not to discount the significance of the new output of artisan-authors like Paré, Palissy, Dürer, Tartaglia *et al*. It is merely to note that learned men accustomed to teaching and preaching had been pioneering in translation and abridgement even before self-taught authors set to work. When one recalls that Nicole Oresme presented his royal master with French translations of Aristotle's *Politics* and *Ethics* one may be less inclined to regard Tartaglia's translation of Euclid as 'departing from ordinary scholarly practices' and less likely to assume that 'no professor would have bothered to make a vernacular transla-tion.'[73] In fact, the idea of conveying Euclidean geometry to laymen

---

[69] Clusius' work for Plantin consisted partly of translating Dutch, Spanish, Portuguese, and French scientific works into Latin. See Sarton, *Six Wings*, pp. 143–4. Schmitt, 'Essay Review' 1, 166–8, notes that Stevin was more influential in Latin than in Dutch. See also reference to Galileo's *Sidereus Nuncius*, n. 24 above.

[70] That English friars prized novel anecdotes that kept congregations awake (and were reluctant to share them with colleagues) is noted by Smalley, *English Friars*, pp. 37–44. Smalley also notes that despite new *exempla* the content of sermons remained traditional. Stale and hackneyed themes made it even more desirable to use fresh and novel anecdotes.

[71] A fourteenth-century collection of sermons thus contains a prologue by its compiler stating that 'modern man who admires novelty' was being given a 'novel collection in a novel style.' Rouse and Rouse, 'The Texts Called Lumen Anime,' p. 28. See also remarks about an 'avid public interest in novel things' made in connection with an Italian sermon of 1305–6 noted in Rosen, 'The Invention of Eyeglasses,' p. 34.

[72] This was the case with Pecham's *Perspectiva Communis*, according to Lindberg's introduction, *John Pecham*, p. 17.

[73] Drake, 'Early Science,' p. 51. On Oresme's translations, see references given by C. R. Sherman, 'Some Visual Definitions,' p. 319 n. Oresme's prefaces, cited by Sherman, contain the topoi which vernacular translators democratized after printing.

and of exploiting the new presses to do this was vigorously advocated fifty years before Tartaglia by Luca Pacioli, who was a doctor of divinity and on the faculty of several universities.

The celebrated portrait of Pacioli by Jacopo de' Barbari which shows the friar teaching Euclid to the future Duke of Urbino does not do justice to Pacioli's unconventional role as a pioneering public lecturer and science-writer whose work was ransacked by others for a century or more. As a pedagogue, the friar probably owed much to the Venetian 'school of the Rialto' where he had studied as a youth; as a publicist he was also clearly indebted to the Venetian presses.[74] At the same time, he reflected attitudes that had been common among Franciscan preachers in many regions from the thirteenth century on. 'Pacioli had the common touch. In his book, he turned away from scholars and directed his voice to the public.'[75] Far from considering vernacular translations beneath him, Pacioli urged that Euclid be made available in the vernacular because 'the subject matter will bear more fruit if there are more people to read it.'

Pacioli understood the need...for mathematics and a study of Euclid... He had the native good sense to see that a printed book in mathematics would not get far unless Arabic numerals were used and unless the native language was resorted to in order to reach the greatest number of students.[76]

Dedicated to a Duke of Urbino and partly subsidized by Marco Sanuto, Pacioli's major treatise, the *Summa de arithmetica, geometria et proportionate* (Venice: Paganini, 1494), was deliberately written in the vernacular for 'if written in Latin, each and everyman could not understand it.'[77] Thereafter, it was translated into Latin and numerous other tongues. It was excerpted in countless sixteenth-century works, including mathematics texts used in college courses. Its contents were

74 J. B. Ross, 'Venetian Schools,' p. 531 points to the key study by Nardi, 'La scuola di Rialto' which relates Pacioli's activities to the school of the Rialto and the latter to Paduan Aristotelianism. Dr Ross's own article contains a wealth of new data on a pedagogue who edited several volumes for the Aldine press: Giovanni Battista Egnazio.
75 R. E. Taylor, *No Royal Road*, p. 197. In a similar vein, see remarks of Alessandro Piccolomini, Archbishop of Patras on the need for vernacular translation to benefit Italian engineers and architects (as reported by Biringuccio), cited by Rose and Drake, 'The Pseudo-Aristotelian "Questions,"' p. 85.
76 R. E. Taylor, 'Luca Pacioli,' p. 183. Pacioli's revision of the Latin translation of Euclid done by Campanus of Novara for Pope Urban IV (first printed by Erhard Ratdolt, Venice, 1482 and used by Copernicus) appeared in Venice in 1509. It was done partly to rescue Campanus' reputation from attack. See Rose, 'Humanist Culture.' p. 99.
77 R. E. Taylor, *No Royal Road*, p. 187.

paraphrased by Bishop Tunstall and Jerome Cardano.[78] That Pacioli himself reproduced ('plagiarized'?) large portions of earlier scribal treatises was made clear by the author himself and is often noted in later literature.[79] Less often noted is the way this fifteenth-century encyclopedic work linked double-entry bookkeeping and business arithmetic with Pythagorean harmonies and the music of the spheres. Fibonacci's practical Book of the Abacus was thus brought together with treatises composed by commentators on Euclid, such as Campanus of Novara, who stressed divine proportion, golden sections and the like. As an eclectic mélange of classical and Arabic, scholastic and mercantile treatises, Pacioli's *Summa* represents something of a landmark. Within the covers of this one book could be found all the varied aspects of mathematics known to his day. As a friar and theologian who numbered quattrocento artists among his close friends, Pacioli bridged the gulf between schoolmen and humanists. He paid homage in his preface not only to scholastic culture heroes such as Aristotle, Isidore of Seville, Boethius, Bartolus, and Duns Scotus, but also to Renaissance artists – to Verrocchio, Mantegna, Piero della Francesca and Alberti.[80] He converted Piero's treatise on perspective from script into print and from Latin into a vernacular tongue while inserting it as a section of his Italian treatise *On Divine Proportion*.[81] Just as he expounded the mysteries of double-entry bookkeeping for merchants, so too he underlined the importance of the study of Euclid for surveyors, architects, and other 'universal men.'

Engravers and type designers – such as Dürer and Tory – were

---

[78] For indications that parts of the *Summa* entered into the two chief arithmetic texts that replaced Boethius in sixteenth-century college courses, see remarks on Bishop Tunstall's *De Arte Supputandi* (1522) in Stillwell, *Awakening Interest in Science*, p. 71 and comments on Cardano's *Ars Magna* (1545) by Ore, foreword to G. Cardano, *The Great Art*, p. vii. On how Tunstall and Cardano replaced Boethius as required texts at Oxford by 1549 see Johnson, *Astronomical Thought*, pp. 83–4.

[79] His discovery of a ms. version of Fibonacci's *Liber Abaci* in the Venetian library of San Antonio di Castello is noted by Rose, *Italian Renaissance of Mathematics*, p. 83.

[80] See preface to Luca Pacioli's *Summa* (tr. R. E. Taylor), p. 191. In reconciling Plato with Aristotle and the schoolmen, Pacioli was following the path set forth by Cardinal Bessarion in his widely read *In Calumniatorum Platonis* (first printed in Latin in 1469). Kristeller, *Renaissance Concepts*, p. 101.

[81] Sarton, *Appreciation*, p. 135. Pacioli is scolded by Vasari for stealing and publishing as his own Piero's treatise. Vasari, *Lives*, p. 93. Piero's treatise *De Prospectiva Pingendi* is described by Panofsky in *Albrecht Dürer* (1 vol. ed.), pp. 249, 251 as an unpublished work which did not get printed until 1899. Dürer's trip to Bologna in 1506 to learn the 'secret' of perspective from a master (who may have been Pacioli) is noted on pp. 251–2. Of course, the Italian edition of Piero's treatise was still in a foreign tongue to the Nuremberg artist.

especially attracted to this aspect of Pacioli's work. The effort to design letters that conformed to classical canons, and the belief that ancient lettering had been modelled on the same lines as Vitruvian man produced some remarkable human alphabets and experiments in type design.[82] According to Panofsky, Dürer's printed treatise on regular polygons helped to acquaint 'coopers and cabinet makers with Euclid and Ptolemy and...professional mathematicians with...workshop geometry.' The Italian friar performed a comparable service, and probably contributed something to Dürer's treatise itself. When considering the expanding vogue for Vitruvian man, the nesting 'perfect' solids that captivated Kepler throughout his life, the 'geometrical spirit' that Pascal opposed to intuition, or even ideal cities laid out with divine proportions in mind, Pacioli's early printed treatises are worth a longer look. As an editor of Euclid, his work also deserves more attention as providing themes reworked later by Elizabethans such as John Dee.[83]

In the year 1570...a very important book was printed by John Day in London. It was the first English translation of Euclid by H. Billingsley, citizen of London. The translation is preceded by a very long preface in English by John Dee in which Dee surveys all the mathematical sciences both from the point of view of Platonic and mystical theory of number and also with the purpose of being of practical utility to artisans. In this preface, Dee makes many quotations from Vitruvius...gives the Vitruvian theory of architecture ...using not only 'Vitruvius the Romaine' but also 'Leo Baptista Albertus a Florentine.'[84]

[82] Morison, *Fra Luca Pacioli*, p. 7. John Lewis, *Anatomy of Printing*, pp. 55–6 also offers relevant references and illustrations. Efforts to achieve the impossible task of reconciling human proportions with Roman inscriptions and Euclidean geometry, are described by Lewis (p. 56) as straining logic to the breaking point. Obsession with symmetry and insistence on perfect congruence leads, beyond the 'architecture of humanism,' to a kind of 'crazy' logic, reflected in the utopian schemes for perfect cities of the seventeenth century or in Kepler's preoccupation with perfect solids (see chap. 7, n. 43 below). Perspective renderings of alphabet forms and manuals on perspective partly inspired by Pacioli's work are also illustrated by Mayor, *Prints and People*, 173–8. Dürer's attempt to force Gothic letters into a system based on modules is well illustrated in Panofsky's *Albrecht Dürer* (1 vol. ed.), figures 6a–7b, pp. 258–9.

[83] See description of the plan of 'Christianopolis' in Yates, *The Rosicrucian Enlightenment*, pp. 147–8, where emphasis on the mathematical sciences is attributed partly to John Dee's influence. In considering the Euclidean and Vitruvian features that are prominent in continental utopian schemes in the seventeenth century, Pacioli's *Summa* and *Divine Proportion* seem to me to be more seminal than the later writings of Dee or Fludd. Dee's trips to Italy brought him into contact with Pacioli's successors such as Federico Commandino (who published a manuscript attributed to Euclid brought to him by Dee). See Rose, 'Notes and Correspondence.' On Dee's stay with his Antwerp printer, Sylvius, see chap. 2, n. 168, volume 1 above.

[84] Yates, *The Art of Memory*, p. 347.

In view of these references and of the contents of the work he was introducing, one might expect that Dee was not unfamiliar with Pacioli's
eclectic work. Indeed he mentions 'Frater Lucas de Burgo' along with
Tartaglia, Dürer *et al.* as precursors of his effort to bring Euclid to
'unlatined people.' The Italian universities, Dee argued, did not feel
themselves 'disgraced or their studies anything hindered' by Pacioli's
large volumes 'in vulgar speche.'[85]

Later on, to be sure, Dee's preface was put to anti-Aristotelian and
anti-academic purposes that were quite alien to the Franciscan friar.
Thus the 'preface before Euclide' by the 'expert and learned Dr John
Dee' was used as ammunition by a Puritan divine, urging curriculum
reform at the English universities while attacking 'Aristotelians' and
the 'supine negligence of the schools.'[86] Pacioli, however, was writing
before later battle lines were drawn. In keeping with his protean role
as a 'father of double-entry bookkeeping,' translator of Piero della
Francesca, mentor of Leonardo da Vinci and doctor of divinity, he
displayed an ecumenical frame of mind. After the initial privilege
granted to his wide-ranging work expired, sections of the *Summa*
were published separately. 'The Perfect School for Merchants' and
'Divine Proportion' tended to go their separate ways. But for the ten-
year interval, 1494–1504, a printed vernacular mathematical encyclopedia had managed to link the most heavenly with the most mundane
concerns.

Pacioli was probably the most wide-ranging, influential and forceful
advocate of mathematics for the layman during the first century of
print. His work repeatedly stressed utilitarian, popular, and progressive
themes. For Zilsel this indicates that Pacioli 'must have had close contacts with artist-engineers and merchants.'[87] In the Marxist scheme
adopted by Zilsel, it is as if friars and scholars were not permitted to
initiate 'progressive' trends once early capitalists had appeared on the

[85] John Dee, Preface, *The Elements of Geometrie of the Most Ancient Philosopher Euclide of Megara* (tr. and ed. Henry Billingsley) (London, John Day, 1570), pp. Aiij v–Aiiij r. (I am indebted to Alice McGinty for bringing this reference to my attention.) On John Day, see recent mono- graph by Oastler.

[86] John Webster, passages from *Academiarum Examen* (London, 1654). Cited by Pagel, 'News, Notes and Queries.' Webster's eulogy of Dee provoked a rebuke from an Oxford professor, Seth Ward, who likened Webster's 'canting discourse' to that of a 'moping Friar' while deprecating the school of mathematical enthusiasts such as Dee and Fludd and praising Baconian experimental philosophy. Yates, *Rosicrucian Enlightenment*, pp. 186–7. For full account of this debate see Debus, *Science and Education*.

[87] Zilsel, 'The Genesis,' p. 342, n. 31.

scene. The initial impulse to contribute to public knowledge always has to come from merchants and artisan-engineers. Yet priests often activated presses more readily than did guildsmen. There is no question that Pacioli was on friendly terms with artists such as Piero della Francesca and Leonardo da Vinci. But it was Piero who composed a Latin treatise and the friar who put it into the vernacular and got it circulated in print.[88] It is quite possible that Pacioli secured the help of Leonardo for the design of illustrations for his *Divine Proportion*,[89] but the initiative for making the work available to architects and surveyors came from the friar and not the artist-engineer.

The prominent role played by friars – such as Pacioli, Bruno, Foscarini, Campanella, Mersenne and others – as heterodox science-writers and publicists surely deserves more attention. The Franciscan tradition that transmitted the heritage of Grosseteste, Roger Bacon, and John Pecham is also worth noting when considering 'neo-Platonic' or 'Pythagorean' trends in the quattrocento. Pecham's *Perspectiva Communis* offers a good example of the kind of science-writing that provided Pacioli with a precedent. But it was designed for friars at Paris and Oxford and clerks at the papal university or monastic seminaries. The different public reached by treatises, such as Pecham's with the aid of early-modern printers is striking. An Italian edition of 1482 was probably consulted by Leonardo da Vinci as well as by other Renaissance artisan-engineers.[90]

The contrast between Pacioli's frequent resort to the new presses and Leonardo's predilection for ciphers and secrecy is also instructive. It underlines my point that the role of the publicist was often more easily assumed by teachers and preachers (by a bishop like Tunstall or a friar like Pacioli) than by artists and craftsmen who were untrained in

---

88 See note 81 above. Note also that L. B. Alberti wrote his major architectural treatise *De Re Aedificatoria* not in Italian for architects but in Latin, under the patronage of Lionello d'Este, for presentation to Pope Nicholas V. This point is underlined by Krautheimer, 'Alberti's Templum Etruscum,' p. 328.

89 According to Keele, 'Leonardo da Vinci's Influence,' p. 361, Leonardo probably learned how to manipulate mathematical roots while working for Pacioli. The extent of Leonardo's collaboration with Pacioli is as difficult to determine as that of Jan Stephan of Calcar with Vesalius. A printed copy of Pacioli's *Summa de Arithmetica* as well as an unidentified vernacular ms. Euclid is listed among Leonardo's books. See items No. 93 and No. 110 in Ladislao Reti, 'The Two Unpublished Manuscripts,' pp. 81 ff.

90 Lindberg (tr. and ed.), *John Pecham*, p. 17. Keele, 'Leonardo da Vinci's Influence,' p. 364 cites Fazio Cardano's Italian translation of Pecham's treatise as influential in Leonardo's work. Eastwood, in a review of Lindberg's edition of Pecham (*Speculum* (1972) p. 324), contends that Pecham's influence on quattrocento artists, such as Ghiberti, has been overplayed. Of course, Ghiberti did not, like Leonardo, have printed vernacular works to consult.

rhetorical and scribal arts. The case of Tartaglia, so often singled out to illustrate 'the frame of mind of gun founders and military engineers,'[91] is also worth examining. The self-taught artisan-author pioneered with a vernacular translation of Euclid, yet he was unwilling to part with the most recent tricks of a reckon-master's trade. Indeed he was infuriated by Cardano's publication of his solution to a cubic equation – even though he was repeatedly credited with the discovery in three separate chapters of Cardano's book.[92]

To the modern scholar imbued with the notion that, as R. K. Merton has put it 'an idea is not really yours until you give it away' (i.e., through publication), Tartaglia's attitude seems strange. Yet...the very notion of individual ownership of ideas was itself novel and strange.[93]

In view of his objections to the publication of his mathematical solution there is need to qualify the familiar portrayal of Tartaglia as a representative of a new non-academic popularizing movement, associated with artisan-engineers and emergent capitalist enterprise. A more wholehearted acceptance of the 'novel and strange' uses of publicity was demonstrated by Jerome Cardano who, unlike Tartaglia, had gone through the schools. As a science-writer Jerome Cardano was following an example set by his natural father. Fazio Cardano was a university professor whose vernacular translation of Pecham's treatise on optics has already been noted as having been consulted by Leonardo da Vinci among others.[94] Leonardo took advantage of printed materials to increase his mastery of numerous fields. But he also retained the secretive habits of medieval craftsmen. His behavior – like that of Tartaglia – may remind us that Latin grammars had circulated more freely in the later middle ages than did 'mysteries' transmitted within guilds.

The desire to collaborate more closely with craftsmen had long been expressed by university scholars, such as Vincent of Beauvais, Albertus

---

[91] Zilsel, 'Genesis,' pp. 337–8; see also Drake, 'Early Science,' pp. 50–2.

[92] Ore, foreword to *The Great Art*, pp. ix–xi, offers a detailed account of this intriguing priority struggle. Tartaglia actually 're-discovered' the contested solution (for the special cubic equation $x^3 + ax = b$) and when imparting the secret to Cardano claimed he made Cardano swear an oath 'never to publish it and put it down in cipher.' The opening sentence of the *Ars Magna* (p. 7) suggests the rudimentary state of acknowledgments in the sixteenth century. 'This art originated with Mohamet, the son of Moses the Arab. Leonardo of Pisa is a trustworthy source for this statement.'

[93] Mahoney, *The Mathematical Career*, p. 7.

[94] See n. 90 above. On Leonardo's study of printed technical literature, see n. 135 below.

Magnus or Roger Bacon.[95] Medieval schoolmen indeed often seemed more eager to learn from guildsmen than the latter were to publicize what they knew. Here again it seems worth recalling that the spread of glad tidings was cultivated by medieval churchmen but guarding trade secrets was inculcated in medieval apprentices. Insofar as artisan-authors did contribute to sixteenth-century technical literature, they were risking the disapproval of colleagues who felt that guild 'mysteries' were not intended to be disclosed. Their prefaces show their felt need to justify themselves. In resorting to publicity, they were not perpetuating workshop traditions but breaking with them instead.

Even where secrecy had not been enforced during previous centuries, and where letters were mastered by shopkeepers' sons, apprenticeship learning and unwritten recipes were the customary channels for transmitting the tricks of all trades. New techniques or inventions might be mentioned in writing, but this was usually in a sermon that some clerk had transcribed. Before the advent of printing, events of significance, when reported at all, were usually conveyed from the pulpit. 'Lenses were already known in the thirteenth century...For three centuries a kind of conspiracy of silence was entered into concerning them... they became an object of theoretical study only in the sixteenth century.'[96] News of the invention of spectacles was not suppressed by 'a conspiracy' in the later middle ages. But it was conveyed by word of mouth somewhat vaguely in a sermon that was transcribed.[97] By the early seventeenth century, however, technology had gone to press. Reports of optical instruments which were being developed gave rise to priority struggles over inventions such as 'Galileo's tube.' As noted above, movable type had a unique advantage over the other late medieval inventions, for it alone was able to advertise itself. Hence the unusually rapid spread of printing and debates about its inventor's name. Inventors of compass or gunpowder might also be described as

95 Interchanges between the two groups based on personal contact rather than written materials are well described by Shelby, 'Education of Medieval Masons,' pp. 16–18, who suggests how masons and their patrons collaborated on Gothic cathedral building. For reference by Roger Bacon to Magister Petrus' desire to 'learn from metal workers' *et al.* see Zilsel, 'Origins of William Gilbert's Method,' p. 30. Other references are given by Crombie, 'Commentary,' Clagett (ed.) *Critical Problems*, p. 73.

96 Rossi, *Philosophy, Technology*, p. 35. Rossi refers to an article by V. Ronchi, who has underlined the prolonged failure to put lenses to use for scientific purposes (as in telescopes and microscopes) in numerous studies.

97 See Rosen, 'Invention of Eyeglasses' for data on the Lenten sermon delivered at Florence in 1306 by Friar Giordano of Pisa – one of the earliest extant specimens of a transcribed vernacular Italian sermon.

subject to a 'kind of conspiracy of silence.'[98] It was not that such technical inventions were despised or even undervalued until a new class of capitalists came along; it was rather that in the late fifteenth century, functions performed by the pulpit began to be taken over by the press. The advent of printing lessened reliance on oral transmission even while providing powerful new incentives to open closed sketchbooks and publicize the tricks of various trades. The result was an avalanche of technical treatises and teach-yourself books, which had at least as much effect on advanced studies as on procedures followed in workshops.

Just how this early printed literature may have affected actual practices and techniques is a complex question. On the one hand there is evidence to support the sceptical opinion that 'teach-yourself' books proved more helpful to teachers than doers.[99] The opinion that books explaining double-entry bookkeeping were more helpful for teachers of accountancy than for merchants has already been noted.[100] A recent biographer of Fermat makes the same point concerning many presumably 'practical,' problem-solving sixteenth-century arithmetic texts.[101] Similarly Samuel Eliot Morison emphasizes how mariners went on using dead-reckoning and ignoring treatises presumably written for their benefit.

To assume that once an instrument is invented or a rutter or nautical almanac published, every offshore shipmaster is familiar with them is a complete fallacy. The very simple mathematical calculations involved in obtaining latitude from a meridional observation of the sun were too much for most sailors in 1550 and are still too much for many sailors in the present century.[102]

But although some scepticism concerning uncritical claims made for technical literature may be justified, it can also be carried too far.

98 For 'scraps of evidence' pertaining to the invention of the compass, see Kreutz, 'Mediterranean Contributions.' Diverse views on the origin of gunpowder are discussed by Hale, 'Gunpowder and the Renaissance,' pp. 115-17.

99 It is a mistake to assume as does McLean, *Humanism and the Rise of Science*, p. 142, that when John Dee directed his preface at technicians and artisans, he must have hit the target at which he presumably aimed. For useful discussions of general problems associated with relating technical literature to innovation, see Mathias, 'Who Unbound Prometheus?' chap. 3, Cipolla, *Before the Industrial Revolution*, chap. 6.

100 See above, p. 383, volume I. For good description of the professional 'overkill' in early treatises on bookkeeping see Yamey, 'Scientific Bookkeeping.'

101 Mahoney, *The Mathematical Career*, p. 6.

102 Morison, *The European Discovery of America*, pp. 141-2. See also discussion of tables carried by Columbus, pp. 582 ff below.

Whatever the case with double-entry bookkeeping or 'cossist algebra,' or nautical tables, there were printed materials – converting weights and measures, giving distances between important towns or guides to foreign languages and phrases – that probably did provide practical aid. Furthermore learned professional groups often profited from rule books, even though craftsmen went on using rules of thumb. Simple sailors might fail to master improved declination tables but what about cartographers, geographers and astronomers? Were they not likely to put such tables to good use? Even now, journals such as *Popular Mechanics* are rarely read by real mechanics; but they are studied with profit by students who are drawn toward some kind of scientific career. During the first centuries of printing, similar trends prevailed. The young Isaac Newton was stimulated by John Wilkins' *Mathematical Magick* – a 'popular science' treatise which owed something in turn to the works of Simon Stevin and to Galileo's early tracts.[103] Browsing at book fairs and reading at random probably helps to account for the proliferation of 'amateurs' and 'dilettanti' – who joined the scientific societies as gentlemen of leisure without any special institutional affiliations or professional roles. The same activity was common among professional scientists. As already noted, significant and novel services were rendered by technical handbooks which acted as 'silent instructors' during student years.

When dealing with the 'reaction of learned men to the state of technology' at all events, more consideration ought to be given to the precise state in question: had technology gone to press or was it still largely concealed? Beginning with early editions of Vitruvius and Valturius' first illustrated volume on military engines, going on to Biringuccio and Agricola, culminating in the late sixteenth-century works of Besson and Ramelli, the machines that men used in the great workshops and mines and arsenals of Western Europe were made increasingly visible to the armchair traveller. In this light it seems doubtful that the

philosopher of antiquity had as great an opportunity of appreciating the inventiveness of craftsmen as his successors of the sixteenth and seventeenth centuries...The success of craft empiricism was nothing new in...early-modern times...if the philosopher became conscious of its significance for

103 On young Newton, see Manuel, *Portrait*, p. 406 and citation on p. 245, volume 1 above. On
   Wilkins' work, see Shapio, *John Wilkins*, p. 43.

science it was not because such success was more dramatic now than in the past. It was always there to be seen by those who had eyes to see it, and the change was in the eyes of the beholder.[104]

Craft successes must have been more difficult to see as long as oral and scribal transmission prevailed. As discussion of Renaissance book illustration has already indicated, engravings which displayed the engines required to destroy a fortress or to erect an obelisk, did dramatize engineering feats. Readers who turned the pages of Jacques Besson's appropriately named *Theatre of Machines* were witnessing a dramatic spectacle that previous scholars had not seen, just as readers of Agricola and of Vesalius had their eyes opened to 'veins and vessels' that had been less visible before.[105]

In this regard, it is probably misleading to make too much of the continuous scholarly interest exhibited in technology since the twelfth century or to try to demonstrate the 'rising articulateness of higher artisans' by lining up a long series of 'technical treatises'

extending backwards to the sources behind the twelfth century chemical treatises of Adelard of Bath and of Theophilus the priest and forwards through the writings...of Walter of Henley...Cennini...Alberti and the other fifteenth-century German and Italian treatises on military engineering and architecture. The series continues through the sixteenth-century descriptions of crafts, and inventions by such writers as Agricola...and Ramelli down indeed to the Royal Society's projected History of Trades and the plates of the *Encyclopédie*.[106]

The path that led to the *Grande Encyclopédie* was not open in the days of Theophilus the priest. Instead of a gradually 'rising articulateness' there was a fairly abrupt change. Before printing, even the most 'articulate artisans' preferred to keep their sketchbooks closed. They might not have taken

the extra precaution of describing their designs in mirror-writing...but they were strongly inclined to keep their discoveries for themselves. In a world which knew little of copyrights or patents, the inventor had no interest in publicizing his work for others to steal. So long as their secrets remained secrets they were valuable, but once they became public property they were worthless. No wonder that few 'inventors' were prepared to expose their brain-children to the critical judgement of their peers.

[104] A. R. Hall, 'The Scholar and the Craftsman.' p. 15.
[105] See pp. 261–2, volume 1 above.
[106] Crombie, 'Commentary,' Clagett (ed.) *Critical Problems*, p. 77

Even so a patent system was beginning to grow up. Monarchs had less interest...in keeping inventions private and...were ready to grant privileges of copyright as their ancestors had granted lands, making the reproduction of specified inventions illegal for the space of several years. Protected in this way, mechanicians might have begun to think it worth the risk of telling the world of their discoveries in books...The growing market for books of mathematical instruments...could have taught them that publicity was as good a servant as secrecy.[107]

The emergence of mathematical practitioners and instrument-makers as distinctive occupational groups is often associated with new demands for greater precision made by monarchs, bureaucrats and merchants during early-modern times and is accordingly related to middle-class enterprise and expanding dynastic states. The output of mathematical instruments, atlases, globes and 'theatres of machines' should also be related to the new possibility of profiting from disclosing instead of withholding the tricks of varied trades. The new publicity apparatus enabled ingenious individuals to satisfy the long-standing 'public' aims of bureaucrats and army engineers even while serving their own private needs as well. It was not so much that 'monarchs had less interest in keeping inventions private' but that inventors had been given new incentives for making their brain children public.

The reasons for the growing demand for instruments of navigation in the sixteenth century are obvious. But there was also a demand for instruments by surveyors, architects, and miners. The old rule-of-thumb methods were felt to be inadequate; greater precision was now demanded and precise instruments of calculation needed to attain it.[108]

It seems likely that old rule-of-thumb methods had been felt to be inadequate by some groups for many centuries. As Rupert Hall reminds us, interest in precisely predicting the motion of projectiles did not wait until the introduction of gunpowder and cannon into warfare. 'The simplest methods of hurling projectiles – the human arm, the sling, the bow – pose problems of motion no less emphatically than more complex or powerful devices.'[109] The desire to publicize devices and techniques for determining the trajectory of projectiles waited – not for the invention of gunpowder but for opportunities opened up by print.

---

[107] Keller, *A Theatre of Machines*, p. 3.   [108] Keller, *A Theatre of Machines*, p. 3.
[109] A. R. Hall, 'The Scholar and the Craftsman,' p. 16.

The effect of early printed technical literature on science and technology is open to question. That it served as a major vehicle for the expression of a new 'scientific ethos' seems less subject to doubt. The socially conscious, public-spirited and progressive themes sounded in numerous prefaces have been noted in many studies. In expressing a desire to serve the cause of posterity, in setting unselfish service to humanity against guild monopolies and the selfish pursuit of personal glory, sixteenth-century authors repeatedly anticipated later Enlightenment views.[110] But the new values expressed in the prefaces were derived less from old routines pursued in artisan workshops than from reactions to the publicity apparatus furnished by print. By a marvelous alchemy, print transmuted self-seeking activities into public good. To advertise an invention or sea chart did not render it worthless but attracted purchasers to the shops of instrument-makers and map-publishers.

In this respect I agree with those who question Zilsel's emphasis on the strategic role played by workshops and arsenals where men were accustomed to working together and were familiar with ideas of progress that applied to improvements in particular arts and crafts.[111] When accounting for the emergence of an idea of progress one ought not to overlook the accumulation of improvements leading to the perfecting of certain skills among artisans. But a significant strategic role must also be reserved for the shift from script to print. If one looks hard enough, one may find different kinds of progressive themes being played in a limited way in libraries and observatories as well as in workshops or mines during the age of scribes. Print encouraged a fuller orchestration of all such themes and for the first time enabled them to be continuously sustained,

'The idea that technology must be furthered through publication made head-way in the sixteenth century'[112] mainly because technology could be furthered by publication – could 'go to press,' that is – for the first time. Map-publishers such as Ortelius, Mercator, Blaeu, and Hondius sponsored new forms of intellectual cooperation and served astronomers and mariners, historians, and merchant adventurers in new ways – not because they were affiliated with painters and Netherlands guildsmen but because they could take advantage of a new

110 In addition to Zilsel, Rossi et al., see Houghton, 'The History of Trades.'
111 See e.g. Keller, 'Zilsel, The Artisans,' pp. 281–6.   112 Zilsel, 'Genesis,' p. 335.

medium for duplicating charts and books.[113] The 'fading of guild secrecy' was not due to the growth of large-scale enterprise in general but to a particular enterprise represented by the expanding printing industry, that made possible technical publication programs.

In other words, new attitudes toward publicity ought to be related to new forms of publicity. Discussion of how authors of technical treatises dealt with a so-called 'contribution process' should be related to the new kind of 'contribution,' authors who were served by printers could make.[114] Cooperation among artisans and between patrons had long been encouraged by large-scale endeavors. The construction of cathedrals no less than the later manufacture of cannons had called for a pooling of varied talents. Ventures in cooperative data collection, however, could not be continuously or systematically pursued until after printers had set to work.[115] Thereafter authors were likely to write prefaces in which they supplemented traditional scribal themes by expressing their hope that their work might contribute in some way to the betterment of mankind – to a collective and cumulative cognitive advance.

This new concern about making a contribution toward a collective goal, this new desire to serve humanity and posterity, is misinterpreted when described as peculiarly altruistic. 'Knowledge is no longer the business of literati greedy for personal fame and disputing schoolmen,' says Zilsel, in connection with the *Transactions* of the Royal Society.[116] One need only glance at the long list of priority struggles to see that the rise of science entailed no particular decrease in greed or vanity or contentiousness among men of knowledge or inventors of useful things. Socially useful techniques could be publicized in the sixteenth century not because of the rise of a new class but because of the advent of print. Artisan-authors were no less attracted by the lure of new intellectual property rights than were literati and schoolmen. Dürer's preface, which expressed the wish to contribute to a collective endeavor, to augment and improve the art of painting for the benefit

113 See Zilsel, 'Genesis,' pp. 344–5 where Zilsel singles out these map-publishers as exemplifying the new approach.
114 Over-emphasis on craft traditions and neglect of new trends launched by print seem marked in Lilley, 'Robert Recorde and the Idea of Progress.' Lilley's theories are invoked but fail to help Keith Thomas analyze certain 'puzzling phenomena' in *Religion and the Decline of Magic*, p. 430. See also discussion on pp. 245–6, volume I above.
115 Here again, an exception should be made to cover certain major scribal message centers such as the Alexandrian Museum.   116 Zilsel, 'Genesis,' p. 348.

of later generations,[117] was not unrelated to the output of sheets containing giant woodcuts which, 'like the ships of a great merchant, bearing a distinctive flag, carried his initials: 'A.D.' all over the world.'[118] Whatever prefaces said about the glory of God and the good of humanity, the fact remained that contributors to technical literature were not only better able to serve others after printing; they were also better able to serve themselves.

We can discern the first...rudimentary formulations of the new concept of ...scientific progress in many texts written by the 'master craftsmen' and the engineers of the sixteenth century. As justifications for their work the technicians advanced the glory of God and public utility. And this work was viewed as something that would be added to an already existing fund of knowledge destined to be prolonged, perfected and integrated in time through the cooperation of others. Edgar Zilsel in a felicitous image has contrasted the workshop arsenal and *bottega*...where men worked together, to a monk's cell and a humanist's study. Zilsel draws conclusions...that are not wholly acceptable. But we can agree...that the birth of capitalism and ...economic competition led those men to theorize goals...which were... very different and certainly more impersonal than those of individual sanctification or literary immortality.[119]

Even while 'theorizing' about impersonal goals, however, artisan-authors were achieving eponymity. The personal celebrity and literary immortality won by Dürer, Paré, Palissy *et al.* had not been within the reach of guildsmen before.

Not only did these authors seek fame much as had scribal poets, but they were no less attracted than any other social group by the prospect of pecuniary rewards and material gain. It is noteworthy that high-minded passages justifying the writing of books by 'humble' craftsmen often went together with appeals to the reader to visit the author's workshop where 'marvelous things can be seen' and with the inclusion of addresses where instruments were on sale.[120] The important point

117 Cited by Lilley, 'Robert Recorde and the Idea of Progress,' p. 10.
118 Panofsky, *Albrecht Dürer*, p. 44.
119 Rossi, *Philosophy, Technology*, pp. 70–1. Rossi follows Zilsel in citing treatises written by a mixed group of authors ranging from vernacular writing artisans and/or engineers (Tartaglia, Dürer, Paré, Norman) to the Latin-reading astronomer–publisher 'Apianus' and map-publisher Mercator. See Zilsel, 'Genesis,' pp. 343–7.
120 See examples given of Henry Lyte, Robert Norman, Bernard Palissy on p. 241, volume 1 above. W. J. Blaeu also made clear where his maps, globes, and sea charts could be found. Early printers' colophons and booksellers' catalogues were among the first printed materials to treat readers as potential purchasers and guide them to places of sale.

is that selfishness and altruism could be served at the same time. This capacity to satisfy mixed motives needs more attention because it helps to explain the driving power of the press.

This point is just as applicable to learned Latin treatises as to more popular vernacular ones; to the 'brain children' of professors as to those of instrument-makers – if, indeed, the two figures can be kept apart.[121] A certain ambivalence concerning new forms of publicity characterized academicians no less than artisans at first. Both groups contained men who expressed their desire to disclose information for virtuous motives and who became entangled in priority disputes. It has been suggested that 'the craft of philologists like Fichet and Budé was changed by the invention of printing in ways parallel to the crafts of barber surgeons and navigators following the introduction of gunpowder and the compass.'[122] I am arguing, however, that craftsmen *and* scholars, barber–surgeons *and* philologists were affected by the same invention at the same time. When a barber–surgeon like Paré could become a published author, his craft was changed perhaps even more fundamentally than was the case when wounds were made by bullets rather than arrows. In the early-modern era, 'scholarship had as much ground on which to base its view of cumulative advance as had technology' notes a critic of Zilsel.[123] But scholarship and technology also shared common ground, namely the early printers' workshops. The new flow of technical literature required skills cultivated in the schoolroom no less than in urban workshops or mines. In view of the significance assigned to 'rudimentary formulations' of 'the new concept of scientific progress' it is necessary to repeat that texts written *for* craftsmen and engineers were not always written *by* them. Granted that an 'awareness of the...necessity of intellectual cooperation and of the progressive character of knowledge in time is...evident in passages in many "technical" books written in the sixteenth century,' this awareness should not be viewed as peculiar to master craftsmen. It was shared by preachers, teachers, and other learned men.

When analyzing diverse approaches toward new forms of publicity,

---

[121] Galileo combined both roles, inventing his 'proportional compass' while serving as a professor at Padua (see n. 11 above). So did his rival, the Jesuit astronomer, Christopher Scheiner, whose *Exegeses Fundamentorum Gnomonicorum* (Ingolstadt, 1615) contained a new design for an elliptical compass. Rose, 'Renaissance Italian Methods of Drawing the Ellipse,' pp. 399–400. In general the designing of scientific instruments seems to cut across town–gown divisions.

[122] Kinser, 'Ideas of Temporal Change,' p. 710.

[123] Keller, 'Zilsel, the Artisans,' p. 286.

moreover, one must assign due weight to personal idiosyncrasies which often counted more than did occupational roles. Cardano's flair for self-advertisement probably owed as much to temperament as to parental example or professional status group. Vesalius 'rushed into print' but other professors of anatomy did not.[124] Whereas some mathematicians and astronomers ran new presses themselves, others were reluctant even to let their manuscripts get into printers' hands. That Paracelsians tended to favor a paradoxical mixture of publicity with secrecy has been already noted. Bishop Sprat's complaint on this point is worth citing:

> This desire of glory and to be counted *Authors* prevails on all, even on many of the dark and reserv'd Chymists themselves: who are ever printing their greatest mysteries though indeed they seem to do it with so much reluctancy …which makes their style to resemble the smoak in which they deal.[125]

One reason why early-modern trends are peculiarly confusing to the historian of science is that many charlatans and pseudo-scientists were eager publicity-hounds, and many gifted professionals clung to habits shaped by scribes. It took time before the magician could be distinguished from the scientist by his refusal to disclose all that was known about his arts, by his 'smoky' style, and by his reluctance to frame his theories in a form where they could be openly tested and accepted or rejected.

> Furtiveness clung to alchemy. It thus sinned against the open altruism of the true scientific spirit. A precept of science is free interchange. 'Science' said Rutherford, 'depends on the combined wisdom of thousands of men all thinking about the same problem.' The alchemist concealed from others such knowledge as he thought he had. [He] devised secret systems. Cryptic alphabets…anagrams and acrostics masked [his] results.[126]

Rutherford's vision of a cooperative endeavor, which entailed the use of print, had been clearly articulated by Francis Bacon in the early seventeenth century. 'Knowledge of Nature was to be public; indeed, the jealously guarded secrets of craftsmen were to be set out in great collections of "histories." '[127] Bacon condemned magic for its 'non-

---

124 See discussion of the ambitious but long delayed publication program, involving elaborate illustration, of Fabricius in Adelman, *Embryological Treatises of Fabricius*, p. 23. See also Whitteridge, *William Harvey*, p. 19.

125 Sprat, *History of the Royal Society*, part 2, section viii, p. 74. See also discussion of secrecy and publicity, pp. 274 ff, volume 1 above.

126 Sherrington, *The Endeavour*, p. 46.   127 Rattansi, 'Alchemy and Natural Magic,' p. 135.

progressive, non-cooperative methods.' He attacked alchemy for placing too much stress on the 'solitary inspiration of the individual genius,' and for relying on 'special secret transmission' rather than 'normal public channels.' His program for human mastery of nature was predicated on a vast collaborative collective effort that required resort to publication at every stage of the game.[128]

Bacon's program was taken over by the Commonwealth of Learning and later became a hallmark of Enlightenment thought; yet it was by no means commonly shared by the learned men of his own day. Indeed Sir Walter Raleigh took the opposite side. Somewhat soured, no doubt, by confinement in the Tower, Raleigh praised Archimedes for withholding inventions designed 'to enrich a Mechanicall trade and teach the art of murdering men.' He defended 'alchymists and al others that haue...any secret skill,' for not wanting to 'cast away upon men of no worth the long travells of an understanding braine.'[129] As Raleigh's comments may suggest, in the early seventeenth century furtiveness was by no means a clear sign that charlatans were at work. Cryptic alphabets, anagrams and acrostics did not necessarily conceal trickery. The appearance of strange codes and ciphers might be a sign that a mathematical genius was inventing a new language or giving birth to the equivalent of the Pythagorean theorem. (That ancient Egyptians had concealed fundamental equations in their mysterious hieroglyphs continued to be believed until the deciphering of the Rosetta Stone.)[130] Bacon's opposition to secrecy went together with his antipathy to mathematicians and to a language of numbers whose significance he never understood. In the middle ages it should be remembered, secrecy was not peculiar to alchemists. It also characterized mathematicians and mechanics.[131] Acrostics and ciphers continued to attract many mathematicians down to Leibniz and beyond. There were still 'scientific societies' in the early seventeenth century which exchanged information by means of ciphers and codes.[132]

128 Rossi, *Francis Bacon*, pp. 30–5.
129 Cited from Raleigh's *History of the World* (book 1, part 5, chap. 3, section 15) by Rattansi, 'Alchemy and Natural Magic,' p. 136.
130 See Sprat, *History of the Royal Society*, p. 5 on this point.
131 See Gandz, 'Invention of the Decimal Fractions,' pp. 29–30, for description of how the medieval mathematician, Bonfils, deliberately concealed his procedures and substituted easily memorized but cumbersome inelegant 'rules of thumb.' See also references discussed on pp. 277 ff, volume 1 above.
132 On use of ciphers and secret codes by Prince Cesi's Academy of the Lincei see Preserved Smith, *History of Modern Culture* 1, 155–6. The effect of print on codes and ciphers is worth

How furtiveness and the 'true scientific spirit' could still be combined in the early sixteenth century is shown by Leonardo da Vinci's work. The celebrated contrast drawn by George Sarton, between Dürer who turned to print and Leonardo who shunned it, seems instructive in this regard:

> The comparison between these two men is valid because they were interested, roughly speaking, in the same things; the difference between them was that Leonardo accumulated notes and perplexities, while Dürer's thoughts though less deep were more fertile. Dürer would not bother much about a subject unless he had a practical purpose such as the writing of a book. He not only prepared his books as any bookmaker would but he printed them...
>
> Dürer was always practical and earthbound. Leonardo was just the opposite. While Leonardo disdained typography and engraving, Dürer understood immediately the commercial possibilities of both arts...He established himself as printer, engraver, and bookseller...We are well informed about his business dealings because he kept careful accounts of all his receipts and expenditures...signed all his works and often added the date. Leonardo did not bother about such matters. He was as indifferent to chronology as the Hindus...
>
> Dürer was a businessman...capable of taking some interest in scientific questions but he was not a man of science. Leonardo on the contrary was a pure artist, a distinterested inventor, a man of science.[133]

The contrast is vividly, but unfairly, drawn with anachronistic overtones developed at Dürer's expense. The German businessman is used merely as a foil for the romanticized portrayal of the Italian artist and one loses sight of the creative talents that produced the brooding figure of 'Melancholia I.' Dürer deserves no more to be stereotyped as a nineteenth-century bourgeois philistine than do other humanists and artists such as Erasmus or Raphael who also took full advantage of printing and engraving. Coming from an indefatigable and conscientious chronicler such as Sarton, whose many large volumes might well be condemned by romantics for dry-as-dust pedantry, the

separate study. Complex letter–number systems (not unlike those used in the Cabala) had been developed both in connection with scribal memory arts and also for the purpose of indexing or cross-referencing large compilations and anthologies. Handwriting manuals in print made it more difficult for diplomats to assume that written messages would be illegible if they fell into the wrong hands. Beginning with L. B. Alberti's invention of a 'cipher wheel' (which was perhaps inspired by movable type according to Gadol, pp. 207–8) going on to Trithemius' *Steganographia* and *Polygraphia* and culminating in the work of seventeenth-century virtuosi – such as John Wilkins and Leibniz – the arts of coding and decoding were propelled in new directions. David, *Le Débat sur les Ecritures*, pp. 26–7, 29.

133 Sarton, *Six Wings*, pp. 232–3.

portrayal of Leonardo as a 'capricious' bohemian poet and dreamer who turned out to be the true 'man of science' seems somewhat paradoxical. The paradox deepens when one notes that Sarton fully recognized that Leonardo, for all his brilliant scientific work, failed to contribute very much to the science of his day.

His love for science and his zeal need not be argued...but is it possible to ascribe to him a single discovery, except such as are contained implicitly in his drawings?
In order to receive credit for a discovery it is not enough to make it. One must explain it; one must prove very clearly that one has understood it...
One might say that a discovery is not completed until it has been justified in public.
Leonardo's ideas were like seeds that failed to nurture. They remained buried in his notes and drawings...
The most elaborate part of Leonardo's scientific work is that on anatomy, yet this exerted little if any influence...One might say that the evolution of anatomy might be the same if Leonardo had never existed...
One of the greatest men of science in history...remained unknown by his own fault for he did nothing to publish his own discoveries; in most cases indeed he did not even bother to complete them...
Nothing is more curious and perplexing...than the caprices of the mechanical inventor. Leonardo invented and reinvented a whole series of machines, yet he overlooked two of the greatest inventions not only of his own time but of all time: printing and engraving.[134]

Actually Leonardo did not overlook advantages conferred by printed materials to the point of refusing to consult them. As noted earlier, he consulted a fair number of printed texts.[135] His lack of Latin learning limited his range. It led to struggles with word lists and slowed down the progress of his studies in technically sophisticated fields.

Compared to Vesalius, Leonardo was slow to gain a thorough acquaintance with classical anatomy at its best...Ignorance does not place Leonardo's

---

[134] Sarton, Six Wings, pp. 228-9.
[135] The list of Leonardo's collection of books, given by Reti, 'Two Unpublished Manuscripts of Leonardo da Vinci,' pp. 81 ff., shows how his library expanded in the decade after 1497. How the study of newly printed vernacular works by ancients and moderns (especially the illustrations in De Re Militari by Valturius) entered in his work as an engineer is well described by Gille, Renaissance Engineers, pp. 52-3, 122-3, 132, 144. See also Aiton, 'Essay Review,' Studies in History and Philosophy of Science (1970-1); Reti, 'Leonardo and Ramelli,' p. 577. How his anatomical studies were guided by his limited access to technical literature and how belated acquaintance with some of Galen's work enriched his later oeuvre is demonstrated by Kemp in two seminal essays: 'Il Concetto dell' Anima' and 'Dissection and Divinity.'

researches at an empirical advantage...His early dissections tend to reflect partial knowledge of debased traditions.[136]

His later studies show how his knowledge also was enriched by contacts with learned men and their works. But Leonardo himself did remarkably little to enrich the studies of others in turn. The many authorities who repeat Leonardo's favorite dictum 'painting is natural philosophy' might well pause over his own failure to serve the natural philosophers of his day. In view of his preference for 'mute' visual statements against 'blind' verbal ones, there is a certain irony in the fate of his own superbly rendered picture-sequences of embryonic development. These sequences were too 'silent' to speak to sixteenth-century scientists. One other point is worth underlining here: if the development of anatomy as a scientific discipline left Leonardo's observations out of account, this was not because university doors failed to open but because his remarkable sketchbooks remained closed.

3. GALENIC SCIENCE REVIVED AND SURPASSED: RESETTING THE STAGE FOR THE 'NEW ANATOMY'

In the history of anatomy Leonardo da Vinci, the great artist, probably made less of a mark than did the master-printer Charles Estienne. As a member of a scholar–printer dynasty, Estienne was a better Latinist and more erudite than either Leonardo or Dürer. Many of the same skills that were useful for producing polyglot Bibles and multi-lingual dictionaries were also helpful in handling Greco-Latin and Arabic terms used for parts of the body. Such terms, which proved to be a stumbling block for Leonardo, were more easily mastered by an editor and proof reader such as Servetus[137] or by a member of the scholar–printers' dynasty such as Estienne. This urban entrepreneur, who also composed a road guide for French merchants and a handbook

---

136 Kemp, 'Dissection and Divinity,' p. 201. Along with Keele, Kemp accepts Vasari's suggestion that Marcantonio della Torre, professor of anatomy at the University of Pavia, probably guided Leonardo's anatomical studies and was responsible for the Galenic influence that led to Leonardo's improved later work. On Leonardo's word lists, see references given by Augusto Marinoni, book review, *Technology and Culture* (1972).

137 Servetus followed Vesalius in Paris as an assistant to Guinther (or Winter) of Andernach and, like Rabelais, also worked for a Lyons publishing firm (Trechsel) in the 1530s. His work provides a good example of the overlap between Bible study and geographical and medical research. See O'Malley, *Michael Servetus*.

for landed proprietors, had close contacts with university science. When Vesalius as a student in Paris in the 1530s was assisting the distinguished Professor Guinther (or Winter) of Andernach who edited Galen's *Anatomical Procedures*, Estienne was assisting his relative, the Paris printer Simon de Colines, who had charge of publishing the first edition of this important Latin text.[138] Thereafter, Vesalius went on to become a professor while Estienne carried on in the publishing trade. As pioneering authors of new illustrated texts, however, the anatomist-printer and professor were close rivals and spurred each other on.[139]

Beginning about 1520 there was a great rush of anatomical works, one after another of varying degrees of originality. All are...more or less influenced by Galen. Each...has its own merits and its own discoveries; all together represent the 'new anatomy.' It is difficult to distinguish them chronologically for books were often years in publication; one of the distinctions of Vesalius was the way in which he rushed into print.[140]

As noted above, although Vesalius was a young man in a hurry, other anatomists were not. Yet most professors who contributed to this increasingly important academic science in the sixteenth century differed from prior generations in that they had had eventual publication in mind. Many of them helped to prepare plates, and process copy while others consulted printers, engravers, and artists as university professors had never done before. Whether they were engaged helping to supervise illustrations or in copy-editing medical manuscripts or in following polemical pamphleteers, all members of the new generation of anatomy students were encouraged to rethink familiar problems and to handle them along new lines. 'One wrong word may now kill

138 On Vesalius' study of the *Anatomical Procedures* which 'started him on his triumphant career' see Singer (ed. and tr.) *Galen on Anatomical Procedures*, pp. xiii, 2. Among other services rendered by Robert Estienne's stepfather, the printer, Simon de Colines, was that of helping Jean Fernel, the future 'father of physiology' on his way through medical school. See Sherrington, *The Endeavour*, pp. 3-4. Fernel's early publications stemming from his pre-medical work on the *quadrivium* included the *Monolasphaerium* (de Colines, 1526) (which had a title page border bearing *quadrivium* symbols attributed to Oronce Finé) and the *Cosmotheoria* (1527) which contained data on the measurement of the earth, later confirmed by Jean Picard in 1671. Fernel's 'Dialogue' of 1542 also contains a celebrated passage on printing as facilitating both recovery and discovery. See Sherrington, pp. 3-4, 12, 15-17, 21-2. Also Sarton, *Six Wings*, pp. 191-6.
139 See Kellett, 'Two Anatomies,' pp. 342-50 for discussion of litigation between Estienne and his collaborator, de la Rivière in 1539 which alerted Vesalius to their project. See also Rath, 'Charles Estienne.' Charles Estienne's road guide has been noted above, p. 387, volume 1. His *L'Agriculture et la Maison Rustique* (Paris: J. Du Puys, 1564) ran through many editions. It was aimed at proprietors and land management agents.
140 Boas, *Scientific Renaissance*, p. 142.

thousands of men,' noted Rabelais in the course of collating texts by Hippocrates and Galen for the scholar–printer Gryphius who was eager to get editions out for the Lyons book fair of 1532.[141]

That professors had the preparation of a printed edition in mind helps to account for the marked change in attitude which differentiates Vesalius' school from that of previous professors of medicine. The 'attitude of scrupulous diligence' toward 'observation' and 'description of factual data' exhibited by Vesalius and some of his fellow anatomists has been singled out by many authorities. They tend to agree with Rossi that the new attitude placed 'traditional frames of knowledge...in a crisis situation.'[142] Although medievalists occasionally demur, for the most part there is agreement that Vesalius approached his field with a new insistence on 'systematic analytic and meticulous' description, and was less inclined to tolerate 'obscure and enigmatic terms.' Other features that are singled out include the new assertion of the dignity and value of mechanical arts, and the new use of

special illustrative techniques...to translate the results of observation into the clearest, and most comprehensive graphic images possible. It was this desire for clarity, this precise will to avoid mistakes, to place oneself deliberately at a distance from the fabulous view of things, that a work like Vesalius' *De Fabrica* and Agricola's *De Re Metallica* had in common...[143]

In addition to his own views, Rossi cites those of others on how Vesalius introduced 'an acute sense of the importance of minutiae, of the mastery of special methods and of precise and full reporting of observations' into biological science and how 'it became more objectionable to reproduce stereotyped words in the vicinity of correct images.'[144] As a description of new views and attitudes, Rossi's account cannot be faulted. But any explanation of how or why these new views appeared when they did must leave more room for the shift from script to print. Changed approaches to 'communicable knowledge' hinged on the transformation of communication techniques. The 'enormous distance' which separates the outlook of Vesalius or Agricola from that of medieval encyclopedists cannot be fathomed without prior consideration of the new features ushered in by print.

---

141 Kline, 'Rabelais and the Age of Printing,' pp. 8–9. Kline also notes that Rabelais' work on Hippocrates and Galen helped win him a job as a doctor at the chief hospital in Lyons. He has cogent remarks on how assistants in Gryphius' workshop correlated work on medical texts with work on legal and biblical texts.   142 Rossi, *Philosophy, Technology*, p. 49.
143 Rossi, *Philosophy, Technology*, p. 49.   144 Rossi, *Philosophy, Technology*, n. 82.

As discussion of Renaissance book illustration has already indicated, the new visual vocabulary developed by quattrocento draughtsmen and the new arts of engraving were of great importance in transforming the study of anatomy. But no less important was the reconstruction of the Galenic corpus that accompanied publication of all of Galen's works. The admission of barber–surgeons to certain college faculties although it created an uproar was probably of less consequence in reshaping medical school curriculum than was the re-editing of Galen and the output of pocket-sized texts.

in the anti-medieval and anti-Arabic climate of the period, every attempt was made to get...Galenic works into the hands of medical students: thus in 1528 there was published in Paris a series of four handy texts in pocket size ...The rise in importance of the medical school of the University of Paris dates from the renewed interest in Galen indicated by these publications. It was Johannes Guinther of Andernach...a professor at Paris who first published a Latin translation of the newly discovered and most important Galenic text: *On Anatomical Procedures*...Guinther was a medical humanist rather than a practicing anatomist but...[he] did perform...dissections as well as make translations. Vesalius as a student assisted Guinther in preparing the professor's own textbook.[145]

In the middle ages it had been customary also for students to help professors prepare texts as well as copy them out by hand. As a student in Paris in the early sixteenth century, however, Vesalius was less encumbered by the duties of a 'slavish' copyist and could devote more time to copy-editing. When his student days in Paris were over, he combined the activities of a professor with those of an author–editor who was in close contact with artists in Titian's workshop as well as the celebrated scholar–printers of the day.[146] He edited texts for major editions of Galen's collected works. After supervising preparation of the famous woodcuts that were made in Venice he got the manager of a distinguished printing firm to help him convey the finished blocks over the Alps to Oporinus in Basel where *De Fabrica* was seen through the press.[147] Oporinus, the son of a Strasbourg painter named Herbst,

---

[145] Boas, *Scientific Renaissance*, pp. 134–5.
[146] On questions raised about collaboration with Titian's assistants, see p. 267, volume 1 above, for pertinent references.
[147] See letter from Vesalius to Oporinus in Basel dated August 24, 1542 noting that blocks were being entrusted to Nicholas Stopius, manager of Daniel Bomberg's Venetian firm and 'well versed in the humanities.' Saunders and O'Malley, *Illustrations*, pp. 46 ff. See chap. 2, n. 39, volume 1 above for Herrlinger's discussion of refinement and durability of the blocks.

had mastered Latin, Greek, and Hebrew while working for the Amerbachs and Froben in Basel. He became an assistant to Paracelsus and served for a while as town physician and lecturer on medicine in Basel. He eventually formed his own Basel firm, in partnership with Thomas Platter. He extended hospitality to all the leading figures of the 'radical Reformation' and to the Marian exiles as well. He issued the first Latin edition of the Koran. He thus exemplified the protean character of the early scholar–printer. His workshop served as a cross-roads for all kinds of cultural exchange. He was superbly well equipped to supervise the varied tasks entailed in producing a work such as *De Fabrica*.[148]

Partly because it occurred under the aegis of scholar–printers in Venice, Lyons, Paris and Basel, the Galenic revival of the early sixteenth century took a different course than had similar revivals in prior centuries.

Humanism was another force...which played a part in bringing about the scientific revolution...improved editions and translations of...familiar works of Galen as well as the discovery and publication of a hitherto unknown Galenic text...gave a great boost to the study of anatomy...*De Fabrica*...one of the seminal works of the scientific revolution was itself founded to some extent on...Galen's works which [were]...virtually unknown before Vesalius' lifetime.

The rediscovery of classical scientific texts must therefore have a place in any discussion of the origins of the scientific revolution, but it is of course a limited place. The humanists looked back to classical antiquity as the golden age...this idea extends to the science of the ancients. A great feature of the scientific revolution however was that it did improve...upon the...ideas of the ancient world. The rediscovery of classical texts, which gave significant impetus to scientific studies cannot therefore account for the direction which these studies finally took.[149]

In my view the Galenic revival moved in a new direction because methods of transmission had been changed. Not humanism but printing gave the 'great boost' which led researchers to surpass the ancients and move toward new frontiers for the first time. The 'significant impetus'

148 Oporinus' circle is also discussed on p. 446, volume 1 above. Apart from Steinmann's biography, relevant data on his contacts with Vesalius are given by Pagel and Rattansi, 'Vesalius and Paracelsus'; O'Malley, *Andreas Vesalius*, pp. 131–3.

149 Alan G. R. Smith, *Science and Society*, pp. 45–6. For a similar statement concerning the relation between classical revivals and the surpassing of Greek science, see A. R. Hall, 'The Scholar and the Craftsman,' p. 11.

was provided by the new method of duplicating inherited technical literature which freed scholars from scribal labors and provided new means of achieving long sought goals. Vesalius' position *vis-à-vis* Galen was similar to that of Erasmus *vis-à-vis* St Jerome. He was aiming at reconstituting, reforming, and emending rather than replacing or discarding an ancient art. 'Anatomy will soon be cultivated in our academies,' he wrote hopefully, 'as it was of old in Alexandria.' He sought to 'restore from the world of the dead the knowledge of the parts of the human body that had died long ago' – to come closer to a 'pristine' knowledge that had become corrupted and confused. 'The notion of a *prisca medicina* and *anatomia* known to the ancients but lost from view after the Gothic invasions pervades the preface to the *De Fabrica*.'[150]

This notion (which was shared by Paracelsus, Agricola, and many others) seems to be yet another variation played on the familiar Petrarchan theme pertaining to rebirth, reconstruction and recall after an interval of darkness, destruction and forgetfulness. Petrarch, to be sure, had little use for medical studies and scornfully relegated ignoble bodies to doctors while reserving for philosophers and rhetoricians the more elevated education of minds.[151] Vesalius took the position adopted by many Renaissance physicians in the course of interdepartmental wars, that medical arts encompassed both theory and practice, philosophy and experience. The idealized Renaissance physician resembled Vitruvius' ideal architect. He claimed a superior role because his art encompassed all others and linked brain with hand.[152] Vesalius thus anticipated many recent interpretations by deploring the separation of mental from manual skills as indicative of the low state to which medicine had been brought by the ravages of the Goths. Nevertheless when he writes of the loss of the 'elegant compositions of the ancients' and their 'true knowledge of drugs,' when he castigates the 'barbarous names and false remedies' which had been left in the wake of the invasions, and when he celebrates the 'blessed age' which is emerging from 'utter darkness,' he does seem to be replaying a familiar Petrarchan theme.[153]

When trying to account for the ubiquity of this theme in the writings

---

150 Pagel and Rattansi, 'Vesalius and Paracelsus,' p. 324.
151 See chap. 3, n. 260, volume 1 above.
152 On this topos, see references given in chap. 3, n. 251 and n. 257, volume 1 above.
153 See Pagel and Rattansi, 'Vesalius and Paracelsus' for relevant citations.

of pioneers in early-modern science, the main features of scribal transmission deserve more attention than they usually receive. Many authorities seem to find it strange that so many early-modern scientists
thought that they were merely rediscovering 'ancient truths once
clearly perceived.' For the most part this belief is treated as a kind of
collective delusion and traced to some peculiar spell cast by a cult of
antiquity or of the hermetic tradition. There is much speculation, for
example, about the 'strange kind of historicism among the pioneers of
modern science which led them so far into the hermetic tradition...
that they conceived of their science as a rediscovery of ancient truths
once clearly perceived by the gifted and uncorrupted founders of
philosophy.'[154] Yet those virtuosi who believed they were rediscovering
what ancient sages knew were not necessarily being 'led far into
Hermeticism.' Rather they were reflecting long-prevailing attitudes
shaped by the repeated loss of manuscripts and reliance on evidence
supplied by scribes.

In view of what had happened to medical literature over the course
of time, the views expressed by anatomists such as Vesalius, at all events,
seem quite plausible. Anatomical data had been scrambled. Transmission of theoretical treatises on drugs had been separated from the living
experience of practicing apothecaries. Nomenclature had become
confused when manuscripts travelled along Greek–Arab–Latin routes.
Pictures of plants and animals had been corrupted and appropriate
labels had been lost. Certain important Galenic texts had almost
completely disappeared. In the 1530s, Galen's *Anatomical Procedures*
'broke entirely new ground.' Recovery of Galen meant discovery of
natural phenomena to professors and students in Vesalius' day.

Here as elsewhere, the transitory and incomplete revivals that had
occurred under the auspices of particular colleges during the middle
ages ought to be compared with the permanent, total process of recovery that occurred after printers set to work. It was not the practice
of dissection that distinguished sixteenth-century anatomy from that
of the thirteenth century. It was rather the retrieval of medical literature
and the way it was at last secured. The practice of dissection had been
revived at Bologna in the thirteenth century. There, a distinguished
professor of medicine, Mondino, not only used cadavers for demon-

---

154 A. R. Hall, 'Can the History of Science be History?' p. 208. Hall is referring especially to the
now celebrated interpretation of Newton offered by McGuire and Rattansi, 'Newton and the
"Pipes of Pan."'

stration but also prepared a useful and much used anatomy text. After Mondino's death, however, degeneration set in.

In Mondino dei Luzzi [*c.* 1275–1326] medieval anatomy reached its zenith. He dissected for research and...was probably the first teacher since the third century B.C. to demonstrate publicly on the human body. His *Anathomia*, which was printed many times, long remained a popular text. Eager to reconcile authorities he did not venture to assert his own views and perpetuated many mistakes. Good anatomists succeeded Mondino...but there was a general deterioration in the teaching of the subject...The body again became merely an illustration to the words of nobler men. Anatomy degenerated into the repetition of phrases and names.

The curve moves upward again toward the end of the fifteenth century. One factor in this seems to have been pressure in the medical schools for more demonstrative teaching...Another was recognition of human dissection...by the Papacy. The first printed anatomies with figures...in the last decade of the century and the first half of the sixteenth century show a whole group of able...anatomists at work.[155]

In my view, the curve did not merely 'move upward again.' It moved in a new direction, involving correction, feedback, and progressive improvement, rather than corruption and loss. Unlike medieval revivals, the sixteenth-century Galenic revival was not followed by a degenerate phase. On the contrary, full recovery of the Galenic corpus was merely a prelude to an era that saw Galen surpassed. Once the full corpus had been fixed in print it could be subjected to critical scrutiny. It became possible to perceive discrepancies between data and description that had not been perceived or disclosed before. Thus a major step was taken by Vesalius when he became aware that Galen was discussing a vertebra that could be found in the spine of a monkey but not in that of a man.[156] Moreover, the second edition of the *De Fabrica* was an improved version of the first.[157] The opposite was the case with copies of Mondino's long venerated text. *De Fabrica* itself was succeeded by even more elaborate publication programs aimed at surpassing Vesalius' treatise. By provoking a prolonged and vigorous

155 A. R. Hall, *Scientific Revolution*, p. 40. On Mondino's use of dissection as a way of merely demonstrating truths set down by Galenic texts see Singer, 'Confluence,' p. 265.
156 Edwin Clarke, book review, *Medical History* (1964), pp. 380–3, underlines the importance of the recovery of Galen's *Anatomical Procedures* in this connection. See also Pagel and Rattansi, 'Vesalius and Paracelsus,' p. 319.
157 In addition to the improved illustrations noted above, chap. 3, n. 39, volume 1, the merits of the second edition of *De Fabrica* (Basel: Oporinus, 1555) are noted by Adelman, *Embryological Treatises of Hieronymus Fabricius*, p. 60; and O'Malley, 'Vesalius,' p. 306.

debate, Vesalius' criticisms of Galen rendered much the same service to the next generations that was rendered by Copernicus' work.[158] Medical students were no longer presented with one single authoritative corpus of texts that they were expected to learn and then transmit to future generations in turn. They were confronted by alternative views that forced a reassessment of the evidence and encouraged further checking of data against description, leading to the overhauling of inherited schemes.

'Progress in anatomy before the sixteenth century is as mysteriously slow as its development after 1500 is startlingly rapid.'[159] If we are encouraged to regard academic science as impervious to changes wrought by printing, then this kind of reversal is bound to seem 'mysterious and startling.' The contrary is true, when the 'doors of the sixteenth century universities' however tightly 'closed to new scientific ideas' are nevertheless opened to early printers' workshops and to the new interchanges that took place in them.

[158] According to Whitteridge, *William Harvey*, p. 461, Vesalius expressed his growing doubts about the penetration of the septum by pores in the 1555 edition of *De Fabrica*. This probably alerted the next generation to a problem not thrashed out before. The diverse theories and debates that were put forth between the 1550s and 1620s and set the stage for *De Motu* are described by Whitteridge, p. 19 and Adelman, *Embryological Treatises of Hieronymus Fabricius*, p. 23.

[159] Boas, *Scientific Renaissance*, p. 130.

7

RESETTING THE STAGE FOR THE COPERNICAN REVOLUTION

In some ways the early stages of the Copernican Revolution resemble those just sketched in connection with the 'new anatomy.' Like anatomy, astronomy was initially transformed from within, so to speak, by members of a small Latin-writing élite engaged in preserving and transmitting sophisticated techniques first developed in antiquity and later retrieved in the twelfth century. *De Fabrica* and *De Revolutionibus* had more in common than their publication date of 1543.

Vesalius' role in the development of anatomy has many parallels to the role Copernicus played in the development of astronomy. Like Copernicus, Vesalius rejected certain crucial assumptions of his predecessors and replaced them with his own speculations. . . [Each man] produced a comprehensive text that was equal, if not superior to the text that it was designed to replace.[1]

By producing new technical treatises that were no less comprehensive than the old ones and yet diverged from the latter on certain major points, both authors presented the next generation of fellow professionals with alternatives that prior generations had not known. In this way both set in motion a revolutionary sequence whose outcome neither author could foresee. Insofar as they launched a new tradition even while aiming their work at emending an inherited one, both treatises seem to lend themselves to the line of analysis I have been trying out in this book. Both suggest, that is, how old pursuits produced new results after techniques of communication had been transformed.

Yet although the two authors shared some things in common, they reacted to the new arts of printing and engraving in a manner that sharply diverged. Unlike the young anatomist who 'rushed into print,'

---

[1] Steneck, *The Scientific Press*, p. 12.

575

the ageing astronomer circulated handwritten texts, avoided the press and shunned publicity for most of his long life. This contrast seems worth pondering, because it has led many historians of the Copernican Revolution to underrate the printer's role. When dealing with Copernicus' seemingly negative reaction to the medium that Vesalius eagerly employed, several special circumstances need to be kept in mind.

For one thing, the pursuit of disparate disciplines has to be taken into account. Mathematical equations and diagrams were likely to have a more limited appeal than anatomical illustrations which artists as well as anatomists could use.[2] It is not unusual to find sixteenth-century authors of texts devoted to physics or astronomy or other mathematical sciences invoking the sign presumably posted over the entrance to Plato's Academy: 'Without a knowledge of geometry do not enter here.'[3] This warning was displayed on the title page of De Revolutionibus whereas the frontispiece of De Fabrica depicts a dissection being dramatized for all to see. This suggests that there may have been different assumed publics for the two works and that the astronomer envisaged a more restricted circle of readers than did the anatomist. Vesalius also may have been better attuned to publicity by the very nature of his profession being accustomed to perform anatomical demonstrations in front of large audiences. Although Copernicus may have given a few public lectures when visiting Italy, most of his life was spent working in a quiet study, far from theatres and crowds.

As an advocate of a theory presumably regarded as impious by the ancients, seemingly contrary to a literal reading of Scripture, and easily ridiculed by the wits of the day, Copernicus had additional special reasons for shunning publicity and for fearing the reaction it would bring.[4]

---

[2] This point is implied by Gillispie, The Edge of Objectivity, pp. 56–7, when he contrasts 'stunning woodcuts' with 'forbidding calculations.'

[3] See e.g. reproduction of title page – literally illustrating an 'inner circle' of geometers – from Niccolo Tartaglia, Nova Scientia (Venice, 1550; first ed. 1537) and discussion by Steneck, The Scientific Press, p. 9. This theme is discussed by Rosen, 'Copernicus's Attitude,' pp. 281–3. That Leonardo also said only mathematicians should read his work (see e.g. Kline, Mathematics in Western Culture, p. 133) suggests that this theme was favored by others than astronomers and physicists and that the contrast drawn above between exoteric anatomical illustration and esoteric mathematical tables can be overdone.

[4] For details on Copernicus' excision of a passage referring to Aristarchus, his reaction to ridicule presented in a school play, and to the condemnation of Wittenberg theologians, see Rosen, 'Biography of Copernicus,' Three Copernican Treatises, pp. 294; 375, and the same author's article on 'Copernicus' in Dictionary of Scientific Biography, p. 402. How Copernicus probably

I hesitated long whether on the one hand I should give to the light these my Commentaries written to prove the Earth's motion or whether, on the other hand it were better to follow the example of the Pythagoreans and others who were wont to impart their philosophic mysteries only to intimates and friends and then not in writing but by word of mouth...[5]

Apart from expecting adverse reactions to a theory that ran counter to both Scripture and common sense, Copernicus also seems to have had the kind of temperament one might describe as 'introverted.' At least he spent many decades leading a quiet, studious life. By contrast Vesalius appears to have been gregarious and to have relished working in public, close to noisy crowds. Probably such temperamental, as well as occupational, differences ought to be taken into account when considering time spent in printers' workshops, where silence and solitude were difficult to obtain. Copernicus certainly spent much less time in the company of printers and engravers than did other astronomers of note – yet another point of contrast with Vesalius who was often found in such company, as we know. As far as experience of printing went, the expertise commanded by Regiomontanus and the close supervision that later characterized the work of Tycho and Kepler had no counterpart in Copernicus' experience. He left everything in the hands of Rheticus – the printing of tables and texts, and even the choice of places and firms. This lack of interest in the way his data were processed may be related to the somewhat anomalous character of Copernicus' work.

As is often noted, *De Revolutionibus* was by no means a landmark in observational science, but relied on old tables and often corrupted data to support a new theory for computing the movement of the planets about the sun. Here also one may draw a contrast with *De Fabrica*. The carefully prepared and closely supervised illustrations for which Vesalius' work is celebrated indicate a concern with precise and detailed reporting of observed phenomena – a concern that was manifested by Tycho Brahe but was seemingly absent from Copernicus' work.

learned from Giorgio Valla's *De Rebus Expetendis* (Venice: Aldus, 1501) of a relevant passage in Plutarch referring to the ancient condemnation of Aristarchus as an impious heliocentric theorist is noted by Thomas Africa, 'Copernicus' Relation.' An intriguing account of how Galileo and Copernicus differed in their approach to Aristarchus and how a Baroque artist alluded to the condemnation of Copernican doctrines in a portrait of the ancient astronomer, is given by Askew, 'A Melancholy Astronomer.'

[5] Cited by Steneck, *The Scientific Press*, p. 1. See also Rosen, *Three Copernican Treatises*, p. 401, who notes Copernicus' reference to keeping his book 'hidden' four times longer than the interval recommended by Horace.

Although his name has become more famous, Copernicus was in many ways less modern than Vesalius, in particular he had a far less acute sense of the reality of nature: like many medieval men he was far more concerned to devise a theory which should fit an uncritically collected series of observations than to examine the quality of observational material. Tycho Brahe half a century later was the Vesalius of astronomy.[6]

Yet Copernicus was by no means prepared to accept every 'uncritically collected series of observations.' In his *Letter against Werner*, for example, he was keenly critical of a colleague's procedures for dating and placing a particular observation made in the past, and elsewhere he seemed to be a keen-eyed observer of inconsistencies in prior reports.[7]

Here again one must make some allowance for the disparity between scientific disciplines. Unlike anatomists and unlike physicists as well, astronomers have to study observations made at different intervals over long periods of time. Data supplied by the Alexandrians and Arabs were indispensable for anyone concerned with the precession of the equinoxes, for example. The long-term cycles that had to be mastered to achieve successful calendar reform required lining up a series of observations made over the course of hundreds of years; and this task in turn required mastering diverse languages and systems for describing locations in time and space. In this respect, Copernicus' failure to supply the kind of fresh findings that were later provided by Tycho Brahe needs to be balanced against his sustained and zealous efforts to unscramble dusty records made by observers in the past.[8]

If the importance of archival research for astronomers were to receive more attention the early phases of the Copernican Revolution could be more clearly related to concurrent changes transforming libraries and book routes during the first century of print. As a post-print astronomer, Copernicus had an opportunity to survey a wider range of records and to use more reference guides than had any astronomer before him. This obvious point is often obscured by heated debates over the role played by one textual tradition as against another – over how much weight to assign continuous criticism of Aristotle,

---

[6] A. R. Hall, *Scientific Revolution*, pp. 51–2.

[7] How Copernicus' 'careful scrutiny' of predecessors' results led to his finding inconsistencies in the reports of 'two outstanding medieval Muslim observers' is described by Rosen, *Three Copernican Treatises*, p. 388. On *Letter against Werner*, see below, n. 13.

[8] For a different view, chiding Copernicus for failing to reject all earlier observations until he achieved the equivalent of Tycho's observational program see Swerdlow, 'On Copernicus' Theory of Precession,' esp. pp. 50–1.

as against a new revival of Plato or the vogue for Hermetic texts. Granted that such influences may be important in Copernicus' work and are worth investigating; it is also worth pausing over the interplay of many different texts upon his single mind. Given freedom from many hours of 'slavish' copying, given an increased output of dictionaries, and other reference guides; given title pages, book lists, and other rudimentary bibliographical aids, Copernicus was able to undertake a search of the literature on a vaster scale than had been possible before.

Increased access to a variety of records was not only useful when he decided 'to read again the works of all the philosophers upon whom I could lay hand...' in order to canvass possible alternatives to an 'uncertain mathematical tradition.'[9] Access to many records also enabled him to tackle certain technical problems relating to long-term cycles that had remained out of the reach of astronomers who were served by scribes.

My teacher made observations...at Bologna...at Rome...then here in Frauenberg when he had leisure for his studies. From his observations of the fixed stars he selected the one which he made...in 1525... *Then comparing all the observations of previous writers with his own* he found that a revolution of the...circle of inequality had been completed...

To reduce these calculations to a definite system in which they would agree with all the observations, my teacher computed that the unequal motion is completed in 1,717 Egyptian years...and the complete revolution of the mean motion will take 25,816 Egyptian years.[10]

To investigators concerned with celestial cycles that could take over 25,000 years, it must have been helpful to gain increased access to written records and to be supplied with bibliographical guides.

Copernicus undoubtedly learned much from a neo-Platonist professor at Bologna and from the debates conducted by Aristotelians at Padua as well. But Copernicus later abandoned the role of a wandering scholar for long years of study in Frombork. His work indicates that he was acquainted with a vast variety of texts – ranging from the Synoptic Gospels to tables of sines. He made a debut in print in 1509 with a Latin translation of a Greek work: the *Letters* of Theophilactus Simocatta, the first such translation to be printed in Cracow and one

[9] Prefatory Letter to *De Revolutionibus*, cited by Thomas Kuhn, *The Copernican Revolution*, p. 141.
[10] Excerpts from the *Narratio Prima* (1540) of Rheticus, in Rosen, *Three Copernican Treatises*, pp. 111–14. (Italics mine.)

that owed much to Aldus' Venetian press.[11] Although Simocatta is usually described as a minor Byzantine man of letters, students of medieval geography single him out as a seventh-century geographer who indicated knowledge of Asian territories. It seems likely that Copernicus' choice of this author was stimulated by curiosity about geography as well as about Byzantine Greek letters.[12] Certainly he was an assiduous investigator of place names and calendars, of ancient chronologies and coins, as indeed he had to be in order to unravel scribal confusion between 'Nebuchadnezzar' and 'Nabonassar,' or to ascertain the different points taken by past observers for the start of a new year. Neither the Platonic revival nor continued criticism of Aristotle enabled him to line up observations that went back to pre-Christian times, to compare observations made by Alexandrians and Arabs with his own, to establish the 'names of Egyptian months' and the length of 'Callippic cycles' or to point out that a colleague's dating of an autumnal equinox observed by Ptolemy was wrong by at least ten years.[13]

No fundamental astronomical discovery, no new sort of astronomical observation persuaded Copernicus of ancient astronomy's inadequacy or of the necessity for change. Until half a century after Copernicus' death no potentially revolutionary changes occurred in the data available to astronomers...[14]

Shortly before Copernicus was born, however, an actual revolution in book production had begun to affect the technical literature and mathematical tools available to astronomers. As a student at Cracow

[11] A facsimile of Copernicus' translation of the letters of Theophilactus Simocatta from Greek into Latin, first printed by Jan Haller (Kraków, 1509) was shown in the Library of Congress exhibition on Copernicus in 1973. The Greek text used by Copernicus comes from an anthology published in Venice by Aldus in 1499. See Rosen, *Three Copernican Treatises*, p. 325, where interesting connections are traced between the professor of Greek at Bologna (where Copernicus matriculated in 1496) and Aldus Manutius. See also Rose, *Italian Renaissance of Mathematics*, pp. 120–1.

[12] Kimble, *Geography in the Middle Ages*, p. 122 singles out Theophylactus [sic] Simocatta as an Egyptian Greek writing *c*. A.D. 678 about lands bordering on Turkish possessions. The fact that Copernicus' translation was prefaced by a long poem by his former Cracow instructor, George Rabe ('Corvinus') who was a geographer, also suggests that geographical curiosity helped to stimulate the work. On Rabe and printing of the *Letters*, see Rosen, *Three Copernican Treatises*, pp. 337–8.

[13] See *Letter against Werner* in Rosen, *Three Copernican Treatises*, pp. 94–8. A 'reminder that chronology was an important constituent of astronomy' is offered by Ravetz, *Astronomy and Cosmology*, p. 58. The 'immense effort' spent by Copernicus 'merely organizing the Egyptian month' is noted by Gingerich, Commentary, *The Copernican Achievement*, p. 104, n. 9.

[14] Thomas Kuhn, *Copernican Revolution*, p. 131.

in the 1480s, the young Copernicus probably found it hard to get a look at a single copy of Ptolemy's *Almagest* – even in a corrupted medieval Latin form.[15] Before he died, he had three different editions at hand. As a fourteen-year-old in Copenhagen in 1560, the young Tycho Brahe could purchase all of Ptolemy's work, including an improved translation of the full *Almagest* made from the Greek. Soon thereafter, while at Leipzig and still in his teens, Tycho picked up a copy of the *Prutenic Tables* that had recently been computed on the basis of Copernicus' major work.[16] No 'new sort of observation' had affected astronomy in this interval. Nevertheless, the transmission of old observations had undergone a major change. One need not wait until 'a half a century after Copernicus' death' to observe the effect of this change, for it had begun to affect the study of astronomy shortly before Copernicus was born. Copernicus was not supplied, as Tycho's successors would be, with precisely recorded fresh data. But he was supplied, as Regiomontanus' successor and Aldus Manutius' contemporary, with guidance to technical literature carefully culled from the best Renaissance Greek manuscript collections and, for the first time, made available outside library walls. 'By 1543, every

[15] Ravetz, 'The Origins of the Copernican Revolution,' p. 92, states that no copy of the *Almagest* was available in Cracow during Copernicus' student days, but offers no evidence to back up the statement. Ms. copies of the *Almagest* of course are difficult to track down. Since advanced instruction in astronomy was given outside regular university courses in most regions, whatever copies there were, were likely to be less available in university libraries than the texts that were used for 'ordinary' lectures by medical, legal or theological faculties. See e.g. the case of the Swedish master cited by Gabriel, *The College System*, p. 19. That advanced instruction in Aristotle's physics was given in the schools whereas Ptolemaic computation was usually taught outside may help to explain how the two incompatible approaches could co-exist for so long. After printing, as noted in chap. 6, they came into closer contact and conflict. Albert of Brudzewo not only lectured on Peurbach's astronomy at the University of Cracow in 1482–3 but had his lectures printed (at Milan) in 1494–5. He also lectured on Aristotle's *De Caelo* in 1493 when Copernicus was a student at the University and pointed out how it contradicted Ptolemaic views. A Latin translation of Averroës' *Commentary* which described Ptolemaic astronomy as 'computing the nonexistent' was printed at Padua in 1473. That Ptolemy had been previously 'excluded from the schools' and ought to be 'restored' like a 'returned exile' to his 'ancient place of honor' was argued by Rheticus in the *Narratio Prima*. See Rosen, *Three Copernican Treatises*, pp. 132, 141, 195 n. 251, and 274.

[16] Dreyer, *Tycho Brahe*, pp. 14–19. On pp. 81, 131, 135, Dreyer indicates Tycho's persistent concern about new books, his efforts to increase his library and his desire to take advantage of the Frankfurt book fairs. Gade, *The Life and Times of Tycho Brahe*, pp. 54–5, notes that Tycho hoped to meet Christopher Plantin when he went to the fair in 1575. See below, pp. 596–7 for uses to which Tycho put his teenage purchases. Tycho made a point of acquiring Copernicana. He owned and annotated the first and second editions of *De Revolutionibus* and procured the unprinted *Commentariolus* and *Letter against Werner* as well. On the uses of the printed edition of *De Revolutionibus* as a kind of 'textus receptus' among post-Copernican astronomers who glossed their copies and corresponded about passages, see Westman, 'Three Responses to the Copernican Theory,' appendix, pp. 342–3.

important work on ancient astronomy was available in printed editions.'[17]

Given the exaggerated claims made in prefaces to early printed books and given the righteous indignation they have provoked, one hesitates to assign too great a significance to Regiomontanus' role.

It was once usual to see such men as Nicholas of Cusa, Peurbach, and Regiomontanus in the fifteenth century as forerunners of a scientific revival, but more recent estimates of their works serve rather to emphasize the continuity to their thought than to indicate an incipient break with the past.[18]

No doubt the medieval translators of the *Almagest* and compilers of the *Alphonsine Tables* did at least as much to 'restore' astronomy in the West as did many boastful editors who converted medieval translations and tables into print.[19] Not only did a 'recovery' of the *Almagest* occur hundreds of years before Regiomontanus; he also had less to do with the 'discovery' made by Columbus than some of his later compatriots have maintained.

Kepler's tables...accompanied the men who went...on journeys of discovery just as...Regiomontanus' tables had accompanied Columbus... Without themselves having moved very far out into the world, these two Germans had performed important services in the conquest of the earth's globe.[20]

The publication of a so-called practical guide is one thing, putting it into practice is another. We have already noted Samuel Eliot Morison's cogent objections to the notion that sixteenth-century sailors skilled in dead reckoning could be persuaded to use new-fangled

---

[17] Francis Johnson, *Astronomical Thought*, p. 64, n. 62. The one exception: Archimedes' work was printed in Basel the following year and owed something to Regiomontanus' editing. See n. 33 below.

[18] A. R. Hall, *Scientific Revolution*, p. 11. The inflation and deflation of Peurbach and Regiomontanus is discussed by Wightman, *Science and the Renaissance* I, 103. The initial inflationary argument goes back to the sixteenth-century publications of Tanstetter (1514), Melanchthon (1545) and Rheticus who set a theme taken up later by Ramus. German efforts to counter Italian claims to have ended the Dark Ages were present in much of this early history of science literature.

[19] The early sixteenth-century prefaces that boasted of 'restoring' texts and tables (which were actually translated and/or computed during the medieval era) are cited by Thorndike, *History of Magic and Experimental Science*, chapter XVI, pp. 332–77. That sixteenth-century editors such as Tanstetter lacked historical information available to modern scholars and that their references to data 'almost obliterated from human memory' had some validity is not sufficiently appreciated by Thorndike. But the followers of Burckhardt are also prone to overlook the debt owed to medieval scholars for the retrieval and transmission of Alexandrian texts. On the defects of these two approaches, see pp. 300–3, above.

[20] Caspar, *Kepler*, p. 327.

printed devices. Granted Columbus carried a copy of the early printed tables on board, it remains to be shown that he was able to put them to good use.[21]

Here is a case that seems to support the warning issued by many authorities against exaggerating the 'effectiveness of the printed word as a channel for the diffusion of innovations.'[22] But although many sixteenth-century mariners did not put newly printed tables to good use, sixteenth-century astronomers surely did. In the year Columbus set off for the Indies, Copernicus matriculated at Cracow. 'As a student he was able to acquire and to annotate his own printed set of the *Alfonsine Tables* as well as Regiomontanus' *Ephemerides*.'[23] Unlike the stubborn mariners described by Morison, Tycho Brahe fully exploited all the mathematical tools and instruments that inventive printers and engravers advertised. Tycho's efforts to increase the precision of his observations 'would have been useless without trigonometric tables of corresponding accuracy.'[24] Where Regiomontanus pioneered, Ratdolt, Rheticus, Reinhold and others carried on. Lacking logarithms no less than the telescope, Tycho still had on hand paper instruments that astronomers had lacked before.[25] In guiding star-gazers, if not

21 See p. 554 above. See also data in Morison's *Admiral of the Ocean Sea*, pp. 185–6; 653–5. Columbus' exposure to printed materials (especially during his stay with his brother Bartholomew, who was 'a hawker of printed books' in Lisbon in the 1470s) and his expertise in chart-making which are noted by Morison (p. 35) seem to be underplayed once the author gets him under sail. But in this book and others, Morison's distaste for 'armchair admirals' and admiration for unlettered mariners does lead him to raise important questions about the actual usefulness of the 'almanachs, textbooks, charts,' etc. that others stress: e.g. E. G. R. Taylor, *Mathematical Practitioners* (Morison's particular *bête noire*); Waters, 'Science and the Techniques of Navigation,' p. 233. Surprisingly Morison seems to credit the story of Columbus' use of Regiomontanus' tables to predict an eclipse and thus impress credulous Jamaican natives in 1504. 'Si non é vero é ben trovato!' The story shows a mentality Mark Twain later immortalized as that of a Connecticut Yankee emanating from Mediterranean Europe even before Luther's day. Thus the European is shown intimidating 'sullen' 'superstitious' natives, not by using gunpowder or invoking gospel truths, but by exploiting superior knowledge of celestial clockwork conveyed by the printed word.
22 Cipolla, 'The Diffusion of Innovations,' p. 47. See also p. 554 above.
23 Gingerich, 'Crisis versus Aesthetic.' On an early edition of the *Alphonsine Tables* printed by Ratdolt in 1483, see Stillwell, *Awakening Interest*, p. 8. According to Noel Swerdlow, 'The Derivation and First Draft of the Commentariolus,' (pp. 425–6) Copernicus used a 1492 edition (Venice: Johannes Hamman) of the *Alphonsine Tables* along with Ratdolt's 1490 Augsburg edition of Regiomontanus' *Tabulae Directionum* for his *Commentariolus*. See n. 53, below, concerning use of this same *Tabulae Directionum* while Copernicus was studying at Bologna in 1500. On Ratdolt, see pp. 587 ff. below.
24 Cajori, *A History of Mathematics*, p. 132.
25 See Dreyer, *Tycho Brahe*, p. 4; Pannekoek, *A History of Astronomy*, pp. 200–3. On Regiomontanus' pioneering work on trigonometry, see Rose, *Italian Renaissance of Mathematics*, p. 99 and Hughes, ed. and tr., *Regiomontanus on Triangles*; but note errors in Hughes underscored by Rosen, *Three Copernican Treatises*, p. 300, n. 1026.

navigators, the contribution made by the first astronomer–printer was large.

Historical perspectives may be skewed when the role played by early printers is inflated. But they can also be set awry if one goes too far in the opposite direction. Often deflationary tendencies have been carried too far.

> No mutational elements of significance appear to have been introduced in the fifteenth century. There were no major translations or discoveries. The much vaunted version of the *Almagest* initiated by George Peurbach and completed by Regiomontanus was little more than an epitome with few alterations of substance. Both Toscanelli and Regiomontanus professed to be aware that the traditional Ptolemaic–Alphonsine astronomy stood in need of revision, but the observational data and the calculational theory at their disposal were insufficient for the task...[26]

The 'much vaunted version' of the *Almagest was* a noteworthy achievement, given the data which its two authors inherited and the circumstances under which they worked. For one thing, it was much more than a mere 'epitome.' It pointed to unresolved problems in Ptolemaic astronomy and also contained post-Alexandrian data, which Copernicus later put to good use.[27] For another thing, it provided many young astronomers with their first chance to examine specific details given in the *Almagest* – a chance very few astronomers had been granted for a millennium before. Insofar as some of it was based on a corrupted medieval translation from the Arabic and its second author did not fully exploit better versions in Greek, this was because the task of preservation was urgent and plans for future renovation were cut short by premature death.

Because a 'mutational element' was introduced in the fifteenth century – one which eventually doubled the lifetime of the astronomer[28] – renovation continued despite the short lives of Peurbach and

---

[26] Durand, 'Tradition and Innovation,' p. 35.

[27] As Durand notes, 'Tradition and Innovation,' p. 34, n. 21, this point was stressed by Zinner *Leben und Werken*, pp. 60–3. The argument between Thorndike and Zinner over Regiomontanus' significance is briefly described in Durand's annotations. According to Swerdlow, 'Derivation,' pp. 425–6, the virtues of the *Epytoma in Almagestum Ptolemai* 'cannot be overpraised.' It is the 'finest textbook of Ptolemaic astronomy' ever written. But Swerdlow also holds (p. 426, n. 5) that the first printed edition of 1496, done in Venice by Johannes Hamman, was 'very bad.' This was the version Copernicus used. According to Gingerich, 'Copernicus and the Impact of Printing,' p. 204, the student astronomer was indebted to the new medium for having access to the work, even in an impure form.

[28] Laplace's suggestion that logarithm tables 'by shortening the labors, doubled the life of the astronomer' is cited by A. G. R. Smith, *Science and Society*, p. 69.

THE COPERNICAN REVOLUTION

of Regiomontanus. The publication of the *Epitome* was the beginning of a process of retrieval which made more of Alexandrian astronomy increasingly available and provided the next generation of astronomers with purified versions of Ptolemy's work. Before Copernicus died, a Greek text of the *Almagest* (the very same text that had been brought to Venice by Cardinal Bessarion and consulted by Regiomontanus more than a half-century earlier) was published in Basel and permanently secured.[29]

To the jaded modern scholar looking back over five hundred years, early printed editions of the *Almagest* are disappointing – even retrogressive – works.[30] But they opened up exciting new prospects to astronomers in Copernicus' day.

Copernicus studied the *Almagest* very carefully indeed. For the *De Revolutionibus* is the *Almagest*, book by book, section by section rewritten to incorporate the new Copernican theory but otherwise altered as little as might be. Kepler was to remark later that Copernicus interpreted Ptolemy, not nature, and there is some truth in the remark.[31]

Actually, the alternative to interpreting Ptolemy that Kepler had in mind was not really 'nature' but Tycho's data instead. By providing a fully worked out parallel text containing an alternate theory, Copernicus furnished Tycho with a motive for collecting the data Kepler used.[32] He did much to prepare the field, and should not be reproached for dying before others could reap the fruit. As a pre-Tychonic astronomer, he could not have consulted the 'nature' Kepler knew.

As a successor of Regiomontanus, however, Copernicus was better placed to recast the *Almagest* than earlier astronomers had been. He was not the first Western astronomer who had the good luck to gain access to a text setting forth the details of Ptolemaic astronomy. But he was the first for whom this initial stroke of good fortune was followed up by many more. Regiomontanus did little to guide Columbus over-

---

[29] For early printed editions of the *Almagest*, see Stillwell, *Awakening Interest*, pp. 30–1; 33–4. On lists of books owned by or available to Copernicus, see Gingerich, 'Copernicus and the Impact of Printing,' p. 204, n. 8.

[30] Swerdlow's disappointment (see n. 27 above) at the inferior printed version of Regiomontanus' fine ms. *Epitome* is characteristic of the reaction of most specialists who examine fifteenth-century mss. and then compare them with early printed versions.

[31] Boas, *Scientific Renaissance*, p. 74. According to Ravetz, *Astronomy and Cosmology*, p. 55, *De Revolutionibus* actually departs from the *Almagest* more frequently than this oft-cited description suggests. If he is right, it seems ironical that modern historians by themselves acting as 'slavish copyists' of earlier textbooks depict Copernicus as being more of a 'slavish copyist' than he was.

[32] See discussion below p. 597.

seas but he did much to steer Copernicus and his colleagues toward useful technical treatises not only by Ptolemy but also by Archimedes, Apollonius, Heron, Witelo *et al.* He had singled out such works with 'unerring judgement' after studying with Cardinal Bessarion and then serving as a librarian to Matthias Corvinus, King of Hungary, whose vast manuscript collection in Buda rivalled that of Bessarion and of Renaissance Popes. After the library in Buda – which contained many scientific texts taken from Athens and Constantinople among its 50,000 volumes – had vanished, Regiomontanus' book list survived to guide publication programs and armchair travellers for a century or more.[33]

A useful service might be performed by discriminating more clearly between the new functions performed by the first astronomer–printer and those previously performed when astronomers had had to serve as scribes. Until 1470, Regiomontanus pursued a course similar to that followed by his immediate predecessors such as Toscanelli or Peurbach who had also been wandering scholars and versatile servants of cardinals and kings. Insofar as he combined librarianship with astronomy, he followed a pattern that had been characteristic of Alexandrians and Arabs alike. When he left the library in Buda in 1470 to set up his Nuremberg press, however, Regiomontanus crossed an historical great divide. He had, up to then, served colleagues and patrons in

[33] For illustration of this famous book list, see Sarton, 'Scientific Literature,' pp. 115, 163 (figure 42). According to Gingerich, there are only two copies now available at the British Museum and at the Staatsbibliothek in Munich, 'Copernicus and the Impact of Printing,' p. 209, fig. 70. The rich material found in the library of Matthias Corvinus, is noted by Bühler, *Fifteenth Century Book*, pp. 18–19; 96. See also Csapodi, *The Corvinian Library History and Stock*. On Regiomontanus' stay there, his selection of titles for advance list and his posthumous contribution to the edition of Archimedes published in Basel, 1544, see Wightman, *Science and the Renaissance* I, 110; II, 13, n. 38. The edition of Witelo's *Perspectiva*, ed. by Tanstetter and Apianus, published in Nuremberg by Johannes Petreius in 1535 (in Stillwell, *Awakening Interest*, p. 75, n. 254) came two years after *De Triangulis* and eight years before *De Revolutionibus* were issued by the same printer. Regiomontanus' ties to Bessarion and the importance he assigned to using new presses for his program of 'restoring' astronomy are brought out by Rose's chapter on Regiomontanus, *Italian Renaissance of Mathematics*, chap. 4. Since he places 'Regiomontanus in Italy' and focuses exclusively on his Italian heirs, Rose's treatment does not bring out the important role of northern contributors to the trends he traces. In his 'Humanist Culture,' pp. 90–3, Rose also touches on the difficulty of gaining access to Bessarion's collection of scientific mss. after it was bequeathed to Venice and made the nucleus of the Biblioteca Marciana, and implies that there was something of a hiatus in the use made of the collection during the interval between Regiomontanus and the more liberal lending policy inaugurated by Bembo in 1532. The same point is made by Lowry, 'Two Great Venetian Libraries,' (see volume I, chap. 3, n. 164 above). The output of Ratdolt and his co-workers in Venice and Augsburg right after Regiomontanus' death, and that of Nuremberg printers in the early sixteenth century seem all the more important in this light.

a traditional fashion. By gaining the backing of a wealthy Nuremberg citizen to set up a press and observatory, by turning out duplicate tables of sines and tangents, series of Ephemerides and advertisements for instruments, by training apprentices to carry on with the printing of technical treatises and by issuing his own advance publication list, he served later generations in new ways. He died prematurely in 1476. Some of his manuscripts did not get printed until more than fifty years after his death. Others were lost so completely that his ultimate plans for reforming astronomy will never be known. Moreover the great library at Buda that he had culled had its contents dispersed and was sacked by the Turks in 1527. Similar catastrophes had set astronomy back in the past. The course pursued by Regiomontanus gained momentum instead. The serial publications he launched never stopped. Ephemerides and trigonometry tables flowed in an uninterrupted stream which seems to have no stopping point even now. His efforts to train assistants in scientific printing and instrument-making also produced increasingly useful results. Insofar as he embodied the roles of printer and scientist 'in one and the same person,' Regiomontanus was the first but not the last of a new breed.[34] Others carried on where he left off – as did those who prepared *De Revolutionibus* for a Nuremberg press more than sixty years after his death, and as did Erhard Ratdolt and his co-workers did in Venice right away.[35]

Innovations associated with Ratdolt's press: the first 'modern' title page, the first use of Arabic numerals for dating a book, the earliest extant type-specimen sheet, the first list of errata, the first three-color

[34] Hirsch, *Printing, Selling*, p. 146, overdoes the uniqueness of Regiomontanus as a scientist–printer. J. Santritter of Heilbronn who followed Ratdolt in Venice and Peter Bienewitz (or 'Apianus') in Nuremberg are only two of many others who played the same role.

[35] On titles issued by Petreius, the Nuremberg printer of *De Revolutionibus*, see Shipman, 'Johannes Petreius.' Redgrave, *Erwin Ratdolt*, pp. 3–5, notes Ratdolt's probable connection with Regiomontanus in Nuremberg before he set up a press in Venice where he worked from 1476 to 1486, before returning to Augsburg, where he issued the *Tabulae Directionum* (1490) used by Copernicus (see n. 53 below). As noted above, many of Regiomontanus' intellectual heirs who consciously tried to carry on his publication program are omitted from Rose's *Italian Renaissance of Mathematics* which needs to be supplemented by a closer look at concurrent developments north of the Alps. Thus the series of ephemerides launched by Regiomontanus was continued by Johann Stöffler and Jacob Pflaum. Stöffler, a professor at Tübingen who taught Melanchthon, and Johannes Schöner, the Nuremberg mathematician to whom Rheticus addressed the *Narratio Prima* and who wrote a preface to Regiomontanus' treatise on the comet of 1472 (which was posthumously printed in Nuremberg in 1531) are but two of several non-Italian mathematicians who represent important links between Regiomontanus' and Copernicus' work. Eleven books listed on Regiomontanus' advance list which turned up in the library of Johan Scheubel, a professor of mathematics at Tübingen are noted by Hughes, 'The Private Library of J.S.,' p. 417, n. 1.

printed illustrations, the first engraved diagrams in a printed geometry book – are often noted in books aimed at bibliophiles.[36] But their broader significance for the history of science remains to be explored. Ratdolt's *editio princeps* of Euclid, for example, has been described as merely continuing a 'crabbed medieval' manuscript tradition going back to Adelard of Bath.[37] 'The splendour of Greek mathematics,' says Sarton, 'was dimly illustrated' by reproducing the 'poor transla-tion' of Campanus of Novara.[38] Yet the *editio princeps* (which Ratdolt published in Venice in 1482 and Copernicus consulted as a young man) not only made the works of Euclid more available, it also arrested corruption of the text and introduced sharp-edged visual aids.[39] The six-hundred-odd diagrams, which were ingeniously devised for the *editio princeps*, illustrated Euclidean proofs somewhat less 'dimly' than had been done in many hand-copied books. Printed diagrams endowed the *Elements* with a clarity and uniformity that they had not possessed before.[40] Is it too fanciful to suggest that Euclid was associated, there-after, less with Latin verbiage and more with triangles, circles and squares?

What Ratdolt's diagrams did for plane geometry, other early publi-cation programs (beginning perhaps with Luca Pacioli) did for solid geometry – thereby making new use of the artistic invention of focused perspective developed in quattrocento Italy.[41] The sharp and clear perspective renderings of three-dimensional geometric forms that illustrate Pacioli's *Divina Proportione*[42] and other later sixteenth-century

36 See e.g. Mayor, *Prints and People* (opposite plates no. 74 and 75); Updike, *Printing Types* I, 77.
37 Durand, 'Tradition and Innovation,' p. 42.
38 Sarton, 'Scientific Literature,' p. 64.
39 Bühler, 'A Typographical Error,' pp. 102–4, describes how a compositor's slip was caught by Ratdolt who stopped the presses, made a correction and resumed printing, thereby eliminating the error from thirty-five out of thirty-nine copies seen by Bühler.
40 On these diagrams and materials used to produce them, see Mayor, *Prints and People*, plates 74 and 75; Redgrave, *Ratdolt*, p. 16; and Thomas-Stanford, 'Early Editions of Euclid's *Elements*,' pp. 40–1.
41 On Pacioli's relation to Piero della Francesca and other quattrocento artists and his concern with popularizing Euclid, see pp. 548, 551 above. Pacioli's own revision of Campanus of Novara's Latin *Euclid* was printed in Venice in 1509, partly as a riposte to a new translation produced by Zamberti in 1505 which assailed the 'barbarous' Campanus and boasted of the new translator's knowledge of Greek. Rose, 'Humanist Culture,' pp. 98–9. Did Pacioli's edition of the Campanus' *Euclid* also influence Candalla, the French mathematician who shared Kepler's fascination with the properties of regular sclids and whose commentary on Euclid is cited by Kepler? See Westman, 'Kepler's Theory of Hypothesis,' p. 256.
42 See e.g. Octahedron, woodcut from Pacioli's *Divina Proportione* (Venice, Pagano, 1509) in Mayor, *Prints and People*, fig. 174. On question of whether Leonardo da Vinci had a hand in designing these woodcuts in the 1490s while both men were in Milan, see chap. 6, n. 89 above. The effects produced by printed visual aids might be worth considering in connection with

books seem to have supplied the models Kepler had in mind when he envisaged the planetary orbits as a series of nesting 'perfect solids.'[43] It has been noted that *De Revolutionibus* also reflects a new concern with diagrammatic unity and visually symmetrical models.[44] Is it not possible that such concerns owed something to the new forms of book illustration that were ushered in by printing? The Platonic–Pythagorean tradition was not unfamiliar to medieval astronomers. Some Euclidean geometry had entered into the quadrivium as taught in the schools. Astrolabes and mechanical clocks proved mental and manual work could be ingeniously combined. Actual models of a clockwork universe were constructed and discussed.[45] But the visual aids supplied by copyists and illuminators had been infrequent and multiform. As noted above, even theoretical treatises showing that the world was round had not been reinforced by occasional T-O pictograms and sketches conveying flat discs.[46]

Insofar as Copernicus and Kepler shared a conviction that the design of the solar system had to conform to new requirements set by principles of 'fixed symmetry' the novelty of repeated encounters with

the issues raised by Giorgio de Santillana, 'The Role of Art in the Scientific Renaissance,' pp. 33–66. Some cogent remarks are made by Cyril Stanley Smith, 'Art Technology and Science,' but without assigning as much significance as I do to 'colorless linear diagrams' (p. 530).

43 For discussion of the inspiration which came to Kepler in July 1595 while drawing a figure on the blackboard for his class, and for illustrations designed by Kepler for his *Mysterium Cosmographicum* (Tübingen, 1596), see Koestler, *The Sleepwalkers*, pp. 247–61, and critique by Westman, 'Kepler's Theory of Hypothesis,' p. 256. For a suggestive account of Kepler's visual imagination and its indebtedness to picture-books such as Wenzel Jamnitzer's *Perspectiva Corporum Regularum* (1568) see Benesch, *The Art of the Renaissance*, pp. 156–8, 183. Jamnitzer's debt to Dürer's *Unterweisung* seems clear from Benesch (n. 38), and Pacioli's *Summa* also crops up in the same connection.

44 This point is stressed by several authors. See e.g. Hanson, 'The Copernican Disturbance.' Hanson notes (p. 176) how modern textbook illustrations convey a misleading impression of a uniform 'Ptolemaic' system. The significance of Copernicus' reference to 'the design of the universe and the fixed symmetry of its parts' is also brought out by Gingerich, 'Crisis versus Aesthetic,' p. 6.

45 The most celebrated example is the 'Astrarium' that was constructed 1348–64 by Giovanni de' Dondi. See Bedini and Maddison, 'Mechanical Universe,' esp. p. 27, where interest at Cracow (stimulated by Regiomontanus' associate and his successor at Buda, Marcin Bylica) is noted and the copying of mss. of Dondi's treatise on his instrument is held to coincide with Copernicus' student days there. Horsky, 'Astronomy and the Art of Clockmaking,' pp. 25–34 stresses the large numbers of geared clocks in public places as affecting views of the 'machina mundi' among the learned in Copernicus' day. That Copernicus conceived of a divinely constructed clockwork, a 'machina mundi' in contrast to Ptolemy's more pulsating, voluntaristic 'anima mundi' is brought out in a paper by Curtis Wilson, 'Rheticus, Ravetz,' see esp. p. 37. But, of course, Ptolemaic schemes were not always incompatible with notions of clockwork, as is shown by Dondi's 'astrarium' itself. On the existence of ancient Greek geared clockwork calendrical mechanisms, see Price, 'Gears from the Greeks,' and review by Drachmann, *Technology and Culture*, pp. 112–16.   46 See p. 512, above.

identical symmetrical diagrams and with three-dimensional renderings of geometrical forms might be worth further thought. Beginning with early printed editions, new visual aids contained in manuals and text-books made even 'medieval world pictures' easier to see.[47] The anatomy of the eye itself could be rendered by uniform diagrams for the first time.[48] In circulating large numbers of a medieval manual such as Sacrobosco's *Sphaera*, printers may be said to have done the same thing that copyists had been doing before. By supplying an edition of the *Sphaera* with identical polychrome printed diagrams, however, Erhard Ratdolt was doing something copyists had not done.[49]

The addition of polychrome diagrams, moreover, represented only one of several new features that Regiomontanus' former assistant added to technical texts. During the years that Copernicus was coming of age, successive editions of the *Sphaera* were being issued with supplementary data that helped to stimulate a reassessment of conventional views. Ratdolt's 1482 edition of Sacrobosco offers a case in point. He replaced the commentary of Gerard of Cremona by the most up-to-date and sophisticated critique of this same commentary – a critique composed by Regiomontanus himself.[50] This was only one of many instances where Regiomontanus, despite the early demise of his press, managed to exert a posthumous influence on the new generation that was coming of age. His advance book list of 1474 was characteristic of many early printed products in that it promised much more than the publisher actually delivered. But it also pointed the way to future scientific publication programs, setting guidelines that later publishers and vir-

---

[47] See Westman, 'Three Responses,' pp. 322–3 for an intriguing account of how schematic diagrams of the systems of Martianus Capella and Copernicus, which appeared in a text on astronomy published in Venice in 1573, stimulated Tycho Brahe when he was developing his own scheme.

[48] On the inadequacy of medieval drawings illustrating Pecham's *Perspectiva Communis* compared to the new illustrations reflecting Renaissance conceptions that accompanied printed editions of Witelo's, Alhazen's and Pecham's works on optics, see Lindberg, *John Pecham*, pp. 248–9. Lindberg's opinion is questioned by B. S. Eastwood, book review, *Speculum* (1972), p. 326, who sees medieval elements in the illustrations of the 1535 edition of Witelo's *Optics*.

[49] See figure facing p. 16 in Redgrave, *Erwin Ratdolt*. Redgrave notes that the 'beautiful' woodcut diagrams in the 1482 edition were hand-colored; polychrome printing was introduced in the 1485 edition (pp. 17–19).

[50] Redgrave, *Erhard Ratdolt*, p. 19 notes that Ratdolt's 1482 edition contained Regiomontanus' 'contra Cremonensia' along with Peurbach's 'Theoricae Novae.' R. E. Johnson 'Astronomical Textbooks,' p. 295, indicates that this set a vogue. At least eleven editions, issued from Venice between 1482 and 1518, contained Regiomontanus' critique – initially printed in Nuremberg in 1472–4. See Houzeau and Lancaster, *Bibliographie Générale de l'Astronomie* 1, 1e partie, item 2256, p. 552.

tuosi pursued.[51] At the same time, it furnished astronomers who belonged to Copernicus' generation, and for whom bibliographies and reference works were hard to find, with a rudimentary reader's guide. Although the publication program that was launched by Regiomontanus in fifteenth-century Nuremberg was much less newsworthy than the expedition mounted by Columbus, it was more unprecedented than overseas voyages and probably had a more immediate impact on Copernicus' lifetime work. 'Copernicus was probably acquainted with every publication, written, edited or printed by Regiomontanus including, of course, his posthumous trigonometrical treatise De Triangulis.'[52]

There is no room in Sarton's brisk summary to note just how and when the astronomer became acquainted with different texts. In fact, Copernicus was unfamiliar with the major treatise On Triangles – the first full discussion of trigonometry to appear in the Western world – until he was over sixty-five years old. Only in 1539 did he have a chance to look over a copy which was brought to him by Rheticus at that time. The treatise had been left in manuscript for more than fifty years after its author's premature death. The first edition was issued by Petreius in Nuremberg, in 1533 – roughly a decade before De Revolutionibus came off the same press. That Copernicus had already finished his section on trigonometry without any knowledge of his predecessor's treatise suggests how scientific interchange was enfeebled when texts were left in manuscript form. How Regiomontanus' influence was extended by the use of a Nuremberg press is indicated by the fact that Copernicus overhauled his presentation of indispensable theorems after consulting the fifty-year-old work.[53]

In this regard, it is worth reaffirming that 'Europeans of Copernicus' generation' were practicing astronomy in an environment which differed from any in which astronomy had been practiced before. In trying to describe the distinguishing features of the new environment, however, it seems prudent to look more closely at the astronomer in his study before venturing too far outside.

51 This point is overlooked by Thorndike, History of Magic and Experimental Science, p. 339, who makes much of the failure of the defunct Nuremberg press to produce the titles on the advance list. The usefulness of the book list as a guide to sixteenth-century Italian virtuosi and editors is spelled out by Rose, Italian Renaissance of Mathematics, pp. 64, 293.
52 Sarton, Six Wings, p. 257, n. 105.
53 Rosen, 'Biography of Copernicus,' Three Copernican Treatises, p. 326. Rosen also notes how Copernicus acquired a copy of Regiomontanus' Tables of Directions (Augsburg, 1490) in time to use it when making observations in Bologna in 1500.

Until a half a century after Copernicus' death no potentially revolutionary changes occurred in the data available to astronomers. Any possible understanding of the revolution's timing and of the factors that called it forth must therefore be sought principally outside of astronomy within the larger intellectual milieu inhabited by astronomy's practitioners.[54]

Once embarked on a search for new factors to be found 'outside astronomy' within a 'larger intellectual milieu,' the multivariable strategy currently favored by historians makes it difficult to stop short of describing everything that happened around the time Copernicus was born.

The Renaissance had happened...The Commercial Revolution had begun ...men's thoughts were becoming accustomed to a widening horizon. The earth was circumnavigated which proved in more popular fashion its rotundity. The antipodes were found to be quite inhabited...Further...unprecedented religious upheaval contributed to loosen men's thinking... There appeared a number of centres of religious life besides Rome. The rise of vernacular literatures...added their bit...In this ferment of strange and radical ideas, widely disseminated by the recent invention of printing it was not so difficult for Copernicus to consider...and suggest...a shift of the centre of reference in astronomy...London and Paris had become like Rome; in the absence of evidence to the contrary, it is to be conceived that the distant celestial bodies are like the earth...[55]

Granted that printing brought distant events closer, it still seems doubtful that the rise of the vernaculars, challenges to Rome or the consolidation of dynastic states had much effect on Copernicus' efforts to recast Ptolemy's work. To an astronomer engaged in trying to emend Ptolemaic theories, accounts of new-found lands were undoubtedly significant.[56] But even more important was access to data collected by past observers. Insofar as we lose sight of changes affecting the transmission of old records when searching for new factors, multivariable explanations are not much more helpful than monocausal ones. At many points such explanations seem to be positively unhelpful. Particularly where they touch on the problem of the Renaissance, they make it hard to avoid entanglement in a large number of counterproductive disputes.

At present, the two trips over the Alps made by Copernicus (like

[54] Thomas Kuhn, *Copernican Revolution*, p. 131.   [55] Burtt, *The Metaphysical Foundations*, p. 40.
[56] One should not conclude however that news of overseas voyages invariably undermined confidence in Ptolemy's *Geography* and hence of his astronomy as well. Learned men, who believed Ptolemy knew better than the Genoese mariner how to calculate the dimensions of the globe, had their hunch confirmed after Magellan's voyage. See Morison, *Admiral*, p. 384.

countless astronomers before him) are deemed more significant than
the three decades he spent in his Prussian study using facilities that had
never been extended to armchair travellers before. We are encouraged
to think of 'ten years in the sun and in the open intellectual climate of
Italy' in connection with expanding mental horizons. Narrow-
mindedness and Gothic gloom, by contrast are associated with the
tower room in 'crabbed little Frauenburg' where Copernicus 'would
peer through the mists and pore over Ptolemy and the tables of
astronomy.'[57] Yet it was 'in Frauenburg when he had leisure for his
studies' that Copernicus lined up key observations reported by Alexandrians and Arabs and drew conclusions from them.[58] It was there that
Rheticus brought him Greek editions of Euclid and Ptolemy, and several
other significant technical works.[59] Doubtless Copernicus' journey
over the Alps was of major significance for his work. His studies at
Bologna and Ferrara, his visit to papal Rome and his chance to learn
some Greek supplemented his experience at Cracow in many important
respects. Nevertheless the northern student who went to Italy for graduate studies or to learn Greek was a less remarkable phenomenon than
the astronomer who could spend thirty-odd years studying a vast range
of records without leaving home. It is significant that when a Greek
teacher at Bologna died, the northern astronomer could go on mastering
the difficult language with the aid of printed lexicons and guidebooks.[60]

Intellectual horizons probably expanded most rapidly when wandering scholars could stay longer in one place and, instead of setting
out in search of 'walking encyclopedias' or manuscripts in scattered
libraries, could get copies of books sent to them instead. Portable
records combined with a fixed observation-post proved helpful to
Tycho Brahe on his northern isle no less than to Copernicus in his
Prussian tower study. Before trying to account for the achievements of
either man, the question of possible changes affecting 'the data available
to astronomers' needs to be thought through again. The 'larger
intellectual milieu inhabited by astronomy's practitioners' is at present
too vague a concept to be helpful and also too inclusive as a catch-all.

[57] Gillispie, *Edge of Objectivity*, pp. 21–2. See also deployment of familiar stereotypes setting the
'crabbed Gothic lettering of the North' against the 'bold clear typeface of Italian printing'
despite its inappropriateness to editions involved – as noted on p. 490 above.
[58] Rheticus, 'Narratio Prima,' p. 111.
[59] Rosen, 'Biography of Copernicus,' *Three Copernican Treatises*, p. 393.
[60] See account of Copernicus' well-worn copy of Crestone's *Greek-Latin Dictionary* (Modena,
1499) in Rosen, 'Biography of Copernicus,' *Three Copernican Treatises*, p. 323.

This point may be illustrated by drawing on an otherwise very useful study of the Copernican Revolution.

To Europeans of Copernicus' generation, planetary astronomy was... practiced in an intellectual and social environment quite different from any in which astronomy had been practiced before. In part that difference arose from theological accretions...Even more essential changes were produced by the...criticism of men like Buridan and Oresme. But these were medieval contributions and Copernicus did not live during the Middle Ages. His lifetime, 1473-1543, occupied the central decades of the Renaissance and Reformation and novelties characteristic of this later age were also effective in inaugurating and shaping his work.[61]

This eclectic and multivariable approach is in keeping with a practice long honored by historians. Medieval contributions are not neglected; almost everything that happened in the Renaissance and Reformation is presented in review. Background and foreground are carefully distinguished – more carefully than usual, so that implausible far-fetched connections are avoided. The more distant repercussions produced by the Turkish threat, the Protestant revolt, the rise of nation states and of a new commercial aristocracy are assigned brief paragraphs. The voyages of exploration, which helped discredit Ptolemy's *Geography*; the agitation for calendar reform which spurred Copernicus' efforts to overhaul the *Almagest*; and the Greek revival, which contributed to the reconstitution of Ptolemy's texts are featured more prominently. Finally, Renaissance neo-Platonism is discussed at some length as a movement which 'gave a significant new direction to the science of the Renaissance and, in particular, shaped Copernicus' appreciation of mathematical elegance and his preference for a heliocentric hypothesis.'[62]

With the discussion of neo-Platonism, the 'conceptual stage setting' is deemed complete. All the 'novelties that were effective in inaugurating and shaping Copernicus' work' have presumably been introduced. Yet although distant repercussions from movements associated with Columbus, Luther, Machiavelli and Calvin have been duly acknowledged, the consequences of Gutenberg's invention are left out of account. Nothing is said about the installation of new presses, and one might well conclude that the technical literature consulted by sixteenth-century astronomers was still being copied out by hand.

---

[61] Thomas Kuhn, *Copernican Revolution*, p. 123.
[62] Thomas Kuhn, *Copernican Revolution*, pp. 123-31.

To say that the advent of printing ought to be featured more prominently than is done in this case, is not merely to advocate putting another prop on an already over-cluttered stage. I am not asking 'the over-burdened historian' to add yet another item to his long list of 'features of the Renaissance' or even to re-order items so as to give printing 'higher billing.'[63] Instead, I am suggesting that the entire problem of providing an appropriate setting for the Copernican Revolution has to be thought through again.

Once the shift from script to print has been taken into account, the setting which is currently provided appears to need re-adjustment at important points. For one thing, several of the 'novelties' singled out as most significant for Copernicus' work were not entirely novel and probably had been on the scene before. Thus overseas voyages had occurred before Columbus; medieval scholars in Sicily had studied Ptolemy in Greek; and pressure for calendar reform was almost as venerable as the Venerable Bede (a point to be discussed at more length below). For another thing, what was genuinely new about Copernicus' rejection of Ptolemaic astronomy cannot be perceived unless printing is brought into the picture. Insofar as he objected to 'the diffuseness and continued inaccuracy of the Ptolemaic tradition,'[64] Copernicus was objecting to features that characterized all textual traditions shaped by scribal transmission. If he differed from earlier astronomers who had perpetuated this tradition, this was partly because these 'monstrous' features had become more visible and also because he did not have to put up with them any more.

This is not to say that Renaissance 'intellectual currents' were insignificant in Copernicus' work. Scholastic criticism of Aristotle and neo-Platonist views undoubtedly helped to shape the solution he tried out. His recognition that some ancient authorities had believed in heliocentric and/or geokinetic theories owed much to Renaissance classical anthologies produced by Italian humanists, such as Giorgio Valla.[65] But of course his access to several humanist anthologies and

---

[63] Rabb, 'Debate: The Advent of Printing,' p. 139.

[64] According to Thomas Kuhn, *Copernican Revolution*, p. 140, 'these are the two principal characteristics' which Copernicus found objectionable. Other authorities differ on this point. See e.g. Gingerich 'Crisis versus Aesthetic,' pp. 85–97.

[65] See n. 4 above. That Copernicus found support for a sun-centered cosmology in many different ancient sources and that the one citation from the hermetic corpus which appears in *De Revolutionibus* has been overstressed in recent studies is persuasively argued by Rosen, 'Was Copernicus a Hermetist?' p. 171.

his expanded awareness of ancient cosmologies and astronomical theories also hinged on the output of printed editions.[66] Increased access to texts seems especially relevant to a heightened concern with 'inconsistency among the mathematicians.' Moreover something must be said about his chance to work out a new solution – his chance to rework all the Ptolemaic computations in full mathematical detail with the positions of sun and earth reversed. Had this kind of opportunity been extended to European astronomers before printing? Should we not at least pose this kind of question when seeking to understand 'the Revolution's timing and the factors that called it forth'?

> The passage of time...presented a counterfeit problem which ironically was even more effective than the real motion of the planets in fostering recognition of errors in the Ptolemaic method. Many of the data inherited by Copernicus...were bad data...Some had been collected by poor observers; others had...been...miscopied or misconstrued during the process of transmission...The complexity of the problem presented by Renaissance data transcended that of the heavens themselves...[67]

It was not so much the 'passage of time' as it was the conditions of scribal culture that produced this 'counterfeit problem.' As long as these conditions persisted, the problem was not counterfeit, but all too real. Even when they were aware that they had inherited bad data, astronomers could do little to arrest scribal drift, and drifting texts were uncertain indicators of shifting stars. Moreover awareness of error was kept at a low level given necessary reliance on one seemingly authoritative corpus of texts. As long as planetary positions had to be computed on the basis of Ptolemy's instructions, there was no way of using the 'heavens themselves' to act as an independent check. By providing another complete set of instructions, the 'second Ptolemy' freed astronomers from their total dependance on the first.

How recognition of error was fostered by access to two Ptolemies instead of to one is implicit in the oft-cited anecdote about the young Tycho Brahe. Having taught himself astronomy by sneaking books past his tutor and poring over them alone at night, Tycho procured copies of the (Ptolemaic) *Alphonsine Tables*, the (Copernican) *Prutenic Tables* and Stadius' *Ephemerides* (which were based on the latter).

[66] The Aldine collection *Astronomici Veteres* (Venice, 1499) ought to be mentioned along with Giorgio Valla's *De Rebus* in this connection. See Rose, 'Humanist Culture,' p. 99, n. 241.
[67] Thomas Kuhn, *Copernican Revolution*, p. 140.

Tycho soon mastered the use of these tables and perceived that the computed places of the planets differed from the actual places in the sky...He even found out that Stadius had not computed his places correctly from Reinhold's tables. And already while Tycho was a youth only sixteen years of age his eyes were opened to the great fact which seems to us so simple to grasp but which escaped the attention of all European astronomers before him that only through a steadily pursued course of observations would it be possible to obtain a better insight into the motions of the planets.[68]

Tycho's 'eyes were opened' to the need for fresh data partly because he had on hand more old data than young students in astronomy had had before. Even as an untutored teenager he could compare Copernicus with Ptolemy and study tables derived from both.[69] Contradictory predictions concerning the conjunction of planets encouraged him to re-examine the 'writing in the skies.' For the purpose of gathering fresh data, he was also supplied with newly forged mathematical tools which increased his speed and accuracy when ascertaining the position of a given star. In these and in other respects, Tycho's case does not entirely fit that of 'an astronomer who saw new things while looking at old objects with old instruments.'[70] Printed sine tables, trigonometry texts, star catalogues did represent new objects and instruments in Tycho's day. As a self-taught mathematician who mastered astronomy out of books, Tycho was himself a new kind of observer.

Because he lacked recourse to a telescope and yet saw a different writing in the skies than star-gazers had seen before, the findings of the Danish astronomer pose a special problem for historians of science.

Brahe's fine instruments were not required to discover the superlunary character of novas and comets...Maestlin needed only a piece of thread to decide that the nova of 1572 was beyond the moon...The observations... which speeded the downfall of traditional cosmology...could have been made at any time since remote antiquity. The phenomena and the requisite instruments had been available for two millenniums before Brahe's birth, but the observations were not made or, if made, were not widely interpreted. During the last half of the sixteenth century age-old phenomena rapidly changed their meaning and significance. Those changes seem incompre-

---

[68] Dreyer, *Tycho*, pp. 18–19.
[69] In 1574–5, Tycho bought copies of the *Prutenic Tables* and distributed them among the poorest students while lecturing on Copernicus, as the 'second Ptolemy' at the University of Copenhagen. Moesgaard, 'Copernican Influence on Tycho Brahe,' p. 32.
[70] Thomas Kuhn, *Structure of Scientific Revolutions*, pp. 116–17.

hensible without reference to the new climate of scientific opinion one of whose first outstanding representatives is Copernicus.[71]

One wonders how the 'superlunary character of novas and comets' could, in fact, be established before scattered observations of transitory stellar events could be made simultaneously, coordinated with other findings, checked and confirmed. As long as accounts of separate stellar events were transmitted by scribes; as long as separate observers lacked uniform methods for placing and recording what they saw; as long as the most careful observers lacked mastery of trigonometry; how could falling stars be permanently located beyond the moon's sphere?[72] 'The desire to find an orbit for a *purely transitory*, *ephemeral* phenomenon marked an important shift in the theoretical, interpretation of comets.'[73] Maybe Tycho's 'fine instruments' were not needed, but certainly Maestlin's piece of thread was not enough to fix transitory, ephemeral stellar events so firmly that they could be seen to conflict with traditional cosmology.[74]

To understand why these 'age-old phenomena' rapidly changed their meaning in the sixteenth century at all events, it is worth going back, beyond Copernicus, to the thickening literature on comets that commenced shortly after the first press was established at Mainz.[75] Here again Regiomontanus appears as a significant pioneer, with his posthumously published treatise on the comet of 1472 and his sixteen-point program for ascertaining the distance of future comets from the earth. By Maestlin's day, much of the program had been fulfilled. Various

---

[71] Thomas Kuhn, *Copernican Revolution*, p. 209.

[72] That the phrase: 'length of a lance' was commonly used to describe the length of a comet's tail until Regiomontanus is noted by Hellman, 'The Role of Measurement,' p. 43. Tycho's use of Regiomontanus' spherical trigonometry is noted by Wightman, *Science and the Renaissance* I, 123 ff.

[73] Westman, 'The Comet and the Cosmos,' p. 11. (Italics mine.)

[74] That it took more than a piece of thread is suggested by the efforts of Regiomontanus' disciple Vogelinus who tried to work out the parallax of the comet of 1532 and by the sixteen-point program set forth by Regiomontanus himself. See Hellman, *The Comet*, pp. 81–2, 97. Maestlin's own research is described by Westman, 'The Comet and the Cosmos,' pp. 7–30.

[75] Hellman, *Comet*, pp. 74–6, 111–12, notes that the comet of 1472 inspired more treatises and had more observers than did those of 1456 and 1468 and that the volume of reports increased steadily thereafter, due 'partly to the use of printing' and 'partly to the fact that fewer of the later tracts were lost with time.' I think increased preservation was probably related to the new process of duplication and find it indicative that there was no similar continuous thickening of documentation for any interval between the twelfth and fifteenth centuries. According to Bernard Goldstein, 'Theory and Observation,' p. 46, comets did not 'formally enter the realm of astronomy' until Tycho but did 'begin to get treated as astronomical phenomena' in Regiomontanus' day. Goldstein stresses the absence of any 'textual evidence' to 'account for this change of attitude' and makes no reference to the advent of printing.

methods for determining parallaxes had been described by mathematicians, reports of comets had given rise to 'a flood of fugitive literature' and to the compiling and publishing of comet catalogues as well. The comet of 1533 provoked controversial pamphleteering on the part of scattered observers. By 1541, Rheticus was writing a Wittenberg colleague that, 'in this area,' it was known 'that comets originated beyond the lunar sphere.'[76] Continuous publication increased interest and curiosity. The nova of 1572 attracted more observers from all parts of Europe than had ever gazed at a single star before.[77] When Tycho announced his findings, he had to struggle 'to make his voice heard above the din.'[78] He succeeded so well in this unprecedented situation that long after the nova had faded, 'Tycho's star' gleamed too brightly beyond the moon's sphere for cosmologists to ignore it or chroniclers to shift it around. 'Almost every star chart and globe between 1572 and the end of the 17th century showed where [it]... had appeared, encouraging astronomers to watch for its return.'[79]

Stellar events that had been witnessed before the advent of printing could not be pinpointed so precisely and permanently that one man's name could be assigned to one such event. Nor could any one detailed account avoid getting blurred in the course of entering into the public domain. Much as was the case with mundane events when they were woven into tapestries or noted in monkish chronicles, discrete separate events merged into a single mythical category;[80] conventional images and standard formulae smudged carefully observed detail. Jerusalem stayed at the center of the world, comets stayed below the lunar sphere, and neither could be permanently dislodged from their appointed places until scribal transmission had come to an end.

'These stars marked out in gold are those of the Lord Tycho; the

76 For controversy engendered by the Comet of 1533, in which Apianus (d. 1552), Jerome Cardano, Gemma Frisius and Copernicus participated, see Rosen, 'Biography of Copernicus,' *Three Copernican Treatises*, pp. 373–4, where citation from Rheticus' letter is also given.

77 Hellman, *Comet*, pp. 80 ff, stresses Regiomontanus' pioneering role and criticizes Thorndike's deprecatory remarks. She also describes how solutions to finding parallaxes were published by Cardano and Gemma Frisius (pp. 91–6), how the comet of 1556 gave rise to the first publication of comet catalogues, how the Nova of 1572 gave rise to more tracts and observers than any previous stellar event (pp. 110–11), and how Tycho at Hven and Hagecius at Prague were alerted to coordinate their observations of the comet of 1577 (pp. 118 ff). Westman, 'Comet and Cosmos,' p. 8, n. 20 notes that the six-year-old Kepler had been led by his mother to a high place to view it.

78 The phrase comes from Christianson, 'Astronomy and Printing.'

79 Warner, 'The First Celestial Globe,' p. 36.

80 This point is brought out by Nichols, Jr. 'The Interaction of Life,' pp. 51–77.

remaining ones correspond to those observed by the Ancients,' runs an English translation of the Latin text placed on a celestial globe produced by Willem Janszoon Blaeu between 1596 and 1599.[81] Blaeu's 'exceedingly accurate globe' not only made clear what the great modern astronomer had added to skies studied by the greatest star-gazers of antiquity; it also made clear that even more exciting news was destined to be forthcoming from intrepid explorers who had ventured beyond the edge of the known world.

Certain stars nearer to the Antarctic Pole, and avoiding our sight, are not less remarkable for their magnitude than those lying in the northern region, whether by report of the extent of their brilliances or by the annals of writers, nevertheless having delineation as uncertain, we have here omitted the measuring of them.[82]

What Blaeu cautiously omitted in the late 1590s a competitor was able to fill in by 1600, suggesting how competition between profit-driving printers – no less than collaboration among scattered observers – helped to accelerate data collection and push it along new paths. Just as Blaeu was finishing supervision of his plates, an expedition was returning carrying records of uncharted skies. 'At the very end of the century two Dutchmen...working sometimes together, made the first systematic attempt to organize and catalogue the southern stars.' Both men sailed on the 1595–7 voyage of the *Hollandia* and kept records of the observations of the southern skies they made while voyaging in the East Indies. One, the chief pilot, died at sea, but his data carried back to Amsterdam were exploited by Blaeu's chief competitor, Jocondus Hondius for his celestial globe of 1600. No less than fourteen new constellations were displayed on the Hondius globe.

So Blaeu who doubtless expected his first celestial globe to be widely acclaimed and distributed, instead saw it become obsolete just a short time after publication. There was nothing to do but to withdraw it from the market and begin again.[83]

To begin again in the age of print had a different meaning than had been the case in the age of scribes. By 1602, Blaeu turned out an updated smaller globe which contained all the fresh data brought back

---

[81] Warner, 'First Celestial Globe,' p. 36.
[82] According to Warner, 'First Celestial Globe,' p. 36, n. 24, Blaeu is echoing comments made in Tycho's *Astronomiae Instauratae Mechanica*.
[83] Warner, 'First Celestial Globe,' p. 37.

from the Dutch expedition and, in addition, registered a brand-new observation that was uniquely his own. In August, 1600 he had noted a new star of the third magnitude in the constellation Cygnus and this also he placed upon his globe – where it remained to be duplicated repeatedly – long after the star faded from everyone's view.[84] Moreover, he never really did begin all over again. In 1603 the large plates for his first globe, which had been too valuable to discard, were re-used after corrections had been made on them and resulted in the 'now justly famous 34 centimeter globe of 1603' with his own name prominently displayed alongside that of his former master, 'Lord Tycho,' on the revised title text.[85]

According to Wightman, Tycho Brahe was the first Western astronomer to pursue the kind of program that later became characteristic of the Royal Society.[86] He was the forerunner of a new breed of astronomers who were singled out by Bishop Sprat. They 'studied to make it not onely an enterprise of one season or of some lucky opportunity; but a business of time; a steddy, a lasting, a popular, an uninterrupted work.'[87] It does not detract from Tycho's justly distinguished position in the history of astronomy to suggest that he was favored by a 'lucky opportunity' by being born at the right time. No one man however gifted could put so vast a collaborative enterprise as astronomy on a new footing or live long enough to assure that it would be a steady, lasting, popular, uninterrupted enterprise. The 'business of time' lies outside the control of any one generation, let alone that of a single mortal creature. Geoffrey of Meaux's nightly observations of the comet of 1315 suggest that Tycho's program of steady observation to obtain fresh data was not unprecedented.[88] Much as Viking landfalls preceded Columbus, careful star-gazers had been at work before Tycho. What was unprecedented (with new stars

---

[84] After being visible for a few years, Warner says the star faded completely. It reappeared in 1657–8 before fading to the fifth magnitude. The capacity to fix a location for an invisible star so that its reappearance may be detected was greatly enhanced after printing.

[85] Warner, 'First Celestial Globe,' p. 38.

[86] Wightman, *Science and the Renaissance* I, 120.

[87] Sprat, *Royal Society*, part 2, sect. 5, p. 62.

[88] Hellman, *Comet*, pp. 47, 67 ff, describes medieval observations. In her 'Role of Measurement,' p. 43, she notes that Geoffrey's observations were 'unusual in the annals of the era.' Goldstein, 'Theory and Observation,' p. 47, shows that an observer of an eclipse in 1337 noted that the *Alphonsine Tables* were in error but left no evidence of trying to rectify the error. Unless associated with a special message center designed to correct and copy astronomical data, individual observers could do little to change such tables until after the advent of printing. Incentives to compile long lists of numbers in tables were also at a low ebb. See n. 162 below.

and new worlds alike) was the way observed phenomena could be recorded and confirmed.

As the foregoing may suggest, when trying to explain the new sixteenth-century view of 'age-old phenomena' such as novas and comets, the changes wrought by printing need to be taken into account. General references to a turbulent age or even more specific evocation of the 'new climate of scientific thought' represented by Copernicus do not help very much to explain phenomena such as Tycho's star. The neo-Platonic and Aristotelian currents that entered into Copernicus' studies with Italian masters, such as Domenico Maria de Novara, had no counterpart in the young Danish nobleman's case. Indeed Tycho set out to become an astronomer by defying his tutor and teaching himself. He by-passed the traditional master–apprentice relationship by taking advantage of printed materials. It seems likely that his freedom from prevailing cosmological assumptions owed something to his unusual position as a largely self-made astronomer.[89] Symmetry and sun-worship seem to have been subordinated to other concerns in Tychonic astronomy.[90] Its architect did not share Copernicus' aesthetic or metaphysical concerns. The two astronomers were not linked by mutual admiration for a particular classical or Christian textual tradition.[91] As sixteenth-century astronomers they may be distinguished from their predecessors not so much because they were influenced by one or another Renaissance current of thought but rather because they were freed from copying and memorizing and could make use of new paper tools and printed texts.

Whether the sixteenth-century astronomer confronted materials derived from the fourth century B.C. or freshly composed in the fourteenth century A.D., or whether he was more receptive to scholastic or humanist currents of thought seems of less significance in this particu-

89 Tycho's position as an 'autodidact,' is of course a limited one since he did take the usual cycle of undergraduate courses. As noted (pp. 533–4) above, while taking the traditional cycle of studies associated with the *trivium* and *quadrivium*, Tycho was also exposed to new mathematical and linguistic training and some new information (albeit often in a concealed form).

90 The fact that 'symmetry and proportionality' were not respected in the Tychonic scheme offended Maestlin. He strongly opposed Tycho's cosmology on that account. See Westman, 'Comet and Cosmos,' p. 27.

91 One could elaborate on this point by noting that Copernicus had taken a degree in canon law at Ferrara whereas Tycho was trained at a 'Philipist' university where canon law was regarded as a diabolic instrument of the Papal anti-Christ. The possible influence of working with a 'concordance of discordant canons' on Copernicus' approach to discordant Ptolemaic and Arabic texts might be worth further thought – according to Schoeck's paper on 'Copernicus and Humanism.'

lar connection than the fact that all manner of diverse materials were being seen in the course of one lifetime by one pair of eyes. For Copernicus as for Tycho, the result was heightened awareness of, and dissatisfaction with, discrepancies in the inherited data.

For the first time a technically competent astronomer had rejected the time-honored scientific tradition for reasons internal to his science...The astronomical tradition had not previously seemed monstrous. By Copernicus' time a metamorphosis had occurred and Copernicus' preface brilliantly described the felt causes of that transformation.[92]

Copernicus' preface emphasizes the diversity of views held by the authorities who described 'the movements of the sun, moon and planets' according to incompatible schemes. His precursors were 'so unsure of the movement of the sun and the moon that they cannot even explain or observe the constant length of the seasonal year.' When set side by side their systems fail to cohere; 'they use neither the same principles and hypotheses nor the same demonstrations of apparent motions and revolutions.'[93] Too many textbooks have overplayed Copernicus' dissatisfaction with the purported complexity of Ptolemaic celestial machinery.[94] Only a few bring out clearly how his own words express 'nothing else than the knowledge that the mathematicians are inconsistent in these investigations.'[95] In many accounts indeed, Copernicus' dissatisfaction with Ptolemaic astronomy can scarcely be distinguished from that of an untrained layman, baffled by the intricacies of a sophisticated reckoning scheme. But Copernicus' reaction not only needs to be distinguished from that attributed to King Alfonso X; it also needs to be distinguished from that of later contributors to so-called scientific 'revolutions.' It was not predicated on an accumulation of minor discrepancies in the course of prolonged 'normal' research. Copernicus was not simply reacting, as did later critics of Newton, to the inadequacy of a given astronomical theory.[96] He was also expressing concern at his finding that no one theory had been *consistently* used.

His comments point both to the difficulty of lining up observations

---

92 Thomas Kuhn, *Copernican Revolution*, p. 138.
93 Citation from preface to *De Revolutionibus* in Thomas Kuhn, *Copernican Revolution*, p. 137.
94 That this theme has been overdone (to the point of falsifying the number of epicycles required by Ptolemaic astronomers) is persuasively argued by Palter, 'An Approach to the History.' See also Gingerich, 'Crisis versus Aesthetic,' n. 7 and 8.
95 Citation from preface to *De Revolutionibus*, in Thomas Kuhn, *Copernican Revolution*, p. 137.
96 See Thomas Kuhn, *Structure of Scientific Revolutions*, pp. 68–9.

made by predecessors who used diverse reckoning schemes and to the monstrous model that was produced when trying to assemble separate parts 'each excellently drawn but not related to a single body.'[97] In both cases the chief irritant was supplied by inconsistency.

Copernicus and his contemporaries inherited not only the *Almagest* but also the astronomies of many Islamic and a few European astronomers who had criticized and modified Ptolemy's system...There was no longer any one Ptolemaic system, but a dozen or more and the number was multiplying rapidly with the multiplication of technically proficient astronomers.[98]

Insofar as there was a rapid multiplication of incongruous theories this was probably related to the fact that texts had become more numerous after printers set to work. However many colleagues Copernicus had, and however few professional astronomers Europe had known when Regiomontanus was alive, their number probably had not 'multiplied' as fast as had copies of astronomical texts after printers set to work. Although uncertain guidance is offered here, the number of technically proficient astronomers who were equipped to read the *Almagest* in the early sixteenth century actually seems to have been quite small.[99] 'To Europeans of Copernicus's generation, planetary astronomy was almost a new field.'[100]

Now if planetary astronomy was 'almost a new field' to Copernicus' generation it would seem to be an unlikely setting for a breakdown of

97 Cited by Thomas Kuhn, *Copernican Revolution*, p. 138. This passage which invokes aesthetic canons seems to owe something to quattrocento theories developed by humanists such as Alberti, who transposed Aristotelian rules as set forth in the *Poetics* and other classical rhetorical conventions into visual terms and stressed compositional unity when judging a painting. See Baxandall, *Giotto, passim*. How Copernicus' view of God as 'the great artisan' who designed a perfect celestial machine contrasted with Ptolemy's view of the god-like wandering stars is well brought out by Curtis Wilson's paper, 'Rheticus, Ravetz.'

98 Thomas Kuhn, *Copernican Revolution*, pp. 138–9. Just what is meant by a 'dozen or more' Ptolemaic systems in this passage is not entirely clear and entails using the term 'system' more loosely than may be deemed justified by other authorities. When Copernicus himself refers to something 'which the mathematicians call their system' (in the citation given by Kuhn on pp. 137–8) he seems to be implying that the term is not deserved. Previous authorities have questioned whether Ptolemaic astronomy can be associated with any 'system' but Goldstein, 'The Arabic Version of Ptolemy's *Planetary Hypotheses*,' part 4, *passim* shows that there was a definite order of planets set forth in the full Ptolemaic text.

99 See references to the 'small group of Europeans' and 'small group equipped to read Ptolemy's treatise,' Thomas Kuhn, *Copernican Revolution*, p. 135, as against later passages asserting *De Revolutionibus* 'was widely read,' and that 'the book's large audience ensured it a small but increasing number of readers equipped to discover Copernicus's harmonies' (p. 186). The 'wildly diverse' estimates of the size of the first edition of *De Revolutionibus* which probably ranged between 500 and 800 copies, are discussed by Gingerich, 'Copernicus and the Impact of Printing,' p. 207.

100 Thomas Kuhn, *Copernican Revolution*, p. 123.

'normal science' to occur. Jerome Ravetz has suggested that early sixteenth-century science was not well enough organized to fit a pattern followed in later scientific revolutions.[101] His suggestion fits in well with the views offered here. Scribal transmission produced a fundamentally different pattern from the flow of information after print. The conditions that permitted Alexandrian achievements were not 'normal' but exceptional. Accurately copied tables were exceptional as well. 'Firmly established expectations that things will go right' had not begun to characterize those who sought to chart every planet's wandering course.

Instead of confronting an unprecedented 'break*down*' of a 'normal research effort,'[102] in other words, sixteenth-century European astronomers were just beginning to take advantage of a technological break-*through* which set continuous problem-solving on its later 'normal' path. To depict Copernicus' preface as 'one of the classic descriptions of a crisis state' in astronomy and to attribute his rejection of Ptolemy to a 'breakdown in normal technical puzzle-solving'[103] seems ill-suited to a situation when 'normal' puzzle-solving was barely getting under way, corrupted scrambled records were just beginning to get sorted out and fresh data had not yet been systematically collected.

By the early sixteenth century an increasing number of Europe's best astronomers were recognizing that the astronomical paradigm was failing in application to its own traditional problems. That recognition was prerequisite to Copernicus' rejection of the Ptolemaic paradigm and his search for a new one.[104]

The chief 'traditional' problem for astronomers in Western Christen-

---

101 Ravetz, *Astronomy and Cosmology*, p. 44. Ravetz is referring specifically to the kind of 'normal science' that is described in Kuhn's *Structure of Scientific Revolutions* as I am also doing throughout this discussion.

102 'As time went on...the net result of the normal research effort of many astronomers' pointed toward a crisis for the Ptolemaic paradigm according to Thomas Kuhn, *Structure of Scientific Revolutions*, pp. 68–9.

103 Thomas Kuhn, *Structure of Scientific Revolutions*, p. 69.

104 Thomas Kuhn, *Structure of Scientific Revolutions*. When Kuhn says (p. 67), 'On this point historical evidence is entirely unequivocal, the state of Ptolemaic astronomy was a scandal before Copernicus' announcement,' the actual 'point' that provoked scandal seems to be unclear. In his footnote, Kuhn refers the reader to A. R. Hall's discussion of how tables of eclipses and church calendars were awry. On the question of the calendar which was 'the most notorious,' according to Hall, historical evidence is not unequivocal and the scandal is centuries-old. The role of calendar reform in 'intensifying the crisis' is also underlined by Kuhn in 'The Function of Measurement,' 181, no. 39. A very long-simmering 'steady-state' crisis seems to be entailed. (The validity of Kuhn's use of the term 'crisis' is also questioned by Gingerich in 'Crisis versus Aesthetic.')

dom was posed by church calendars failing to align Easter with the vernal equinox. Awareness of this failure may have served as a prerequisite for the Copernican Revolution. But it did not take 'an increasing number of Europe's best astronomers' in the sixteenth century to recognize the problem. It had been a concern of Christian Churchmen from the early middle ages on.

Had 'normal' puzzle-solving been feasible for the astronomers of Latin Christendom, it seems likely that calendar reform would have been accomplished well before Copernicus was born. Full technical mastery of Alexandrian and Arabic computations represented a relatively recent achievement for a sixteenth-century Western astronomer. In contrast, pressure for calendar reform, 'a pressure that made the puzzle of precession particularly urgent' had been a significant feature of the culture of Latin Christendom in Roger Bacon's day. Indeed the Church's sponsorship of the study of astronomy and its contribution to the retrieval of Alexandrian scientific texts was partly predicated on the need for help with this perennial problem. A 'long list of Christian scholars had called for calendar reform.' Many popes took a special interest in the matter. It loomed large at various church councils.[105]

One is reminded of repeated efforts to establish trilingual studies. There was nothing new about perceiving that the calendar was awry in Copernicus' day; just as there was nothing new about acknowledging the need of help from trilingual scholars to emend the Vulgate.[106] As in the latter case, so too in the former, novelty lay in the steps that were taken to achieve a long-desired goal. Although agitation for calendar reform had persisted for centuries, implementation had been frustrated for reasons that have yet to be made clear.

On this issue no two specialists seem to agree. (It is even difficult to discover whether Copernicus' work was helpful or irrelevant to the Gregorian reform that was finally carried through.)[107] Most accounts

---

[105] Sarton, Six Wings, p. 70. For repeated church requests, see also Thorndike, History of Magic and Experimental Science, p. 18.

[106] See p. 340, volume I above.

[107] Ravetz, Astronomy and Cosmology, p. 40, says that calendar reform 'was impossible before Copernicus' who provided the methods and data which rendered the Alphonsine Tables obsolete. Rosen, 'Galileo's Misstatements About Copernicus,' pp. 328–9, says, 'the Gregorian Calendar owed nothing to Copernicus' and was not based on the Prutenic Tables but rather on the mean tropical year as defined in the Alphonsine Tables. A seemingly authoritative reference from the journal of the Pontificia Academia Scientarium, kindly supplied by Robert Palter, helps to clarify this question. According to de Kort, 'Astronomical Appreciation,' the length of the Gregorian Year was based on a value adopted from the Alphonsine Tables but the length of the month 'was taken from Copernicus's data as used in the Prutenian Tables' (p. 57).

imply that official inertia was primarily responsible. Unsolved astronomical problems are rarely discussed, and it is difficult for the nonspecialist to ascertain whether they played an important role or indeed any role at all. Some studies state that only 'simple arithmetic and common sense' were required,[108] and others imply that the technical problems had been surmounted several centuries before Copernicus set to work. 'The reform of the Julian calendar was a limited and quantitative problem which medieval writers set out to solve and in fact solved.'[109] It is clear that a short-term reform of the Julian calendar was undertaken in the thirteenth century and that guidelines for further reform were also proposed.[110] Tinkering with the ancient Roman calendar was not quite the same as replacing it, however, and medieval calendar reform seems to have left the latter task unfulfilled. 'In improving the calendar' Rheticus complained on his teacher's behalf, 'most scholars enumerate various lengths of the years as computed by writers. But they do this in a confused way and come to no conclusion...'[111]

To arrive at a firm conclusion on an issue of this kind would have been exceedingly difficult in the age of scribes. According to Jerome Ravetz, most accounts tend to underestimate the technical difficulties that had to be surmounted in order to achieve the Gregorian reform. It was not as easy a task, Ravetz argues, as hindsight (based on Gauss' eighteenth-century formula) makes it appear. In his view, the Gregorian reform could not occur until after 'inequalities appearing from records of the past' had been mastered – as Copernicus set out to do.[112] If Ravetz is right, the conditions of scribal culture ought to be featured more prominently for having frustrated previous efforts at thoroughgoing reform.

It does seem misleading, at all events, to attribute the prolonged delay to 'institutional reluctance to apply scientific results' and to draw

Of course using the *Prutenic Tables* does not imply acceptance of Copernican geokinetic theories. Erasmus Reinhold who compiled the *Tables*, for example, did so without accepting the Copernican scheme.

108 Sarton, *Six Wings*, p. 70.
109 Crombie, 'Rejoinder,' pp. 318–19.
110 See e.g. account of later adjustments in the calendar which had already been reformed by Grosseteste, made by Peter Nightingale in 1292. Nightingale's program encompassed a seventy-six-year period and detailed instructions for re-adjustment thereafter (which were followed in 1369 and 1440) according to Pedersen, 'The Life and Work of Peter Nightingale,' p. 6.
111 Rheticus, 'Narratio Prima,' p. 127.
112 Ravetz, *Astronomy and Cosmology*, pp. 7, 9, 38–9, 51–2. On p. 38, n. 23, Ravetz suggests that Sarton's approach is too naive.

analogies with the English postponement until 1752 and the Russian failure to move until 1918.[113] Even apart from uncertainty about 'scientific results,' medieval officials were handicapped by the difficulty of 'publishing' such results and of ensuring their uniform adoption. Institutional incapacity as well as possible reluctance must be taken into account.

It would have been an extremely simple matter once in every 308 years to prepare and publish a new table of Golden Numbers giving effect to this simple correction. But this was not done. The dread of innovation or some sort of superstitious regard for the established table apparently prevented any change.[114]

For one thing, this particular correction appears 'simple' only after the proper formula has been devised – after it is known that '235 lunations fell short of 19 Julian years by 1 hour and 29 minutes every 308 years.'[115] Before there was agreement on just these points, the case was not simple at all. For another thing, reluctance to instruct officials to change numerical tables every three centuries and eight years would have been sensible, not 'superstitious' in an era when there was no way of publishing 'errata' of any kind, when copies of written instructions were likely to drift over the course of a single century and when heavy reliance on oral transmission meant one had to arrange for changing memorized formulae – a dangerous procedure indeed. It became relatively easy to train clerks to handle Dominical letters after they were laid out in printed tables. But formidable mnemonic feats were required of the Oxford clerks who studied the computus from the thirteenth to the sixteenth centuries. To help them learn the required 260 lines of hexameter, each finger was assigned six joints and all sixty joints were used.[116] Before printed calendars, it was 'an arduous mathematical feat' merely to 'find a day that corresponded to a given date.'[117]

In view of the difficulty of ensuring conformity with the existing system any 'dread of innovation' was soundly based. It seems mis-

[113] Crombie, 'Rejoinder,' pp. 318–19.   [114] Philip, *The Calendar*, p. 68.
[115] Philip, *The Calendar*, p. 68.
[116] Bosanquet, *English Printed Almanacks*, p. 59. See also discussion of vernacular rhymes in a manual on the *Computus* written by Alexander de Villedieu and taught to students at the Paris college of Ave Maria in the fourteenth century, Gabriel, *Garlandia*, p. 110.
[117] D. E. Smith, *Le Comput*, p. 13. This publication also contains a discussion of early printed versions (beginning with a Strasbourg manual of 1488), of other medieval mnemonic works, and of finger exercises such as those illustrated in a 1504 Lyons publication (pp. 28, 49).

guided, at all events, to attribute postponement of reform to 'inner quarrels of the Church' which prevented any measure being taken until the late sixteenth century. When the measure was finally taken, Western Christendom was no less quarrelsome than it had been before. The more plausible explanation offered by Kuhn, who points to the expansion of dynastic states and burgeoning bureaucracy, also seems somewhat doubtful to me. To suggest that the '...size of political, economic and administrative units placed a new premium upon an efficient and uniform means of dating' seems to put the cart before the horse.[118] It was not the high value assigned to calendar reform but the means of achieving this long-desired goal that was new in the sixteenth century. Calendar reform had been a church-sponsored project at the outset, and remained one to the end. It was so little valued by secular statesmen that Protestant officials in well-consolidated realms were willing to bow to anti-Papist sentiment and postpone its adoption for many decades.

That the project was assigned high priority by medieval churchmen rather than by early-modern state officials is worth underlining, for it points to some neglected religious roots of Western science. Investigation into calendrical problems was the accidental by-product of sacred concerns that were peculiar to the Christian faith and that centered on commemorating the miracle of the Resurrection. The definition of Easter made at the Council of Nicea kept Western mathematicians and astronomers at work on a set of problems that evaded solution throughout the age of scribes. Was there any other religious community that celebrated a sacred festival so peculiarly sensitive to errors in solar and lunar tables or so insistent that the puzzle of the precession of equinoxes be solved?[119]

The complexity of the Christian Church calendar, like that of its polyglot Bible, can best be appreciated when set against Moslem simplicity. 'We are a people who do not write and do not count' said Mohammed. Not sixty knuckles and hundreds of lines of hexameter but only ten fingers shown three times with the thumb folded on the third time were needed by the faithful of Islam to measure the passing

[118] Thomas Kuhn, *Copernican Revolution*, p. 124. Pannekoek, *History of Astronomy*, p. 219 attributes the delay to 'inner quarrels' of the Church.

[119] Calendrical problems spurred the development of mathematical science in China according to Needham, *Science and Civilisation* III, 152. But successful reform was achieved only after the arrival of Western missionaries in the seventeenth century. See d'Elia, *Galileo in China*, appendix, pp. 61 ff.

of the months.[120] The same Semitic calendar that was complicated by the Christians at Nicea was drastically simplified by Mohammed who eliminated intercalations and ignored the solar cycle. The length of every year was arbitrarily fixed at twelve lunar months, and seasonal changes were irrelevant to the celebration of Ramadan. Over the course of centuries the Moslem calendar became increasingly out of phase with the solar cycle (by now it is forty years off) but the growing discrepancy did not serve as an irritant. Moslems 'simply ignored the law of nature in their regulation of their time scheme.'[121] This is not to say that all the sacred concerns of the Moslems were indifferent to the laws of nature. Problems posed by orienting all mosques toward Mecca in an expanding empire, for example, may have spurred study of astronomy and geography among the Arabs.[122] But a different set of problems was posed for Christians by a celestial clockwork that perversely moved out of phase with annual commemoration of the central miracle of their faith.

Throughout the middle ages, the movable feast of Easter, indeed, served as a focal point where studies of astronomy and of chronology, of sacred history and of profane all converged. Not only were solar and lunar cycles difficult to reconcile, but Passover also had to be kept out of Easter's way. Ancient Jewish and Roman time schemes had to be mastered. The puzzling precession of the vernal equinox could not be set aside nor could contradictions in the gospels be left out of account.[123] The problems posed by Easter help to explain why Chris-

120 Sayili, *The Observatory in Islam*, p. 22, cites Al Bîrûnî's version of Mohammed's statement in this connection.
121 Philip, *The Calendar*, p. 26. Data on how the Christians complicated and the Moslems simplified a luni-solar calendar inherited from the Jews are also contained in Archer, *The Christian Calendar*, pp. 39–52.
122 According to Sayili, *The Observatory in Islam*, pp. 23–5, taxes and harvests were affected by the absence of a solar calendar or of any intercalated years in Islam. For a brief interval in the eleventh century, the Malikshâh Observatory introduced reckoning according to a solar calendar but this lasted only twenty years (1072–92). The orientation of mosques allowed for so much latitude (up to forty-five degrees error or more) that this problem provided less impetus to astronomy than might be thought. Non-sacred concerns, such as desert navigation, *did* stimulate the Arabs, however, to develop some observational techniques well in advance of those available in the West in Columbus' era. (See e.g. Morison, *Admiral*, p. 184.)
123 The additional complications posed by the Council of Nicea's insistence on avoiding 'judaising Easter' are described by Philip, *The Calendar*, pp. 63, 78. Archer, *The Christian Calendar*, pp. 18, 53, argues that the decision was predicated, not on animosity toward the Jews, but to avoid the inconsistency of celebrating the Resurrection before or on the same day as the slaying of the Paschal Lamb which prefigured the crucifixion. One need not adopt an either/or approach. Probably both anti-Semitism and allegorical consistency played a role. The fact that no calendar can avoid Easter's occasionally coinciding with Passover is only one of many complications that persistently challenged the ingenuity of Christian clerks.

tian astronomers down to Newton's day were so often preoccupied with biblical chronology,[124] and why Christian churchmen going back to Bede's time, devoted so much effort to graphing the planets, compiling tide-tables and instructing future priests in the mysteries of the computus.

computistical material did much to stimulate the use of tables and diagrams. Although the tables abound in error...their construction stimulated at least scientific ratiocination...It is possible but by no means proved that such astronomical graphing influenced the application of graphing techniques to problems of local motion and qualitative changes in the fourteenth century.[125]

The early medieval graphs described by Clagett did not merely have some indirect bearing on the future development of fourteenth-century mechanics. They also point more directly to the inclusion of planetary astronomy in the sacred concerns of Christians even during the early middle ages. They offer evidence that concern with uniformity, regularity and a mathematical order in nature was manifested in church schools even before Aristotle's *Logic* re-entered the West. The 'craze for the dialectic' came well after a strong 'habit of definite exact thought' had been implanted in Christian culture. Among professional astronomers, of course, this habit went back to pre-Christian times. But even after ancient astronomy had been lost and before it was again retrieved, the same habit was being inculcated among novices who tried to master the computus in order to become Christian priests. By a seeming paradox, their most sacred festival kept Christian energies bent toward puzzle-solving of a purely scientific kind.

In this regard one might take issue with modern writers who project a more recent warfare between science and theology into earlier eras. 'Comets and monsters were of greater moment to medieval piety than the daily sunrise and normal offspring.'[126] The news value of the odd as opposed to the ordinary event is still rated high even in these impious days. Insofar as they viewed dog-biting men as more newsworthy than man-eating dogs, monkish chroniclers had more in common with modern journalists than with medieval natural philoso-

[124] Kepler's many references to J. J. Scaliger's *De Emendatione Temporum* (1583) and his correspondence with the author about ancient chronology are noted by Palter (ed.) *Johannes Kepler 1571–1630*, Catalogue, item no. 118. An entire section in this catalogue: *VI. Calendars and Chronology* points to many other relevant titles. The case of Newton has inspired a special study: Manuel, *Isaac Newton Historian*. On Scaliger's work see Grafton, 'Joseph Scaliger and Historical Chronology.' [125] Clagett, *Greek Science*, pp. 162–5.
[126] Zilsel, cited by Lewis Feuer, *The Scientific Intellectual*, p. 249.

phers who graphed planetary movements and studied the tides. Insofar as the daily sunrise was part of a celestial clockwork that was persistently out of phase with Easter, it could not be ignored by pious clerics and was a source of constant concern. Their very belief in a supernatural event encouraged learned churchmen to persist with investigations of the order of nature. The desire to commemorate a miracle on the proper holy day forced repeated inquiries into cyclical movements of a non-miraculous kind.

Until the advent of printing, scientific inquiries about 'how the heavens go' went hand-in-hand with religious concerns about 'how to go to heaven.' Astronomers were needed to help commemorate Gospel truths. After printing, however, the study of celestial mechanics was propelled in a new direction and soon reached levels of sophistication that left calendrical problems far behind. With the output of printed tables, moreover, training priests to master the computus lost many of the virtues it had formerly possessed. Complex mnemonics, parchment volvelles and other devices designed to help with 'Easter date computation, Golden Numbers, Sunday Letters and all the rigamaroles of the passion for calendrics that afflicted the scholarly church'[127] eventually receded into a dimly remembered Gothic past. That intelligent adults had actually been preoccupied with child-like jingles such as 'Thirty days hath September...' made medieval men seem strangely 'retarded' to scholars who lived in an 'enlightened' age. Churchmen and astronomers continued to move apart to the point where it now seems odd to think of their having ever been committed to a joint enterprise.

The calendrical problems posed by Easter – like the linguistic ones posed by the Bible – turned out to be peculiarly sensitive to changes wrought by print. The Koran did not provide the same incentive that the Vulgate did to master strange tongues or dig up ancient scrolls. The observance of Ramadan did not supply the religious motives that Easter did to go beyond the *Almagest* and ascertain the long-term slow-motion movements of the stars. Their most sacred festival as well as their holy scriptures acted to keep Christian men of learning constantly pressing against the limits imposed by scribal culture. Special religious motives helped to provide the initial impetus for what later appeared to be an almost sacriligious 'Faustian' quest.

[127] Price, 'The Book as a Scientific Instrument,' p. 102.

Evidence of this special concern was clearly present in the book that launched the Copernican Revolution. Even though Copernicus originally set out to emend Ptolemaic astronomy without giving much thought to calendrical problems,[128] a concern with these problems did play a significant part in guiding his research during the last thirty years he spent revising his *magnum opus*. For a decade he 'concentrated on the unequal length of the seasons and explanations of this inequality.'[129] His prolonged investigation was not without a significant result:

In Copernicus's mature *Revolutionibus*, this fixed apsidal line was replaced by a moving terrestrial aphelion.

This discovery, doubtless connected with Copernicus's intensified investigation of the length of the year was based in part on a careful scrutiny of the results obtained by his predecessors. It is sometimes said that Copernicus had too much faith in the observations of earlier astronomers. But in this instance he could not be incredulous, since he found an incompatibility in the position of the solar apogee as reported by two of the most outstanding medieval Muslim observers between whom he had to choose.[130]

The recruitment of mathematicians and astronomers to help with calendar reform thus acted very much as did the use of trilingual scholars to help with scriptural emendation. In urging Copernicus to work further on the calendrical problems that the fifth Lateran Council had not solved, Paul of Middelburg was doing something many other learned churchmen had done before. In accepting the assignment Copernicus was also serving in a conventional role.[131] For astronomers as for biblical scholars, however, unanticipated consequences resulted when new means came to the aid of those who were pursuing old goals. Copernicus set out to reform Ptolemy much as Erasmus had set out to re-do Saint Jerome – in order to serve the Church, not subvert it.

---

[128] Rosen, 'Biography of Copernicus,' *Three Copernican Treatises*, p. 360, points out that the *Commentariolus* was undertaken before Copernicus was asked to help with calendar reform and indicates little concern with the topic. Other good reasons for rejecting Ravetz's suggestion 'that Copernicus' reconstruction of astronomy sprang from the problem of calendar reform' are set forth by Wilson, 'Rheticus, Ravetz,' pp. 4–5. The problem *did* enter into Copernicus' revision of Ptolemaic astronomy, but at a later stage. See n. 131 below.

[129] Rosen, 'Biography of Copernicus,' *Three Copernican Treatises*, p. 362.

[130] Rosen, 'Biography of Copernicus,' *Three Copernican Treatises*, p. 388.

[131] On the invitation addressed to Paul of Middelburg (1445–1533) Bishop of Fossebrone, by Pope Leo X to help with calendar reform and on how Copernicus was 'spurred' by the urging of Paul of Middelburg in 1515 to investigate the topic more closely see Rosen, 'Biography of Copernicus,' *Three Copernican Treatises*, pp. 359–62. How Paul of Middelburg's own calendrical research led him toward Hebrew studies is discussed by Offenberg, 'The first use of Hebrew.'

'Never, perhaps, has such a conservative and quiet thinker had such an upsetting effect upon men's minds and souls...'[132]

De Revolutionibus itself must be a constant puzzle and a paradox for...it is a relatively staid, sober and unrevolutionary work...In every respect except the earth's motion the De Revolutionibus seems more closely akin to the works of ancient and medieval astronomers...than to the writings of succeeding generations...who made explicit the radical consequences that even its author had not seen in his work...[133]

The 'radical consequences' that ensued from Copernicus' 'sober and unrevolutionary work' might seem somewhat less puzzling if the new powers of print were taken into account. As things stand now, however, these powers tend to be mainly confined to functions associated with publicity and propaganda. Accordingly, they seem to loom large in the early stages of the Lutheran revolt and to recede to the point of vanishing in the first phases of the Copernican Revolution. Whether they are called into play to spread Lutheran tracts or Copernican theories, it should be noted, the new presses make a belated appearance as agents of change. But although early printers have to wait until 1517 before their presence on the stage of history is acknowledged in Reformation studies, they are assigned significant functions thereafter. News of the ninety-five Theses spread far and fast; Luther's German Bible set records as a bestseller. Whether one is willing to accept Arthur Koestler's verdict or not, one must admit that by contrast with the stir Luther made, the reception of Copernicus was very subdued. According to Koestler, this posthumous publication 'created less of a stir than Rheticus' First Account of it. Rheticus had promised that the book would be a revelation; it turned out to be a disappointment... it raised no particular controversy either in public or among professional astronomers...[134]

Many authorities, to be sure, regard Copernicus' failure to attract

---

[132] Boas, Scientific Renaissance, p. 69.

[133] Thomas Kuhn, Copernican Revolution, p. 134.

[134] Koestler, Sleepwalkers, p. 213. The 'book that nobody read' is so described on p. 191. For sharp attack on Koestler's 'ludicrously unhistorical' judgment, see Rosen, 'Biography of Copernicus,' Three Copernican Treatises, pp. 406–8. Actually, sufficient controversy was created for the Italian publicist, Doni, to portray two Florentines disputing the hypothesis as a theory refuted in sermons – in I Marmi (Venice, 1552) and for Du Bartas to include verses ridiculing it in his popular poem: 'La Semaine' of 1587. See Preserved Smith, Origins of Modern Culture, pp. 52–3. A full account of sixteenth-century publicity pro and con cannot be given here. Recent studies have outdated the pioneering monograph by Dorothy Stimson, The Gradual Acceptance of the Copernican Theory of the Universe (New York, 1917) as noted in a review by Erna Hilfstein and Edward Rosen of a recent Polish book by Barbara Bienkowska.

publicity as less deplorable than does Koestler. When Whitehead, for example, contrasts the 'quiet' rise of modern science with the 'popular' religious uprising that 'drenched Europe in blood,' it is to suggest that diffident scientists were really better Christians than were quarrelsome monks: 'Since a babe was born in a manger, it may be doubted whether so great a thing happened with so little stir.'[135] Kuhn regards the 'quiet' reception of *De Revolutionibus* as useful for the purposes of subversion. By making his work 'unreadable to all save the most erudite,' Kuhn suggests, Copernicus actually fashioned 'an almost ideal weapon' for the struggle that lay ahead. By the time opposition was mobilized, professional astronomers had come to rely on Copernicus' mathematical techniques and had become accustomed to computing planetary positions from a moving earth. The geokinetic theory had already achieved 'victory by infiltration' before it came under strong official attack. Kuhn even argues that printing helped to consolidate this victory by making it more difficult 'to suppress the work completely' – a somewhat debatable point.[136]

Whether effective opposition was eventually blunted because *De Revolutionibus* was printed and not copied out by hand is a matter for debate. There can be no dispute, at any rate, that early printers play a much less conspicuous and much more problematic role in the Copernican Revolution than in the Reformation. Not only did sixteenth-century printers fail to rally behind the Copernican cause as they did behind the Lutheran one, they also did much to popularize Ptolemaic views.[137] As noted above, their propensity for backing the 'wrong' astronomical theory is repeatedly used as a warning not to

135 Whitehead, *Science and the Modern World*, pp. 11–12. Particularly after Galileo turned to print, the 'quiet rise of modern science' was less remote from the noisy clash of rival faiths than this passage suggests. See chap. 8, below, for critique of Whitehead's view.

136 Thomas Kuhn, *Copernican Revolution*, p. 185. Given the technical nature of the work, and given the less rigorous character of censorship before printing, it seems unlikely that an attempt would have been made 'to suppress the work completely' had it been in ms. form. As it was, *De Revolutionibus* lent itself easily to expurgation thus rendering 'complete' suppression unnecessary. That it could be used *without accepting the earth's motion* should also be kept in mind. See n. 107 above on Reinhold's work as an example.

137 Koestler, *Sleepwalkers*, p. 191 points to fifty-nine editions of Sacrobosco's *Sphaera*, nineteen reprints of Clavius's *Treatise*, nine reprints of Melanchthon's textbook and other reprints of Ptolemy's *Almagest* and Peurbach's *Planetary Theory* to come up with a total of 'a hundred reprints in Germany' before 1600 as against the one reprint of *De Revolutionibus* and thus validate his description of a 'worst seller.' This is somewhat like comparing the number of editions of Einstein's *Die Allgemeine Relativitätstheorie* with those of all textbooks and popularizations based on 'classical' Newtonian theories during the past fifty years. As noted above, moreover, many editions of old titles contained supplements which pointed toward a new astronomy.

exaggerate the effects of print. The most debased version of this over-done thesis appears in a well reviewed volume by a former curator of prints at the Metropolitan Museum of Art:

Before the age of Galileo, Descartes and Newton, printers tended to leave scientific innovations in manuscript. Commercially they were right, for in 1543 when Johann Kepler [sic] proved that the planets circle around the sun and not around the earth, his founding treatise of modern astronomy sold so slowly that it did not need reprinting for 23 years.[138]

As long as functions performed by early printers are confined to the 'spread of new ideas,' as long as they are associated with conversion and propaganda (or even with subversion and infiltration) they are bound to seem less effective when dealing with the new astronomy than with new approaches to the Gospel. Of course *De Revolutionibus* does appear to be a 'worst seller' when set against Lutheran Bibles and tracts. But this kind of juxtaposition would also make Vesalius appear to have produced a 'worst seller.'

Vesalius's work did not at once have the important success that it deserved; only with difficulty and slowly were the truths established that he had audaciously put forth...the teachings of Galen continued to occupy an important place in the universities for another century...[139]

In many surveys, sixteenth-century anatomy books are just as likely as astronomical treatises to be subjected to a 'cultural lag' – an illusory lag, which is based on ignoring all the advantages that hindsight has con-ferred. If the 'wrong' theories of Galen and Ptolemy continued to circulate and be taught in the second half of the sixteenth century this was partly because the 'right' theories developed by Kepler and Harvey had not been spelled out fully. Sixteenth-century printers and pro-fessors naturally failed to anticipate what Kepler and Newton would make of Copernicus' work. Given the difficult technical nature of *De Revolutionibus* and given the fact that five editions of the *Narratio Prima* were also being put on the market during the same century, it seems remarkable that the Basel printer 'Henricpetreius' thought a second

[138] Mayor, *Prints and People*, text below fig. 108. Page references cannot be given, for there are no page numbers in this book – which may help to explain how the substitution of Kepler for Copernicus went uncorrected. This kind of boner is too obvious to do much harm (apart from reinforcing two-culture divisions). But the false opinion that scientific innovation did not get into print until the seventeenth century is more insidious and skews perspectives on the 'century of genius.'

[139] Castiglioni, *A History of Medicine*, p. 425. On the debates engendered by *De Fabrica*, see above, p. 574.

edition was worth issuing twenty-three years after the first[140] and that a third one was deemed worthwhile by W. J. Blaeu's Amsterdam firm in 1617.[141]

As we have seen, there are significant differences between *De Fabrica* and *De Revolutionibus* and between the two authors' attitudes toward print. Nevertheless it seems more appropriate to compare two scientific treatises published in 1543 than to set Copernicus next to Darwin and Marx – and throw in Luther for good measure as well!

The Darwinian revolution struck like lightning, the Marxian took three-quarters of a century to hatch. The Copernican revolution...spread in a slower and more devious manner than all. Not because the printing press was new, or the subject obscure; Luther's theses created an immediate all-European turmoil though they were less easy to compress into a single slogan than 'the Sun does not go round the Earth but the Earth goes round the Sun.'[142]

Actually, geokinetic theories had been publicized by slogans decades before the publication of *De Revolutionibus*. The view 'that the earth moves but the sun stands still' was assigned to a pamphlet written by Copernicus as early as 1514.[143] Koestler himself mentions the relatively catchy title of Calcagnini's treatise 'concerning how the Heavens rest; the Earth moves' – a treatise probably inspired by Cusa and 'echoing an idea...much in the air.'[144] It was not the lack of a catchy slogan but the presence of lengthy and complicated calculations that prevented *De Revolutionibus* from achieving bestsellerdom. Nothing suggests that Copernicus' few readers were disappointed or that hopes raised by Rheticus seemed to be betrayed when the large work was finally

[140] The *Narratio Prima* was printed first at Danzig and then at Basel, 1540–1. A third edition was coupled with the 1566 Basel *De Revolutionibus*; a fourth and fifth with Kepler's *Mysterium Cosmographicum*, Tübingen, 1596 (under Maestlin's supervision) and at Frankfurt, 1621. Rosen, *Three Copernican Treatises*, p. 11; Dreyer, *A History of Astronomy*, p. 349. On the decision to print a second edition of *De Revolutionibus* see Rosen, 'Biography of Copernicus,' pp. 406–7 and on Heinrich Petri, 'Henric-petri' or 'Henricpetreius' (1527–79) heir to a distinguished Basel dynasty and husband of a Froben widow, see entry no. 16 in Benzing, *Buchdrucker-lexicon*, p. 24 and chap. 2, n. 175, volume 1 above.

[141] Koestler, *Sleepwalkers*, p. 458 passes over this important third edition, published by Blaeu in 1617 soon after *De Revolutionibus* was condemned. He gives uninformed readers the mis-taken impression that no one bothered to reprint *De Revolutionibus* since it was outdated by Tycho's observations, Kepler's discoveries and Galileo's telescope. On the timing of Blaeu's publication, see discussion, below, p. 676.   [142] Koestler, *Sleepwalkers*, p. 149.

[143] According to Rosen, 'Biography of Copernicus,' *Three Copernican Treatises*, p. 343, there is no question that this description of a pamphlet which is contained in an inventory of a Cracow doctor's library referred to the *Commentariolus*, i.e., the first draft of Copernicus' 'geokinetic and heliostatic theory.'   [144] Koestler, *Sleepwalkers*, p. 209.

published. On the contrary, the evidence suggests the magnitude of the task performed by the 'second Ptolemy' impressed even those sixteenth-century astronomers who failed to adopt Copernican views.[145] (That an 'unreadable' work often commands more awe and respect than an easy-to-read one is suggested by the reception of Einstein's 'general theory of relativity.') It is the twentieth-century science reporter who experiences disappointment when looking over the book that purportedly started it all. In the 1550s and 1560s, heliocentricity was not devoid of intriguing implications and Elizabethans who read about the 'most aunciente doctrine of the Pythagoreans lately revived by Copernicus' do not seem to have been disappointed.[146] Nevertheless the Copernican hypothesis did not stir readers' interest in the same way as did the latest news about a royal marriage or the election of a Pope. Insofar as the heavens were deemed newsworthy, controversy over the meaning of a given planetary conjunction was likely to attract the largest number of pamphleteers.

To historians of science, Regiomontanus is 'newsworthy' for having edited an epitome of the *Almagest*, for launching a continuous series of *Ephemerides* or for posthumously providing a pioneering text on trigonometry. Almost a century after his death, the work of his that was most exciting to Elizabethan literati was an astrological verse concern-

145 Tycho's tribute in a Copenhagen lecture to the 'second Ptolemy' in 1574 is noted above, n. 68. Dreyer, *History of Astronomy*, p. 349 cites Urstisius' praise of Copernicus as a 'truly divine genius' in a work printed in 1573; Ravetz, *Astronomy and Cosmology*, p. 49 notes that even Clavius hailed Copernicus as the 'restorer of astronomy.' Westman's 'Three Responses' brings out the respectful attention as well as the diverse reactions elicited by *De Revolutionibus* as viewed by professional astronomers who belonged to the circle around Melanchthon and who transmitted diverse aspects of the Copernican heritage to the next generation.
146 Thomas Digges, *A Perfit Description of the Caelistiall Orbes according to the Most Aunciente Doctrine of the Pythagoreans, lately Revived by Copernicus and by Geometrical demonstrations approved* was first published in 1576 as a supplement to a reissue of his father's (Leonard Digges) ephemerides: *The Prognostication Everlasting* and was reprinted at least six times by 1605. See Johnson, *Astronomical Thought*, pp. 100–2. Since this treatise contained large portions of Book I of *De Revolutionibus* it also argues against the 'worst-selling' thesis. The printer of the *Prognostication Everlasting*, Thomas Marsh (or Marshe) also published in 1556 the celebrated *Ephemeris Anni 1557* which contained the *Prutenic Tables* (issued only five years previously) rearranged for the meridian of London by John Feild and containing a preface by John Dee, mentioning Copernicus and Reinhold. See Bosanquet, *English Printed Almanacks*, pp. 33–4; Dreyer, *History of Astronomy*, pp. 346–7. When Koestler, *Sleepwalkers* says the Copernican theory 'was practically ignored until Kepler and Galileo' (p. 213) he sets Thomas Digges aside as a 'non-astronomer' although Digges contributed to Tycho's work on the Nova of 1572. The early interest in the Copernican theory shown by English Cantabrigians who matriculated in the 1540s and frequented the libraries of Cheke and Sir Thomas Smith is underlined by Johnson, *Astronomical Thought*, p. 89. The 1556 catalogue of Sir Thomas Smith's library testifies to the innovative role of early printers and the long reach of Regiomontanus.

ing the world's end.[147] The outpouring of sixteenth-century printed material devoted to portents and prognostication ought not to be dismissed as sheer rubbish. As previous discussion of Tycho's star suggests, useful observations might come as by-products of the mounting public excitement. Markets for *Ephemerides* were enlarged, astronomical instrument-makers could flourish and serial publication was encouraged by intense interest in eclipses and conjunctions.[148] Moreover, the sheer volume of conflicting prophecies and predictions may have helped eventually to undermine the confidence of some readers in the validity of astrology.[149] Nevertheless, there is no positive correlation between the publicity value and the scientific worth of any treatise in any age.

Even after Galileo stirred the Republic of Letters, and scientific curiosity was stimulated among princes and poets, the news value of the oddity outstripped that of the ordinary. Sober discussion of celestial or terrestrial mechanics still did not achieve the same sales as did more sensational 'pseudo-scientific' reports. Moreover, the scientist never did achieve the same position as the evangelist. Even in the heyday of Enlightenment, Methodist tracts and hymnals kept presses humming and new Bible societies used the powers of print to the full. Furthermore, entertainment was never outsold by instruction. The Royal Society celebrated the banishing of ghosts and goblins from its precincts. Romantic novelists, visionaries, and Grub Street hacks found a large reading public who were more entranced than disenchanted by such stuff.

It may be worth noting that the situation has not changed much over the course of recent centuries. The number of astronomers and mathematical physicists has greatly increased. It still remains proportionately small compared to the audience tapped by Gothic tales of witchcraft, reports of flying saucers, and the like. The news value of a weeping statue or of a haunted house is still likely to hold its own against a

---

[147] Aston, 'The Fiery Trigon,' n. 66.

[148] According to Bosanquet, *English Printed Almanacks*, p. 4, few prognostications were issued in written form before print. See Keith Thomas, *Religion and the Decline of Magic*, pp. 283–389 on the outpouring of fugitive literature in Tudor and Stuart England.

[149] Thomas, *Religion and the Decline of Magic*, pp. 335 ff says that 'massive and repeated errors' did not diminish the demand for prognostications but also notes (p. 300) that a Council of State in 1652 issued a paper, stating that eclipses were natural events without political implications, in order to counteract the impact of anonymous pamphlets. The effectiveness of prognostications was also diminished according to Thomas, p. 350, by increasingly accurate predictions, such as that offered by Halley's comet.

treatise on astrophysics or a story about a quasar. However popular the American journal, *Popular Mechanics*, its sales never rivalled those of printed horoscopes – or of Bibles for that matter.

It is also worth noting that spreading news came naturally to sixteenth-century evangelists whereas keeping secrets was conventional among the followers of Pythagoras. This situation *did* change. Trade secrets were advertised, arcana were disclosed. Unwritten recipes entered the public domain. Science became 'public knowledge' and as such was separated from 'furtive' magic. Yet even after this transformation it is interesting to observe that scientists are still more uneasy about publicity than are evangelists (or journalists or performing artists of any kind). Secretive attitudes, at all events, were entirely conventional in Copernicus' day (even Newton retained them much later on). It seems unwarranted to expect a sixteenth-century astronomer to share the attitudes of the modern science reporter.[150]

Kepler, whom Koestler does not describe as 'timid' or 'devious,' also had a thesis that could be compressed into a simple statement. Yet Kepler's demonstration that planets do not move in circles caused little more of a stir than did the heliocentric views Copernicus had previously set forth. At least the thesis set forth in *De Revolutionibus* managed to reach Kepler. The latter's work was so 'supremely unreadable' that its important contents passed Galileo by.[151] Elliptical orbits failed to make contact with parabolic curves until later on.[152]

[150] Koestler, *Sleepwalkers*, pp. 149–50 accuses Copernicus of being 'infatuated with the Pythagorean cult of secrecy,' 'arrogantly obscurantist' and 'anti-humanist' in contrast to Erasmus, Reuchlin, von Hutten, Luther *et al*. That the Pythagorean cult was quite compatible with many forms of Northern humanism and shared by Reuchlin among others is clear from many studies. See e.g. Spitz, *The Religious Renaissance*, and 'Reuchlin's Philosophy.'

[151] See chap. 5 above, pp. 501–3; n. 152. How other readers were eventually persuaded to study Kepler's difficult prose and to extricate important theorems from them is discussed below, p. 631.

[152] See Boyer, *History of Mathematics*, p. 358 for suggestive remarks about ellipses and parabolas and also for a relevant discussion of Kepler's work on the measurement of the volume of liquid in barrels. Here again, the addition of uniform sharp-edged diagrams to texts needs more attention. Problems associated with conic sections must have been clarified thereby. 'How many mathematicians are there who will undertake the labor of reading through the Conics of Apollonius of Perga?' asked Kepler (Boas, *Scientific Renaissance*, p. 305). In medieval Latin manuscripts the theorems of Apollonius (like those of Euclid) could not speak unambiguously and directly to 'reason's inner ear' partly because they were not presented clearly to the eye. The transmission of Apollonius' *Conics* is well covered by Rose, 'Renaissance Italian Methods of Drawing the Ellipse,' where Rose notes the 'weak' medieval tradition, the plans of Regiomontanus to publish a new translation based on the Greek text, the printing of excerpts by Giorgio Valla in his *De Rebus* (1501) and other editions up to that of Commandino (Bologna, 1566). Rose's article also contains valuable data on methods of constructing conic sections and new instruments devised for this purpose. Koestler, *Sleepwalkers*, pp. 330–1,

Whereas Copernicus' failure to attract as many followers as Luther did is attributed to a cowardly penchant for secrecy, contemporary neglect of elliptical orbits is seen merely as the price Kepler paid for being ahead of his time. The double standard is particularly inconsistent because Copernicus had even fewer contemporaries who could follow his arguments with Ptolemy than Kepler did. Only astronomers who were equipped to read the *Almagest* could be expected to judge the 'Second Ptolemy's' work. As noted above, the number of astronomers who were thus equipped probably was not large.[153]

It is indeed mainly because Copernicus belonged to such a restricted professional group that historians rarely think about the impact of printing when dealing with his work. If the effects of printing are confined to dissemination, and circulation figures are stressed, it will scarcely seem to matter whether the *De Revolutionibus* was printed or not. Much useful astronomical data continued to be transmitted during the early-modern era without getting into print. Copernicus is often said to have studied some of Regiomontanus' works before they went to press;[154] Tycho obtained some of Copernicus' manuscripts; Kepler inherited all of Tycho's papers. Until as late as 1854, the posthumous circulation of Copernicus' 'Letter against Werner' was handled by scribal transmission.[155] Is it not conceivable that copies of *De Revolutionibus* might have reached the restricted group equipped to make use of it by the same means?

Many authorities seem inclined to answer this question affirmatively. Accordingly, they postpone considering changes in communications until the appearance of learned periodicals in the seventeenth century. They may argue, as does Thorndike, that since professional scientists

speculates about Kepler's unconscious 'fixation' or 'biological bias' because of his failure to recognize ellipses in egg-shaped curves. It might be more helpful to investigate the presence or absence of clear diagrams of conic sections in early mathematical texts.

153 See n. 99 above.

154 But see evidence provided by Rosen and discussed above, p. 591 showing that *On Triangles* was *not* seen by Copernicus until Rheticus brought him the first printed edition on his visit to Frombork in 1539.

155 See Rosen, introduction, *Three Copernican Treatises*, p. 8 for suggestion that such sixteenth-century hand-copied letters served the function later performed by printed articles and book reviews. That Tycho obtained a second- or third-hand transcription of the *Letter Against Werner* and that mss. turned up both in Berlin and Vienna in the nineteenth century is also noted (pp. 8–9, n. 15). Swerdlow, 'Derivation of Commentariolus' also notes that a ms. of Copernicus' *Commentariolus*, which was owned by Tycho, served as the basis for further copies. His comments on the corrupt texts of the later copies are indicative of problems posed by scribal transmission at any time. Since the data inherited from Tycho by Kepler was in fresh, *uncopied* form, scribal transmission is irrelevant to this latter case.

could serve each other adequately by handwritten interchange, early printing merely propagated error, spreading a little learning more thinly over a greater surface of the public-at-large. Or they may take a more positive view as does Stillman Drake, who welcomes the breaking of an academic monopoly and the tapping of scientific talents outside university walls. Whether Latin-reading professional élites are regarded as progressive or reactionary, there seems to be agreement that they were fairly adequately served by scribes.

The medieval university community was clearly relatively small and homogeneous...A large number of copies of any given work was never necessary within that community whether we think of this as a single university, of several universities in a geographical area, or even as all the universities in Europe. It was unlikely that a person living in the university community would long remain unaware of the existence of a significant work related to his particular interests. If a copy was not immediately at hand, it is probable that the scholar who told him of the existence of the work would also be able to outline the nature of its contents.[156]

The argument seems sufficiently plausible to win general assent. Yet I think it neglects the obstacles posed by scribal culture and seriously overestimates the services it rendered academic élites. Even the most intrepid 'wandering scholars' seeking access to highly valued technical texts had much more difficulty than we are likely to recognize, given problems posed by books locked in chests or chained in collegiate and ducal libraries. Throughout the later middle ages, teaching and preaching orders kept copies in different places but use was confined exclusively to fellow friars. Lay faculties were equally reluctant to allow important texts to circulate outside cloistered walls.[157] Given restricted access to diverse collections, there was little more free trade in ideas than there was open interchange of guild secrets. The academic community was not homogeneous and the texture of learning was remarkably variegated. The high level of sophistication achieved by one group of fellows in a particular college or a monastic order often went unshared in other lecture halls. Regional barriers were much more formidable in the age of scribes than they were after annual book

---

156 Drake, 'Early Science,' p. 48.
157 See Gabriel, *College System*, p. 28; Humphreys, *The Book Provisions of the Medieval Friars 1215–1400, passim.* See also problem of gaining access to the Bessarion manuscripts in the Marciana experienced by Poliziano in 1491 (Rose, 'Humanist Culture,' p. 93) and experience of Budé viewing the Florentine codex of the *Digest* as noted on p. 103, volume I above.

fairs began. During the later middle ages, for example, knowledge of tangent functions scarcely moved beyond Paris and Oxford.[158] Before the advent of printing the full *Almagest* was rarely available in any college libraries at all.

It would not be of much help to a student of astronomy to know that there was in existence a great composition by an ancient hand. His imagination might be stimulated from hearing someone outline its contents, but his capacity to make use of the work would go unfulfilled. Could Tycho have 'taught himself' astronomy merely by overhearing astronomers converse? Further, would he have felt compelled to reappraise the evidence without having two conflicting tables to examine? The difference between having a full treatise on hand when drawing diagrams and compiling tables and having to go by a report about its contents is worth pausing over. It helps to explain why astronomy remained in a pre-Copernican state for so long. Even Koestler grudgingly admits that Copernicus' 'disappointing' treatise won for its author a 'certain repute' because it served as a basis for the *Prutenic Tables* which Erasmus Reinhold published eight years after *De Revolutionibus*. However unsatisfactory as popular reading matter, these tables were 'welcomed' as a 'long overdue replacement for the Alphonsine Tables.' As previous remarks suggest, the new tables may have been historically significant not so much as a 'replacement' for the old ones but rather as an alternative set that encouraged further checking against the writing in the sky. At all events, they were put into use very quickly – as the case of the young Tycho Brahe shows:

On 17 August, 1563 at the age of seventeen while Vedel was asleep he noticed that Saturn and Jupiter were so close together as to be almost indistinguishable. He looked up his planetary tables and discovered that the Alphonsine tables were a whole month in error...and the Copernican tables by several days.[159]

Koestler not only provides a retelling of Gassendi's often-told tale, he

158 Hughes, introduction, Regiomontanus' *On Triangles*, p. 7. Northern Europe was poorly supplied with trigonometry texts for a long time. Even after his student days at Tübingen in the late sixteenth century, Kepler remained ignorant of the 'science of the sine' and the 'computation of triangles' until he borrowed a text from a doctor traveling through Gratz from Italy. Only later on did he gain access to copies of Euclid and Regiomontanus. See Koestler, *Sleepwalkers*, p. 583, n. 20. Rheticus' undertaking the separate publication (by Luther's favorite firm) of the first two chapters (on plane and spherical trigonometry) of Book I of *De Revolutionibus: De Lateribus et Angulis Triangulorum* (Wittenberg: Johannes Lufft, 1542) probably performed a more useful service than is often recognized.
159 Koestler, *Sleepwalkers*, p. 287. The *Prutenic Tables* are discussed on p. 213.

also offers an equally familiar gloss.[160] Tycho's shock at the disparity between predictions and outcome is taken to indicate a new habit of mind. It is also contrasted with the 'almost hypnotic submission to authority,' associated with reliance on Ptolemy and inherited data, manifested by all previous astronomers, including Copernicus.[161] In 1563 the *Prutenic Tables* were twelve years old. Before puzzling over why Tycho had put his two sets of tables to a new use, it ought to be noted that no one had been supplied with two full sets of tables to put to use before.[162]

It was not because he gazed at night skies instead of at old books that Tycho Brahe differed from star-gazers of the past. Nor do I think it was because he cared more for 'stubborn facts' or precise measurement than had the Alexandrians or the Arabs. But he did have at his disposal, as few had before him, two separate sets of computations based on two different theories, compiled several centuries apart which he could

---

[160] On Gassendi's efforts to amass biographical data while assembling Tycho's works see Christianson, 'Tycho Brahe's Facts of Life,' pp. 21–2. Gassendi's role as a kind of latter-day Vasari to the chief Renaissance astronomers is worth further study. See his *Tychonis Braheii ...Vita. Accessit Nicolai Copernici, Georgii Peurbachii et Joannis Regiomontanii* (The Hague: A. Vlacq, 1654). According to Dreyer, *Tycho*, p. 127, Gassendi also got data on Tycho from Willem Janzoon Blaeu, the founder of the Dutch map-publishing dynasty, whose work is discussed above, pp. 480, 600–1. With his own engraved icons of the great astronomers and printed output, Tycho helped to create his own posterity. He is also included in Ramus' *Scholarum Mathematicarum* (Basel, 1569) (having made that author's acquaintance in Augsburg). From Ramus to Gassendi to Fontenelle and ultimately to Voltaire's eulogy of Newton, members of the French Republic of Letters (often propelled by Huguenot or foreign presses), took the lead in celebrating the star-gazers who produced the new astronomy. Italian initiative in this field represented by Bernardo Baldi's *Vite dei Matematici* composed between 1587–95, failed, characteristically, to be fully implemented by print. See Rose's *Italian Renaissance of Mathematics*, chap. 11. Italian presses were responsible for immortalizing Tycho, Kepler, Galileo (as well as Ptolemy, Sacrobosco, Kircher, Scheiner *et al.*) by placing them on a moon map in an anti-Copernican work by an Italian Jesuit: Giovanni Battista Riccioli's *Almagestum Novum Astronomiam Veterem* (Bologna, 1651). That Riccioli's work fixed the nomenclature of lunar formations until recently is noted by Van de Vyer, 'Original Sources.'

[161] Koestler, *Sleepwalkers*, p. 199.

[162] In addition to working with Reinhold in Wittenberg and probably helping in the preparation of the *Prutenicae Tabulae Coelestium Motuum* (Tübingen: Ulricus Morhardus, 1551) Rheticus also began several monumental projects, entailing diverse series of trigonometric tables that were extended and completed by such successors as Viète, L. Valentine Otho and Bartholomaeus Pitiscus. Sarton, *Appreciation*, p. 161 marvels at the amount of labor involved in compiling such tables by hand. So does Koestler, *Sleepwalkers*, p. 189, who suggests Rheticus needed this kind of 'occupational therapy' to keep sane. The new freedom from having to copy out earlier tables and the knowledge that new ones once compiled could be preserved by print ought to be taken into account. The interval between Regiomontanus and Napier – a pre-logarithmic but post-print interval – might be singled out as a distinctive phase in the history of mathematical sciences, since it inspired a special kind of intellectual labor. No doubt desk calculators will soon lead future historians to marvel at how much was accomplished in the way of dreary labor with slide rules, during the last few centuries. Like the logarithm, the slide rule is another much neglected print-made innovation.

compare with each other. The study of records was no less important for Tycho than it had been for the astronomers of the past. Like his predecessors he had no telescope to aid him. But his observatory, unlike theirs, included a library well stocked with printed materials as well as assistants trained in the new arts of printing and engraving. For he took care (and went to much trouble and expense) to install printing presses and a paper mill on the island of Hven.[163]

Given the more than fifty assistants at work on the island, and the stream of publications that issued forth, Tycho's 'Uraniborg' has been suggested as a possible prototype for Bacon's 'Salomon's House' and for the later Royal Society[164] 'Uraniborg' did see collaboration and publication applied to astronomical observation on a scale the Western world had not seen before. Insofar as Tycho's observations were made with the aid of instruments, he could tap the talents of engravers who 'knew the meaning of "within a hair's breadth." '[165] He also exploited the arts of engraving to display astronomical instruments for readers of his books. His own printing press is displayed in his most celebrated self-portrait.[166] Ever since he started to sneak books past his tutor, he profited greatly from the product of other presses. In these respects, he differed from his predecessors in ways that need to be underlined. The deliberate use of publicity to channel excitement about ephemeral stellar events and thus encourage precise recording of fresh observations on a vast scale was one of Tycho's most lasting and unheralded accomplishments. The Danish astronomer was not only the last of the great naked-eye observers; he was also the first careful observer who took full advantage of the new powers of the press – powers which enabled astronomers to detect anomalies in old records, to pinpoint more precisely and register in catalogues the location of each star, to enlist collaborators in many regions, fix each fresh observation in

---

[163] Gade, *The Life*, p. 102 describes the 'blank check' given Tycho by the Danish King for paper supplies throughout Denmark and Norway, which turned out to be inadequate, leading to the establishment of a mill on the island of Hven. Dreyer, *Tycho*, pp. 239 ff, describes Tycho's remarkable trip, made with the printing press loaded on to the baggage van, to Copenhagen and Rostock in 1597–8. [164] Christianson, 'Astronomy and Printing.'
[165] It is intriguing to note the line which reaches from Tycho to Moxon's *Mechanick Exercises* via W. J. Blaeu who worked for Tycho and instructed Moxon in the more advanced typographical arts of the day. E. G. R. Taylor, *Mathematical Practitioners*, pp. 92, 231–3. Moxon was one of the few instrument-makers and printers who was admitted as a fellow to the Royal Society.
[166] This engraving of Tycho showing his great mural quadrant and assistants at work is in his *Astronomiae Instauratae Mechanica* which was dedicated to Rudolph II and was printed by a Hamburg printer in 1598. See easily available illustration in Boas, *Scientific Renaissance*, pp. 96–7.

permanent form and make necessary corrections in successive editions.
The unusual fate of Tycho's star has already been noted. The expansion of his star catalogue is equally worthy of note.

The *Tabulae Rudolphinae* remained for more than a century an indispensable tool for the study of the skies...The bulk of the work consists of...rules for predicting the positions of the planets and of Tycho's catalogue of 777 star places enlarged by Kepler to 1,005. There are also refraction-tables and logarithms put for the first time to astronomic uses; and a gazeteer of the towns of the world, their longitudes referred to Tycho's Greenwich – the meridian of Uraniborg on Hveen.[167]

Koestler's estimation of the value of printing 'unreadable' technical works seem to change after his hero Kepler has set to work. One might compare his high opinion of the *Rudolphine Tables* with his deprecatory references to Copernicus' *De Revolutionibus*, while keeping in mind that he assumes both works were published in first editions of the same size.[168]

Kepler's heroic struggles over the course of four years to get his valuable work into print during the turmoil of the Thirty Years War, suggest how political and religious events impinged on scientific developments – much as they did on biblical scholarship. The *Rudolphine Tables*, very much like the Antwerp Polyglot produced by Plantin's press, indicates how rapidly new and precise information accumulated after print and how many obstacles had to be overcome by the masterbuilders of the new monuments of erudition.[169] As an overseer of a technical publication program, who saw a manuscript of 568 pages

167 Koestler, *Sleepwalkers*, pp. 410–11. The improvements made by Tycho's 777 star catalogue over that of Ptolemy and the Arabs are noted by Warner, 'First Celestial Globe,' p. 30. On the composition and contents of *Rudolphine Tables*, see also Caspar, *Kepler*, p. 327, who notes that a plan to add a world map was frustrated at the last minute. The 'refraction tables' owed much to the publication of various works on optics, particularly Witelo's which, having been on Regiomontanus' advance list, was printed by Petreius in Nuremberg in 1535, and was among the books Rheticus brought to Copernicus in 1539.
168 According to Koestler, *Sleepwalkers*, pp. 191; 410, each edition consisted of one thousand copies but there seems to be no sound basis for this guess. The estimates of Gingerich are noted above, n. 99.
169 On research spurred by publication of polyglot Bibles, see Preserved Smith, *Origins of Modern Culture*, p. 251, and discussion, pp. 337 ff, volume 1 above. Kepler's biblical research and work on technical chronology is discussed by Caspar, *Kepler*, pp. 317–19. That chronological tables and gazeteers were necessary supplements to both types of publication and that both also required mastery of trilingual studies points to the overlapping of research interests among biblical scholars and astronomers. The latter were among the first group of scholars to raise questions about the dating of the birth of Jesus, for example. See Caspar, *Kepler*, p. 228. Both studies of Newton by Manuel: *Portrait of Newton* and *Isaac Newton, Historian* contain a wealth of data on Newtonian research into scriptural chronology and calendrical problems.

through the press, the dreamy, mystical, 'sleepwalking' astronomer also seems to be cast in an uncharacteristic role. Kepler spent many hours of each day in the printing house, coped successfully with political emergencies and personnel problems, procured adequate supplies of paper, supervised the punch-cutting of symbols, the setting of type and finally – in the guise of a travelling salesman – set out in the company of tradesmen to peddle his finished products at the Frankfurt book fair. While he was at Ulm during the final stages of the four-year ordeal, Kepler found time to help local officials solve problems pertaining to weights and measures. As an ingenious gadgeteer, he provided Ulm with a new standard measuring device.[170] That he was capable of using his hands as well as his head is also shown by the fact that he himself designed the frontispiece to his massive work.[171]

The House of Astronomy as envisaged by Kepler is modelled on Baroque lines that may seem somewhat dream-like – even surreal – to modern eyes. Like the memory theatres described by Frances Yates, it presents oddly assorted motifs closely juxtaposed. Ancient sages and modern masters are displayed in a temple of eclectic design. Muses representing the mathematical sciences stand around the dome, while the German imperial eagle hovering above (hopefully) furnishes patronage and gold. Not only the reference to financial sponsorship from on high but also the instruments hanging on pillars and the printing press engraved on a wall at the base suggest that the 'sleepwalker' had his practical side.[172]

It seems significant that Koestler's romantic biography contains a

[170] Caspar, *Kepler*, pp. 317–24. Kepler's previous work on barrels: the *Stereometria*, also indicates his skill in solving practical problems. Koestler, *Sleepwalkers*, pp. 406–9, also describes the long ordeal and (p. 415) notes Kepler's later, eighteen-month long struggle to procure type and machinery and install a press in his own lodgings in Sagan, in order to publish *Ephemerides* for the years 1629–36.

[171] The actual engraving was made by a Nuremberg craftsman: Georg Coler, who placed his name at the base. As noted above, both practical and manual tasks had been undertaken by astronomers and mathematicians in the middle ages. They had helped to design astrolabes and sundials and had served as mint masters even before the advent of printing. Thereafter they collaborated closely with instrument-makers, engravers and type-designers and often turned their own talents to such work. Thus it seems unnecessary to invoke a 'puritanical' ethos to account for such a phenomenon as Newton's willingness to grind lenses (see e.g. Manuel, *Portrait of Newton*, p. 47).

[172] The print shop actually occupies two of the five panels visible at the base. Immediately to the right of the central panel (showing the isle of Hven) are two printers at a press and beyond, the extreme right-hand panel shows a compositor at work with pieces of type and a wooden frame. Kepler's high regard for the new art of printing (which he associated with the revival of ancient writers and the advent of new theology, medicine, astronomy et al.) is clear from citation in Rosen, 'In Defense of Kepler,' pp. 141–9.

description of this same frontispiece which omits the press and the other instruments. Despite his praise of the 'Tabulae Rudolphinae' as an 'indispensable tool,' and as Kepler's 'crowning achievement in practical astronomy,' Koestler seems almost contemptuous of the tedious 'herculean donkey work' such tables entailed. One can understand why he might sympathize with Kepler's weary reaction to the 'treadmill of mathematical computation,'[173] but it seems unfair to withhold sympathy from Kepler's predecessors, who deserved it perhaps even more. The compiling of hand-copied tables had much more of a 'treadmill' character than was the case after print. The herculean analogy also seems to be better suited to labors performed in the age of scribes, when astronomers knew that their tables would be refilled with errors almost as soon as they had been cleansed.

As is often the case, when the shift from script to print is ignored, the incapacity to achieve precise error-free results is attributed to indifference or stupidity. Earlier astronomers are belabored for wasting their 'life work' by providing seafarers and star-gazers with bad tables instead of good.[174] Kepler is commiserated with for toiling away at his dreary task, and little or nothing is said about the labor-saving devices that came to his aid. Napier's name is not in the index; his logarithms are not mentioned in the text. Only a footnote preserves Maestlin's grudging comment, 'It is not fitting for a professor of mathematics to manifest childish joy just because reckoning is made easier.'[175] But although some astronomers may have been inhibited about expressing their joy, it is incumbent on historians to take note of it. To compare Kepler's tables with those derived from Copernicus' work, without pausing over the new tools that had been supplied in the interim is not only unfair; it is to miss a chance of understanding how Alexandrian astronomy came to be surpassed.

For it is really beside the point whether Copernicus was timid and devious or Kepler frank and bold. The point is, rather, that the flow of information had been reoriented to make possible an unprecedented cumulative cognitive advance. In using Napier's logarithms for the Rudolphine Tables Kepler was doing something his master could not do. Although Tycho had hoped to put such tables to use, they were not

173 Koestler, Sleepwalkers, p. 407. On p. 411 the frontispiece is described without mention of the two panels containing printing equipment. A similar omission is in Caspar's description upon which Koestler's account relies. 174 Koestler, Sleepwalkers, p. 124.
175 Koestler, Sleepwalkers, p. 590, n. 5.

published until the Danish astronomer had died. Tycho had, however, been able to compare the *Prutenic Tables* with the *Alphonsine Tables* as Copernicus could not do, for the latter were compiled from the older man's posthumous work. In reworking all of Ptolemy's computations, in charting every planet's course as from a moving earth, did Copernicus also achieve something that could not have been accomplished in the age of scribes? The answer is necessarily speculative, yet it seems likely that a complete recasting of the *Almagest* – like a thorough-going calendar reform – required freedom from hours of copying and access to reference works that were rarely available to astronomers after Alexandrian resources had been dispersed.

Perhaps the most significant contribution made by Copernicus was not so much in hitting on the 'right' theory as in producing a fully worked out *alternative* theory and thus confronting the next generation with a problem to be solved rather than a solution to be learned. In the frontispiece to Riccioli's *Almagestum Novum* of 1651, the Copernican and Tychonic schemes are diagrammed on either side of a scale held by a muse while the Ptolemaic scheme is displayed on the ground with the notation: 'I will arise only if I am corrected.' The fact that the balance is tilted in favor of Tycho or that the notion of 'restoring' Ptolemy is retained should not distract attention from the novelty of presenting three clearly diagrammed alternative planetary models within a single frame.[176] Much as contradictory scriptural commentaries encouraged recourse to the text of the Good Book itself, so too did conflicting verdicts rendered by the 'little books of men' encourage a persistent checking against the 'great book of Nature.'

By the time Kepler was a student at Tübingen, astronomers had to choose between three different theories. A century earlier, when Copernicus was at Cracow, students were fortunate to gain access to one. The fact that Kepler's teacher Maestlin gave instruction in all three schemes has been cited to show that university instruction was backward and resistant to innovating currents from outside.[177] That a given student at one university was being instructed in three different ways of positioning the sun and earth when computing planetary orbits seems to me to indicate a remarkable change.[178] All three authorities

---

[176] For more conventional treatment of Riccioli's work see Stimson, *Gradual Acceptance*, pp. 77–8.
[177] Drake, 'Early Science,' p. 49.
[178] By Newton's day, undergraduates in English colleges could study contradictory versions by reading Gassendi's *Institutio Astronomica*, which went through at least six editions between

fell short of correctly describing planetary orbits. Tycho's brand-new scheme no less than Ptolemy's very old one was destined to be discredited later on. But after 1543, commentaries, epitomes, or addenda devoted to one master's work had been superseded by a confrontation with alternatives that forced some sort of choice. Given the hundreds of years that had been spent compiling, retrieving and preserving the *Almagest*, the appearance of two alternative full fledged planetary theories in the course of a single century does not point toward cultural lag or the presence of an inertial force. On the contrary, it points toward a cognitive breakthrough of an unprecedented kind.[179]

Furthermore it should be noted that alternative theories were accompanied by alternative sets of tables which also forced astronomers to make choices and focused special attention on key stellar events. Exclusive reliance on the *Alphonsine Tables* until the 1540s might be contrasted with the array of six different sets of tables confronting astronomers in the 1640s. Detailed instructions in the use of six different sets were actually provided by Galileo's friend Rienieri in a single work: the *Tabulae Medicae* of 1639. By then, the idiosyncratic experience of the young Tycho, who checked two conflicting tables against the writing in the skies, was becoming commonplace. The accuracy of competing tables was tested by simultaneous observations made from different places and by many eyes. Challenges were being issued in the form of open letters alerting all European astronomers to observe a particular stellar event and recheck their findings against different predictions.

Astronomers could compare the predictions of the tables with the actual observed positions of the sun, moon and planets and could then compare the results with those of rival astronomical theories...could decide whether it was worth while to undertake the difficult and laborious work of mastering Kepler's methods...[180]

1647 to 1702 and was later used as a textbook in eighteenth-century Harvard and Yale. See Palter (ed.), Kepler Catalogue, item no. 93. Stimson, *Gradual Acceptance*, p. 90, notes that 'spheres according to the Ptolmean, Tychonean and Copernican systems with books for their use' were available at a London bookseller in 1670.

179 See Thomas Kuhn, *Structure of Scientific Revolutions*, p. 77 for comment on importance of confrontation with alternative theories.

180 Russell, 'Kepler's Laws,' p. 7. See also p. 13 for data on contrast between one set of tables available in 1550 as against six sets in 1660. The long struggle of one astronomer, Peter Cruger, with Kepler's 'obscure' writings which moved him to pray, like King Alfonso, for some simpler solution and his eventual conversion in 1629 which led him to reappraise Kepler's important *Epitome Astronomiae Copernicanae* 'previously read and thrown aside' is recounted in fascinating detail on p. 8.

In 1631 Gassendi, following a suggestion made by Kepler, published an open letter to the astronomers of Europe asking them to observe the transit of Mercury across the sun and noting it was due to take place on November 7, 1631. Here is an example of a collaborative effort in simultaneous observation that was made possible by print and had been impossible in the age of scribes. The new process of feedback operated in this instance as well. A German observer who accepted the challenge not only found the *Rudolphine Tables* gave the most accurate prediction. He also published a pamphlet in 1632 which informed the reading public of his findings, outlined Kepler's theory and referred interested readers to Kepler's publications for further details.[181]

To return for a moment to the problem posed by Galileo's neglect of Kepler's discovery of elliptical orbits. According to Rosen, Galileo felt a natural reluctance to struggle with Kepler's turgid prose. He was put off by 'the longwinded theological speculations, mythological allusions and autobiographical meanderings in which Kepler concealed his genuine achievement.'[182] If we accept this explanation, then the question remains as to how this sort of reluctance was overcome so that the 'genuine achievement' was finally disclosed. From recent accounts describing how astronomers became convinced of the superiority of the *Rudolphine Tables*, one may see the important role played by the publishers and editors of *Almanacks* and *Ephemerides* who were spurred by competitive conditions to investigate rival claims made by different astronomers and who were eager to hit on the most foolproof schemes. Resistance to strange logarithms and seemingly cumbersome procedures, as well as reluctance to struggle with Kepler's formidable prose were overcome once a given publisher became persuaded by demonstrations (such as Gassendi's) that better tables could be printed only by mastering Kepler's techniques.[183] One English almanack publisher who entered flourishing popular markets during the English civil war concluded that Kepler was the 'most subtile mathematician

[181] Russell, *Kepler's Laws*, pp. 10–11.   [182] See citation above, p. 501.

[183] In addition to data given in Father Russell's article cited above, see Curtis Wilson, 'From Kepler's Laws,' where the 'open' dispute over elliptical orbits between Ismael Boulliau and Seth Ward in the 1630s and 40s is described (pp. 100–19) and the conversion of Noel Duret, a publisher of *Ephemerides* is noted (p. 100, n. 29). The articles of Wilson, Russell and Whiteside contain evidence which runs counter to views expressed by Hetherington 'Almanacs,' pp. 275–9. Hetherington deprecates Wing's 'sketchy' treatment (p. 277), whereas Whiteside 'Before the Principia,' shows how Newton picked up Wing's references (to Salusbury's translation of Galileo, for example) and used them to guide his reading.

that ever was' and described his work as 'the most admirable and best restauration of astronomy of any that did precede him.'[184] This publisher was Vincent Wing, author of the *Astronomia Britannica* that was later read and annotated by Newton.[185] By the time Newton had come of age, the *Rudolphine Tables* and the *Epitome Astronomiae Copernicae* had begun to drive out competitors – at least in regions where there was a free trade in ideas. Elliptical orbits, at long last, could make contact with parabolic curves.

Shortly before Copernicus was born, Regiomontanus left his post as chief librarian to the King of Hungary to set up in Nuremberg the first scientific press known to the world. Soon after Copernicus died, Tycho Brahe sent off to Wittenberg to secure expert help so that he could set up a printing office, and when he left Denmark he brought a press along. That the struggle to get his tables into print loomed large among Kepler's many ordeals has already been outlined above. From his youthful quarrels over priority to his last smuggled manuscript, Galileo's career hinged on exploiting the new powers of the press. When such examples are invoked it is relatively easy to see that the new presses were important in the activities of many who helped to shape the Copernican Revolution. It seems plausible to argue that they ought to figure more prominently in our accounts. But the case seems more doubtful when we think about Copernicus in his tower or all the manuscripts stuffed in Newton's desk drawer. The two men who inaugurated and completed the Copernican Revolution not only wrote for Latin-reading colleagues. They both procrastinated about seeing their manuscripts into print, shied away from publicity and spent little time in the printing-house, if any at all.

The fact that they exhibited ambivalence toward the printing press and retained esoteric, élitist attitudes does not mean that Copernicus and Newton were unaffected by the shift from script to print. On the contrary, secretive philosophers who set out to voyage on strange seas of thought were much better equipped for their long journeys by printers than they had been by scribes, as the following comments suggest:

at the beginning of Newton's final year as an undergraduate (1664) his notebooks give us...different signs...he gave up an exclusive diet of reading

[184] Russell, 'Kepler's Laws,' pp. 18–19.
[185] Wilson, 'From Kepler's Laws,' pp. 123–4. Whiteside, 'Before the Principia,' pp. 5ff.

the ancients...and plunged into the moderns...we can trace the... flowering of...genius as he came to know the scientific writings of the men of his own century...He devoured books by Boyle and Hooke...took careful notes on his reading in the *Philosophical Transactions*...read and made notes on Galileo's *Dialogues*...and Descartes' *Principles of Philosophy*; from Descartes he copied out an English version of the principle of inertia... As we turn the pages of his notebooks we can see his mind leap from summaries of his reading to his own new principles and results...He began to think of gravity as a force extending as far as the moon...Newton's chief mentor was Descartes. From the latter's *Geometrie*, a veritable mathematical bible in Schooten's richly annotated second Latin edition, he drew continuous inspiration over the two years from the summer of 1664...In those two years a mathematician was born...His only earnest regret must have been that he had yet found no outlet for communicating his achievement to others. The papers...throb with energy and imagination but yet convey the claustrophobic air of a man completely wrapped up in himself, whose only real contact with the external world was through his books...[186]

The image of Newton in his mother's apple orchard at Woolsthorpe is so full of mythical overtones[187] that trips made to bookstalls or to a neighboring rector's library are likely to get overlooked.

In recent years, Pope's couplet on Newton: 'Nature and Nature's laws lay hid in night;/God said, Let Newton be! – And all was light,' has become unconvincing even as poetic hyperbole. The *Principia* did not spring full blown...Newton's...process of discovery was often tortuous...While the story of the apple may be true, it was a long way from the initial insight in his mother's garden to the finished mathematical proofs.[188]

Perhaps the story of the apple also should be demythologized. The 'initial insight in a maternal garden' might be reinterpreted in the light of Whiteside's careful review of Newton's miraculous years.[189] This is not to deprecate the importance of time spent in a maternal garden watching apples fall. Idle reveries release unconscious energies that

[186] Whiteside (ed.), *The Mathematical Papers of Isaac Newton I: 1664–1666*, cited by I. B. Cohen, book review, *The Scientific American*, pp. 139–44. In an additional passage, Cohen refers to 'the arithmetical symbols of Oughtred' which seems to support the suggestion by Taylor, *Mathematical Practitioners*, p. 347, that Oughtred's *Clavis Mathematica* had replaced Recorde's sixteenth-century textbook in mid-seventeenth century English schools.

[187] For a glimpse at some of the myth-making entailed (by Voltaire and Hegel among others) see Robert Gorham Davis, 'Speak of the Devil,' p. 55.

[188] Manuel, *Portrait*, p. 151.

[189] On Newton's visits to the library of Humphrey Babington, rector of Boothby Pagnell which was three miles north-east of Woolsthorpe manor house; on his use of Isaac Barrow's fine private library in Cambridge and on his book purchases, compare Manuel, *Portrait*, pp. 81–2, 98; with Whiteside, 'Newton's Marvellous Year.'

seem essential for many creative acts. But it was the library not the orchard that had undergone the greatest change and that furnished the shy undergraduate with his chief means of making 'contact with the external world.' Even more than Tycho Brahe, Newton was 'uniquely a self-taught man' who seems to have learned more by reading on his own than from talking to tutors or attending lectures in the schools. His observations of falling bodies, like his experiments with prisms, were shaped by close study of many printed texts, beginning with childish experiments with recipes for making paints.[190] Given his intense curiosity and introverted personality, silent scanning probably offered a welcome substitute for verbal interchange. At all events, it seems desirable to think of the young Newton as being equipped with more than 'his prism and silent face.' If we want to know why the fall of the apple and the colors thrown on the wall conveyed patterns that had been unperceived before, then we ought to note the unprecedented free mental play with printed tables and formulas, diagrams, and equations that marked his apprenticeship years.

It is also worth remarking that Copernicus in his isolated tower and Newton in his lonely chamber were persuaded in the end to part with their manuscripts and thus make their contributions to the science of their day. Thanks in large part to good offices performed by intermediaries such as Rheticus and Halley, public knowledge was vastly enriched. When he was over sixty years old, Rheticus welcomed the young Otho who had come to work for him: 'You come to see me at the same age as I myself went to Copernicus. If I had not visited him, none of his works would have seen the light.'[191] Insofar as 'nature and nature's laws' were contained in Newton's mass of notes, Halley also deserves considerable credit for bringing them 'to light.'

It was he who first undertook to report Newton's solution to the Society and he who undertook to bear both the cost and burden of publication when the Society had drained its treasury in printing Willoughby's *De Historia Piscium*.[192]

The importance of these expensive ventures in scientific publication is too often discounted. The willingness to undertake them in certain

190 Lohne, 'Isaac Newton,' offers a description of the teenage Newton in Woolsthorpe, studying recipes for mixing paints, preparing dyes and printing ink (p. 128). Whiteside, 'Before the Principia,' describes the 'self-taught' Newton's reading in detail.
191 Koestler, *Sleepwalkers*, p. 190.
192 Manuel, *Portrait*, p. 154.

realms and the reluctance to do so in others is worth further thought. For the problem of gaining access to publication outlets forced science into contact with religion and politics in a manner that remains to be assessed. To a preliminary exploration of this issue, the following chapter is addressed.

8

SPONSORSHIP AND CENSORSHIP
OF SCIENTIFIC PUBLICATION

I. INTRODUCTION

This chapter serves as a companion piece to the previous one. There I argued for the need to reset the stage for the Copernican Revolution. Here I will employ a similar approach to Galileo's trial. There will be no attempt at detailed coverage of the episode itself or at a comprehensive survey of all the issues it raised. My main purpose in dealing with the trial is to show that the problem of access to publication outlets was a pivotal issue – one that has been unduly neglected and needs to be given more weight. I also hope to show how this same issue enters into other related problems and provides a kind of missing link between episodes on battlefields and adventures in ideas. In the following discussion, special consideration will be given to two interrelated problems.

First, there is the problem of connections between the Reformation and early-modern science. Second, there is the relevance of external social institutions to the internal, relatively autonomous, life of science. By bringing out the significance of the role of publication, I hope to suggest a fresh approach to both problems. I hope, that is, to throw some new light on connections between Protestants and scientists, and also to suggest how the external regulation of the book-trade impinged on scientific theories and creative acts.

Let me start with the vivid contrast drawn by Whitehead and others between the quiet, peaceful rise of science with its world-wide repercussions and the bloody clash of rival faiths that disrupted Western Christendom alone. According to Whitehead, the rise of science contrasts 'in every way' with the contemporary religious movement.[1] The

---

[1] Whitehead, *Science and the Modern World*, p. 12.

new philosophy won adherents without resort to fire or sword, without forced conversion or any manipulation of mass minds; whereas the Reformation unleashed a popular uprising that drenched Europe in blood for a century and a half. George Sarton draws the same lesson from observing the peaceful collaboration between the Catholic Copernicus and the Protestant Rheticus during the mid-sixteenth century when religious zeal was at its height. The 'sublime' quest for truth, Sarton says, placed the activities of scientists 'au-dessus de la mêlée.'[2] Finally, when Sir Herbert Butterfield views the scientific revolution in the perspective of world history, he says it outshines everything since the rise of Christianity and reduces the Reformation to the rank of a 'mere episode, a mere internal displacement within the system of Medieval Christendom.'[3]

Such contrasts, however valid, seem to be carried so far that they detach early-modern science from its historical moorings and cut all its connections with the forces that brought it forth. A most significant connection from my point of view was provided by the felt need of scientists to publish their results. By placing more emphasis on access to publication outlets and on the fate of the firms which got the printing done, one may see how even minor episodes on the battle-fields of Western Europe could affect major achievements of the human mind.

'In a generation which saw the Thirty Years War and remembered Alva in the Netherlands,' says Whitehead, 'the worst thing that hap-pened to men of science was that Galileo suffered an honorable deten-tion and a mild reproof before dying peacefully in his bed.'[4] One would scarcely imagine from this passage that there might be some connection between troop movements in the Netherlands and what Galileo achieved. Yet because the Dutch won their war of independence (a very minor scuffle, from world history's view) scientific publication outlets were open to Galileo that might otherwise have been closed. Worse things *could* happen to men of science in the seventeenth century than being 'honorably detained and mildly reproved' for a given publica-tion. One might not be able to publish at all. Galileo, whose last major treatise had been smuggled out to Holland, could probably die with his mind at peace. But there were less fortunate investigators who

---

[2] Sarton, 'Quest for Truth,' p. 62.
[3] Butterfield, *The Origins of Modern Science*, p. viii.
[4] Whitehead, *Science and the Modern World*, p. 12.

went to their graves with voluminous of manuscripts left to gather dust.

In this regard, Whitehead's celebrated dictum ought to be emended: 'In the year 1500, Europe knew less than Archimedes...yet in the year 1700, Newton's *Principia* had been written.'[5] In 1700, the *Principia* had not merely 'been written.' Thanks to Halley, who stepped in when the Royal Society's publication funds were exhausted, it had been issued in printed editions and discussed in all the major learned journals of Europe. It had been made known throughout the Commonwealth of Learning in a Latin review which stimulated major revisions in the second edition of 1690, and which led Leibniz to turn out three articles even before he had seen Newton's work. It had been publicized for the Republic of Letters in a French translation of a long review-essay which may have been written by John Locke.[6]

To stop short before Halley's intervention is to leave the revolution launched by Copernicus still incomplete, with Newton's papers still piled in disarray on his desk. Many accounts do stop short in just this way. They follow the activities of virtuosi up to the point where experiments are performed, observations recorded, theories framed and treatises composed. But they stop short of the point where manuscripts are handed over to printers and actual publication occurs. In this way the 'internal' life of science is disconnected from the external social forces which shaped it from birth. Even the most elegant experiments were destined to wither on the vine if cultivated too long in private and deprived of exposure in the end. That publication will be forthcoming is too often taken for granted. It is simply assumed that intermediaries such as Rheticus or Halley will perform whatever tasks are needed, or that scientists themselves will see to it that the services of printers are

5 Whitehead, *Science and the Modern World*, p. 16.
6 Axtell, 'Locke's Review of the *Principia*,' pp. 152–61, describes the English pre-publication notice by Halley in the *Philosophical Transactions*; the Latin review in the *Acta Eruditorum* and the French review in the *Journal des Sçavans* as well as the unsigned French review, which upheld Newton against the Cartesians, and appeared in Jean LeClerc's *Bibliothèque Universelle*. Axtell's attribution of this unsigned review to Locke and his high estimation of its significance is questioned by I. B. Cohen, *Introduction*, p. 46, n. 9. In an evaluation of the early reviews (pp. 145–62) Cohen argues that the long Latin review in the *Acta* is more worthy of attention. As noted by Aiton, 'Essay Review,' *History of Science*, the *Acta Eruditorum* account not only led Newton to revise his text, but stimulated Leibniz to publish three papers even before he read the *Principia* itself. Yet the review which appeared in LeClerc's journal, however unworthy, was more likely to attract attention from the chief publicists of the Republic of Letters. It set a theme that Enlightenment *philosophes* exploited to advantage for the next century and makes one question the verdict of Jacob, 'Early Newtonianism,' pp. 142–6, that one must wait for the Boyle lectures before Europeans learned of Newton's scientific accomplishments.

secured. These necessary services, however, hung in the balance for many virtuosi three centuries ago.

While Kepler was busy with the publication of his presentation of the Copernican theoretical structure...Copernicus' work was banned. In the summer of 1619...he received...news that the first part of his *Epitome* which appeared in 1617 likewise had been placed on the Index of prohibited books. The news alarmed Kepler...He feared that should censorship be granted in Austria also, he could no longer find a printer there...He pictured the situation so black that he supposed he would be given to understand he should renounce the calling of astronomer...[7]

Kepler was reassured by his friends that his worst fears were exaggerated. They wrote to tell him that his book could be read, even in Italy, by learned men who secured special permits. One Venetian correspondent suggested, shrewdly, that authors often benefited from having their books banned. In Italy, he wrote, 'books by distinguished German scholars even if prohibited would be secretly bought and read so much the more attentively.'[8]

Similar reassurances are still being issued by historians who discount the significance of the Catholic condemnation of pro-Copernican works.[9] Once publication has been assured, it may well be advantageous to have one's book banned in certain regions. But when one is having trouble getting technical printing completed, official proclamations aimed at frightening printers are not advantageous at all.[10] As these remarks suggest, to understand the circumstances confronting seventeenth-century scientists we need to assign more significance to the act of publication and to the role of intermediaries who got the printing done. If this were done, moreover, one might be able to draw significant connections between the rise of modern science and seemingly extraneous political events. For the outcome of dynastic and religious wars obviously affected the kind of publication-programs that could be undertaken in a given realm. It determined the degree of risk that printing a given work entailed. Forms of piety and patronage, licensing and censorship, literacy and book-reading habits varied from region to region in accordance with this outcome. Since the distribution of

[7] Caspar, *Kepler*, p. 298.   [8] Caspar, *Kepler*, p. 299.

[9] See e.g. citations from Ben-David given in text below (pp. 654, 656) and comment by A. R. Hall, *Scientific Revolution*, p. 77 that 'the significance of Galileo's summons to Rome is easily exaggerated.'

[10] Kepler's difficulties during the Thirty Years War in trying to obtain printers and keep necessary presswork going are described by Caspar, *Kepler*, pp. 310–22.

printing industries can be determined with a fair degree of accuracy, the 'geography of the book' can be mapped out; and the movement of printing centers can be correlated with the fixing of religious and dynastic frontiers.

What about the movement of scientific centers? Obviously it is more difficult to trace. Indeed it is open to question whether there were any real centers of scientific activity when clusters of print shops were first formed. The printer can be readily identified before the role of the scientist had clearly emerged. The latter is still a problematic creature, as current definitions suggest. In the early-modern era, it may be a mistake to use the label at all.[11] The distribution of talents contributing to 'scientific' advances in the early-modern era hinges on a wide variety of activities (mathematical techniques, instrument-making, data collection and so forth). The question of where and how to apply the term 'scientist' to men who did not regard themselves as such is open to dispute. Furthermore, from the 1500s to the 1640s, investigations now regarded as 'scientific' were still largely un-coordinated. Scattered regions containing varied clusters of talents – an observatory on a Danish island, groups of instrument-makers in Nurem-berg, lens-grinders in Amsterdam or Jesuit astronomers in Rome – dot the map somewhat randomly. Some highly energetic 'centers,' such as Tycho's Uraniborg or Mersenne's 'Letterbox' or Rudolph II's court at Prague, were so short-lived and so dependent on the movements of a particular individual that their location cannot be taken as proving any rule.[12]

Given inevitable uncertainty over the location of the 'main centers' of scientific activity, there is bound to be disagreement over the factors that encouraged their formation and early growth. There are those who argue that a prime role during the strategic 'take-off' phase was played in Catholic regions, especially in Italy where the Platonic revival flourished, the study of natural philosophy was propelled by lay university faculties, and the first scientific societies appeared.[13]

[11] The 'scientist' – a term first popularized by William Whewell – has been plausibly defined (by Derek da Solla Price) as anybody who has contributed at least one article to a professional scientific journal. But by this definition, the creature is called into being only after the appearance of a learned periodical press. This seems to put Descartes, Galileo, Kepler and Harvey in an occupational limbo and to bisect the 'century of genius' in an unhelpful way.
[12] How the cluster of talents mobilized by Rudolph II evaporated after his death is well described by Evans, *Rudolf II and His World*, p. 192.
[13] On the primacy of Italy, see references in chap. 5, section 2, above.

There are those who look instead to regions that broke away from Rome. They believe Protestant teachings spurred a new systematic investigation of God's open book. Some single out Wittenberg, rather than Padua, as *the* university which served as the seed-bed for modern science; while others play variations on Max Weber's theme by emphasizing Calvinist centers such as Leiden and Puritan academies established elsewhere.[14] Yet another school regards all universities and confessions as too conservative and tradition-bound, and looks to heterodox circles and non-academic groups, represented by 'invisible colleges' and 'schools of the night.' 'The presence or absence of Protestantism' is thus regarded by Frances Yates as less significant than the 'Hermetic–Cabalist' tradition. Virtuosi such as Newton owed less to Anglican bishops and Puritan divines than to the Renaissance Magus who sought to play the 'pipes of Pan.'[15] Yet others argue that Newton's mathematical physics ought not to be confused with his alchemy or theology, and agree with Edward Rosen: 'out of Renaissance magic... came not modern science, but modern magic.'[16] They stress the demystifying aspects of the new philosophy, its open and public character, and the predictive powers that made it useful to practical men. For the most part, they identify science with materialism and regard it as incompatible with belief in a spirit world. Anti-clerical circles and libertine groups are thus singled out, along with the revival of pre-Christian pagan views associated with atomism and hedonism.[17]

[14] Dannenfeldt, 'Wittenberg Botanists' cites a relevant passage from Ferdinand Cohrs, *Philipp Melanchthon, Deutschlands Lehrer*: 'At no other university did mathematics and the natural sciences bloom as at Wittenberg' (p. 242). (This view goes back to Peter Ramus who praised German efforts in order to spur French kings.) For opinion that the main centers later passed from Catholic Italy and Lutheran Germany to Calvinist circles elsewhere in Europe, see Mason, 'The Scientific Revolution,' and Hooykaas, 'Science and the Reformation,' which also offers a good summary of Lutheran and Calvinist views. In his *Humanisme*, p. 86, Hooykaas cites Ramus' praise of Germany as the 'nursery of mathematics' and his tributes to Melanchthon and the Wittenberg school. The more insular debate over Anglican, Puritan, Latitudinarian, deist, academic and non-academic influences in the Royal Society has given rise to a large literature – too large to be covered here. The updated bibliography (up to 1970) given in the 1970 edition of Merton, *Science, Technology*, pp. 266–73, may be consulted along with essays collected by Webster, ed. *The Intellectual Revolution*.

[15] In addition to Yates, *Rosicrucian Enlightenment*, p. 227, McGuire and Rattansi, 'Newton and the "Pipes of Pan,"' and Rattansi's several articles, see also critical essays by A. R. Hall, 'Magic, Metaphysics,' and Rossi 'Hermeticism,' both in *Reason, Experiment and Mysticism* (ed. Righini Bonelli and Shea).

[16] Rosen, 'Was Copernicus a Hermetist?' p. 171. Westman's 'Magical Reform' is a devastating critique of Yates.

[17] Demystification and disenchantment are themes that go back at least to the Enlightenment *philosophes* and their nineteenth-century admirers: Comte and Marx. The rejection of the occult and the shift away from magic is stressed by Rossi in his book on *Francis Bacon* as well

Finally there are the eclectics who find some truth in all views even while holding to a multivariable approach. No one region or institution, tradition, creed or class played a strategic role in the great collaborative venture, which was itself composed of diverse methods and pursuits.[18] Competing claims for the primacy of diverse 'external' forces when taken all together tend to cancel each other out. The way is paved for a reassertion of the autonomy of activities which owed something to all groups but nothing special to any one. We are back to Sarton's 'sublime quest for truth,' envisaged as a neutral and nonpartisan cerebral activity unaffected by the clash of warring creeds and conducted 'au-dessus de la mêlée.'

Although all these arguments have some merit, none in my opinion goes far enough. Discussion of research activities ought to be accompanied by consideration of publication of results. In the search for seedbeds or nurseries, moreover, early printers' workshops deserve a closer look. So too does the problem of how scattered circles were linked and how they began to cooperate on many different fronts. However they differ, the various interpretations now offered share in common a tendency to assume that coordination was inevitable and that the flow of information would not be disrupted or cut off. As we have seen modern authorities take more for granted than a seventeenth-century printer or virtuoso could.

The issues of communication and coordination are not neglected in all studies, to be sure. But when they are raised, it is usually in a form that detaches research from publication and leaves the role of intermediaries out of account.

From a convent in Paris, Mersenne...drew into his epistolary network most of the leading scientists of his day irrespective of religion or nationality, even to the extent of admiring the work of Bacon, Harriott and Oughtred. Though based in Paris, the circle was Western European in scope. It connected Descartes in Holland, Gassendi and Peiresc in Provence, Schickard

as in his other essays. Anti-clerical views are prominent in Andrew White's old *Warfare of Science with Theology* which more recent works still cite although it is misleading on Protestant censure of Copernicus (see strictures offered by Hooykaas, 'Science and Reformation,' pp. 238–9, n. 100; 104). Anti-clericalism is also evident in many later positivist accounts, such as those of Wolf and Randall cited above in chapter 5. Feuer borrows from Randall *et al.* in order to stress materialist and epicurean currents in *The Scientific Intellectual*.

18 The need for a multivariable approach is underscored by A. R. Hall, 'On the Historical Singularity.' That the English use of the singular form 'science' (in contrast to the European preference for 'les sciences') obscures the diversity of plural enterprises is suggested by Charles Schmitt's 'Essay Review' on 'Mechanics in 16th Century Italy,' p. 175, n. 45.

in Tübingen, Hortensius in Leyden, Galileo in Florence and Van Helmont in Brussels...It was upon these foundations and not upon economic developments confined to particular geographical areas that scientific research advanced...

The intellectual Europe of the age of Galileo took no account of later national boundaries. Nor, curiously enough, do religious differences seem relevant, despite the shadow of the Thirty Years War.[19]

By conducting his wide-ranging correspondence, Mersenne undoubtedly helped to coordinate the varied activities of scattered virtuosi, and he did so while steering clear of trouble with authorities. Yet the fact that Mersenne's letterbox was located in Paris does not really offer an adequate clue to its celebrated contents. Private correspondence had been handled by friars in Paris convents for centuries. It was the open letter addressed to Europe at large that was new. Mersenne's letterbox was distinctive because it was plugged into a much larger communications network created by print. This larger network had several nodal points – all located outside Paris in northern Protestant regions, beyond the borders of France.

The mistaken impression that a network centered in Paris provided the foundations for seventeenth-century scientific advance derives from the common practice of detaching early scientific communications and organization from the output of the scientific press. Centers are located by considering all the diverse forms of interchange and research activities which stop short of publication. Thus encounters at Peiresc's residence in Provence and at the Paris 'Cabinet des Frères Dupuy,'[20] taken together with Minorite Friar's letterbox, give rise to the impression that there was a 'translatio studii' from Galileo's Italy (where the first societies were formally organized) to Mersenne's France. But although a few promising scientific publication programs were initiated by enterprising Frenchmen during the age of Mersenne, none received continuous support; all were at some point interrupted or curtailed.[21]

---

[19] Kearney, 'Puritanism and Science,' pp. 108–9.
[20] Harcourt Brown, Scientific Organizations, discusses these meeting places.
[21] Difficulties experienced by Théophraste Renaudot (whose 'Feuilles du Bureau d'Addresse' may be described as the 'first scientific periodical,' according to Harcourt Brown) and by Denis de Sallo who launched the Journal des Sçavans are noted in Brown, Scientific Organizations, pp. 21–4; 195. On Renaudot's career as an enterprising pioneer in scientific journalism (who influenced Samuel Hartlib among others) see also Solomon, Public Welfare, passim. On de Sallo and his Journal see Birn, 'Journal des sçavans.'

Mersenne's own efforts were so frequently blocked that he has been described in a recent study as a 'publicist manqué.'[22] By remaining publicly discreet on the burning issues of the day (to the point of doctoring a publication sent to Rome) even while condemning 'mystical-magical' practices, the friar did what he could to neutralize science and set suspicions at rest.[23] But he was not really able to remain 'au-dessus de la mêlée.' Rather he was forced into contact with underground channels, becoming involved in a clandestine book-trade that got works listed on the Index quickly translated and into print.[24]

In these clandestine efforts the key role of intermediary was not played by Mersenne but by a Genevan diplomat who was stationed in Paris. Elias (Élie) Diodati did as much to bring Galileo's work 'to light' as Rheticus did for Copernicus or Halley for Newton. A member of the celebrated Protestant family which had left northern Italy for Geneva in the sixteenth century; a cousin of the Diodati who translated the Bible,[25] Elias also belonged to an inner circle of erudite 'free-thinking' Frenchmen. He participated actively in the meetings held at Peiresc's residence in Provence and at the Paris 'Cabinet des Frères Dupuy.' Pierre Gassendi, Gabriel Naudé and La Mothe Le Vayer were his three closest friends.[26] Travelling frequently on commercial and

22 Whitmore, The Order of Minims, p. 21. The conflict between Mersenne's potential for pioneering in 'haute vulgarization' and his need to preserve a measure of clandestinity is also brought out on p. 150.

23 On Mersenne's preparing a special version of the Questions Théologiques – which substituted passages on music for astronomy – to be sent to Rome after his hearing of Galileo's condemnation, see two articles by Hine, 'Mersenne and Copernicanism,' p. 30; 'Mersenne Variants.' Mersenne's efforts to separate magic from science are noted by Yates, Giordano Bruno, chap. 22. On this point the pioneering study is Lenoble, Mersenne.

24 The French translation of Herbert of Cherbury's deist treatise: De Veritate, was made by Mersenne and 'printed clandestinely through his good offices' shortly after the work was placed on the Index, as is noted in a letter of 1640 sent to Comenius, according to D. P. Walker, Ancient Theology, p. 170. The route by which De Veritate travelled to Peiresc in Aix, Campanella in Rome, Mersenne and Gassendi in Paris is noted by Krivatsky, 'Herbert of Cherbury's De Veritate.' Elias Diodati, in London during 1632–3, took copies back with him to France. On other useful services performed by Diodati and Mersenne see Ornstein, The Role of Scientific Societies, pp. 140–1; Hine, 'Mersenne,' p. 30; Drake, Discoveries and Opinions, p. 171, n. 33.

25 When de Santillana, The Crime of Galileo, p. 173 describes Elias Diodati both as Galileo's Paris correspondent and as the Tuscan emigré 'who had had a great part in the French translation of the Bible,' one wonders if he has confused Elias with his cousin Jean (or Giovanni) who had 'a great part' in the Italian translation of the Bible (1605) and who also prepared a French translation of Sarpi's History of the Council of Trent (1621) as noted on p. 412, above.

26 See Pintard, Le Libertinage Erudit I, 129–30; 175–6. Elias Diodati's contributions to the Strasbourg publication of the censored Lettera of Foscarini and Galileo's Letter to the Grand Duchess are noted in II, 593. Readers of Spink, French Free Thought, are left unaware of Elias Diodati's existence. Whereas Pintard includes him in the close-knit quartet whose other three members

diplomatic missions to the central cities of Western Europe, he developed useful contacts with publishers, booksellers, couriers and postal officials. He served in Pintard's words as a 'colporteur de la République des Lettres' well before the era of Jean LeClerc and Pierre Bayle. In this capacity he brought the 'new philosophy' out of convents and secluded villas and into contact with the world of the Elseviers – acting more boldly than his French Catholic comrades dared. He accompanied Grotius on a voyage, sustained Campanella in Paris, publicized Francis Bacon and won a following for Lord Herbert of Cherbury, the 'father of Deism,' in France. Although his name often appears in small print in Galileo studies, he seldom receives adequate recognition for his energetic and successful efforts to get the works of the imprisoned virtuoso translated, printed, and well publicized abroad.

The same thing can be said of Diodati's most important ally, the Dutch printer Louis Elsevier. Among visits made to Galileo's residence in Arcetri, where he was confined as a political prisoner, few were as historically significant as the visit made by this member of the great Dutch publishing firm.[27] Yet few of the visitors who saw the celebrated prisoner have been so neglected in later accounts.

'Intellectual Europe in the age of Galileo' was fundamentally affected by the movement of printing industries away from older cultural centers. The seventeenth-century knowledge industry was not based in Paris, nor did villas in Florence and Provence contribute as much as did the presses of the Dutch Netherlands to sustaining scientific research. Indeed Colbert was dissuaded from prohibiting the entry of Dutch printed books into France, despite his concern about their subversive content and adverse impact on the Paris printing industry, by the argument that French *savants* could not do without them.[28] During the seventeenth century, it has been suggested, more books were printed in the United Provinces than in all other countries taken together.[29] The

were Gassendi, Naudé, and Le Vayer; Spink discusses the same trio and substitutes Gui Patin for Diodati as the fourth member.
[27] Elias Diodati's correspondence with Galileo concerning Louis Elsevier's visit in 1635 and Elsevier's contacts with Mersenne are described in the editors' introduction to Mersenne's *Les Nouvelles Pensées de Galilée*, ed. Costabel and Lerner I, 17–24. On the Elsevier firm and its founder's links with Plantin, see D. W. Davies, *The World of the Elseviers, passim.*
[28] Febvre and Martin, *L'Apparition*, pp. 374–5. The preference for Dutch printers and their products exhibited by Englishmen under Charles I which provoked a complaint from Laud is noted by Haley, *The Dutch*, p. 123.
[29] This statement, made by de La Fontaine Verwey, 'The Netherlands Book,' p. 29, is based on guesswork, as is noted by Haley, *The Dutch*, p. 123.

contrast between the meagre scientific output of the most populous, powerful, well-consolidated realm in Europe and the abundant one of the small, loosely federated Dutch realm underscores a point made in an earlier chapter, that nation-building worked at cross-purposes with the expansion of printing industries. It was the powerlessness of central courts and the strength of the towns which secured for Dutch entrepreneurs a *de facto* if not a *de jure* free press.[30]

The significance of Dutch presses for the expansion of Western science is obliquely acknowledged by Sir Herbert Butterfield in a passage which, however, places them on the stage of history almost one hundred years too late.

In this period the changes were not by any means confined to France... The movement was localized however and it is connected with a humming activity which was taking place, say from 1660 not only in England, Holland and France but also actually between these countries - the shuttle running to and fro and weaving what was to become a different kind of Western culture. At this moment the leadership of civilization...moved in a definite manner from the Mediterranean...to the regions farther north...

Not only did England and Holland hold a leading position, but that part of France which was most active in promoting the new order was the Huguenot or ex-Huguenot section, especially the Huguenots in exile... who... - after 1685 - after the Revocation of the Edict of Nantes - ...fled to England or became the intermediaries for the publication in Holland of journals written in French communicating English ideas...[31]

The important role played by a French language press, run by exiles in the Netherlands, in publicizing the 'new philosophy' and in forcing a 'crisis of the European conscience' is certainly worth underlining; for it is too often ignored. 'French Huguenots made no mark scientifically' argues Kearney. 'In Holland Cartesianism came under heavy fire.'[32] Yet French Huguenots manning Dutch presses provided some Cartesians, such as Malebranche, with important opportunities to make their mark.[33] Nevertheless, the 'humming activity' that occurred

30 See p. 405, volume I, above. J. L. Price, *Culture and Society*, chapter 7 brings this point out more clearly than do other authorities writing about the Dutch press.
31 Butterfield, *Origins of Modern Science*, pp. 140–1. This description is based on Hazard, *La Crise de la Conscience*. See especially I, chapter III where Hazard describes the movement of culturally influential centers from Catholic South to Protestant North.
32 Kearney, 'Puritanism and Science,' p. 109.
33 Martin, *Livre à Paris* II, 874–9, offers pertinent data about Malebranche. Haley's account of what the support of his Rotterdam printer, Reiner Leers, meant to Pierre Bayle is cited on p. 420, volume I above.

in the late seventeenth century also needs to be related to events that preceded the Revocation of the Edict of Nantes in France (and that also antedated the establishment of the Royal Society in England). The seventeenth-century cosmopolitan French language press which conveyed the ideas of Newton and Locke to the Republic of Letters was really a latecomer to the 'world of the Elseviers.' The wars of Dutch independence had ushered in a golden age of printing in Holland (and had established at Leiden a great Protestant university) before the Edict of Nantes had even been proclaimed. A third edition of Copernicus' prohibited *De Revolutionibus*, the works of Descartes and Galileo (and of Bacon, Comenius, Hobbes, Grotius, Gassendi *et al.*) were being turned off Dutch presses before this Edict had been revoked.[34] The 'humming activity' that propelled scientific advances toward the end of the seventeenth century did not originate in a Paris convent. Nor did it start with the Huguenot exodus of the 1680s or even with earlier programs launched by Francis Bacon, Galileo and Descartes. It began with defeats suffered by the Spanish Habsburgs in the sixteenth-century Dutch wars – minor scuffles on a corner of the globe, to be sure, but with world-wide repercussions nonetheless.

The divergent publication programs pursued by Plantin's two sons-in-law – by the Catholic Jan Moretus, who stayed in Antwerp; and the Protestant Frans Raphelengius, who went to Leiden – point to differences characterizing publication policies in Catholic and Protestant Europe as a whole.[35] When considering problems associated with such divergence, it seems odd to find that Jesuit publishers in Peking (where Jesuit policy soon led to condemnation from Rome) attract more attention than do the successors of Plantin who worked so much closer to home.[36] During the age of Galileo, Catholic Antwerp specialized in serving the needs of Catholic churchmen. Protestant Amsterdam diversified and served lay readers all over the globe. Insofar

---

34 The penetration of French cultural influences into Holland before the 1680s is described by Haley, *The Dutch*, pp. 190 ff. See also Gustave Cohen, *Ecrivains Français en Hollande, passim.* Italian Protestant refugees who (like the Diodati clan) prospered in Geneva after their mid-sixteenth-century exodus, also contributed something to the cosmopolitan French language press that developed in Holland. See Barnes, *Jean LeClerc, passim.*

35 On these divergent policies as delineated by Vöet, *The Golden Compasses* I, 197, see pp. 408–9, volume I above.

36 Both Rabb, 'Religion and the Rise of Modern Science,' p. 117 and Koestler, *The Sleepwalkers*, p. 495 discuss Jesuit astronomical publication in seventeenth-century China as if it was pertinent to Protestant–Catholic policies in Europe. Yet Jesuit teachings in China brought them into disrepute in Rome (as is shown by Hazard, *La Crise* I, 29).

as the pace of scientific publication quickened in the seventeenth century, it did so outside regions that followed the Counter-Reformation policies set in Rome.

This is not to say that the activities of Jesuit astronomers and missionaries in China should be overlooked. It is useful to recall that the intellectual conquest of Asia by Western science was inaugurated under Catholic auspices and connected with calendar reform.[37] Jesuit successes in China help to remind us what the previous chapter has tried to bring out; namely, that the study of astronomy had long been encouraged by the Roman Church. Religious motives for deciphering the writing in the sky pre-dated the Reformation. So too did belief that God, as the Author of Nature, was pleased by study of His work. Religious motives for scientific inquiry, in other words, were too deeply rooted in Western Christendom to be regarded as a special by-product of Protestantism.

2. DIVERGENT PROTESTANT AND CATHOLIC PUBLICATION POLICIES

By stressing the new implementation rather than the older motivation, one might be in a better position to handle the much-debated question of how Catholic-Protestant divisions were related to early scientific advance.

After all, the rise of science is the topic under discussion. The question is not why Protestantism proved to be more flexible in the long run, but rather what part religion played in stimulating the great advances in anatomy, physics and astronomy which are known as the scientific revolution. Most of these advances had taken place by the end of the 1630's. By 1640, with the work of Galileo, Harvey and Descartes virtually complete, one can safely say that science had risen...[38]

Instead of looking for direct connections between Protestantism and

---

[37] Rabb, 'Religion and the Rise of Modern Science,' p. 133 says that Counter-Reformation popes, such as Paul III and Gregory XIII, 'at least welcomed the findings of the new astronomy which paved the way for calendar reform.' But the connection between Copernicus' work and the Gregorian Reform is very tenuous, as is noted in chap. 7, n. 107, above. To my knowledge there is no evidence of any pope welcoming 'the findings of the new astronomy' (unless one interprets 'new' to include data incorporated into Ptolemaic or Tychonic schemes). According to the introduction (by Donald Menzel) to Pasquale D'Elia, *Galileo in China*, p. vii, the Jesuits did circulate news of Galileo's discoveries and helped with reform of the Chinese calendar but because of the Injunction of 1616 and Sentence of 1633, they never did teach a heliocentric system in their Chinese publications.

[38] Rabb, 'Religion and the Rise of Modern Science,' p. 112.

science, it might be more helpful to begin by considering the role played by printers 'in stimulating the great advances.' Once this role has been brought out, the 'part played by religion' is more likely to fall into place. For example, it becomes easier to see that a more positive role was played by Protestant publishers than by Catholic ones in bringing the work of Galileo and Harvey and Descartes to the point of being 'virtually complete.' One is also less likely to feel safe about assuming that 'science had risen' in 1640 when the fate of continental publishing centers was still being affected by the shifting fortunes of the Thirty Years War. Finally one will probably be inclined to go beyond the mere acknowledgement that 'Protestantism proved more flexible in the long run,' and note that Catholic policy was less stimulating from the first.

When the new presses are left out of account, it may seem plausible to argue: 'It is only by ignoring the enormous Catholic scientific activity' between the 1540s and 1640s that 'major claims can be made for the importance of Protestantism.'[39] Once technical publication is brought into the picture one may fully acknowledge Catholic activity and still make 'major claims' for the way Protestants encouraged and Catholics discouraged its development and expansion. 'The lack of noticeable difference between Protestant and Catholic resistance to change... must be explained away if the reformed religion is considered inherently more conducive to science or in any way responsible for the rise of the new form of inquiry.'[40] When resistance to changes wrought by printing is brought into the picture, the difference between the two confessions is not merely noticeable: it is striking. The common practice of treating anti-Copernican *statements* made by sixteenth-century Protestants as if they were equivalent to anti-Copernican *measures* taken by seventeenth-century Catholics is, in this regard, misleading. It leads many historians astray. For example, Bronowski and Mazlish seriously misinform their readers by asserting that Luther's contempt for Copernicus 'strangled' the scientific revolution in Germany.[41] (The achievements of Rheticus, Reinhold, Maestlin, Kepler notwithstanding!) Theological statements do not represent the same

---

39 Rabb, 'Religion and the Rise of Modern Science,' p. 117.
40 Rabb, 'Religion and the Rise of Modern Science,' p. 113.
41 Bronowski and Mazlish, *The Western Intellectual Tradition*, p. 124. The assertion is coupled with a remark that 'in 1596, Kepler had taken refuge with the Jesuits.' But this was the date when Kepler's first work was published under Maestlin's sponsorship in Tübingen – scarcely an indication of how the Copernican Revolution was being strangled.

kind of resistance to change as do measures taken to prevent publication.[42] The latter threatened the life of science as the former did not.

Protestant printers often ran afoul of authorities by producing political or theological tracts, but when serving mathematicians and astronomers they were left in relative peace. This was not merely true in late seventeenth-century England when (it is often said) religious zeal had begun to lose its force. It was also true in the age of Luther and Melanchthon when zeal was at its height. The evangelical drive which powered the presses of Wittenberg and other centers of the Reformed religion encouraged the expansion of book markets from the first. At the same time the theology of the reformers, drawing on older Christian traditions, also promoted scientific research.[43] The positive impulse thus given both to the establishment of printers' workshops and to scientific publication programs was, to my knowledge, never checked or reversed. Thus anti-Copernican pronouncements made by Luther and Melanchthon did not deter the Wittenberg professor Rheticus or the Nuremberg printer Petreius from getting the Catholic astronomer's work into print.[44] The Protestant theologian Andreas Osiander, who

[42] See Rabb, 'Religion and the Rise of Modern Science,' p. 122 where the 'earlier hostility of the Protestants' is balanced against later Catholic 'official opposition' with the suggestion that 'roles were reversed.' Kepler's sufferings 'at the hands of German theologians and professors' and the fact that the leading reformers 'openly and vehemently' opposed the heliocentric theory is made equal to the condemnation of 1616 and Galileo's forced recantation. Yet the reformers' 'open, vehement' opposition consisted of one statement by Luther (possibly made in 1539 and later recorded in the Table Talk) and one by Melanchthon made in 1541 along with a later criticism of Copernican theory in Melanchthon's published textbook. At no point did this opposition lead to arresting or even delaying publication of the three editions of De Revolutionibus or of works promoting and publicizing its contents. On Kepler's troubles with the Tübingen faculty see p. 654 below.

[43] Hooykaas, 'Science and Reformation,' p. 214 contains relevant discussion on Protestant views. The positive role played by German Lutherans is documented by J. W. Montgomery, 'Cross, Constellation and Crucible' (not to be confused with same author's two-volume biography of Andreae: Cross and Crucible). The promotion of botanical and astronomical studies by northern universities, subject to Melanchthon's reforms which was publicized by Peter Ramus is described by several authorities. See n. 14 above. Westman, 'The Melanchthon Circle' offers the most thorough recent investigation into the complex positions of members of the Wittenberg school of astronomers.

[44] Rosen, Three Copernican Treatises, pp. 400–1 speculates that the hostile statements did deter Rheticus from going on beyond the preliminary trigonometry section with a Wittenberg printer and caused him to turn to Petreius in Nuremberg instead. (He had used Luther's printer, Hans Lufft, for the separate section: 'Sides and Angles of Triangles' (Wittenberg, 1542) and Lufft later printed Melanchthon's Initia Doctrinae Physicae, which contained an anti-Copernican passage.) But Petreius had indicated interest in publishing De Revolutionibus as early as 1540 and his previous output and reputation made him a logical choice. (See Shipman, 'Johannes Petreius.') Moreover, Petreius himself was closely linked to the Wittenberg theologians and collaborated with one of them, Osiander, in preparing De Revolutionibus for publication. The question of Rheticus' departure from Wittenberg has been examined by

took over editorial chores, did connive with the publisher to add prefatory remarks: 'Ad Lectorum' which implied that the author was
setting forth a purely fictitious scheme.[45] Osiander's position is taken
by many authorities to indicate that Protestant theology, just like
Catholic theology, prevented astronomers from attempting to do more
than 'save the appearances' and forbade assigning any physical reality
to a given planetary model. Yet Osiander's comments did not deter
Protestants from publishing different views. On the contrary, it provoked Peter Ramus into issuing a celebrated challenge, offering his
chair at the Collège Royale to anyone who could devise an 'astronomy
corresponding to the truth of the heavens'; to anyone, that is, who
could avoid resorting to 'false' hypotheses, such as those described in
Osiander's 'Ad Lectorum.' The Ramean challenge, in turn, spurred
Kepler to claim that he had earned the right to the French chair by
demonstrating the physical truth of the geokinetic scheme.[46] Thus
although Protestant and Catholic theologians did adopt very much the
same position – both assigning a provisional hypothetical status to
geokinetic theories – Protestant publicists and astronomers were not
deterred from rejecting this position, in marked contrast to Catholics
after the condemnation of 1616.

Even before the 1616 condemnation and after Luther and Melanchthon's pronouncements, Catholic publishers still did less than did
Protestants to promote the Copernican cause. In this regard, too much
emphasis on Copernicus' position as a Catholic canon who relied on
Church patronage most of his life can be misleading: 'While Copernicus was aided by a Protestant mathematician,' says Sarton, 'he received
his greatest encouragement from prelates...His book was published

Elert, *The Structure of Lutheranism*, pp. 420–2, who concludes that Rheticus' espousal of Copernicanism was unrelated to this move.

45 Osiander's positive contributions to the publication of *De Revolutionibus* and his intention of
safeguarding the work by tacking on the celebrated 'Ad Lectorum,' which assigned a purely
hypothetical status to the Copernican system, is brought out by Wrightsman, 'Andreas
Osiander's Contribution.' That the 'Ad Lectorum' (although anonymously presented) was by
Osiander (who openly admitted authorship to Petrus Apianus) was known to many of the
professional astronomers and astronomical publishers of the next generation. See Rosen,
Three Copernican Treatises, p. 404 and Alexandre Koyré, *La Révolution Astronomique*, p. 99,
n. 13.

46 Curtis Wilson, 'Newton and Some Philosophers.' See esp. pp. 246; 250–2 where relevant
citations are discussed. Kepler had written to Maestlin about the Ramean challenge in 1597
but made his claim in print with the *Astronomia Nova* of 1609. There also he made the first
public disclosure that Osiander had falsified Copernicus' views by tacking on unauthorized
remarks to the *De Revolutionibus*. In this way, he publicly aired the chief issues that provoked
the condemnation of 1616.

under the highest Catholic auspices.'[47] In his career as a churchman, Copernicus was aided by several Catholic prelates and he had his major treatise dedicated to a Catholic pope.[48] Nevertheless the actual work of publishing *De Revolutionibus* was done under *Protestant* auspices. Beginning with Rheticus' *First Narration*, works describing or promoting Copernican theories, whether under the guise of a new astronomy or as 'the ancient doctrine of the Pythagoreans lately revived,' never ceased to come from Protestant presses. It is worth noting that this point applies just as well to the mystical Copernicanism of Catholic friars such as Giordano Bruno and Tommaso Campanella as to such English virtuosi as Thomas Digges and William Gilbert. The imprints of Venice and Paris on the first editions of Bruno's works were fictitious. It was during Bruno's stay in London between 1583 and 1585 that the English printer John Charlewood printed his six major treatises. Charlewood belonged to a group of London publishers who obtained both profits and patronage by taking advantage of free publicity provided by the Index. He engaged in 'surreptitious' operations, turning out works in foreign vernaculars, bearing foreign imprints and aimed at continental markets.[49]

In contrast to the active role played by Protestant firms in propelling early Copernicanism, Catholic presses seem to have been relatively inactive – until Galileo's *Sidereus Nuncius* was published in the spring of 1610. An overnight sensation, *The Starry Messenger* not only catapulted its author into the position of an international celebrity, it also did for astronomy what had been done for theology by Luther's early tracts – stimulating literary excitement and generating publicity of a new kind. 'The extent and rapidity of the spread of Galileo's telescopic discoveries can scarcely be exaggerated. Only five years after *The Starry Messenger* appeared, the principal facts announced by Galileo were published by a Jesuit missionary in Peking.'[50] Not only were Jesuit presses in China activated, but so too were Italian printers in Venice and Rome. The

---

[47] Sarton, *Six Wings*, p. 61.
[48] Rosen, *Three Copernican Treatises*, p. 406 suggests that the dedication to Pope Paul III taken together with Osiander's 'Ad Lectorum' saved *De Revolutionibus* from being placed on the Index sooner than it was. Copernicus' rejection of Cardinal Schönberg's request to have his writings copied and of his friend Bishop Tiedemann Giese's plans to get his work published is noted by Rosen, *Three Copernican Treatises*, p. 393. When de Santillana says *De Revolutionibus* was 'sponsored' by Schönberg and that Giese 'assisted at its publication' (*The Crime of Galileo*, p. 22, n. 14) he seems, like Sarton, to overplay Catholic involvement in the actual publication.
[49] Woodfield, *Surreptitious Printing*, p. 20.
[50] Drake, *Discoveries and Opinions*, p. 59, n. 1.

Republic of Letters, which had previously looked to Wittenberg and other northern centers for the most sensational fast-breaking stories, began to turn back toward Italy once more. Even in England the accomplishments of earlier English virtuosi were overshadowed by literary excitement generated by reports of what could be seen through 'Galileo's tube.' 'It is "the Italian's moon" and the "Florentine's new world" we find in English poetry, not the same moon as it had appeared to Hariot in London and to Lower in Wales.'[51] For the first time in many decades, Italian publishers were able to take advantage of the excitement generated by a new bestselling author who appealed to a vernacular-reading public.[52] A flurry of pamphlets brought profits to local firms, and probably helped to spur fresh observations along with sales of instruments and books. But this promising windfall for Italian publishers lasted only five or six years. The stimulus supplied by Galileo ricocheted to the benefit of foreigners in the end. The 'dangerous consequences' of 'spreading' Copernican views 'among the people by writing in the vernacular'[53] were arrested by the decree of the Congregation of the Index in 1616. Open promotion of Copernican theories and indeed any vernacular treatise dealing with astronomy or physics became risky for Catholic printers and thus all the more profitable for Protestant ones. This occurred in the early seventeenth century, it should be noted – well before the works of Descartes *et al.* were 'virtually complete.'

One may agree that Galileo's *Letter to the Grand Duchess Christina* reflected a 'long-standing continental tradition' and expressed views that were by no means peculiar to Protestants like Francis Bacon, but were common among many Catholic virtuosi as well.[54] But it should also be noted that had Galileo had only Catholic compatriots to aid him, this very same *Letter* would have never seen the light of day. In 1635–6, Elias Diodati and Louis Elsevier, aided by other friendly

---

[51] Nicolson, *Science and Imagination*, p. 34.

[52] The *Letters on Sunspots* which contained Galileo's first unequivocal endorsement of the geo-kinetic theory in print (and was published in Rome in 1613 under the auspices of the Lincean Academy) was deliberately written in the vernacular. Galileo knew that he could not only appeal to potential Italian patrons in this way but could also delay swift retaliation from his foreign rival, the Jesuit father Christopher Scheiner (who was using the pseudonym, 'Apelles'), by writing in a 'colloquial tongue' the Latin-reading, German Jesuit could not understand. See letter to Paolo Gualdo, cited by Drake, *Discoveries and Opinions*, pp. 84–5.

[53] Citation from the letter sent to Kepler, August 13, 1619, which described the 'practical effect of the prohibition' aimed at Foscarini's vernacular work in Langford, *Galileo, Science*, p. 104.

[54] Rabb, 'Religion and the Rise of Modern Science,' p. 117.

virtuosi and Strasbourg printers, collaborated to make *Letter to the Grand Duchess Christina* along with the forbidden *Dialogues* available in Latin to the Commonwealth of Learning.[55] This collaborative effort has been deemed significant by a sociologist of science because it marked the emergence of 'an active "scientific lobby" in Protestant Europe.' In Ben-David's view, the trial of Galileo was blown up by scientific publicists in Protestant regions simply in order to gain more substantial official patronage for their cause. Although the case provided an occasion of energetic lobbying and thus helped to heighten the collective consciousness of the growing scientific community, he believes that it was insignificant in and of itself.

The first notable opportunity for the emergence of a distinctly Protestant science policy was provided by the persecution of Galileo...A group of Protestant scholars in Paris, Strasbourg, Heidelberg, and Tübingen decided ...to translate Galileo's work into Latin. In this endeavor they received general support from several Protestant communities otherwise not notable for their tolerance of Copernican ideas. Copies of the original work were obtained through doctrinally rigid Geneva; one member of the group was from Tübingen University where only some time before Kepler had been prevented from earning a theological degree...It is difficult to conclude how long the Galileo case was used to link science with Protestantism: It was not in any case a major factor in the establishment of science...[56]

As far as I know, there is no evidence that 'Protestant communities' such as Geneva or Tübingen had ever been notable for their *in*tolerance of 'Copernican ideas.' Kepler's troubles with the Tübingen faculty came chiefly from his Calvinist leanings and from scruples that prevented him from adhering to the Lutheran Formula of Concord.[57] It was via lectures given at Tübingen, after all, that Michael Maestlin first opened Kepler's eyes to the defects of Ptolemaic astronomy and to the advantages of the Copernican scheme. As a professor at Tübingen also, Maestlin obtained the University Senate's approval for the publication of Kepler's first book and spent many days in the workshop personally supervising the actual printing of his student's work. When the *Mysterium Cosmographicum* was published in 1596, it was accompanied by a fourth edition of the *Narratio Prima*. Rheticus' brief de-

---

[55] See Drake, *Discoveries and Opinions*, p. 171, n. 33 for discussion of Elias Diodati's role in the Strasbourg printing of this tract in 1636 and of rigorous Catholic efforts to suppress it. Costabel and Lerner note (p. 17) that Louis Elsevier bore the cost of the Strasbourg publication.
[56] Ben-David, 'The Scientific Role', p. 571.
[57] See Caspar, *Kepler*, pp. 52, 188, 205, 258–9.

scription of the Copernican theory was thus published under the auspices of Tübingen, twenty years before Copernicus went on the Index and forty years before a so-called 'Protestant lobby' was formed.

As for 'doctrinally rigid Geneva,' the myth that Calvin was anti-Copernican has been discredited for some time.[58] Calvin was too ignorant of Copernicus to have taken any stand on his work. He supported Aristotelian theories since they seemed to be accepted by the scientific experts of his day. But in supporting the ancient philosophers, he also argued against using the Bible to serve as a guide to astronomy and thus helped to pave the way for the eventual separation of theology from scientific research. Far from supporting a rigid anti-Copernicanism, Calvinist arguments were used by Kepler and by pro-Copernican Dutch theologians – not only by Remonstrants but also by some of the more zealous anti-Arminian leaders who won out at the Synod of Dort.[59]

Unlike Tübingen and several other Lutheran centers, Geneva produced little in the way of scientific publication. But Calvinist Holland produced a great deal. In view of the services rendered by Dutch printers to virtuosi of all lands, it seems misleading to say that in 'small self-contained Protestant communities such as those in Geneva...in most places in Germany and later in the seventeenth century, in Holland, science fared worse than in the great Catholic centers of Italy, France and Central Europe.'[60] For virtuosi seeking publication outlets the great Catholic realms offered very little, the smaller Protestant communities offered much more.

There were Dutch Calvinists, to be sure, who refused to regard the Bible as irrelevant to any concern and who opposed the new philosophy as contrary to Scripture. The Voetian party, headed by the rector of Utrecht, thus denounced Cartesians and Copernicans and found them guilty of associating with Arminians and libertines. At no point, however, did the quarrels of theologians prevent Dutch printers from serving Copernicans, Cartesians and scientific investigators of all kinds.[61] In small German Protestant communities such as Strasbourg and Frankfurt, printers were also much better able to serve scientists (as well

58 Rosen, 'Calvin's Attitude.' (See also exchange in *J. of the History of Ideas* (1961) XXII, 382–8.)
59 Hooykaas, 'Science and Reformation,' pp. 227; 234–5.
60 Ben-David, 'The Scientific Role,' p. 570.
61 See Hooykaas, 'Science and Reformation,' pp. 234–5 for discussion of the position of the two Dutch Calvinist groups: the anti-Copernican Voetians and the pro-Copernican Cocceians and p. 239, n. 104, for objections to A. D. White's misleading account of this issue.

as a wide variety of heterodox groups) than was the case in the larger realms that were on friendly terms with Counter-Reformation Rome. That Galileo's friends turned to Leiden and Strasbourg in the 1630s was not the result of some new development but of book-trade patterns that had long since been laid down.

Many Protestant professors and churchmen objected to the new astronomy. Several Catholic virtuosi presided at its birth. The fact remains that Protestant authorities interposed few obstacles in the way of scientific publication and actively encouraged (however inadvertently) expanding lay book markets which attracted printers to Protestant realms. The Counter-Reformation Church pursued a contrary course. Beginning with the banning of vernacular Bibles and the prohibitions issued against other secular bestselling works, Catholic printers were subject to pressures that worked against diversification and that led to greater and greater reliance on turning out 'safe' devotional literature and on serving a clerical clientèle.

Here again a word of warning is needed. Serving a clerical clientèle did not invariably render a disservice to science. Seventeenth-century Jesuits furnished much useful data for serious astronomers. Profit-driving lay printers who served vast markets by churning out prognostications were not invariably helpful to scientific advance. Parallels often drawn between the 'Protestant who interpreted God's word for himself and the scientist who interpreted nature for himself' need to be handled with caution. 'Everyman his own scientist' is a slogan that Puritan pamphleteers often seemed to push too far. 'Culpeper translated into English the sacred text of the College...He hoped it would make everyman his own physician as the Bible made everyman his own theologian...'[62] Culpeper was neither the first nor the last to question the usefulness of Latin prescriptions and medical degrees or to encourage more self-help among long-suffering patients.[63] In the early-modern era, doctors rarely did more good than harm, and there was

---

[62] Hill, *The World Turned Upside Down*, p. 240. For further discussion of these trends see Brock-bank, 'Sovereign Remedies,' two articles by Rattansi, 'Paracelsus and the Puritan Revolution' and 'The Helmontian-Galenist Controversy in Restoration England,' Debus, *Science and Education* and now Charles Webster, *The Great Instauration, passim.*

[63] For examples of sixteenth-century vernacular translations being promoted on behalf of French surgeons, see references to the Jouberts, father and son, chap. 6, n. 48, above. Renaudot's 'Présence des Absens' discussed by Solomon, *Public Welfare,* pp. 17; 175–6 (and described pp. 246–7, volume I above) is a fine example of the same trend (described by Webster and Hill in connection with Puritan revolutionaries) being promoted by a French Protestant publicist in Richelieu's pay who provoked hostility from the French medical establishment.

every reason to be critical about the way physicians were trained. Yet even in that benighted era, the advancement of medical science still owed much to Latin treatises on anatomy, physiology and embryology.

Insofar as they encouraged literacy among surgeons and apothecaries and pressed for more mathematics as against Greek and Latin in the schools, the campaigns led by the more radical Protestant pamphleteers were not unhelpful to science. But they could also take an excessively anti-intellectual form. As previous chapters suggest, there is a difference between surpassing the ancients after mastering their technical literature and simply attacking the ancients while imitating Paracelsus and burning old books.[64]

The Protestant doctrine...proclaimed the duty of everybody to read the book of Scripture for himself. As a consequence...the duty to read the book of nature without regard to the authority of...Aristotle, Pliny, Ptolemy, Galen was put forward...everybody...might be a priest to the book of creation in defiance...of the ancient authorities. When Palissy was derided because of his ignorance of the classical languages...he proudly answered... I have no book but heaven and earth and it is given to everyman to know and read this beautiful book.[65]

As an artisan-author Palissy both contributed to public knowledge and produced a new ceramic glaze. In his public lectures he spelled out a program that was taken up by Francis Bacon and proved highly significant later on. Nevertheless, the attack on learned authorities and the defense of everyone's right to read the 'book of nature' for himself was not always helpful to the advancement of science. Did not later fundamentalists stand on much the same ground, when they claimed the right to judge Darwin's teachings for themselves? Even Galileo, who appealed on occasion over the heads of Latin-reading professors to the ordinary 'horse sense' of intelligent compatriots, pointed out that understanding the organs of the human body or the movement of the stars called for special training and required much more than merely looking with untutored eyes.

The eyes of an idiot perceive little by beholding the external appearance of a human body, as compared with the wonderful contrivances which a careful

Such phenomena provide necessary background for dealing with the later pre-revolutionary struggle between Mesmerists and physicians in which Marat figured prominently – as described by Darnton, *Mesmerism, passim.*

64 See pp. 472, above. On Paracelsus' burning of Avicenna's *Canon* in 1527 (in imitation of Luther's burning of a Papal bull) reported by Sebastian Franck in his *Chronica* (Strasbourg, 1531), see Pagel, *Paracelsus*, pp. 20–1.   65 Hooykaas, 'Science and Reformation,' pp. 215–16.

and practiced anatomist or philosopher discovers...Likewise that which presents itself to mere sight is as nothing in comparison with the...marvels that the ingenuity of learned men discovers in the heavens by long and accurate observation...[66]

In another celebrated passage, Galileo again underlined his conviction that the 'book of nature' although always open to public inspection, was not really 'given to everyman to know and read.'

Philosophy is written in this grand book, the universe which stands continually open to our gaze. But the book cannot be understood unless one first learns to comprehend the language and read the letters in which it is composed. It is written in the language of mathematics.[67]

The language of mathematics certainly differed from Latin or Greek, but not because it was as easy to learn as one's mother tongue. On the contrary, it became increasingly sophisticated in the course of the seventeenth century and was subject to incremental change. 'Newton was as incomprehensible to the average mechanic as Thomas Aquinas. Knowledge was no longer shut up in the Latin Bibles which priestly scholars had to interpret; it was increasingly shut up in the technical vocabulary of the sciences which the new specialists had to interpret.'[68] There are not only affinities but there are also contradictions that have to be considered when applying a 'priesthood of all believers' doctrine to the study of nature. As Rabb suggests, the parallels and analogies that are frequently drawn between early Protestant and early scientific thought 'do not prove the existence of any significant connection between the two movements.'[69]

I agree that mere analogies prove nothing and believe they are sometimes pushed too far. Yet here again by assigning more significance to publication programs one may find some valid connections that still remain to be drawn. For example, the larger the vernacular reading public, the larger the pool of potential scientific talent that could be tapped, and the more craftsmen would be encouraged to disclose trade secrets by printing treatises and attracting purchasers to their shops.

[66] 'Letter to the Grand Duchess Christina' in Drake, *Discoveries and Opinions*, p. 196. Galileo's use of the term 'horse sense' in his explanation of why he was using the vernacular in the *Letters on Sunspots* is in his letter to Paolo Gualdo, Drake, *Discoveries and Opinions*, p. 85. (On this letter, see also n. 52, above.)

[67] 'The Assayer,' in Drake, *Discoveries and Opinions*, pp. 237–8.

[68] Hill, *World Turned Upside Down*, p. 239.

[69] Rabb, 'Religion and the Rise of Modern Science,' p. 120.

New and useful interchanges between publishers and readers were also encouraged by the social penetration of literacy. When authors of atlases and herbals called on their readers to send in notes about coast-lines or dried plants and seeds, a form of data collection was launched in which 'everyman' *could* play a supporting role. Pliny's *Natural History* and Ptolemy's *Geography* were not burned by Paracelsians or Puritans. Yet they were permanently outmoded in the end. Even the output of prognostications probably stimulated sales of almanacs and ephemerides and may have encouraged some readers to buy telescopes, thereby stimulating instrument-makers to turn out more pamphlets designed to bring purchasers to their shops.[70]

The expansion of a large and variegated public for their products was especially important for booksellers, map-publishers, instrument-makers, mathematical practitioners, and other contributors to applied sciences, whose prefaces are often cited when the new scientific ethos is described. Reijer Hooykaas has described how

The defenders of the 'new' science called upon the unlearned to contribute to the knowledge of natural history, geography and physics by communicat-ing their observations on birds and flowers, on ebb and flood tide, on celestial phenomena and the...magnetic needle. Travellers and mariners especially were invited to do so.[71]

Hooykaas plausibly links such invitations to Protestant notions per-taining to a priesthood of believers and to the belief that 'everyone should read the book of nature according to his capacities.' Yet the men who solicited responses from readers were not all of them devout Protestants or conscious defenders of a 'new science.' In many in-stances they were acting rather as conscientious manufacturers of globes, maps and almanacs or of other guidebooks or instruments, who hoped to attract purchasers, outdo competitors and ensure steady sales by building up their reputation as makers of reliable and useful products.

In repudiating vulgar Marxism, Hooykaas writes, somewhat in-dignantly, that Protestant insistence:

---

[70] Copernican doctrines were thus publicized by Leonard Digges' *Prognostications Everlasting*. The 1595 Catalogue of Andrew Maunsell (noted above, pp. 106-7, volume I for defining 'science' along modern lines) carried mention of 'Leon. Diggs gent. his Prognostication everlasting... whereunto is added by T. Diggs his sonne A perfect description of the Celestiall Orbes according to the most ancient doctrine of the Pythagorians. Latelie revived by Copernicus & etc. Reprinted by Tho. Orwin 1592.' (Thomas Digges' celebrated translation of the first part of *De Revolu-tionibus* first appeared in 1576 as is noted in chap. 7, n. 146, above).

[71] Hooykaas, 'Science and Reformation,' p. 216.

on the benefit that may come to mankind from useful inventions...is not a manifestation of the capitalistic mentality of a rising merchant class hiding mammonistic intentions behind a pious pretence. Genuine love for God and one's fellow beings is the main driving force...[72]

Here again it seems mistaken to set one motive against another, when 'having it both ways' is what most human beings seek. Insofar as technical publication was spurred, the driving force was fueled not by love of God *or* Mammon but by love of God *and* Mammon – and of one's compatriots and of oneself – in short by the very same powerful mixture of altruistic and self-serving motives which propelled early Bible-printing along with map-publishing and instrument-making. (For some time indeed the two activities went hand in hand, for new gazeteers and other technical guides were often prepared to supplement Bible editions.) I would imagine that the chance to serve God and help mankind, even while making money and establishing one's name was just as attractive to instrument-makers, reckon-masters, and map-publishers in Catholic realms as in Protestant ones. But official Church policies diverged significantly. Catholic enterprise was braked in a manner that encouraged Protestants to move into high gear. Thus the same censorship policies that discouraged Catholic Bible printers and curtailed their markets, later closed up scientific publication outlets in Catholic lands. The same forces that encouraged expanding markets for vernacular Bibles also favored interchanges between readers and publishers of useful vernacular works.

3. BLOCKING THOUGHT EXPERIMENTS, SPONSORING CREATIVE ACTS

Of course, some authorities question whether useful vernacular treatises and Baconian programs should be linked to true scientific advance. They stress a series of creative acts by a small group of virtuosi who gave the century of genius its name. Collecting facts or promoting 'useful knowledge' are set aside by this school as irrelevant to the investigations of Pascal, Harvey, Kepler, Galileo, Malpighi, and other great men.

The Scientific Revolution was surely utilitarian only to a limited degree. The classical experiments were anything but useful in their application... The improvement of man's lot on earth was an irrelevant consideration...

[72] Hooykaas, 'Science and Reformation,' p. 216.

What has been said about Pascal applies equally to Kepler's planetary investigations, Galileo's mechanics, Mersenne's study of music, the Cartesian theory of the universe, Harvey's discovery of the circulation of the blood and Newton's *Principia*. Intellectual curiosity is relevant here, not crude utilitarianism...A sociological investigation...must concentrate attention not upon technology and economic need but upon the social and intellectual conditions which favored the development of originality.[73]

Once again it seems possible to avoid an either-or approach. Intellectual curiosity *and* useful trigonometry texts entered into 'Kepler's planetary investigations.' In laboring over the *Rudolphine Tables* during the Thirty Years War, Kepler himself produced a work that was designed to do more than satisfy 'intellectual curiosity,' a work that proved useful to editors of ephemerides and publishers of sky maps. Activities such as compiling tables of functions, or developing logarithms and slide rules also involved the production of useful tools and at the same time spurred new creative acts.

In this connection it is worth recalling Laplace's dictum that logarithm tables doubled the life of the astronomer. Consideration of the intellectual labor saved by printed materials points to aspects of early-modern scientific activities which are neglected by those sociologists of science who emphasize the Puritan work ethic. Present guidelines, derived from Max Weber, focus attention on the appearance of a set of values that discouraged unrelieved idleness on the part of a leisure class.[74] Something more should be said about the new *leisure* that printing gave to a *learned* class. Within the Commonwealth of Learning, systematic work habits were coupled with released time *from* grinding labor. Thought experiments required time off from slavish copying and freedom from compiling long tables of numbers by hand. Less reliance on memory work and rote repetition in lecture halls also brought new mental talents into play. Printing enabled natural philosophers to spend more time solving brain teasers, designing ingenious experiments and new instruments; or even chasing butterflies and collecting bugs if they wished.

In this particular connection I agree with Lewis Feuer (although elsewhere I think he overdoes the theme) that it is a mistake to dwell only on the ascetic attitudes scientists displayed.[75] Cardano's anticipation of

---

[73] Kearney, 'Puritanism and Science,' p. 108.
[74] Merton, *Science, Technology*, p. 96.
[75] Feuer, *Scientific Intellectual, passim*.

probability theory which stemmed from his own penchant for gambling did not found a new science since his *De Ludo Aleae* (unlike his *Ars Magna*) was not published until after Pascal's and Fermat's works. Nevertheless card playing, betting and dice throwing (which were notoriously antipathetical to Puritanism) contributed to the development of probability theory in the seventeenth century.[76] Pascal's Jansenism linked him with Puritan theology but his celebrated 'wager' about the existence of God had distinctly *un*Puritan overtones. The pleasure principle should not be ruled out when considering the rapid development of new puzzle-solving techniques by men who were aptly described as *dilettanti* and *amateurs*. 'Homo Ludens' as well as 'Homo Faber' was encouraged after printing to use his mental energies in new ways – as the modern chess player or bird watcher may suggest. Early-modern science owed something to playfulness and 'idle' curiosity as well as to piety and profit-seeking drives.

Even black-robed Latin-writing professional lawyers, physicians, and astronomers took advantage of new leisure by browsing at book fairs and indulging in mathematical fun and games. The use of print to mobilize European talents by issuing open letters and challenges was not confined to sponsoring inventions deemed useful by bureaucrats and capitalists, such as methods of finding longitude at sea. Newton's image of himself as a child playing on the seashore diverting himself 'by finding a smoother pebble or prettier shell than ordinary' seems to be singularly at odds with a work ethic and even somewhat pagan in its implications.[77] The satisfaction of pure intellectual curiosity, as Hugh Kearney says, needs to be given due weight.

[76] Ore, *Cardano: The Gambling Scholar*, pp. 176–7. The *Ars Magna* was published in 1545 by the same Nuremberg firm of Petreius which published *De Revolutionibus* in 1543.

[77] This celebrated metaphor may have been picked up from a sermon by John Donne (as suggested by Christopher Hill, 'Newton and His Society,' p. 46, n. 96) or both Donne and Newton may have been drawing on common classical–Christian topoi. The Renaissance humanist Vergerius was fond of referring to the practice favored by Scipio and Laelius 'who sought rest for exhausted minds in aimless walks along the shore, picking up pebbles and shells as they went' in order to refute this idle indulgence and suggest (à la Dr Arnold) that strenuous recreation and purposeful work were better as restoratives. See Woodward, *Vittorino*, p. 116. (Ironically the humanist seems fonder of the work ethic than the presumably puritanical seventeenth-century scientist.) Newton's further comment that 'the great ocean of truth lay all undiscovered around him' evokes a favorite theme of Baroque engravers: i.e. the legend of St Augustine who, while pondering the mystery of the Trinity beheld a child with a seashell trying to empty the ocean and realized that his human efforts to comprehend the divine mystery were equally hopeless. The first graphic rendition was in the third (illustrated) edition of Cesare Ripa's *Iconologia* (Rome, 1603), p. 109. See *Baroque and Rococo Pictorial Imagery*, Item no. 3, 'The Deity.'

Nevertheless, even the most seemingly impractical cerebral feats and all the 'classical experiments' mentioned by Kearney required repeated recourse to various printed materials. Tables and charts were not turned out in idle moments by members of a leisured class. The output of better maps and globes, the new ventures in data collection which led to improved estimates of the dimensions of the earth were helpful to pure science as well as to applied.[78] When publishers competed to get news from an expedition the minute it docked or instrument makers took time off to advertise their wares, such actions contributed to *all* kinds of scientific experiments – whether they were aimed at bearing fruit or intended only to shed light.

Even when considering only the light-shedding experiments performed by a very small number of highly gifted men, the many practical problems posed by publication still have to be taken into account. Where publication outlets were imperiled, speculative freedom was also endangered. Official censorship could affect even the hidden life of the mind. One wonders, for example, whether the 'Cartesian Theory of the Universe' was ever fully disclosed, even to Descartes himself. When hearing of Galileo's fate in 1633, he stopped working on his grand cosmological treatise and perhaps clipped the wings of his own imagination by this negative act.[79] Newton's creative energies could be given freer rein. Conditions that guarantee speculative freedom are probably related to the 'development of originality.' They are also related to mundane matters involving economics, technology, and affairs of church and state.

78 W. J. Blaeu's contributions to terrestrial measurement are described by Keuning, *Willem Jansz. Blaeu*, pp. 22–4 who notes the use made of them by Jean Picard. The latter's 1672 expedition (which had simultaneous measurements of the altitude of Mars taken in Cayenne and in Paris and secured more accurate estimates of the sun's mean distance from the earth) is cited in Newton studies by many authorities (see Butterfield, *Origins of Modern Science*, p. 120) who suggest Newton delayed final calculations for the *Principia* until seeing Picard's results in a publication of 1684. (This suggestion was queried by Florian Cajori in his appendix to *Sir Isaac Newton's Mathematical Principles*, p. 663 who shows Newton already had used a fairly accurate value derived from an earlier Dutch measurement by Snell (in 1617) and by Norwood, when correcting a table of distances in his emended version of Varenius' *Geographia Generalis emendata et illustrata ab Isaaco Newton* (Cambridge, 1672). But, of course, Newton may well have waited for Picard's well substantiated verdict while using those of Snell and Norwood as the most reliable to date. Newton's work on Varenius' *Geographia* is described by Manuel, *Portrait*, p. 117 as useful for his chronological research. It entered into his astronomical calculations as well.

79 Descartes' letter to Mersenne describing his decision to withdraw his treatise on 'Le Monde' from publication after learning of Galileo's recantation is discussed by Hine, 'Mersenne and Copernicanism,' p. 30. His prudent handling of problems posed by French censorship and use of Dutch firms is described by Martin, *Livre à Paris* II, 874–6.

By 1640, we are told, 'science had risen.' The work of Descartes, Galileo and Harvey was 'virtually complete.' But Descartes' work was surely incomplete. The complete *Monde* was never issued, even in a posthumous form. By 1640, moreover, Kepler's laws had not won acceptance. Three alternative planetary models and six sets of conflicting tables were in circulation. Elliptical orbits were still far from making contact with parabolic curves. During the same interval, the fate of the continental publishing firms that were used by Kepler, Galileo, and Harvey also hung in the balance and hinged on the shifting fortunes of war. Perhaps it is *un*safe to say that science had risen – especially in those regions where printers were being subject to new controls. In Italy, for example, a clandestine book-trade had taken hold, and scientific publication programs were winding down. One might be better advised to think less of science as 'rising' among Galileo's compatriots than of its going underground. At least it was able to go abroad, thanks to the help provided by the Royal Society, whose efforts at underwriting foreign work deserve to be better known.

For it was not just large and costly volumes of English virtuosi, such as Willoughby, that made the financing of the *Principia* difficult for the Royal Society. It was also the expense of undertaking to publish (and illustrate lavishly) significant contributions by Italians who worked in their native land and yet found it awkward to publish there. For example, all the major treatises of Marcello Malpighi, indeed every work that he published after 1669, were published by the Royal Society.[80] Much as Copernicus was served by Rheticus, Galileo by Diodati or Newton by Halley, so too was Malpighi served, not by Italian colleagues, but by Henry Oldenburg and by Robert Hooke. These Secretaries of the Royal Society furnished the great embryologist with the most recently published technical literature. (It was easier to wait for books from England than to turn to local booksellers by that time.) They solicited contributions and assured him repeatedly of the fine reception accorded his papers by the 'company of philosophers abroad.'[81] In general, they provided the Italian virtuoso with the en-

[80] Adelman, *Marcello Malpighi* I, 669–726. Kearney, 'Puritanism and Science,' p. 109 cites Malpighi's contributions as evidence that Italian scientific activity was not affected by religious and political events. See also Rabb, 'Religion and the Rise of Modern Science,' p. 123, for a similar interpretation of Italian academies and virtuosi, which overlooks the question of publication outlets.

[81] Adelman, *Marcello Malpighi* I, 670. See pp. 712–15 for discussion of new treatises sent by Oldenburg, all in Latin so that Malpighi could read them.

couragement and group support he lacked at home. That the atmosphere in Italy was less receptive, Malpighi's many letters show. Even while expressing some concern about possible reprisals for engaging in the 'commerce with Protestants' Malpighi also commented that a friend had mentioned there were advantages in having works 'condemned by Italian censors sail to England to be printed.'[82]

This opportunity was advantageous not only to Malpighi but to the Commonwealth of Learning at large, as Oldenburg recognized at the time. His correspondence with the Italian embryologist shows that the Secretary of the Royal Society was fully aware of the special service the press was rendering to scientific advance.[83] Having assured the anxious author that his history of the silkworm was to be published 'in splendid style,' Oldenburg noted that publication would 'bring out the opinion of all the learned, and perhaps where you have not yet seen clearly, they will shed fuller light.'[84] With these words, Oldenburg underscored a theme which has been running through this book; namely that printing rendered a special service to the learned Latin-reading community. Publication would not serve to acquaint 'everyman' with Malpighi's highly technical treatise on the silkworm. But it would 'bring out the opinion of all the learned,' that is, it would elicit contributions from other qualified investigators who could check observations, repeat experiments or devise new tests and present fresh data. Given Oldenburg's clear understanding of the value of scientific publication and the vigorous efforts he made on its behalf, it seems odd that this aspect of his activities is not acknowledged more often.

As things stand now, recognition of the important services rendered by printing to the scientific community, a recognition that was shared by Renaudot as well as by the founders of the Royal Society, is likely to be obscured by the debate over the so-called 'Baconian' movement and whether it was peripheral or central to seventeenth-century scientific advance. Those who scornfully dismiss the 'Baconians' as promoters rather than as real scientists and those who uphold the same group (while depicting them as embattled Puritans trying to bring down

---

82 Adelman, *Marcello Malpighi* 1, 347. Malpighi was not the only Italian virtuoso who turned to England for help. A 1661 letter from Vicenzo Viviani to Robert Southwell, a future president of the Royal Society, urging promotion of Viviani's work reads like 'the letter of a sales manager to a favorite travelling salesman,' according to Middleton, *The Experimenters*, p. 282.
83 Oldenburg's appreciation of the uses of publicity and of the need to improve scientific communications systems was also shared by others associated with the Royal Society. See Shapiro, *John Wilkins*, pp. 32; 223.   84 Adelman, *Marcello Malpighi* 1, 674 (Letter of March 25, 1669).

Latin-reading élites) serve to reinforce each other. The special functions rendered by the underwriting of costly technical publications tend to be discounted by both sides.

Along with the special services rendered by Royal Society publications, the special threats posed by press censorship also are likely to be discounted. It has become increasingly fashionable to muffle the repercussions of Galileo's trial and to view the stir it caused as a consequence of clever Protestant propaganda.

It is very doubtful whether the dramatic events of the condemnation of Galileo were in themselves of far-reaching significance. The indignation aroused...probably increased the popularity of science. There is no sign of cessation of scientific activity following the condemnation...It is true that the activities of the Lincei were curtailed...but some of its members... continued to be active...and participated in the foundation...of the Cimento...[85]

Although scientific activity did not cease in Italy after 1632, studies of the *Lincei*, the *Cimento*, the *Investiganti*, and of individual members of these societies show how it was being crippled. The *Lincei* had to discontinue the study of physics and astronomy; its short-lived successor, the *Cimento*, which relied entirely on the personal patronage of a Medici duke, was disbanded ten years after its formation. Two of its members were imprisoned by the Inquisition. Its collective papers: the 'Saggi' ('Examples' or 'Samples') were published in 1667, but could not be purchased in Italian bookshops.[86] Indeed it required action once again by the Royal Society for the *Saggi* to become known abroad.[87]

A brief comparison of the policy of the Royal Society with that of its Italian counterpart, the *Cimento*, in the 1660s seems worth making if only to suggest how divergent publication policies might serve to stimulate or to stifle scientific advance. With the *Transactions*, the Royal Society launched a continuous series[88] that attracted an expanding list

[85] Ben-David, 'The Scientific Role,' p. 571.
[86] Ornstein, *The Role of Scientific Societies*, pp. 76, 78–9, 812; Middleton, *The Experimenters, passim.*
[87] The *Saggi* was translated into English by Richard Waller and published by the Royal Society in 1684. Oldenburg's impatient and eager letters awaiting receipt of copies of the Italian version in 1665–6 are in Middleton, *The Experimenters*, p. 289.
[88] The series was *almost* uninterrupted. There was a hiatus between 1687 and 1691 before Richard Waller took over and previous difficulties were experienced between 1665 and 1669 due to plague, the fire of London, and Oldenburg's imprisonment in the Tower (for corresponding in French with a virtuoso). See Stimson, *Scientists and Amateurs*, pp. 107–8; Margaret Espinasse, 'Decline and Fall of Restoration Science,' pp. 347–69.

of subscribers and readers all over the world. The *Cimento* issued only one single compendium, whose first edition could not be locally bought or sold. The *Transactions* encouraged signed contributions and attracted authors even from abroad with the lure of fame. Its editors took measures to ensure the protection of intellectual property rights by dating contributions and adjudicating priority disputes. The *Saggi* tried to protect contributors from persecution by leaving them anonymous. It thereby deprived them of the incentive to make a public contribution while achieving personal fame.[89]

As an institution which failed to survive... [the *Cimento*] shows us something interesting about... the 'reward structure' of science. Within the social system of modern science, one of the primary incentives for... original research is the desire for recognition and status... The Academy failed... because the enthusiasm of its most talented researchers was dampened by the anonymity of its only publication.[90]

Adverse publication policies also hurt the chief scientific society of Naples, as Max Fisch's article on the Academy of the Investigators suggests. Its members were often on the verge of publication but almost never ventured over the brink. One of them, Tommaso Cornelio, postponed publication to the point where he 'lost credit' for significant work in anatomy and physiology. English virtuosi, although slower in their research, were quicker to win eponymous fame.[91] It has been suggested that Naples should have a place alongside Padua, Florence, Copenhagen, Paris, and London as a center of seventeenth-century scientific activity.[92] Seventeenth-century Naples contained many distinguished virtuosi. But it was not a good location for any scientist who hoped to get his major works into print before he himself expired. Cornelio's master, Marco Aurelio Severino, left seventy-seven volumes of unpublished manuscript materials behind him when he died of the plague in 1656. As a host to many English visitors and a careful reader of Harvey's pioneering studies, he had

[89] See Ornstein, *The Role of Scientific Societies*, pp. 88–90 on first edition of the *Saggi* and p. 130 on Oldenburg's handling of problem of 'plagiary.' For sophisticated sociological analysis of the role played by the *Transactions* editors, see Merton and Zuckerman, 'Patterns of Evaluation in Science.'

[90] Westman, book review, *Renaissance Quarterly* (1974) p. 223.

[91] Fisch, 'The Academy of the Investigators' I, 528. See also discussions of constant postponement of publication by another member of the *Investiganti* (Joseph Valetta) on pp. 544–5. A similar pattern is traced by Whitmore, *The Order of Minims*, with regard to the friars of Mersenne's order in France. See n. 128 below.

[92] Schmitt, 'A Garin Compendium,' p. 420.

written hopefully to England in search of publication outlets there.[93] Severino's former mentor, Tommaso Campanella, was eventually rescued from his Neapolitan prison by the good offices of a pope and he found refuge in a Parisian convent not far from Mersenne. But his *Apologia Pro Galileo*, written in Naples in the fateful year 1616, had to be smuggled out by German disciples to be published under Rosicrucian auspices in Frankfurt.[94]

In the year 1616 the head of the Carmelite Order, Foscarini, was silenced for arguing that Copernicanism might be in harmony with Scripture. The Anglican bishop, Thomas Sprat, who said much the same thing later in the century, also provoked opposition. Thus Henry Stubbe, an English physician, was moved to write: 'A Censure upon Certaine Passages Contained in the *History of the Royal Society* As being Destructive to the Established Religion and the Church of England.'[95] Unlike Foscarini and his printer, however, Bishop Sprat and his colleagues could afford to view this kind of 'censure' with relative equanimity. Controversy attracted publicity and helped to boost sales. The author of the *History of the Royal Society* was protected by all the forces that rallied Englishmen behind the anti-Papist cause. 'Without a doubt,' ran one of the arguments which allowed press censorship to lapse in England, 'if the late King James had continued on the throne ...books against Popery would have...been deemed offensive...'[96] Unlike members of the *Cimento*, the apologist for the Royal Society could draw on the heritage of biblical humanists and vernacular translators to provide religious sanction for the new undertaking. The Anglican Church and the Royal Society may both lay claim to the achievement of a 'Reformation' said Sprat:

both have taken a like course to bring this about; each of them passing by the corrupt copies and referring themselves to the perfect originals for instruc-

93 Schmitt and Webster, 'Harvey and M. A. Severino.'
94 The disciples were Tobias Adami and Wilhelm Wense, both friends of Andreae who got the *City of the Sun* also printed in Frankfurt. Yates, *Rosicrucian Enlightenment*, pp. 137–8. On Frankfurt firm associated with Rosicrucians, see Evans, *The Wechel Presses*, pp. 281–2. On Campanella's *Apologia Pro Galileo* see also Grant McColley's introduction to *The Defense of Galileo of Thomas Campanella* and McColley, 'The Debt of Bishop John Wilkins.' On Boyle's approval of Hartlib's plan to produce English translations of Campanella's *City of the Sun* and Andreae's *Christianopolis* see Rattansi, 'Social Interpretation of Science,' p. 20
95 Ornstein, *Role of Scientific Societies*, p. 132. R. F. Jones, *Ancients and Moderns*, pp. 249–62 has long excerpts from Stubbe's 'Censure.' That Stubbe was ironically attacking, not defending, the Anglican church is argued in James Jacob's forthcoming study.
96 Item no. 15, 'The House of Commons' Reasons for Not Renewing the Licensing Act (1695)' cited from *Lords' Journals* XV, 545 by Vann, ed. *Century of Genius*, p. 7.

tion; the one to Scripture, the other to the huge Volume of Creatures. They are both accused unjustly by their enemies of the same crimes, of having forsaken the Ancient Traditions and ventured on Novelties. They both suppose alike that their Ancestors might err; and yet retain a sufficient reverence for them...[97]

Sprat's reference to retaining 'a sufficient reverence' suggests that the establishment of public knowledge entailed some measure of prudence and self-restraint. Even in England, protection and patronage were likely to be withheld from those who pressed controversial causes too far. This was especially true during the Restoration when men were weary of civil war. Virtuosi, who were easily confused with magicians and sorcerers, and who still numbered some astrologers and alchemists in their midst, had particular reasons to be prudent in pressing their cause. The claim to bring about a 'Reformation' was associated with Rosicrucian and revolutionary manifestos and was by no means free of political implications.[98] Moreover, there was still a residual confusion between the 'true experiments' of virtuosi and the charlatan's mystico-magical tricks. The experimenters were also vulnerable as 'amateurs' and as founders of unauthorized 'invisible colleges' to being classed with zealous Puritans and levellers who had attacked Latin learning, university faculties and the granting of any professional degrees.[99]

In securing support for the new form of 'public knowledge,' the founders of the Royal Society used tactics similar to those deployed by Mersenne.[100] They took care to present the study of nature in its most neutral, innocuous guise; treading a cautious middle path between Hobbist 'atheistical materialism' on the one hand and occult 'Familias-tical-levelling Magical' trends on the other.[101] Even while upholding

[97] Sprat, *History of Royal Society*, part 3, sect. 23, p. 371.

[98] See passage calling for a 'general reformation of the world' in Boccalini's *Ragguagli di Parnaso* (Venice, 1612–13) translated as *Advertisements from Parnassus* by the Earl of Monmouth (London, 1669) as cited by Yates, *Giordano Bruno*, pp. 408–11. As Yates shows, Boccalini's tract was translated into German and incorporated into the first Rosicrucian Manifesto (Cassel, 1614). See also Yates, *The Rosicrucian Enlightenment*, chap. x. Special insular concerns also entered into the effort to disassociate the Royal Society from belief in occult and hermetic texts. Early reactions to James I's *Demonologie* are described by Rattansi, 'Alchemy and Natural Magic.' (See also n. 101, below.)

[99] See n. 62 above for coverage of attacks on English universities by Puritan sectaries.

[100] According to Yates, *Rosicrucian Enlightenment*, p. 111, the 'Mersenne-Fludd controversy held the attention of all Europe.' It was set off by Mersenne's *Questione in Genesim* of 1623. How this landmark in 'demythologization' was related to the Rosicrucian furore is also discussed by Yates in her *Giordano Bruno*, pp. 435 ff.

[101] Prior, 'Joseph Glanvill,' suggests how one effort to disassociate English science from atheism and materialism (à la Hobbes) led, paradoxically, to the claim that belief in witchcraft was scientifically valid.

claims to Reformation, welcoming contributions from artisans, and advocating the use of unadorned vernacular prose, Bishop Sprat emphasized the apolitical non-partisan character of the Society. Not only poetry and magic, but also religion and politics were banned. There is more than a hint of a suggestion in Sprat's apologia that the neutral scientific society had taken over functions once assigned to the medieval Church by providing a peaceful sanctuary for factions who were otherwise at each other's throats. Later Addison asserted that the Society was established less to promote natural knowledge than 'to keep out of politics many of the greatest Geniuses of the age who might otherwise have set their country in a flame.'[102] The 'innocent amusements' which diverted the virtuosi were depicted in a manner calculated to distract attention from earlier Puritan zeal and in a way that evoked an Edenic freedom from original sin. Within the refuge provided by the study of nature, Anglicans and Puritans could behave as did inhabitants of a 'peaceable kingdom' where lions lay down with lambs. 'The Beautiful Bosom of *Nature* will be Expos'd to our view; we shall enter into its *Garden* and taste of its *Fruits* and satisfy ourselves with its plenty.'[103] The heretical implications of this vision of science as restoring the prelapsarian paradise on earth have been brought out by many authorities. The paradoxical implications of associating large-scale data collection, expanding knowledge industries and periodical publication with medieval images of enclosed gardens, modest maidens and forbidden fruit remain to be explored.

4. RESETTING THE STAGE FOR GALILEO'S TRIAL

For Italian virtuosi, at all events, no similar refuge could be constructed; flaming swords still barred the way. The 'book of nature' was not open to public inspection, but was subject to expurgation, and large tracts were declared out of bounds. Libraries were ransacked and printers were imprisoned. Fear of persecution led to a different kind of self-censorship than that enjoined upon members of the Royal Society, who had to stay clear of politics and theology but could wander freely within nature's realm.

historians have not thrown much light upon the rise of the Index. They have not brought out the actual differences it made in each case in each place...

[102] From *The Spectator* 262 (31 Dec., 1711), cited by Espinasse, 'Decline and Fall,' p. 353.
[103] Sprat, *History of The Royal Society*, part 3, section 1, p. 327.

the silent battles that were...fought behind the scenes about certain works, publishing houses, the sales and the circulation of books brought in from abroad...Everything vital and new that had been produced during a century and half of cultural effort was now being mutilated and suppressed...

The secret history of the great battle which was supposed to protect the Catholic world from the progress of European knowledge is still to be written...it is difficult to understand the atmosphere of suspicion, secretiveness and suppression which dominated the world of culture in the age of Galileo. Everything became dangerous...Heresy was ferreted out from dictionaries and traced in the collections of apothegms; it was believed to be hidden in the very names of the printers and had to be exterminated there...[104]

Since 1965 when Garin published the above passages, several historians have thrown more light on the 'silent battle' as it was fought out in particular regions of Italy. Thus John Tedeschi has studied documents pertaining to the situation in Florence between 1592 and 1606 and has described the 'unmitigated confusion' and interminable delays which led to the ruin of booksellers and printers. Tedeschi agrees with Garin concerning the 'devastating effects on Italian culture of Roman censorship practices.'[105] Paul Grendler, who has followed the situation in Venice over a longer interval (1540–1605), draws a picture that is somewhat less black-and-white; for Venetian policy was often at odds with that of Rome. Thus Grendler describes both the initial delay in implementing Roman edicts when they were first issued and the eventual curtailment of the power of clerical censors by officials who weathered the interdict crisis. He also suggests that 'mutilation and suppression' of innovative literature was not entirely successful, even when collaboration with Roman inquisitors was the order of the day. Between 1570 and 1590, Venetian virtuosi continued to obtain forbidden works. 'The Inquisition was unable to stop illicit traffic' and could not 'halt clandestine importation of ultramontane titles.' Profits from this traffic, however, did not line the pockets of Venetian printers. The latter were hard hit by the two decades of collaboration with Rome which benefited their foreign competitors. The 'ban on publication of prohibited titles was almost totally effective' and this 'dealt a lasting blow' to local booksellers and publishing firms.[106]

[104] Garin, *Science and Civic Life*, pp. 85–6.
[105] Tedeschi, 'Florentine Documents,' pp. 579–605.
[106] Grendler, 'The Roman Inquisition,' pp. 48–66. (This article summarizes the findings which are now spelled out in more detail in Grendler's book by the same title.)

Italian virtuosi, in sixteenth-century Venice at least, seem to have kept in touch with innovative literature from abroad. Later Venetian literati contributed much to pro-republican and anti-papist propaganda and also to the prolonged struggle for a free press. But what about the access of virtuosi and literati to funds for publication programs and to printers and patrons willing to risk carrying them out? Because this question is rarely posed, the most telling blows to early-modern science dealt by clerical censorship are often overlooked. Instead of pointing to the clear and present threats posed by the decree of 1616 and the trial of 1633, careful distinctions are drawn between different theological positions taken by churchmen on the two occasions. These theological subtleties, however intrinsically interesting, still strike me as being somewhat beside the point.[107]

The decree of 1616 described the doctrine of Copernicus as contrary to Scripture and therefore not to be defended or held. Nevertheless, we are told, the Copernican theory could still be presented as an hypothesis (albeit as an indefensible and absurd one). Moreover, 'if there were any Catholic astronomers who had no doubt that the Copernican system was true' they did not have to violate their inner conviction of certitude. The decree requiring 'interior assent' came from a fallible authority and those who had no doubt 'were excused.'[108] Interior assent could be withheld. But what about external dissent? On the strategic issue of publication, recent Catholic apologists have singularly little to say. Catholic scientists who had no inner doubts (and were certain that Copernicus was right) were still expected to remain silent, or pay a high price for failure to prove their case. At least this conclusion seems to follow from Galileo's trial.

Galileo had... openly disobeyed the express prohibitions against his theory and plainly failed in his attempt to prove the Copernican astronomy. Still it is hard to see the logic of the sentence. There was no reason to condemn the *Dialogue* outright. It... defended the new astronomy as true on physical grounds. If this was objectionable, Galileo's book, like Copernicus' *De Revolutionibus*, should have been suspended until corrected and made more hypothetical. As for Galileo personally the most that should have been given

---

[107] See for example, Langford, *Galileo, Science*, pp. 98–104. For a good summary of literature on the diverse theological and philosophical positions that are entailed, see Nelson, 'The Early Modern Revolution' pp. 1–40 (see esp. bibliography and appendices). Nelson does more to bring out the revised opinions of Cardinal Bellarmine's biographer, Father Brodrick, than other authorities do.

[108] Langford, *Galileo, Science*, p. 103, n. 50.

him was a penance for disobeying Bellarmine's admonition...As for the decree of the Index, it was aimed at books, not authors.[109]

Obviously the prelates who presided over the condemnation of 1633 did not view the issues in quite the same light as does a modern Catholic scholar such as Langford. Although the latter contends that the case of Galileo is too often lifted out of its historical context, his difficulty in understanding 'the logic of the sentence' suggests an incomplete success in reconstructing the mentality of seventeenth-century churchmen. At all events, any decree that was aimed at books was bound to hit printers and authors as well. Whatever interpretation is placed on the edicts of 1616 and 1633, it can scarcely be doubted that they had an inhibiting effect on scientific publication programs in Catholic lands. When it asserted that the old world-system had to be maintained as long as the new one was inadequately proved, and when it forbade further 'attempts to demonstrate' that the new system was 'true in fact'[110] the Church was not encouraging suspension of judgment or urging further investigation of the matter. The condemnations not only curtailed scientific publication programs, they also did much to block 'thought experiments' based on envisaging the Copernican scheme as physically real.

Poor Borelli! He was truly on the road to the great discovery...He renounced all theory beyond the brute, experimental fact and by this very means barred the road to progress. Hooke and Newton had more courage. It is the intellectual audacity of Newton just as much as his genius which permitted him to overcome the obstacles that stopped Borelli ...[111]

When comparing Hooke and Newton with Borelli, one cannot afford to confine the terms of discussion to 'internal' factors alone. Of course, the state of the art and the special talents of the gifted puzzle-solvers have to be considered. But one must also give due weight to unevenly distributed 'external' forces. Otherwise an unfair comparison will result. Borelli may or may not have been less courageous and less audacious than Newton. Surely he had fewer incentives to spur him on and more formidable obstacles to surmount.

Insofar as anti-Copernican edicts might be taken as a challenge to come up with more adequate proof of heliocentric schemes, they were much more likely to be taken in this way by Protestant than by Catho-

[109] Langford, *Galileo, Science*, pp. 150–1. [110] Langford, *Galileo, Science*, pp. 98–9.
[111] Koyré, *La Révolution Astronomique*, p. 506 (translation mine).

lic scientists. Ramus had taken Osiander's preface as a challenge. His open letter to Europe's astronomers helped to spur Kepler on. But when Galileo failed to come up with certain proof, the case was closed – at least as far as papal writ could reach. It is difficult to envisage a member of an Italian scientific society acting as Halley did, urging Newton to overcome his hesitations and to bring his grand design to completion, and then supervising its publication and assuring it favorable publicity. Friends of Catholic virtuosi were more likely to dissuade them from taking the condemned theory too seriously. Even without friends to dissuade them, devout Catholics would feel qualms about moving ahead on their own.

Thus members of the *Cimento* devoted themselves to careful laboratory experiments while avoiding large-scale theories and holding thought-experiments in check. 'It is dangerous to make original conjectures, so look again before giving it to a printer,' ran a note found among the papers of those responsible for preparing the *Saggi* for publication in Italy.[112] The fear of publishing subversive subject-matter led to excluding from the *Saggi* potentially interesting investigations and discussions of comets. Not only cosmology but also astronomy represented a potentially dangerous field after 1633. Even Borelli, who chafed at anonymity and eventually left Tuscany in order to publish on his own, resorted to a pseudonym when publishing one treatise on comets and masked the Copernican implications of a passage before releasing his *Theoricas Mediceorum Planetarum*.[113] The defense of plain-speaking by spokesmen for the Royal Society such as Sprat was not aimed only at excluding poets, rhetoricians and fabulists from the Commonwealth of Learning. It had positive as well as negative aspects. It reflected a recognition that 'Aesopian' language, when effective enough to fool censors, often deceived fellow scientists and sometimes inhibited clear thinking by oneself.

Perhaps enough has been said to suggest that the picture of flourishing Italian scientific activity drawn by several authorities needs to be qualified. Even though the *Cimento* was founded and did important

---

[112] Middleton, *The Experimenters*, p. 72.
[113] Settle, 'Borelli, Giovanni Alfonso, 1608–1679,' *Dictionary of Scientific Biography* II, 306–14. Although he did win patronage and publication support from Queen Christina after her conversion to Catholicism, Borelli's career ended badly – as a poverty-stricken political suspect teaching elementary mathematics in Rome. Settle's description of the setbacks suffered by seventeenth-century Italian science (p. 306) should be contrasted with the bland dismissal by other authorities of the impact of the anti-Copernican decrees.

work, its own scientific publication program was crippled; others in Italy had suffered damaging blows. But then Italian technical publication had already experienced many set-backs in the past. A recent account of the fate of the mid-sixteenth-century *Accademia Venetiana* is instructive in this respect. The *Accademia* had an ambitious program to 're-establish Venice's reputation as the leading publishing center.' It planned to enlist the aid of Paul Manutius' publishing firm and to issue editions of many important scientific works. Founded in 1557, the *Accademia* was incapable of meeting the high costs entailed in securing supplies of paper, the services of printers, editors, and rentals of bookshops and went bankrupt in 1561.[114] Given the pressure being exerted from the Papacy in the 1550s to control printing firms and bring Venetian censorship in line with the Index; given the difficulties experienced by Venetian bookmen stemming from official policies during subsequent decades, it would seem the founders of *Accademia* had chosen the wrong time for launching their ambitious project. But when one surveys developments over the course of the next century, it seems that the time never did come when Italian publication outlets were free of the risk of being abruptly closed off.

In this regard, the stage is set just as awkwardly for Galileo's trial as for other major historical events. The placing of *De Revolutionibus* on the Index by the decree of 1616, and the prohibition of the *Lettera* by Paolo Antonio Foscarini (a sixty-four page treatise published in 1615 by a Carmelite friar, which argued that the Copernican theory was physically plausible and theologically sound) are discussed in many studies. The hard lesson learned by Foscarini's printer, Lazaro Scoriggio, however, is rarely taken into account. 'By the beginning of February 1616 Galileo...felt...victory was in sight. He wrote to secure permission...for a visit to Naples, probably to see Foscarini and if possible Campanella and to organize the campaign in favor of Copernicus...'[115]

On March 5 the decree pertaining to Copernican doctrines was officially published. Foscarini's *Lettera*, which sought to reconcile Copernican views with Scripture, was 'altogether prohibited and condemned.' *De Revolutionibus*, however, was merely 'suspended until it be corrected.' The distinction between the prohibition of the theologi-

---

[114] Rose, 'The Accademia Venetiana.' In his *Italian Renaissance of Mathematics*, Rose has a chapter on Bernardino Baldi (d. 1617) who set out to be the Vasari of mathematicians, collected 200 or so 'Lives' but failed to get his *Vite de' Matematici* into print.

[115] Drake, *Discoveries and Opinions*, pp. 218–20.

cal argument and the suspension of the astronomical treatise is frequently stressed by Catholic apologists and by others who try to soften
the effect of the blow. Thus Langford suggests that it was 'not really
a serious setback to progress in astronomy' and Koestler argues that,
despite the mistaken impression of 'the man in the street,' the 'effect of
the decree on scientific discussion and research was to leave things
almost exactly where they had been.'[116] Neither notes, that in 1617,
one year after the decree, the Amsterdam printing firm (run by the
noted Dutch astronomer, globe-maker and map-publisher, Willem
Janszoon Blaeu) brought out a third edition of De Revolutionibus.[117]
Perhaps Blaeu, like many of his competitors was hoping to trade on the
advantages of being listed on the Index. Perhaps he had laid plans for
a 1617 publication date long before. Whatever the case, Blaeu's edition
appeared at a time when scientific publication programs bearing on
physics and astronomy were being caught up in a familiar pattern –
one that had already affected Erasmus, Boccaccio, Rabelais, Luther,
and Machiavelli. New opportunities to profit from banned titles were
extended to Protestant firms. At the same time new risks and un-
certainties were posed for scientific publishers in Catholic lands.
Virtuosi engaged in scientific research were not unaffected by this turn
of events. A member of the Lincei resigned, accusing Galileo of upholding forbidden views.[118] Galileo withdrew his plan to visit Naples
ostensibly because of 'bad roads.' As Drake suggests, after March 5,
1616, the 'road to Naples was...bad...in more than one sense.' 'The
printer who had published Foscarini's book there was soon to be
imprisoned and the author died that same year under obscure
circumstances.'[119] The road to Naples never did improve, so far as
scientific publication programs were concerned.

Very much like Luther during the decade after 1517, Galileo during
the decade after 1633 could count on the support of numerous publishers, printers, and booksellers to render papal actions ineffective even
while they made profits on the side. The fate of the banned Dialogue
demonstrated once again the advantage that accrued to Protestant
publishers from purveying titles listed on the Index, and the attraction

[116] Langford, Galileo, Science, pp. 58–9; Koestler, The Sleepwalkers, p. 458.
[117] The editor of this edition which bore the title Astronomia Instaurata was Nicolas Müller, a professor of mathematics at Gröningen. According to various authorities, Müller was not a Copernican himself but his corrections made the third edition an improvement over the previous versions.   [118] Ornstein, Role of Scientific Societies, p. 76.
[119] Drake, Discoveries and Opinions, pp. 219–20.

exerted even by fairly recondite scientific treatises that were designated as forbidden fruit.[120] According to de Santillana's colorful account, the black market profits made by the *Dialogue* were high:

> priests, monks, prelates even, vie with each other in buying up copies of the *Dialogue* on the black market...the black market price of the book rises from the original half-scudo to four and six scudi [almost a hundred dollars in American currency] all over Italy.[121]

Galileo's *Dialogue on Two World Systems* was such a provocative and polemical treatise, however, it almost seemed to court censorship in a way that is quite atypical of most serious scientific work. The same thing cannot be said of his later treatise which helped to found classical physics: the *Discourses on Two New Sciences*.

No great cosmic or philosophical questions intrude into this unimpassioned treatise...it is about as controversial and stirring as some freshman lecture on mechanics, of which indeed, it is the ultimate source.

The crowning irony of Galileo's career is that the failure of the great *Dialogues* should be so much more interesting than the success of the unobjectionable *Discourses*.[122]

It is hard to think of a better example of the kind of 'pure science' that is naturally placed 'au-dessus de la mêlée' than the 'ultimate source' of a 'freshman lecture on mechanics.' Yet the dull 'unobjectionable' *Discourses* were also caught up in the fray. They were not deemed unobjectionable by those who kept Galileo under house arrest; their success was not uninteresting when one considers the means by which it was brought out. Given an ageing but resolute political prisoner, whose captors had forbidden him to publish or even write anything ever again; a Dutch printer's visit to Italy and the smuggling of a manuscript in a diplomat's pouch, the ingredients do not lack interest. They could be woven into a narrative involving considerable suspense.

120 A key figure in the English exploitation of the publicity value of Galileo's being on the Index was Thomas Salusbury who (copying a procedure used for expurgated passages in Scripture by Bodley's Librarian, Thomas James) translated the treatises (and expurgated passages from works designated as forbidden in the Indexes of 1616 and 1619) and published them by popular subscription soon after the Restoration of 1660. See Stimson, *The Gradual Acceptance*, p. 90. According to Nicolson, 'English Almanachs,' pp. 22–3, Salusbury's English translations from the Italian and Latin versions of Galileo's works were advertised by Vincent Wing, the almanac publisher, whose work was annotated by Newton. Since the latter came into contact with Galileo's work through the Salusbury translation, the propagandist accomplished a useful task. 121 de Santillana, *The Crime of Galileo*, p. 325.
122 Gillispie, *The Edge of Objectivity*, p. 52.

The book was completed in 1636 when Galileo was seventy-two. As he could not hope for an imprimatur in Italy, the manuscript was smuggled out to Leiden and published by the Elseviers. But it could also have been printed in Vienna where it was licensed, probably with imperial consent, by the Jesuit Father Paulus.[123]

One wonders what grounds there are for Koestler's optimism concerning possible Viennese publication, in view of the risk of reprisals Viennese printers would have to run. There were, after all, many powerful officials in Vienna who disapproved of the licensing and viewed any support of Galileo as a subversive act. Koestler's account, here as elsewhere, seems to underrate the forces of reaction and needs to be balanced against evidence supplied by other accounts.

as soon as the *Discourses on Two New Sciences* is licensed in Olmutz by the bishop and then in Vienna, obviously under direct imperial orders by the Jesuit Father Paulus, the other Jesuits start in hot pursuit after the book. 'I have not been able' writes Galileo...in 1639, 'to obtain a single copy of my new dialogue...Yet I know that they circulated through all the northern countries. The copies lost must be those which, as soon as they arrived in Prague were immediately bought up by the Jesuit fathers so that not even the Emperor was able to get one.' The charitable explanation would be that they knew what they were doing. Someone at least may have understood that Galileo's work in dynamics went on quietly establishing the foundations of the system that he had been forbidden to defend. But they were like that gallant man of whom Milton speaks who thought to pound in the crows by shutting the park gate.[124]

When considering factors that affected the quiet establishment of the foundations of modern science, the difference between getting published by the Elseviers in Holland and being licensed by Father Paulus in Vienna is worth keeping in mind.

'Fortunate Newton!' Einstein exclaimed, 'Happy childhood of science! To him nature was an open book whose letters he could read without effort.' As the case of 'poor Borelli' may suggest, Newton was fortunate not only in being a genius who was born in the right century. He was lucky to be born in the right country as well. After the advent of printing, all talents alike had been freed from certain previous limits set by hand-copying and memory work. But unevenly distributed

---

[123] Koestler, *The Sleepwalkers*, p. 494. For account of complex negotiations between Galileo and François de Noailles which disguised the handing of the *Discourses* over to Louis Elsevier, see Costabel and Lerner, pp. 18–20. [124] de Santillana, *The Crime of Galileo*, p. 326.

literacy rates governed access to the new form of public knowledge and even among literate élites incentives, penalties and rewards varied in accordance with divergent policies pursued by varying régimes. 'Sir Isaac,' wrote his nephew, Conduitt, 'had the happiness of being born in a land of liberty where he could speak his mind – not afraid of Inquisition as Galileo...not obliged as Descartes was to go into a strange country and to say he proved transubstantiation by his philosophy.' There is a certain irony here, for Newton was much more averse to 'speaking his mind' than was Galileo. Even in the *Principia*, he told a friend, he intentionally wrote in 'a cryptic and complicated manner to discourage ignorant quibblers.'[125] Like Copernicus, he was by nature secretive and inclined toward the old esoteric scribal tradition. All the more reason to give credit to the enthusiastic sponsors of scientific publication who encouraged these reticent geniuses to expose their writings to many eyes.

In analyzing the remarkable cluster of talents that marked the century of genius, consideration of random elements supplied by a gene pool may be usefully supplemented by closer study of specific historical determinants.[126] The *Académie des Sciences*, writes Charles Gillispie, was a better-designed and more professional organization than the Royal Society.

But this admirable design was frustrated by the waywardness of genetics. The scientific minds which matured in France under Louis XIV were far less fertile than those of the generation of Descartes and Pascal, far less productive than the cluster of English genius which crowded in upon the Royal Society in Newton's time.[127]

In addition to the 'waywardness of genetics,' one ought to consider the exodus of Huguenot printers and paper-makers, and the press policies adopted by both King and Académie. Did they not help to set back scientific productivity? Neither Descartes nor Pascal had felt free of constraint. During the last third of the century the odds were, if anything, stacked even higher against virtuosi seeking publication outlets in France. Manuscripts containing ample evidence of 'fertile minds' tended to pile up in Paris convents as they did in Naples and

---

125 Manuel, *Portrait*, pp. 267, 365.
126 See cogent remarks by Merton, *Science, Technology*, chap. 9. Merton's treatment of social interaction and communication on pp. 220–4 needs to be supplemented in my view by further consideration of the consequences of printing.
127 Gillispie, *Edge of Objectivity*, p. 112.

Rome.[128] Even closet philosophers taking up residence abroad were necessarily sensitive to decisions made by censors in Rome; although they were often indifferent to the nature of the political régime and welcomed patronage from all quarters, including Catholic prelates, aristocrats or kings.

In this regard, it seems necessary to qualify the usual description of science as an enterprise that was especially characteristic of bourgeois capitalism, sober Puritans and a 'rising middle class.'[129] One may grant that a deeper social penetration of literacy encouraged the tapping of more talents and more chance for useful feedback. One may grant also that expanding mercantile enterprise was linked to the expansion of data collection. One may grant finally that many major scientific publication programs were launched by prospering firms such as those of the Estiennes, Oporinus, Plantin, the Elseviers and the Blaeus – few of whom were orthodox Catholics, all of whom were sober business-men and profit-driving entrepreneurs. Nevertheless the support of royal, aristocratic and clerical patrons was also of great importance both to the early printers and to the virtuosi they served. Mechanical toys and ingenious gadgeteers had long been welcome at different courts. Mathematical wizardry along with botanical gardens and zoos continued to flourish under princely protection (as the names of Leibniz and Gauss may suggest). The rulers of several minor principalities on the fringes of the large Bourbon realm were often more helpful to the cosmopolitan French language press than were the entrepreneurs who monopolized the French book-trade in Paris. Despite the com-bination of Puritan attacks on Charles I and Laud with attacks on Ptolemaic and Galenic theories, the connection between early-modern political revolutions and scientific ones is tenuous at best. When Galileo appealed over the heads of Latin-writing professors to the lay vernacular

---

[128] According to Sauvy, *Livres saisis à Paris*, 1678–1701 was the most rigorous period of press censorship during the Ancien Régime. Martin, *Livre à Paris* II, chap. IV also contains relevant data. Hahn, *The Anatomy of a Scientific Institution*, chap. I describes the adverse policy of anonymity and other difficulties which inhibited publication down to 1699. The visit to Charles Plumier in his Paris convent in 1698 by the English zoologist, Martin Lister, seems similar to visits by English virtuosi to Severino and other members of the *Investiganti* in Naples earlier in the century. Friar Plumier (who belonged to the same order as Mersenne) had trouble finding a publisher for his work on American voyages and left masses of un-published manuscripts at his death. See Whitmore, *The Order of Minims*, pp. 186–97. Whit-more also notes difficulties with publication experienced by the *Académie des Sciences*, its inability to get any copies of the *Philosophical Transactions* sent to it during war time, and the damaging effects of excluding friars, such as Plumier, from membership (pp. 109; 189–90).

[129] See e.g. Gillispie, *The Edge of Objectivity*, pp. 114–15.

reading public, he was not enlisting the support of commoners against aristocrats. On the contrary, he repeatedly solicited help from princely patrons to free him from clerkly academic chores and, not incidentally, to protect him from the enemies his publications might provoke.[130]

The need for official protection and for official approval of publication programs probably contributed to the movement to purify science of associations with sorcery and magic. Calvinist disapproval of magic, along with prayers for intercession by supernatural powers, has been plausibly related to this movement by followers of Max Weber. But Anglican and Catholic campaigns against witches and sorcerers also need to be taken into account. When searching for connections between 'religion and the decline of magic,' pressures exerted by censorship deserve consideration. Concern about censorship probably encouraged Catholic virtuosi to press the cause of mechanism especially hard. Mersenne, Gassendi and Descartes thus cast the soul out of nature with particular zeal. When royal controls over printing were swept away during the Commonwealth, however, the more radical English Puritans sided with the Paracelsians and believers in the occult.[131] As was the case with the Mesmerists in eighteenth-century France, these English revolutionaries contributed little if anything to the 'disenchantment of the world.' Even after the Restoration, the 'new philosophy' that was promoted by the Protestant Royal Society was somewhat less mechanistic than the Catholic Cartesian version. Newtonian theories left more leeway for attractive and repulsive forces and more room for Nature's God to behave in mysterious ways.[132]

It was undoubtedly easier for English authorities – whether Puritan, Anglican or both – to regard scientific pursuits as innocuous than was the case in realms where clandestine book routes carried lectures on physics along with all kinds of subversive stuff. Although French Cartesians went further in purging science of magic and tried hard to stay clear of theological debate, they were less successful in neutralizing the new vocation than were the turncoat Puritans who became bishops

130 See e.g. Galileo's complaints to his prospective Medici patron about his teaching chores and his statement, 'I should like my books (dedicated always to my lord) to become my source of income' in his 'Letters on Sunspots,' Drake, *Discoveries and Opinions*, p. 62.

131 See Debus, *Science and Education*; Webster, *The Great Instauration*, and two essays by Rattansi: 'Paracelsus and the Puritan Revolution,' p. 28, 'The Social Interpretation of Science,' pp. 1–33.

132 Westfall, 'Newton and the Hermetic Tradition,' *passim*, discusses the non-mechanistic elements in Newton's ideas of force. Burtt, *Metaphysical Foundations* and Koyré, *From the Closed World* deal with neo-Platonic concepts associated with 'action at a distance' and 'absolute space.'

under the restored Stuart king. In the 'English rehearsal for the European Enlightenment of the eighteenth century, only one feature was missing. There was no hostility to Christianity.'[133] There was also less trouble with clerical censors. Indeed, after the Glorious Revolution, freedom of the press came to England for good. Across the Channel in France, as Voltaire noted, things were ordered differently. Programs associated with the advancement of learning, the spread of literacy and instruction in 'popular mechanics' were not neutral or peaceful in the Bourbon realm. To appreciate the difference one need only compare the quiet reception of Chambers' *Cyclopedia* in England with what happened to the project to translate it into French.

At all events, the description of science as a neutral, value-free enterprise 'au-dessus de la mêlée' was developed by men who were far from neutral on issues pertaining to press censorship and who were committed to achieving a free trade in ideas.[134] Did this commitment disguise an ulterior motive associated with the vested interests of a 'capitalistic bourgeoisie'? It may be easier to agree that it constituted an accurate appraisal by virtuosi of conditions that were essential for their work.

On this one issue the currently unfashionable and undeniably old-fashioned 'Whig interpretation of history' may still have a useful message to convey. Milton's plea for the 'liberty of Unlicenc'd Printing' and his comments in *Areopagitica* about visiting Galileo 'grown old as a prisoner of the Inquisition for thinking in Astronomy otherwise than the Dominican licensers thought' ought not to be lightly dismissed as *nothing* but anti-Papist propaganda – although it certainly was that. Granted that the case of Galileo was exploited to the hilt by Protestant publicists and pamphleteers such as Milton himself, it was not merely used to link science with Protestantism. It disclosed a link that had been forged ever since printing industries had begun to flourish in Wittenberg and Geneva and had begun to decline in Venice and Lyons. The continuous operation of printing firms beyond the reach of Rome was of vital concern to Western European scientists. The case of Galileo simply drove this lesson further home.

[133] Gillispie, *Edge of Objectivity*, p. 114.
[134] In his *History of The Royal Society*, part 2, p. 64, Sprat expressed the desire of the virtuosi to make the Society 'the general Banck and Freeport of the World.'

CONCLUSION:
SCRIPTURE AND NATURE
TRANSFORMED

The elements which go into the making of 'modernity' may be seen...
first...in the sixteenth and seventeenth centuries. Some historians attributed
the change to the liberation of men's minds during the Renaissance and the
Reformation. Today many historians would be more likely to stress the
conservatism of these two movements...Their emphasis tends instead to
fall on...'the Scientific Revolution.'

By this is meant above all the imaginative achievements associated with
the names of Copernicus, Galileo and Newton...Within the space of a century and a half a revolution had occurred in the way in which men regarded
the universe. Most of this was made possible by the application of mathematics to the problems of the natural world...

All this is by now well known...though many of the details are still to
be worked out...What is not clear is how it all came about...[1]

This book has been aimed at developing a new strategy for handling the
issues posed by the above citation. It seems futile to argue over 'the
elements which go into the making of modernity,' for 'modernity'
itself is always in flux; always subject to definitions which have to be
changed in order to keep up with changing times. As the age of Planck
and Einstein recedes into the past, 'achievements associated with Copernicus, Galileo and Newton' will probably come to share the fate of the
achievements of earlier Renassiance humanists and Protestant reformers.
Indeed recent interpretations of Copernicus show that his work is
already coming to seem more and more conservative; less and less
associated with emancipation from traditional modes of thought.
Pointing early-modern science toward an elusive modernity leads to
invidious comparisons between 'liberating' later movements and

[1] Kearney, introduction, *Origins of the Scientific Revolution*, p. xi.

earlier 'conservative' ones and brings us no closer to understanding 'how it all came about.'

To ask historians to search for elements which entered into the making of an indefinite 'modernity' seems somewhat futile. To consider the effects of a definite communications shift which entered into each of the movements under discussion seems more promising. Among other advantages this approach offers a chance to uncover relationships which debates over modernity only serve to conceal. Thus one may avoid entanglement in arguments over whether the first-born sons of modern Europe were to be found among the humanists of Renaissance Italy, or whether we must wait for the Pope to be defied by Luther, or for the Calvinists to turn Geneva into a Protestant Rome; or whether genuine modernity came with the scientific revolution or should be postponed even further until industrialization. Energies can be directed toward the more constructive task of discerning, in each of the contested movements, features which were not present in earlier epochs and which altered the textual traditions upon which each movement relied.

By setting aside the quest for theoretical 'modernizing' processes and focusing attention on the paradoxical consequences of a real duplicating process, it should be possible to handle periodization problems more deftly. We may see how movements aimed at returning to a golden past (whether classical or early Christian) were reoriented in a manner that pointed away from their initial goal and how the very process of recovering long-lost texts carried successive generations ever farther away from the experience of the Church Fathers and of the poets and orators of antiquity. We may also see how lay humanists, priests and natural philosophers alike shared the common experience of acquiring new means to achieve old ends and that this experience led in turn to a division of opinion and ultimately to a reassessment of inherited views.

To adopt this strategy does not make it possible to provide a complete answer to questions of 'how it all came about' but does open the way to supplying more adequate answers than have been offered up to now. Thus we would be in a better position to explain why long-lived scientific theories were deemed less acceptable even before new observations, new experiments, or new instruments had been made.

It is one of the paradoxes of the whole story with which we have to deal that the most sensational step leading to the scientific revolution in astronomy was taken long before the discovery of the telescope – even before... improvement...in observations made with the naked eye...William Harvey...carried out his revolutionary work before any serviceable kind of microscope had become available...even Galileo discusses the ordinary phenomena of everyday life[and]...plays with pellets on inclined planes in a manner that had long been customary...[2]

Current efforts to account for this seeming paradox do not take us very far. We are asked to guess about a transformation that took 'place inside the minds of the scientists themselves,' when they 'put on new thinking caps' to gaze at the unchanging heavens. Yet the technical literature upon which astronomers relied had undergone change even before the 'new thinking caps' were put on. More careful consideration of the shift that altered the output and intake of this literature would help to explain the timing of the 'sensational step' and also help us analyze its relationship to other 'modernizing' trends.

When considering Copernicus' intellectual environment, changes wrought by printing deserve a more central place. Present tactics either encourage us to wander too far afield compiling lists of everything that happened and marvelling at the general turbulence of the times, or else trap us into prolonging old debates – between Platonists and Aristotelians, scholastics and humanists; Catholics and Protestants, Anglicans and Puritans, even, on occasion, between Italians, Germans, Danes and Poles. By placing more emphasis on the shift from script to print, many diverse trends may be accommodated without resort to an indiscriminate mélange and in a way that avoids prolongation of intellectual feuds. The sixteenth-century astronomer may be seen to owe something to the neo-Platonists and to the Renaissance Aristotelians; to his masters in Catholic Poland and Italy and to a disciple from Protestant Wittenberg later on; to calculations made by ancient Alexandrians, observations made by medieval Arabs and to a trigonometry text compiled in Nuremberg around the time he was born.

We are less likely to set Plato against Aristotle or any one textual tradition against another when we appreciate the significance of setting many disparate texts side by side. The character of Copernicus' studies and of the currents of thought which influenced him are certainly

[2] Butterfield, *Origins of Modern Science*, p. 1.

worth studying. But this investigation should not divert us from recognizing the novelty of being able to assemble diverse records and reference guides, and of being able to study them without having to transcribe them at the same time. If we want to explain heightened awareness of anomalies or discontent with inherited schemes then it seems especially important to emphasize the wider range of reading-matter that was being surveyed at one time by a single pair of eyes.

Similarly in seeking to explain why naked-eye observation produced unprecedented results, it is worth paying more attention to the increased output of materials relating to comets and conjunctions and the increased number of simultaneous observations made of single celestial events. Nor should we neglect to note how stars which faded from the heavens (and brief landfalls made on distant shores) could be fixed permanently in precise locations after printed maps began to replace hand-copied ones. Although inferior maps continued to be duplicated and many map-publishers perpetuated errors for a century and more, a process of transmission had been fundamentally reoriented when this replacement occurred. Analogies with inertial motion do not apply to this sort of reversal. When considering a shift in direction it is misleading to draw analogies with uniform motion in a straight line. Since corrupt data were duplicated and thus perpetuated by print, one may say that scribal corruption was prolonged for some time. But one must also take into account that an age-old process of corruption was being decisively arrested and was eventually reversed. With proper supervision, fresh data could at long last be duplicated without being blurred or blotted out over the course of time.

By making more room for new features introduced by typography we would also be better situated to explain the timing of 'the application of mathematics to the problems of the natural world.' By considering the difficulties faced by astronomers, assayers, surveyors, merchants, mint masters and all others who tried to use the language of number in the age of scribes, and by recognizing how new incentives encouraged instrument-makers and reckon-masters to publicize their wares, the victories won by quantitative analysis could be better explained. By paying more attention to the duplication of pictorial statements, we might see more clearly why the life sciences no less than the physical ones were placed on a new footing and how the authority of Pliny, no less than that of Galen and Ptolemy, was undermined.

Even while acknowledging the importance of the empirical movement
and of the slogan 'from books to nature' it should be noted that dissatisfaction with literature inherited from scribes coincided with the
development of new forms of data collection. The advent of printing
made it possible for more of nature to be put into books. Here as elsewhere, claims made for the significance of particular developments in
special fields such as Renaissance art or Renaissance Aristotelianism
need to be coupled with more consideration of how separate developments (the separate talents of painters and physicians, for example)
could be coordinated and combined. When Agricola and Vesalius hired
illustrators to render 'veins' or 'vessels' for their texts, they were
launching an unprecedented enterprise and not simply continuing
trends that manuscript illuminators had begun.

The advantages of issuing identical images bearing identical labels
to scattered observers who could feed back information to publishers
enabled astronomers, geographers, botanists and zoologists to expand
data pools far beyond all previous limits – even those set by the
exceptional resources of the long-lasting Alexandrian Museum. Old
limits set by the pillars of Hercules and the outermost sphere of the
Grecian heavens were incapable of containing findings registered in
ever expanding editions of atlases and sky maps. The closed world of
the ancients was opened, vast expanses of space (and later of time)
previously associated with divine mysteries became subject to human
calculation and exploration. The same cumulative cognitive advance
which excited cosmological speculation also led to new concepts of
knowledge. The closed sphere or single corpus, passed down from
generation to generation, was replaced by an open-ended investigatory
process pressing against ever advancing frontiers.

In attempting to explain 'how it all came about,' finally, new elements involving coordination and cooperation deserve not only more
attention but also a more central place. When searching for the nurseries of a new philosophy, it seems unprofitable to linger too long in
any one region, university, court or town – or focus too much attention
on any one special skill or special scientific field. Certain universities,
ateliers or lay academies may be singled out for special contributions.
But the chief new feature that needs further attention is the simultaneous tapping of many varied talents at the same time. As the chief
sponsors of field trips, open letters, advertisements for instruments and

technical handbooks of all kinds, early printers ought to receive as much attention as is currently given to special occupational groups such as Paduan professors, Wittenberg botanists or quattrocento artist-engineers. Publication programs launched from urban workshops in many regions made it possible to coordinate scattered efforts and to expand the scope of investigations until (like the Blaeu *Grand Atlas*) they became truly world-wide.

Attempts to account for the rapid growth and expansion of scientific enterprise during the century of genius may be handled in much the same manner as treatments of nurseries, seed-beds and births. In explaining the 'acceleration of scientific advance,' there is much disagreement over whether to stress the role played by individual genius, the internal evolution of a speculative tradition, a new alliance between intellectuals and artisans, or a host of concurrent socio-economic or religious changes affecting the 'environment against which these discoveries took place.'[3] To say that argument over such issues is pointless, because *all* these 'factors' were at work, still leaves open the question of how and why they became operative when they did. Unless some new strategy is devised to handle this question, the old argument will break out once again. Since it perpetually revolves about the same issues, diminishing returns soon set in. One advantage of bringing printing into the discussion is that it enables us to tackle the open question directly without prolonging the same controversy *ad infinitum*.

As previous remarks suggest, the effects produced by printing may be plausibly related to an increased incidence of creative acts, to internally transformed speculative traditions, to exchanges between intellectuals and artisans, and indeed to each of the contested factors in current disputes. Thus we need not invoke some sort of 'mutation in the human gene pool' to explain an entire 'century of genius' nor do we need to deny that random motives (both personal and playful) entered into the successful puzzle-solving of the age. Without detracting from the strong personal flavor of each separate creative act, we may also make room for the new print technology which made food for thought much more abundant and allowed mental energies to be more efficiently used.

A similar approach would also take us further toward bridging the false dichotomy between the life of science and that of society at large.

---

[3] Kearney, 'Puritanism, Capitalism and the Scientific Revolution,' p. 81.

Changes wrought by printing had a more immediate effect on cerebral activities and on the learned professions than did many other kinds of 'external' events. Previous relations between masters and disciples were altered. Students who took full advantage of technical texts which served as silent instructors were less likely to defer to traditional authority and more receptive to innovating trends. Young minds provided with updated editions, especially of mathematical texts, began to surpass not only their own elders but the wisdom of ancients as well. Methods of measurement, records of observations and all forms of data collection were affected by printing. So too were the careers that could be pursued by teachers and preachers, physicians and surgeons, reckon-masters and artist-engineers. 'It is easy to agree with...contentions that a neat separation of internal and external factors is out of the question...but, as G. R. Elton wrote several years ago, there is work to be done rather than called for.'[4]

Before work can be done, however, some promising avenues of inquiry have to be opened up and more attention given to the presence of new workshops alongside older lecture halls. Printed materials should be allowed to affect thought-patterns, facilitate problem-solving, and, in general, penetrate the 'life of the mind.' Printers themselves must be allowed to work with Latin-writing professors as well as with vernacular-writing publicists and pamphleteers. In other words, the divisions that are often assumed to separate scholars from craftsmen, universities from urban workshops need to be reappraised.

This point applies to theories which internalize scientific problem-solving to the extent of ignoring the communications revolution and neglecting its possible relevance to the lectures and studies of learned men. It also applies to theories which deny that churchmen and school-men are capable of launching innovating trends. In this respect, Marxist theories of class struggle seem to be more of a hindrance than a help. To set an avant garde of early capitalists against a rear guard of Latin-reading clerks does little to clarify medieval developments and much to conceal the new interchanges that came after print shops spread. There are perfectly good reasons for associating printers with merchants and capitalists. There are none for detaching them from association with professors and friars – especially in the age of scholar-printers, when close collaboration was the rule. Indeed preachers and

---

[4] 'Toward a New History,' *Times Literary Supplement*.

teachers often turned to new forms of publicity with less conflict than did artisans accustomed to preserving trade secrets. Early printers were invited to set up presses in monasteries and colleges, while schoolmasters and tutors were much in demand as editors and translators. The formation of lay cultural centers outside universities and of the vernacular translation movement was of major significance. But no less significant were changes that affected university faculties and students seeking professional degrees. When Latin-writing professional élites are insulated from the effects of the new technology, internal divisions within the scholarly community become more puzzling than they need be and a rare opportunity to watch 'external' forces enter into the 'internal' life of science is lost.

These points carry beyond the special field of the history of science to the more general problem of relating socio-economic and political developments to intellectual and cultural ones. Attention focused on a communications shift encourages us to relate mind to society and at the same time to avoid forcing connections between economic class and intellectual superstructure, in order to fit a prefabricated scheme. Plausible relationships can be traced by taking into account the connecting links provided by a new communications network which coordinated diverse intellectual activities while producing tangible commodities to be marketed for profit. Since their commodities were sponsored and censored by officials as well as consumed by literate groups, the activities of early printers provide a natural connection between the movement of ideas, economic developments and affairs of church and state.

The policies pursued by merchant publishers offer a useful corrective to the conventional wisdom which opposes 'forward-looking' centralizing rulers and nation-building statesmen to 'backward' petty principalities and late medieval walled city states. The printing industries represented a 'forward-looking,' large-scale enterprise which flourished better in small loosely federated realms than in well consolidated larger ones. Printers also injected into diverse Protestant literary cultures foreign secular ingredients which will appear anomalous unless the peculiar workings of a censored book-trade are taken into account. When tracing the movement of ideas from Catholic South to Protestant North, factors which led to the prior movement of printing industries ought to be given due weight. How the center of gravity of the Republic of Letters shifted from sixteenth-century Venice to late seventeenth-century Amsterdam warrants special consideration in any social history of ideas.

When searching for the 'seedplots of Enlightenment thought' the *modus operandi* of the more celebrated master printers (such as Aldus Manutius, Robert Estienne, Oporinus, Plantin) deserves a closer look and so too does the relatively aristocratic nature of their clientèle. As Martin Lowry's forthcoming biography of Aldus points out; when the Venetian printer discarded the large folio in favor of a smaller octavo format he was aiming at serving the convenience of scholar–diplomats and patrician councillors of state. He was not thinking, somewhat absurdly, of tapping popular markets with texts devoted to classical Greek works. From the Aldine octavo of the 1500s to the Elsevier duodecimo of the 1630s the circulation of convenient pocket-sized editions altered circumstances within the Commonwealth of Learning, first of all. Before assuming that an altered world view implies the rise of a new class, it seems worth devoting more thought to intellectual regroupment among Latin-reading élites. By this means we may also rectify an imbalance created by current emphasis on popularizing trends and mass movements.

In this age when the paperback book is probably doing more to change the process of science education than all the new teaching methods, it should not be difficult to appreciate the intimate connection between the printer's craft and that of science...

If science helped give birth to the printed book, it was clearly the printed book that sent science from its medieval habits straight into the boiling scientific revolution...It was of course the rapid dissemination of knowledge to whole new classes that created the modern new attitudes to both science and religion at the end of the fifteenth century.[5]

This statement may have some validity with regard to the religious Reformation, but does not seem to apply to early-modern science. Mentelin's German Bible appeared in 1460, and forty years of vernacular Bible-printing (along with the increased output of other devotional literature) need to be considered when setting the stage for the Lutheran Revolt. But despite the early date of Regiomontanus' Nuremberg press (1474), the end of the fifteenth century still seems much too early to think of scientific knowledge being 'rapidly disseminated to whole new classes' by means of the printed word. Even later on, as we have

[5] Price, 'The Book as a Scientific Instrument,' pp. 102–4.

noted, Latin treatises by Copernicus, Harvey and Kepler were not disseminated in the same manner as Lutheran Bibles, broadsides and tracts. Bestsellerdom was reserved for prognostications and Sacrobosco's *Sphaera*. In 1500, Latin-learning was still restricted, scientific translation movements were just getting under way, the corrupted materials which were being duplicated had not yet been sorted out. To jump from 'the birth of the printed book' to the creation of 'modern new attitudes' so precipitously and by means of popularization raises doubts about assigning any significance to the advent of printing for scientific change. The precipitous jump also detaches the Reformation from the Copernican Revolution, while reinforcing the view that mobilization of 'whole new classes' is the only conceivable motor of major historical change.

The evangelical impulse which powered early presses had the most rapid spectacular consequences and provoked mass participation of new kinds. But this should not divert attention from more subtle yet equally irreversible transformations which altered the world view of Latin-reading élites. Several new features other than dissemination which were introduced by printing entered into the scientific revolution and played an essential part in the religious reformation as well. In relating the two movements we need to consider the way old attitudes were being implemented within learned communities, before expecting new attitudes to be created, let alone knowledge to be disseminated to whole new classes. Even when dealing with evangelical trends, this approach has merit. Earlier attitudes exhibited by Lollards, Waldensians, Hussites and the Brethren of the Common Life were being newly implemented by printing before full-fledged Protestant doctrines were born. In setting the stage for the Reformation, moreover, some attention must be given to those many pre-Reformation controversies which had less to do with vernacular translation than with trilingual studies and learned exegesis of Latin texts. In the scholar–printer's workshop, editors of patristic and of Alexandrian texts had a common point of encounter. More attention to changes affecting textual transmission among learned élites should bring us closer to understanding how different strands of early-modern intellectual history may be related to each other. In particular, it may help to clarify the relationship between religious and scientific change.

Thus we may see that the fate of texts inherited from Aristotle,

Galen and Ptolemy had much in common with that of texts inherited from Saint Jerome. Just as scribal scholars had all they could do to emend Saint Jerome's version and to protect it from further corruption, so too did medieval astronomers labor to preserve and emend Ptolemy's *Great Composition*. Much as trilingual studies, repeatedly called for, did not get launched until after the advent of printing; so too was reform of the Julian calendar frequently requested and never obtained. After the advent of printing, Jerome's version was protected from further corruption only to be threatened by the annotations of scholars who had acquired mastery of Hebrew and Greek. Similarly, Ptolemy's work was no sooner emended and purified than it too came under attack. As the 'second Ptolemy,' Copernicus (despite his personal distance from print shops) was cast in much the same role as was Erasmus who had set out to re-do the work of Saint Jerome. Both men set out to fulfill traditional programs: to emend the Bible and reform the Church; to emend the *Almagest* and help with calendar reform; but both used means that were untraditional and this propelled their work in an unconventional direction, so that they broke new paths in the very act of seeking to achieve old goals.

The new issues posed by sixteenth-century path-breaking works also led natural philosophers and theologians to divide along similar lines. Conservatives within both groups were placed in the awkward position of departing from precedents even while defending the *status quo*. Defenders of Aristotle and Galen who sought to fine professors for departing from fixed texts resembled those defenders of Jerome's translation who censored scholars for annotating scriptural editions. At the same time many churchmen and lay professors were attracted by new opportunities extended by printers to reach a wider audience, win new patrons and achieve celebrity. Members of both groups contributed their services as editors, translators, and authors to popular as well as to scholarly trends. Theologians who argued for a priesthood of all believers and translated Bibles were in much the same position as the friars, physicians and schoolmasters who compiled craft manuals and translated mathematical and medical texts. The vernacular translation movement not only enabled evangelists to bring the Gospel to Everyman but also tapped a vast reservoir of latent scientific talent by eliciting contributions from reckon-masters, instrument-makers and artist-engineers. Protestant encouragement of lay reading and self-help was especially favorable for interchanges between readers and publishers – which led to the quiet displacement of ancient authorities, such as Pliny, and to expansive data collection of a new kind. Finally the same censorship policies and élitist tendencies that discouraged Catholic Bible-printers eventually closed down scientific publication outlets in Catholic lands.

But although Protestant exploitation of printing linked the Reformation to early-modern science in diverse ways, and although scientific publication was increasingly taken over by Protestant printing firms, evangelists and virtuosi were still using the new powers of print for fundamentally different ends. The latter aimed not at spreading God's words but at deciphering His handiwork. The only way to 'open' the book of nature to public inspection required (paradoxically) a preliminary encoding of data into ever more sophisticated equations, diagrams, models and charts. For virtuosi the uses of publicity were much more problematic than for evangelists. The case of Galileo may be misleading in this regard. Exploiting his flair for publicity and gifts as a polemicist, he *did* act as a proselytizer for the Copernican cause. Catholic friars such as Bruno, Campanella and Foscarini also exhibited a kind of evangelical zeal in the same cause. So, too, did Rheticus, in his master's behalf. Nevertheless the downfall of Ptolemy, Galen and Aristotle did not come about as a result of cartoons and pamphleteering. Scientific change follows a different pattern than religious revivals. Publication was indispensable for anyone seeking to make a scientific contribution but the kind of publicity which made for bestsellerdom was often undesirable. Even now, reputable scientists fear the sensational coverage which comes from premature exposure of their views. Early-modern virtuosi had even better reasons for such fears. Many Copernicans (including Copernicus himself) took advantage of printed materials while shrinking from publicity. Many Puritan publicists and disciples of Francis Bacon proselytized on behalf of a 'new science' without favoring or even comprehending the technical Latin treatises which marked significant advance.

Visionary schemes for promoting useful knowledge, belief in science for the citizen and mathematics for the millions did, to be sure, enter into the views of the group responsible for launching the *Transactions* of the Royal Society. Nevertheless, contributions to this pioneering scientific journal were of significance insofar as they accomplished the purpose Oldenburg conveyed in his letter to Malpighi: to 'bring out the opinion of all the learned.' To make possible consensual validation by trained observers, experimenters and mathematicians entailed a different use of the press than efforts to spread glad tidings to all men. Eventually, access to scientific journals and societies was shut to all save a professionally trained élite. The rise of modern science entailed the discrediting, not only of Aristotelians, Galenists or Ptolemaists but also of self-proclaimed healers, 'empirics' and miracle workers who attacked book learning while publicizing themselves. From Paracelsus through Mesmer and on to the present, the press has lent itself to the purposes of pseudo-scientists as well as those of real scientists, and it is not always easy to tell the two groups apart. Distinguishing between scientific journals and sensational journalism is relatively simple at present. But during the early years of the Royal Society when sightings of monsters and marvels were still being credited and recorded, the two genres were easily confused. Confusion was further compounded by the workings of the Index which lumped dull treatises on physics with more sensational forbidden tracts and transformed advocacy of Copernicanism into a patriotic Protestant cause.

Thus an English Paracelsian did not find it incongruous to place the secretive Latin-writing Catholic Copernicus in the company of Lutheran reformers for having 'brought Ptolemeus' Rules Astronomicall and Tables of Motions' to 'their former puritie.' His argument suggests that Protestants linked the fate of the Vulgate with that of the *Almagest* – along lines which are by now familiar to the readers of this book. Much as the Protestants had purified Scripture, he said, 'by expelling the clowdes of Romish religion which had darkened the trueth of the worde of God,' so too Copernicus had purified tables which had become corrupted 'by a long excesse of time.'[6] Copernicus was thus cast in much the same conservative role as the editor of the London 'Polyglotte' who claimed in his Prospectus to have freed the Scriptures 'from error, from the negligence of scribes, the injury of times, the wilful corruption of sectaries and heretics.'[7] This relatively

---

[6] Cited by Allen Debus, *The English Paracelsians*, p. 59, from a treatise by 'R. Bostocke Esq.,' London, 1585. Although Bostocke's comment seems to be pointed at the *Prutenic Tables* which were compiled by Erasmus Reinhold who used calculations in Copernicus' *De Revolutionibus* but rejected the geokinetic hypothesis, it probably implied, in the author's mind, support of the latter hypothesis.

[7] Brian Walton's *Prospectus* for the London 'Polyglotte' of 1657 is cited by Hendricks, 'Profitless Printing.'

conservative Erasmian theme with its emphasis on emendation and purification also lent itself to the purposes of those who sought to legitimize the Royal Society, as is suggested by the often-cited comment from Bishop Sprat's *History of the Royal Society*. The Royal Society and the Anglican Church, the Bishop said, 'both may lay equal claim to the word Reformation,'

the one having compassed it in Religion, the other purposing it in Philosophy...They both have taken a like course to bring this about each of them passing by the corrupt copies and referring themselves to the perfect originals for their instruction; the one to Scripture the other to the huge Volume of Creatures...[8]

It seems significant that when such remarks are cited by historians they are not seen to relate to the shift from script to print (despite the reference to the passing by of 'corrupt copies') but are used instead to reiterate the Bishop's three-hundred-year-old claim that the Reformation and the scientific revolution are somehow connected. As long as printing is left out of account this thesis seems destined to engender an inconclusive debate. To leave printing out of the picture is not only to conceal significant links but also to overlook equally important disjunctions.

Scriptural and scientific traditions had taken a 'like course' in the age of scribes. By the time of the Reformation, however, they had come to a parting of the ways. Even while providing both biblical scholars and natural philosophers with new means of achieving long-lived goals, the new technology had driven a wedge between the two groups and was propelling them in different directions.

Until the advent of printing, scientific inquiries about 'how the heavens go' were linked with religious concerns about 'how to go to heaven.' Erasmus and Copernicus had shared a common interest in deciphering ancient place names and dating old records. Insofar as the movable holy festival of Easter posed problems, astronomers were needed to help the Church commemorate Gospel truths. After the advent of printing, however, the study of celestial mechanics was propelled in new directions and soon reached levels of sophistication that left calendrical problems and ancient schemes of reckoning far behind. The need to master philology or learn Greek became ever more

---

[8] Sprat, *History of the Royal Society*, part 3, section 23, p. 371. This citation appears in works by S. F. Mason, D. S. Kemsley, R. Hooykaas and others mentioned in chap. 8 above.

important for Bible study and ever less so for nature study. Indeed, difficulties engendered by diverse Greek and Arabic expressions, by medieval Latin abbreviations, by confusion between Roman letters and numbers, by neologisms, copyists' errors and the like were so successfully overcome that modern scholars are frequently absent-minded about the limitations on progress in the mathematical sciences which scribal procedures imposed.[9] From Roger Bacon's day to that of Francis Bacon, mastery of geometry, astronomy or optics had gone together with the retrieval of ancient texts and pursuit of Greek studies. But by the seventeenth century, Nature's language was being emancipated from the old confusion of tongues. Diverse names for flora and fauna became less confusing when placed beneath identical pictures. Constellations and landmasses could be located without recourse to uncertain etymologies, once placed on uniform maps and globes. Logarithm tables and slide rules provided common measures for surveyors in different lands. Whereas the Vulgate was followed by a succession of polyglot editions and multiplying variants; the downfall of the *Almagest* paved the way for the formulation by Newton of a few elegant simple universal laws. The development of neutral pictorial and mathematical vocabularies made possible a large-scale pooling of talents for analyzing data, and led to the eventual achievement of a consensus that cut across all the old frontiers.

Vesalius' recourse to pictorial statements like Galileo's preference for circles and triangles suggests why it is unwise to dwell too long on whether treatises were written in the vernacular or in Latin, and why parallels between evangelical reformers and early-modern scientists should not be pressed too far. Many proponents of the new philosophy favored plain speaking and opposed mystification just as did evangelical reformers. Nevertheless the language employed by new astronomers and anatomists was still incomprehensible to the untutored layman and did not resemble anything spoken by the man in the street. For the most part, it was an *unspoken* language quite unlike that favored by

---

9 Such absent-mindedness is reinforced by modern editions such as the splendid volume on medieval manuscript versions of Archimedes by Clagett, *Archimedes* where the author has taken pains to exclude 'corrupt and senseless readings,' to reconstruct diagrams where figures were obscure and incorrect, to convert a mixture of Roman numerals and rhetorical expressions into consistently used Indo-Arabic numerals, etc. (pp. xv, 36–7); in short: to eliminate just those aspects of major technical works which gave the most trouble before print. On confusion over terms such as cipher and zero which came from the same Arabic word, see Dantzig, *Number*, p. 32.

Protestants who preserved links between pulpit and press in seeking to spread the Word. Recourse to 'silent instructors' conveying precisely detailed non-phonetic messages helped to free technical literature from semantic snares. 'The reign of words' had ended, noted Fontenelle in 1733, 'things' were now in demand. Two hundred years earlier, verbal dispute was already being abandoned in favor of visual demonstration.

I dare affirm a man shall more profit in one week by figures and charts well and perfectly made than he shall by the only reading or hearing the rules of that science by the space of half a year at the least.

So wrote Thomas Elyot in 1531, in the course of recommending courses in drawing to educators.[10]

Publication before printing had often entailed giving dictation or reading aloud. In contrast to scribal culture which had fostered 'hearing the rules of a given science,' print culture made possible the simultaneous distribution of 'well made figures and charts.' In this way, it not only transformed communications within the Commonwealth of Learning, but laid the basis for new confidence in human capacity to arrive at certain knowledge of the 'laws of Nature and of Nature's God.'

What threatened the very foundations of the Church was the new concept of truth proclaimed by Galileo. Alongside the truth of revelation comes now an independent and original truth of nature. This truth is revealed not in God's words but in his work; it is not based on the testimony of Scripture or tradition but is visible to us at all times. But it is understandable only to those who know nature's handwriting and can decipher her text. The truth of nature cannot be expressed in mere words...[but]...in mathematical constructions, figures and numbers. And in these symbols nature presents itself in perfect form and clarity. Revelation by means of the sacred word can never achieve...such precision, for words are always...ambiguous... Their meaning must always be given them by man...In nature...the whole plan of the universe lies before us.[11]

This famous passage brilliantly describes a major intellectual transformation but stops short of explaining why it happened when it did. Cassirer's description needs to be supplemented by noting that 'mathematical constructions, figures and numbers' had not always presented themselves 'in perfect form and clarity.' 'To discover the truth of

---

[10] Cited from *Boke called the Gouvernour* (1531) by Watson, *The Beginning of Teaching*, p. 136.
[11] Cassirer, *The Philosophy of the Enlightenment*, p. 43.

propositions in Euclid,' wrote John Locke, 'there is little need or use of revelation, God having furnished us with a natural and surer means to arrive at knowledge of them.'[12] In the eleventh century, however, God had not furnished Western scholars with a natural or sure means of grasping a Euclidean theorem. Instead the most learned men in Christendom engaged in a fruitless search to discover what Euclid meant when referring to interior angles.[13]

A new confidence in the accuracy of mathematical constructions, figures and numbers was predicated on a method of duplication that transcended older limits imposed by time and space and that presented identical data in identical form to men who were otherwise divided by cultural and geographical frontiers. The same confidence was generated by pictorial statements which, as Sir Joseph Banks observed, provided a common measure which spoke 'universally to all mankind.' It was conveyed by the maps to which Kenneth Boulding assigns an 'extraordinary authority greater than that of all sacred books.'[14] But it was not generated by the scholarly controversies which accompanied the expanding editions of the sacred book of Western Christendom.

Even while the study of nature was increasingly freed from translation problems, the study of Scripture was becoming more ensnared. Not only did vernacular translations fragment the religious experience of the peoples of Latin Christendom and help to precipitate prolonged civil wars; but successive polyglot versions brought the erudite scholars of the Commonwealth of Learning no closer to finding the pure original words of God. Tycho Brahe, confronted by conflicting astronomical tables based on corrupted data, could carry out his vow to check both versions against a 'pure original' – against fresh observation of uncorrupted 'writing in the sky.' But dissatisfaction with corrupted copies of Saint Jerome's Latin translation could not be overcome in the same way. Instead it led to multilingual confusion and a thickening special literature devoted to variants and alternative theories of composition. The mystical illumination which had presided over creation flickered ever more dimly as pedants argued about how to date the event and how to authenticate versions of Genesis. Baroque monuments of erudition, which had been designed to obtain a clear view of the

---

[12] John Locke, *An Essay on Human Understanding*, book IV, chap. XVIII.
[13] See chap. 5 n. 133, above, for reference to Southern's account of Fulbert of Chartres.
[14] See chap. 5 n. 46, above, for reference to Sir Joseph's comment. For discussion of Boulding's disassociated transcript, see pp. 478 ff, above.

divine will, not only fell short of their objective. In the end, they made it seem more elusive than before.

It is surely one of the ironies of the history of Western civilization that Bible studies aimed at penetrating Gothic darkness in order to recover pure Christian truth – aimed, that is, at removing glosses and commentaries in order to lay bare the pure 'plain' text – ended by interposing an impenetrable thicket of recondite annotation between Bible-reader and Holy Book. In his inaugural lecture at Wittenberg, the young Philip Melanchthon scornfully referred to the neglect of Greek studies by angelic doctors, to the superficial glosses of ignorant scribes and to the soiling of sacred Scriptures with foreign matter. He called for a return to the 'pure' Greek and Hebrew sources.[15] But the more trilingual studies progressed, the more scholars wrangled over the meaning of words and phrases and even over the placement of vowel points. The very waters from which the Latinists drank became roiled and muddy as debates among scholars were prolonged. Hobbes and Spinoza both plunged into Bible study and found in the sharp clarity of Euclidean proofs a refreshing contrast to the murky ambiguities of scriptural texts. Sir William Petty protested against teaching boys 'hard Hebrew words in the Bible' and contrasted the profitable 'study of things to a Rabble of Words.'[16] We have already encountered Sir Thomas Browne's preference for 'Archimedes who speaketh exactly' as against 'the sacred text which speaketh largely.' Robert Boyle might endow a lecture series to reconcile scriptural revelation with the mathematical principles of natural philosophy; Isaac Newton might struggle to prove Old Testament tales conformed to a chronology that meshed with celestial clockwork. God's 'two books,' nevertheless, had come to a parting of the ways.

One day in the eighteenth century, some Swedish scientists discovered a certain alteration in the shores of the Baltic...the theologians of Stockholm made representations to the Government that 'this remark of the... scientists, not being consistent with Genesis must be condemned.' To whom reply was made that God had made both the Baltic and Genesis...if there was any contradiction between the two works, the error must lie in the copies we have of the book than in the Baltic Sea of which we have the original.[17]

[15] Melanchthon's lecture is cited in Hillerbrand (ed), *The Reformation*, pp. 59–60.
[16] Petty's comments, are cited by Jones, *Ancients and Moderns*, p. 91.
[17] Arthur Wilson, *Diderot*, p. 143.

Thus the effect of printing on Bible study was in marked contrast with its effect on nature study. This contrast is concealed when one places an exclusive emphasis on popularizing themes, and couples the spread of vernacular Bibles with that of technical texts. It is also obscured by the anti-papist propaganda which linked the emendation of the *Almagest* with that of the Vulgate. Corruption by copyists had provided churchmen and astronomers with a common enemy; but once this enemy was vanquished, former collaborators took divergent paths. To observe this divergence requires studying internal transformations within a Commonwealth of Learning where Latin Bibles had long been studied although full polyglot editions had not been seen. In addition to new problems posed for this community by polyglot versions of sacred words, old limits set on data collection and new advantages provided by printed tables, charts and maps also need to be taken into account. One may then set the stage for Enlightenment thought without resorting to vague concepts such as 'modernity' or becoming entangled in debates over bourgeois ideology. At least in my view the changes wrought by printing provide the most plausible point of departure for explaining how confidence shifted from divine revelation to mathematical reasoning and man-made maps.

The fact that religious and scientific traditions were affected by printing in markedly different ways points to the complex and contradictory nature of the communications shift, and suggests the futility of trying to encapsulate its consequences in any one formula. When considering Protestant iconoclasm or increased Bible-reading, it may seem useful to envisage a movement going from 'image to word'; but one must be prepared to use the reverse formula 'word to image' when setting the stage for the rise of modern science. In the latter case, printing reduced translation problems, transcended linguistic divisions and helped to bridge earlier divisions between university lectures and artisan crafts. In religious affairs, however, the communications shift had a divisive effect; permanently fragmenting Western Christendom along both geographic and sociological lines. Not only were Catholic regions set off from Protestant ones but within different regions religious experience was also internally bifurcated. Loss of confidence in God's words among cosmopolitan élites was coupled with enhanced opportunities for evangelists and priests to spread glad tidings and rekindle faith. Enlightened deists who adhered to the 'Laws of Nature and Nature's

God' were thus placed at a distance from enthusiasts who were caught up in successive waves of religious revivals.

In all regions the ebb and flow of religious devotion affected diverse social strata at different times. But the Bible became 'the treasure of the humble,' with unpredictable consequences only in Protestant realms. Among Protestants, the universalistic impulse to spread the Gospel far and wide had special paradoxical results. Vernacular Bibles authorized by Protestant rulers helped to Balkanize Christendom and to nationalize what had previously been a more cosmopolitan sacred book. Bible-reading householders acquired an enhanced sense of spiritual dignity and individual worth. An 'inner light' kindled by the printed word became the basis for the shared mystical experiences of separate sects. Yet even while spiritual life was being enriched, it was also being tarnished by commercial drives. Where indulgence sellers were discredited, Bible salesmen multiplied.

In print shops especially, old missionary impulses were combined with the demands imposed by an expanding capitalist enterprise. In the early-modern print shop, however, several other impulses also converged. Was the driving power of capitalism stronger than the long-lived drive for fame? Both together surely were stronger than either one alone. Did not the presses also offer rulers a way of extending their charisma and furnish significant help to impersonal bureaucrats as well? Among map-publishers, reckon-masters and artisans, as we have seen, printing acted by a kind of marvelous alchemy to transmute private interest into public good. It also catered to the vanity of pedants, artists and literati. When dealing with the new powers of the press, one may make a sound case for a multivariable explanation even while stressing the significance of the single innovation. The mixture of many motives provided a more powerful impetus than any single motive (whether that of profit-seeking capitalist or Christian evangelist) could have provided by itself. In this sense the use of early presses by Western Europeans was 'over-determined.' The convergence of different impulses proved irresistible, producing a massive irreversible cultural 'change of phase'.

The early presses which were first established between 1460 and 1480 were powered by many different forces which had been incubating in the age of scribes. In a different cultural context, the same technology might have been used for different ends (as was the case in China and

Korea) or it might have been unwelcome and not been used at all (as was the case in many regions outside Europe where Western missionary presses were the first to be installed). In this light one may agree with authorities who hold that the duplicating process which was developed in fifteenth-century Mainz, was *in itself* of no more consequence than any other inanimate tool. Unless it had been deemed useful to human agents it would never have been put into operation in fifteenth-century European towns. Under different circumstances, moreover, it might have been welcomed and put to entirely different uses – monopolized by priests and rulers, for example, and withheld from free-wheeling urban entrepreneurs.

Such counter-factual speculation is useful for suggesting the importance of institutional context when considering technological innovation. Yet the fact remains that once presses were established in numerous European towns, the transforming powers of print did begin to take effect. The new shops themselves interacted with the urban élites who received them in a manner that produced occupational mutations and intellectual regroupment. Here again, one may agree that even when acting as agents of change, early printers could be effective only in combination with other forces. Indeed, the very fact that they functioned as catalysts and as coordinators was of special significance. However much one may wish to stress reciprocal interaction and avoid a simplistic 'impact' model; one must leave room for the special features which distinguish the advent of printing from other innovations.

One cannot treat printing as just one among many elements in a complex causal nexus for the communications shift transformed the nature of the causal nexus itself. It is of special historical significance because it produced fundamental alterations in prevailing patterns of continuity and change. On this point one must take strong exception to the views expressed by humanists who carry their hostility to technology so far as to deprecate the very tool which is most indispensable to the practice of their own crafts.

The powers which shape men's lives may be expressed in books and type, but by and of itself printing...is only a tool, an instrument, and the multiplication of tools and instruments does not of itself affect intellectual and spiritual life.[18]

[18] Archer Taylor, 'The Influence of Printing,' p. 13.

Intellectual and spiritual life, far from remaining unaffected, were profoundly transformed by the multiplication of new tools for duplicating books in fifteenth-century Europe. The communications shift altered the way Western Christians viewed their sacred book and the natural world. It made the words of God appear more multiform and His handiwork more uniform. The printing press laid the basis for both literal fundamentalism and for modern science. It remains indispensable for humanistic scholarship. It is still responsible for our museum-without-walls.

SOME FINAL REMARKS

This book has stopped short in the age of the wooden hand press. It has barely touched on the industrialization of paper-making and the harnessing of iron presses to steam. Nothing has been said about the railway tracks and telegraph wires which linked European capitals in the mid-nineteenth century, or about the Linotype and Monotype machines which went together with mass literacy and tabloid journalism. The typewriter, the telephone, and a vast variety of more recent media have been entirely ignored. Too much territory has been traversed too rapidly as it is. Because contrary views have been expressed, however, it is necessary to point out that the process that began in the mid-fifteenth century has not ceased to gather momentum in the age of the computer print-out and the television guide. Indeed the later phases of an on-going communications revolution seem altogether relevant to what is happening within our homes, universities, or cities at present. In particular, they are relevant to apocalyptic pronouncements about contemporary Western culture delivered by modern intellectuals and literati.

Since the advent of movable type, an enhanced capacity to store and retrieve, preserve and transmit has kept pace with an enhanced capacity to create and destroy, to innovate or outmode. The somewhat chaotic appearance of modern Western culture owes as much, if not more, to the duplicative powers of print as it does to the harnessing of new powers in the past century. It may yet be possible to view recent developments in historical perspective provided one takes into account neglected aspects of a massive and decisive cultural 'change of phase' that occurred five centuries ago.

Some of the unanticipated consequences that came in the wake of Gutenberg's invention are now available for retrospective analysis – certainly more than could be seen in Bacon's day. Others are still unfolding, however, and *these* unanticipated consequences are, by definition, impossible to gauge at present. Few, if any, of the changes we have outlined could have been predicted. Even with hindsight they are difficult to describe. Clearly, more study is needed, if only to counteract premature leaps in the dark. A continuous accumulation of printed materials has certain disadvantages. (The voracious appetite of Chronos was feared in the past. A monstrous capacity to disgorge poses more of a threat at present.) But the capacity to scan accumulated records also confers certain modest advantages. We may examine how our predecessors read various portents and auguries and compare their prophecies with what actually occurred. We may thus discern over the past century or so a tendency to write off by premature obituaries the very problems that successive generations have had to confront.

This impulse to end tales that are still unfolding owes much to the prolongation of nineteenth-century historical schemes, especially those of Hegel and Marx which point logical dialectical conflicts toward logical dialectical ends. The possibility of an indefinite prolongation of fundamentally contradictory trends is not allowed for in these grand designs. Yet we still seem to be experiencing the contradictory effects of a process which fanned the flames of religious zeal and bigotry while fostering a new concern for ecumenical concord and toleration; which fixed linguistic and national divisions more permanently while creating a cosmopolitan Commonwealth of Learning and extending communications networks which encompassed the entire world. At the very least, this book may have indicated the premature character of prevailing grand designs and of the fashionable trend-spotting that extrapolates from them. For the full dimensions of the gulf that separates the age of scribes from that of printers have yet to be fully probed. The unevenly phased continuous process of recovery and innovation that began in the second half of the fifteenth century remains to be described.

To draw any further conclusions about the force, effect, or consequences of the advent of printing on the basis of these chapters would also be premature. My conjectures have been based on uneven knowledge of pertinent data, much of it drawn from unreliable general accounts, and all of it relevant to very few regions. Too many gaps have been filled in by logical inference. To set forth views that may be invalid can be justified when it paves the way for more educated guesswork based on more empirical evidence. A more troublesome issue is posed by speculations that resist invalidation because imponderables are involved. However many crude generalizations may be discarded or refined, there seems to be no way of excluding such imponderables when dealing with this particular topic. One might conceivably measure the varying output of different kinds of printed materials, analyze their contents, examine their distribution, estimate their rate of consumption. There is no way of measuring what may be 'read into' any given text or to assess the effect of 'action at a distance' without resorting to speculation. No one may claim to read the minds of other readers without leaving room for uncertainty; it is even more difficult to read the minds of those who have long since gone to their graves. Imponderables of this kind have, however, to be included in any effort to find out how things happened as they did. When silent, invisible interactions are ignored because they defy precise analysis, more mysterious spirits, ethics, and isms are likely to take their place. There are advantages in defining margins of uncertainty with some precision and thereby holding conspiratorial myth-makers at bay.

'He would be a bold man' says Somervell in discussing certain popular nineteenth-century English novelists, who would deny them 'an influence on general elections.'[19] Historians who exclude reading habits and belles lettres from their work appear to be cautiously avoiding intractable data where firm conclusions are impossible. Yet it may be rash, not cautious, to base analyses on 'hard facts' while leaving 'soft' or 'mushy' issues to others. Possibly such issues appear softer and mushier than need be because most practitioners of *Ideengeschichte*, literary historians, and belles lettrists, have inherited a venerable tradition of proud ignorance of matters material, mechanical, or commercial. It is futile to condemn intellectual divisions of labor. The 'universal bibliography' compiled by Conrad Gesner in the sixteenth century was not only the first of its kind. It was also the last attempt by a single scholar to achieve comprehensive coverage of every work in print. Increasing specialization is inevitable, given an expanding knowledge industry. Granted that intensive cultivation of different fields must be separately undertaken, there is still no warrant for

---

[19] Somervell, *English Thought*, p. 8.

allocating all the 'hard' facts to some fields; all the 'soft' ones to others. Specialists must reckon with both, whatever historical changes they may choose to explore.

Those who are concerned with the 'shaping of the modern mind' might profitably focus more attention on data-processing within early workshops where laboratories of advanced erudition were maintained and where tangible commodities were produced and distributed in measurable quantities. Despite invented accommodation addresses, most publications may be placed and dated with a fair degree of accuracy. Their contents may be tabulated and analyzed. Shifting centers of production and distribution networks may also be located on real maps. Studies pertaining to the 'social history of ideas' and comparative studies of many other kinds would probably be illuminated by more precise analysis of these matters. Those who are concerned with the shaping of modern society – with political economy, legal institutions, or affairs of church and state – however, have to deal with issues that cannot be handled by rigorous quantitative analysis. For they are confronted by the more indirect effects of the consumption of printed materials. Problematic issues pertaining to literacy, book-reading, and new mental habits cannot be avoided when dealing with 'rationalization,' 'modernization,' 'centralization,' élite regroupment, religious divisions, upward mobility, rising expectations, or entrepreneurial organization. While changes affecting paper production, credit or contracts may be related fairly directly to the expansion of printing industries, the same is not true of changes associated with class consciousness or, indeed, any form of group identity. Scepticism is called for about theories pertaining to a meeting of minds or a touching of hearts. Such theories must nonetheless be framed in order to come to terms with changes that affected consciousness and identity and hence necessarily engaged human thoughts and feelings. Thus a salutary inversion of customary alignments might result from exploring the consequences that came in the wake of the printing press. A greater respect for hard facts and material technologies among humanist scholars and intellectual historians; more appreciation of the role played by imponderables and the reality of intangible phenomena among those who investigate socio-economic, political, or institutional changes could, conceivably, lead to more fruitful collaboration between groups of specialists.

Many advantages would, I believe, be gained by following Bacon's advice. Of them all none seems more important than seeing how many of the facts of life that are presently being kept apart actually belong together.

BIBLIOGRAPHICAL INDEX

Given the survey of relevant literature in the first chapter of this book and the space devoted to historiography in other sections, it seemed redundant to supply a bibliographical essay. A conventional comprehensive bibliography was also ruled out on the grounds that more than a hundred pages of book titles constituted an inefficient use of space. This index will enable readers to retrieve full titles of all the works cited in the footnotes while displaying the full range of studies used for my book. Important works that were consulted but are not cited in specific footnotes have been listed without entries. Readers who want to keep up with the most recent work should note that 1976 is my cut-off date and should consult the special periodicals cited in chapter 1 (note 2) volume I, where notices of relevant new studies are to be found.

Adams, Henry. *The Education of Henry Adams: An Autobiography* (Cambridge, Mass., 1918). **x.**

Adamson, J. W. *The Illiterate Anglo Saxon and Other Essays* (Cambridge, 1956). Consulted but not cited.

'The Extent of Literacy in England in the Fifteenth and Sixteenth Centuries: Notes and Conjectures,' *The Library*, 4th ser. x (1929) 163–93. **62.**

Adelmann, Howard B. Introduction to *The Embryological Treatises of Hieronymus Fabricius of Aquapendente* (Ithaca, New York, 1942). **476, 562, 573-4.**

Marcello Malpighi and the Evolution of Embryology (5 vol. Ithaca, New York, 1967). **664-5.**

Adhémar, J. 'L'Estampe et la Transmission des Formes Maniéristes,' *Le Triomphe du Maniérisme Européen* (Amsterdam, 1955). **82.**

Africa, Thomas. 'Copernicus' Relation to Aristarchus and Pythagorus,' *Isis* 52 (1961) 403–9. **577.**

Aidan, Francis (Cardinal Gasquet). 'Roger Bacon and the Latin Vulgate,' *Roger Bacon Essays*, ed. A. G. Little (Oxford, 1914) 89–99. **339.**

Aiton, E. J. 'Essay Review,' *History of Science* 11 (1973) 217–30. **638.**

'Essay Review,' *Studies in History and Philosophy of Science* I (1970–71) 265–73. **565.**

Allen, P. S. *The Age of Erasmus* (Oxford, 1914). **19, 175.**

Erasmus: Lectures and Wayfaring Sketches (London, 1934). **81.**

'Erasmus' Relations with his Printers,' *Transactions of the Bibliographical Society* XIII (Oct. 1913–March 1915) 297–323. **401.**

Allen, Ward, tr. and ed. *Translating for King James: Notes Made by a Translator of the King James Bible* (Vanderbilt University Press, 1969). **360.**

Allison, A. F. and Rogers, D. M. *A Catalogue of Catholic Books in English Printed Abroad or Secretly in England, 1558–1640* (London, 1964). **354.**

Altick, R. *The English Common Reader. A Social History of the Mass Reading Public 1800–1900* (Chicago, 1963). **65, 130-1, 134, 149, 153, 361, 364, 422.**

Ames, Joseph. *See* Thomas F. Dibdin.

Arber, Agnes. 'From Medieval Herbalism to the Birth of Modern Botany,' *Science, Medicine, and History. Essays ... In Honor of Charles Singer*, ed. E. A. Underwood (2 vol. Oxford, 1953) I, 317–36. **266, 487.**

Archer, Peter, S.J. *The Christian Calendar and the Gregorian Reform* (New York, 1941). **610.**

Ariès, Philippe. *Centuries of Childhood: A Social History of Family Life*, tr. R. Baldick (New York, 1962). **431-2.**

L'Enfant et La Vie Familiale sous L'Ancien Régime (Paris, 1973). **431.**

Armstrong, Elizabeth. *Robert Estienne, Royal Printer* (Cambridge, 1954). **75, 87, 387, 399, 401, 411, 442, 447.**

Arnold, Klaus, ed. and introduction to Johannes Trithemius, *In Praise of Scribes – De Laude Scriptorum*, tr. R. Behrendt (Lawrence, Kansas, 1974). **14-15, 94-5, 97, 200.** *See also* Johannes Trithemius.

Artz, Frederick. *The Development of Technical Education in France, 1500–1850* (Cambridge, Mass., 1966). **351.**

Askew, Pamela. 'A Melancholy Astronomer by Giovanni Serodine,' *The Art Bulletin* XLVII (March 1965) 121–8. **577.**

Aston, Margaret. *The Fifteenth Century: The Prospect of Europe* (London, 1968). **310.**

'The Fiery Trigon Conjunction: An Elizabethan Astrological Prediction,' *Isis* 61 (1970) 159–87. **619.**

'John Wycliffe's Reformation Reputation,' *Past and Present* 30 (April 1965) 23–52. **304, 345.**

'Lollardy and the Reformation: Survival or Revival?' *History* XLIX (1964) 149–70. **304.**

Review article, *Shakespeare Studies* IV (1968) 388. **415.**

Atkinson, Geoffroy. *Les Nouveaux Horizons de la Renaissance Française* (Paris, 1935). **303.**

Auerbach, Erich. *Literary Language and its public in late Latin Antiquity and in the Middle Ages*, tr. R. Manheim (New York, 1965). **334.**

'The Author and his Ghosts,' *Times Literary Supplement* (Sept. 22, 1972) 1121. **122.**

Axtell, J. L. 'Locke's Review of the *Principia*,' *Notes and Records of the Royal Society of London*, XX (1965) 152–61. **638.**

Bachman, A. *Censorship in France from 1715 to 1750* (New York, 1934). **145.**

Bacon, Francis. *Francis Bacon. A Selection of His Works*, ed. S. Warhaft (College Classics in English, ed. H. Northrop Frye) (Toronto, 1965). **455.**

Bagrow, Leo. *History of Cartography*, rev. and ed. R. A. Skelton (Cambridge, Mass., 1964). **53, 469, 512, 514.**

Bailey, John E. 'Dee and Trithemius' Steganography,' *Notes and Queries* (May 24, 1879), 5th ser. XI, 401–2, 422–3. **96, 137.**

Bainton, Roland. *Here I Stand: A Life of Martin Luther* (New York, 1950). **307.**

'Interpretations of the Reformation,' *The American Historical Review* LXVI (Oct. 1960) 74–84. **378.**

'Man, God and Church,' *The Renaissance: Six Essays* (New York, 1962) 77–96. **238.**

Review, *The Journal of Modern History* 43 (June 1971) 309–10. **445.**

Baker, Herschel. *The Wars of Truth* (Cambridge, Mass., 1952). **321.**

Baldwin, T. W. *William Shakespere's Small Latine & Lesse Greeke* (2 vol. Urbana, Ill., 1944). **350.**

Barber, Elinor. *The Bourgeoisie in Eighteenth Century France* (Princeton, 1955). **539.**

Barnes, Annie. *Jean Le Clerc et la République des Lettres* (Paris, 1938). **137, 321, 332, 420, 647.**

Barnett, S. W. 'Silent Evangelism: Presbyterians and the Mission Press in China, 1807–1860,' *Journal of Presbyterian History* 49 (Winter 1971) 287–302. **317.**

Baron, Hans. *The Crisis of the Early Italian Renaissance* (rev. edn, 1 vol. Princeton, New Jersey, 1966). **185.**

'The *Querelle* of the Ancients and Moderns as a Problem for Renaissance Scholarship,' *Journal of the History of Ideas* XX (Jan. 1959) 3–22. **123, 185.**

'Toward a More Positive Evaluation of the Fifteenth Century Renaissance,' *Journal of the History of Ideas* IV (Jan. 1943) 21–49. **251, 521, 526.**

Baroni, Victor. *La Contre Réforme devant la Bible* (Thèse de Doctorat) (Lausanne, 1943). **349.**

Baroque and Rococo Pictorial Imagery: The 1758–1760 Hertel edition of Ripa's Iconologia, ed. E. A. Moser (New York, 1971). **662.**

Basalla, George, ed. and introduction. *The Rise of Modern Science: External or Internal Factors?* (Lexington, Mass., 1968). **459.**

Bataillon, Marcel. *Erasme et L'Espagne. Recherches sur l'Histoire Spirituelle du XVIe Siècle* (Paris, 1937) chap. xi. Consulted but not cited.

Etudes sur le Portugal au Temps de l'Humanisme (Coimbra, 1952). Consulted but not cited.

'Philippe Galle et Arias Montano,' *Bibliothèque d'Humanisme et Renaissance* II (1942) 132–60. **20.**

Bate, W. Jackson. *The Burden of the Past and the English Poet* (Cambridge, Mass., 1970). **192.**

'Battle of the Senses,' *Times Literary Supplement* (March 1, 1963) 156. **40.**

Baumann, F. E. 'Mutianus Rufus and Natural Religion: A Test Case,' *Renaissance Quarterly* XXIX (1976) 567–98. **273.**

Baxandall, Michael. *Giotto and the Orators: Humanist Observers of Painting in Italy and the Discovery of Pictorial Composition 1350–1450* (Oxford, 1971). **232, 293, 604.**

Painting and Experience in 15th Century Italy (Oxford, 1972). **293.**

Beardsley, Theodore S. 'The Classics and Their Spanish Translators in the Sixteenth Century,' *Renaissance and Reformation* VIII (Toronto, 1971) 2–9. **360, 408.**

Beaujouan, Guy. 'Motives and Opportunities for Science in the Medieval University,' *Scientific Change: Symposium on the History of Science*, ed. A. C. Crombie (New York, 1963) 219–36. **382, 537.**

Beazley, C. R. *The Dawn of Modern Geography* (3 vol. Oxford, 1906). **516.**

Bebb, P. N. 'The Lawyers, Dr. Christoph Scheurl and the Reformation in Nürnberg,'

The Social History of the Reformation (Festschrift for Harold Grimm) ed. L. P. Buck and J. W. Zophy (Columbus, Ohio, 1972) 52–73. **308, 404.**

Bec, Christian. *Les Marchands Ecrivains; Affaires et Humanisme à Florence 1375–1434* (Paris, 1967). **62.**

Bedini, S. A. 'The Instruments of Galileo,' *Galileo, Man of Science*, ed. Ernan McMullin (New York, 1967) 256–92. **525.**

Bedini, S. A. and Maddison, F. R. 'Mechanical Universe,' *Transactions of the American Philosophical Society* 56 (Oct. 1966) 3–67. **589.**

Ben-David, Joseph. 'The Scientific Role; The Conditions of Its Establishment in Europe' (1st pub. in *Minerva* IV (1965) 15–20), *Western Civilization: Recent Interpretations*, ed. C. D. Hamilton (2 vol. Chicago, 1973) 556–78. **654–5, 666.**

Benesch, Otto. *The Art of the Renaissance in Northern Europe* (rev. edn, London, 1965). **589.**

Benjamin, F. S. and Toomer, C. J. *Campanus of Novara and Medieval Planetary Theory* (Madison, Wis., 1971). **465, 512, 536.**

Bennett, H. S. *English Books and Readers 1475–1557* (Cambridge, 1952). **62, 104–5, 127, 130, 139, 358, 361.**
English Books and Readers 1558–1603 (Cambridge, 1965). **358.**
'The Production and Dissemination of Vernacular Manuscripts in the Fifteenth Century,' *The Library*, 5th ser. I (1947) 167–78. **11.**

Benton, John, ed. and introduction. *Self and Society in Medieval France: The Memoirs of Abbot Guibert of Nogent (1064?–c. 1125)* (New York, 1970). **236.**

Benzing, Josef. *Buchdrucker-Lexicon des 16 Jahrhunderts* (Deutsches Sprachgebiet) (Frankfurt, 1952). **99, 206, 307, 371, 617.**

Berelson, Bernard and Janowitz, Morris. *Reader in Public Opinion and Communication* (Glencoe, Ill., 1953). **8.**

Bergendorff, C. *See* Luther. *Luther's Works.*

Berger, Samuel. *Histoire de la Vulgate pendant les premiers siècles du Moyen Age* (Paris, 1893). **328.**

Berkvens-Stevelinck, Christiane. 'Prosper Marchand, Auteur et Editeur,' *Quaerendo* V (1975) 218–34. **143.**

Berry, B. M. 'The First English Pediatricians and Tudor Attitudes toward Childhood,' *Journal of the History of Ideas* XXXV (1974) 561–77. **431.**

Berry, Lloyd, introduction. *The Geneva Bible: A Facsimile of the 1560 Edition* (Madison, Wis., 1969). **305, 360, 364, 415.**

Berry, W. T. and Poole, H. W. *Annals of Printing: A Chronological Encyclopaedia from Earliest Times to 1950* (London, 1966). **4.**

Besson, Jacques. *A Theatre of Machines* (1579) ed. Alexander G. Keller (New York, 1965). **240, 262, 557.**

Besterman, Theodore. *The Beginnings of Systematic Bibliography* (Oxford, 1936). **94, 98.**

Bevan, E. R. and Singer, Charles, eds. *The Legacy of Israel* (Oxford, 1927). Includes articles by Box, G. H.; Singer, Charles.

Bietenholz, P. G. *Basle and France in the Sixteenth Century: The Basle Humanists and Printers in their contacts with Francophone Culture* (University of Toronto Press, 1971). **187, 399, 405, 407, 419, 441–2, 446, 540.**

Billanovich, R. 'Petrarch and the Textual Tradition of Livy,' *Journal of the Warburg and Courtauld Institutes* XIV (1951) 137–208. Consulted but not cited.

Binz, Louis. *Vie Religieuse et Réforme Ecclésiastique dans le diocèse de Genève pendant le Grand Schisme et la Crise Conciliaire (1378–1450)* (2 vol. Geneva, 1973). **314.**

Birn, Raymond. '*Livre et Société* After Ten Years: Formation of a discipline,' *Studies on Voltaire and the Eighteenth Century* CLI–CLV (1976) 287–312. **29, 146.**

'Le Journal des Savants sous L'Ancien Régime,' *Journal des Savants* (1965) 15–35. **120, 643.**

'Pierre Rousseau and the Philosophes of Bouillon,' *Studies on Voltaire and the Eighteenth Century* XXIX, ed. T. Besterman (Geneva, 1964). **145.**

Bissels, Paul. *Humanismus und Buchdruck: Vorreden Humanistischer Drucke in Köln* (Nieuwkoop, 1965). **206.**

Black, M. H. 'The Printed Bible,' *Cambridge History of the Bible*, Vol. 3. *The West from the Reformation to the Present Day*, ed. S. L. Greenslade (Cambridge, 1963) 408–75. **11, 80–1, 106, 206, 304, 328–9, 349, 367, 377, 411.**

'The Typography of Luther's Bible and its Influence,' *Gutenberg-Jahrbuch* (1969) 110–13. **206.**

Review of Steinberg's *Five Hundred Years*, *The Library*, 5th ser. XIV (1959) 300–2. **80, 206.**

Blades, William. *The Life and Typography of William Caxton . . . with Evidence of His Connection with Colard Mansion, The Printer at Bruges* (2 vol. London, 1861). **38.**

Blaeu, W. J. *The Light of Navigation*: Facsimile of 1612 Edition, ed. and introduction by R. A. Skelton (London, 1964). **480–1.**

Blagden, C. *The Stationers Company, A History 1403–1959* (London, 1960). **120.**

Blake, N. F. *Caxton and His World* (London, 1969). **38, 375, 383.**

Caxton: England's First Publisher (London, 1975). **112.**

Bland, David. *A History of Book Illustration* (2nd edn, Berkeley, 1969). **85–6.**

Blau, J. *The Christian Interpretation of Cabala in the Renaissance* (New York, 1944). **278.**

Blench, J. W. *Preaching in England in the late Fifteenth and Sixteenth Centuries: A Study of English Sermons 1450–c. 1600* (Oxford, 1964). **426.**

Bloch, Eileen. 'Erasmus and the Froben Press: the Making of an Editor,' *Library Quarterly* XXXV (April 1965) 109–20. Consulted but not cited.

Bloch, Marc. *The Historian's Craft*, tr. P. Putnam (New York, 1964). **xv.**

Bluhm, Heinz. *Martin Luther, Creative Translator* (St Louis, Mo., 1965). **341, 368.**

'The Sources of Luther's September Testament: Galatians,' *Luther for an Ecumenical Age: Essays*, ed. Carl S. Meyer (St Louis, Mo., 1967) 144–71. **356.**

Blumenthal, Joseph. Introduction. *Art of the Printed Book 1455–1955* (New York, 1973). **48.**

Blunt, Anthony. *Artistic Theory in Italy 1450–1600* (1st edn 1940, Oxford, 1966). **232, 254, 325.**

Boas, George, ed. and tr. *The Hieroglyphics of Horapollo* (Bollingen Series, XXIII) (New York, 1950). **279, 288.**

Boas, Marie. *The Scientific Renaissance* (New York, 1962). **220, 265, 468–9, 494, 499, 502, 509, 530, 567, 569, 574, 585, 614, 620, 625.**

Boase, T. R. 'Vasari: the Man and the Book.' (Mellon lectures given at the National Gallery, Washington, D.C.) **233.**

Bober, Harry. Review of *The Göttingen Model Book*, ed. H. Lehmann-Haupt, *Speculum* XLIX (April 1974) 354–8. **54, 65, 82.**

'Boccaccio's Dante,' *Times Literary Supplement* (Nov. 4, 1965) 969. **319.**

Bohnstedt, J. W. *The Infidel Scourge of God*. Transactions of the American Philosophical Society (Philadelphia, 1968). **303.**

Bolgar, R. R. *The Classical Heritage and Its Beneficiaries: From the Carolingian Age to the End of the Renaissance* (New York, 1964). **181, 212, 217, 222, 224, 244, 272.**

ed. *Classical Influences on European Culture A.D. 500–1500* (Cambridge, 1971). Includes article by Gerlo, A.

ed. *Classical Influences on European Culture A.D. 1500–1700* (Cambridge, 1976). Includes article by Oestreich, G.

Bollème, Geneviève. *Les Almanachs populaires aux XVIIe et XVIIIe siècles* (Paris, 1969). **386.**

Bonelli Righini, M. L. and Shea, W. R., eds. *Reason, Experiment and Mysticism in the Scientific Revolution* (New York, 1975). **641.** Includes articles by Debus, A.; Hall, A. R.; Rossi, P.

The Book of Common Prayer (1559) ed. John Booty (Charlottesville, Va., 1976). **365.**

Borchardt, F. 'Etymology in Tradition and in the Northern Renaissance,' *Journal of the History of Ideas* xxix (July–Sept. 1968) 415–29. **277.**

Bosanquet, E. F. *English Printed Almanacks and Prognostications, A Bibliographical History to the Year 1600* (London, 1917). **386, 608, 618–19.**

'English Seventeenth-Century Almanacks,' *The Library*, 4th ser. x (1930) 361–97. **386.**

Bossy, John. 'The Counter Reformation and the People of Catholic Europe,' *Past and Present* 47 (May 1970) 51–70. **426.**

Botein, Stephen. 'Meer Mechanics and an Open Press,' *Perspectives in American History* ix (1975) 127–225. **381.**

Botfield, Beriah, ed. *Praefationes et Epistolae Editionibus Principus Auctorum Veterum* (Cambridge, 1861). **20, 320, 392.**

Boüard, Michel de. 'Encyclopédies Médiévales, Sur la "Connaissance de la Nature et du Monde" au Moyen Age,' *Revue des Questions Historiques* 58 (1930) 258–305. **513.**

Boulding, Kenneth. *The Image* (Ann Arbor, Mich., 1961). **81, 479.**

Boumans, René. 'The Religious Views of Abraham Ortelius,' *Journal of the Warburg and Courtauld Institutes* xvii (July–Dec. 1954) 374–7. **448.**

Bouwsma, William. *Concordia Mundi: The Career and Thought of Guillaume Postel (1510–1581)* (Cambridge, Mass., 1957). **340, 343, 448.**

Venice and the Defense of Republican Liberty: Renaissance Values in the Age of the Counter Reformation (Berkeley, 1968). **353, 413.**

'Venice, Spain and the Papacy: Paolo Sarpi and the Renaissance Tradition,' *The Late Italian Renaissance 1525–1630*, ed. Eric Cochrane (New York, 1970) 353–77. **412–13.**

Bouyer, Louis. 'Erasmus in Relation to the Medieval Biblical Tradition,' *Cambridge History of the Bible*, Vol. 2. *The West from the Fathers to the Reformation*, ed. G. W. H. Lampe (Cambridge, 1969) 492–505. **338.**

Box, G. H. 'Hebrew Studies in the Reformation Period and After,' *The Legacy of Israel*, ed. E. R. Bevan and Charles Singer (Oxford, 1927) 315–75. **224, 367, 447.**

Boxer, C. R., et al. *Exotic Printing and the Expansion of Europe, 1492–1840*, catalogue of Exhibition, Lilly Library, Indiana University, 1972. **317.**

Boyd, Julian. 'These Precious Monuments of... Our History,' *The American Archivist* xxii, 2 (1959) 175–6. **116.**

Boyer, Carl. *History of Mathematics* (New York, 1968). **620.**
'Galileo's Place in the History of Mathematics,' *Galileo, Man of Science*, ed. Ernan McMullin (New York, 1967) 232–55. **525.**
Brann, Noel. 'The Shift from Mystical to Magical Theology in the Abbot Trithemius.' Paper given May 5, 1976, 11th Conference on Medieval Studies (Kalamazoo, Mich.). **95.**
Branner, Robert. 'Manuscript Makers in Mid-thirteenth Century Paris,' *The Art Bulletin* XLVIII (March 1966) 65–7. **11, 13, 46.**
'The Soissons Bible Paintshop in Thirteenth-Century Paris,' *Speculum* XLIV (Jan. 1969) 13–34. **11, 13, 46, 328.**
Braudel, Fernand. *Capitalism and Material Life, 1400–1800*, tr. M. Kochon (1st Fr. edn 1967, New York, 1974). **27.**
Bredvold, L. I. *The Intellectual Milieu of John Dryden* (Ann Arbor, 1956). **323, 326.**
Bréhier, Émile. 'The Formation of our History of Philosophy,' *Philosophy and History: The Ernst Cassirer Festschrift*, ed. R. Klibansky and H. J. Paton (rev. edn, New York, 1963) 159–73. **333.**
Bremme, H. J. *Buchdrucker und Buchhandler zur Zeit der Glaubenskämpfe: Studien zur Genfer Druckgeschichte, 1565–1580* (Geneva, 1969). **411.**
Bridenbaugh, Carl. 'The Great Mutation,' *The American Historical Review* LXVIII (Jan. 1963) 315–31. **ix, 364.**
Briel, J. G. C. A. *See* Kingdon, R. M.
Brinton, Crane. *The Anatomy of Revolution* (New York, 1938). **136.**
Brockbank, William. 'Sovereign Remedies: A Critical Depreciation of the Seventeenth Century London Pharmacopoeia,' *Medical History* VIII (1964) 1–13. **539, 656.**
Bronowski, Jacob and Mazlish, Bruce. *The Western Intellectual Tradition: From Leonardo to Hegel* (New York, 1960). **649.**
Bronson, Bernard. 'The Writer,' *Man Versus Society in Eighteenth Century Britain*, ed. J. L. Clifford (Cambridge, 1968) 102–32. **322.**
Brown, Harcourt. *Scientific Organizations in 17th Century France 1620–1680* (New York, 1934). **643.**
Brown, Irene Q. 'Philippe Ariès on Education and Society in Seventeenth and Eighteenth Century France,' *History of Education Quarterly* (Fall 1967) 357–68. **395.**
Brown, Lloyd. *The Story of Maps* (Boston, 1959). **110, 479, 482, 517.**
Browne, Sir Thomas. *The Prose of Sir Thomas Browne*, ed. Norman Endicott (New York, 1967). **18, 471, 483.**
Brun, Robert. *Le Livre Français Illustré de la Renaissance* (Paris, 1969). **544.**
Buck, L. P. and Zophy, J. W., eds. *The Social History of the Reformation* (Festschrift for Harold Grimm) (Columbus, Ohio, 1972). Includes articles by Bebb, P. N.; Cole, R.; Dannenfeldt, Karl.
Bühler, Curt. *The Fifteenth Century Book, the Scribes, the Printers, the Decorators* (Philadelphia, 1960). **6, 14, 19, 49–51, 72, 83, 139, 206, 250, 586.**
Fifteenth Century Books and the Twentieth Century: An Address and a Catalogue of an Exhibition at the Grolier Club (April–June 1952) (New York, 1952). **167–8.**
The University and the Press in 15th Century Bologna, Texts and Studies in the History of Medieval Education, vol. VII (South Bend, Indiana, 1958). **56.**
Review article. *The Library*, 5th ser. VIII (1953) 53–6. **38.**

'Roman Type and Roman Printing in the Fifteenth Century,' *Bibliotheca Docet: Festgabe für Carl Wehmer*, ed. S. Joost (Amsterdam, 1963) 101–10. **204–5.**

'A Typographical Error in the Editio Princeps of Euclid,' *Gutenberg-Jahrbuch* (1966) 102–4. **588.**

Burckhardt, Jacob. *The Civilization of the Renaissance in Italy*, tr. S. G. C. Middlemore, ed. B. Nelson and C. Trinkaus (2 vol. New York, 1958). **45, 48, 221, 226, 228, 237–8, 243, 300, 488–91, 494.**

Burke, Peter. *Culture and Society in Renaissance Italy 1420–1540* (London, 1972). **45, 88.**

Introduction, *A New Kind of History and Other Essays from the Writings of Lucien Febvre* (New York, 1973). **41.**

The Renaissance (*Problems and Perspectives in History*, ed. H. F. Kearney) (London, 1964). **177.**

The Renaissance Sense of the Past (*Documents of Modern History*, ed. A. G. Dickens and A. Davies) (New York, 1970). **257, 300.**

'Fanfare for Princes,' *Times Literary Supplement* (Sept. 10, 1976). **133.**

Burns, Howard. 'Quattrocento Architecture and the Antique,' *Classical Influences on European Culture A.D. 500–1500*, ed. R. R. Bolgar (Cambridge, 1971) 269–89. **83.**

Burns, R. E. Book review. *American Historical Review* LXXIV (Oct. 1968) 181. **290.**

Burrow, John. 'The Medieval Compendium,' *Times Literary Supplement* (May 21, 1976) 615. **122.**

Burtt, E. A. *The Metaphysical Foundations of Modern Science* (1st edn 1932, rev. edn, New York, 1955). **592, 681.**

Butler, Pierce. *The Origin of Printing in Europe* (Chicago, 1940). **6, 17, 89, 95–6, 113, 119, 163, 375.**

Butterfield, Herbert. *The Origins of Modern Science 1300–1800* (rev. edn, New York, 1951). **496, 503, 637, 646, 663, 685.**

The Statecraft of Machiavelli (New York, 1960). **291.**

Butterworth, C. *The English Primers (1529–1545)* (Philadelphia, 1953). **350.**

Cajori, Florian. *A History of Mathematics* (New York, 1919). **583.**

See also Newton, Isaac.

Cambridge History of the Bible (3 vol. Cambridge, 1963–70). Vol. 2. *The West from the Fathers to the Reformation*, ed. G. W. H. Lampe (Cambridge, 1969). Vol. 3. *The West from the Reformation to the Present Day*, ed. S. L. Greenslade (Cambridge, 1963). Includes articles by Black, M. H.; Bouyer, Louis; Crehan, F. J.; Fenn, Eric; Foster, Kenelm; Greenslade, S. L.; Hall, Basil; Jones, D. R.; Lockwood, W. B.; Loewe, R.; Milburn, R. L. P.; Richardson, A.; Robson, C. A.; Sayce, R. A.; Sutcliffe, E. F.; Sykes, N.

Cambridge Modern History, New (14 vol. Cambridge, 1957–79). Vol. I. *The Renaissance, 1493–1520*, ed. G. R. Potter (Cambridge, 1957). Vol. II. *The Reformation, 1520–59*, ed. G. R. Elton (Cambridge, 1958). Includes articles by Hall, A. R.; Hay, Denys; Weiss, R.

Cameron, Kenneth W. Book review. *Renaissance Quarterly* XXIV (Winter 1971) 555. **376.**

Cameron, Richard. 'The Attack on the Biblical Work of Lefèvre d'Etaples (1514–1521),' *Church History* XXXVIII (1969) 9–24. **331.**

Campbell, Anna M. *The Black Death and Men of Learning* (New York, 1966). **295.**

Cardano, G. *The Great Art*, tr. and ed. T. R. Witmer (Cambridge, Mass., 1968). **548, 552.**

Carter, Charles Howard, ed. *From the Renaissance to the Counter Reformation. Essays in Honor of Garrett Mattingly* (New York, 1965). Includes articles by Hale, J. R.; Hay, Denys; Hill, Christopher; Kristeller, P. O.; Smolar, F. J.; Strauss, G.

Carter, Harry. *A View of Early Typography up to about 1600* (Oxford, 1969). **55, 203, 205-7.**

Carter, Harry and Vervliet, H. D. L. *Civilité Types* (Oxford Bibliographical Society Publications, New Ser. xiv) (Oxford, 1966). **202, 205-6.**

Carter, J. W. and Muir, P. H., eds. *Printing and the Mind of Man* (London, 1967). **375.**

Carter, T. F. and Goodrich, C. L. *The Invention of Printing in China and Its Spread Westward* (1st edn 1925, New York, 1955). **27, 376.**

Caspar, Max. *Kepler*, tr. C. Doris Hellman (London, 1948, rev. edn 1959). **582, 626-7, 639, 654.**

Cassirer, Ernst. *The Philosophy of the Enlightenment*, tr. F. Koelln and J. Pettegrove (Princeton, 1951). **698.**

'On the Originality of the Renaissance,' *Journal of the History of Ideas* iv (Jan. 1943) 49-56. **229, 230.**

Castiglioni, A. *A History of Medicine*, tr. E. B. Krumbhaar (rev. edn, New York, 1958). **616.**

Cavallera, Ferdinand. 'La Bible en Langue Vulgaire au Concile de Trente: IVe Session,' *Mélanges E. Podechard* (Lyon, 1945) 37-56. **329, 343-4.**

Chabod, Frederico. *Machiavelli and the Renaissance*, tr. David Moore, introduction, A. P. d'Entrèves (New York, 1965). **185, 293.**

Chalotais, Louis René de Caradeuc de la. *Essay on National Education, or Plan of Studies for the Young*, tr. H. R. Clark (London, 1934). **351.**

Chambers, G. K. 'Sir Thomas Browne, True Scientist,' *Osiris* ii (1936) 28-79. **458.**

Chambers, R. W. 'The Lost Literature of Medieval England,' *The Library*, 4th ser. v (1925) 293-321. **115.**

Charlton, Kenneth. *Education in Renaissance England* (London, 1965). **243, 383, 425.**

Chartier, R., Compère, M. M., Julia, D. *L'Education en France du XVIe au XVIIIe Siècle* (Paris, 1976). **350, 414, 430.**

Chastel, André. 'What is Mannerism?' *Art News* (Dec. 1965), 64. **82.**

Chaucer, G. *The Equatorie of the Planetis*, ed. Derek de Solla Price (Cambridge, 1955). **277, 465.**

Chaunu, Pierre. 'Sur la Fin des Sorciers au XVIIe Siècle,' *Annales: Economies Sociétés Civilisations* xxiv (July-Aug. 1969) 895-911. **434.**

Chaytor, H. J. *From Script to Print* (Cambridge, 1945). **10, 121, 171, 227, 299, 319.**

Chenu, M. D. *Nature, Man and Society in the Twelfth Century*, ed. and tr. J. Taylor and Lester Little (Chicago, 1968). **184-5, 251, 290, 379.**

Chester, Alan G. 'The New Learning: A Semantic Note,' *Studies in the Renaissance* ii (1955) 139-47. **174.**

Chrisman, Miriam Usher. *Strasbourg and the Reform: A Study in the Process of Change* (New Haven, 1967). **370-3.**

Christianson, John. 'Astronomy and Printing,' paper presented at Sixteenth Century Studies Conference, October 26, 1972, Concordia Seminary, St Louis, Mo. **599, 625.**

'Tycho Brahe at the University of Copenhagen 1559–1562,' *Isis* 58 (1967) 198–203. **533-4.**

'Tycho Brahe's Facts of Life,' *Fund og Forskning i Det Kongelige Biblioteks* 17 (1970). **624.**

Cipolla, Carlo M. *Before the Industrial Revolution* (New York, 1976). **244, 554.**

Literacy and Development in the West (London, 1969). **61, 414.**

'The Diffusion of Innovations in Early Modern Europe,' *Comparative Studies in Society and History* 14 (1972) 46–52. **583.**

Clagett, Marshall. *Archimedes in the Middle Ages I: The Arabo-Latin Tradition* (Madison, Wis., 1964). **471, 497, 697.**

ed. *Critical Problems in the History of Science* (Proceedings of the Institute of the History of Science, Sept. 1957) (Madison, Wis., 1959). Includes articles by Crombie, A. C.; Santillana, G. de; Hall, A. R.; Nagel, E.

Greek Science in Antiquity (London, 1957). **611.**

The Science of Mechanics in the Middle Ages (Madison, Wis., 1959). **497, 522, 541.**

Clagett, M. and Moody, E., eds. *The Medieval Science of Weights* (Madison, Wis., 1952). **497.**

Clair, Colin. *Christopher Plantin* (London, 1960). **100.**

'Willem Silvius,' *The Library* 5th ser. XIV (1959) 192–205. **96.**

Clapham, Michael. 'Printing,' *A History of Technology* II *From the Renaissance to the Industrial Revolution,* ed. Charles Singer, E. J. Holmyard, A. R. Hall and Trevor Williams (4 vol. Oxford, 1957) 377–411. **21, 31, 45, 273, 376.**

Clapp, Sarah L. C. 'The Beginnings of Subscription in the Seventeenth Century,' *Modern Philology* XXIX (1931) 199–224. Consulted but not cited.

'The Subscription Enterprises of John Ogilby and Richard Blowe,' *Modern Philology* XXXI (May 1933) 365–79. **367.**

Clapp, V. W. 'The Story of Permanent Durable Book Paper, 1115–1970,' *Scholarly Publishing, A Journal for Authors and Publishers* II (Toronto, 1971) 108 ff. **14, 115.**

Clark, Sir George N. *Early Modern Europe from about 1450 to about 1720* (revised excerpt from *The European Inheritance,* ed. E. Barker and P. Vaucher) (Oxford Paperbacks University Series no. 4) (Oxford, 1966). **169.**

The Seventeenth Century (rev. edn, Oxford, 1947). **29, 460.**

Clarke, Edwin. Review, *Medical History* VIII (1964), 380–3. **502, 573.**

Clifton, Robin. 'The Popular Fear of Catholics in England,' *Past and Present* 52 (Aug. 1971) 23–55. **427.**

Clough, C. H. *Machiavelli Researches* (Naples, 1967). **100.**

Introduction. *The Discourses of Niccolò Machiavelli,* tr. Leslie J. Walker (2 vol. London, 1965). **100.**

Cochin, Augustin. *Les Sociétés de Pensée et la Révolution en Bretagne 1788–1789* (2 vol. Paris, 1925). **149.**

Cochrane, Eric. Book review. *The American Historical Review* 82 (Feb. 1977) 88. **314.**

'Science and Humanism in the Italian Renaissance,' *American Historical Review* 81 (Dec. 1976) 1039–57. **526.**

Cochrane, J. A. *Dr. Johnson's Printer: The Life of William Strahan* (London, 1964). **112.**

Cohen, Gustave. *Ecrivains Français en Hollande dans la Première Moitié du XVIIe Siècle* (Paris, 1920). **647.**

Cohen, I. Bernard. *Introduction to Newton's 'Principia'* (Cambridge, 1971). **638.**

'The Protestant Printing Workers of Lyons in 1551,' *Aspects de la Propagande Religieuse*, ed. H. Meylan (Geneva, 1957) 247–57. **130, 352.**

'Publisher Guillaume Rouillé, Businessman and Humanist,' *Editing Sixteenth Century Texts*, ed. R. J. Schoeck (Toronto, 1966) 72–112. **87–8, 234.**

Review article, *Journal of Modern History* xxx (Dec. 1968) 589. **370.**

'Sixteenth-Century French Arithmetics on the Business Life,' *Journal of the History of Ideas* xxi (1960) 18–48. **384, 392, 542, 544.**

'Strikes and Salvation in Lyons,' *Archiv für Reformationsgeschichte* lvi (1965) 48–64. **87, 250, 392, 406.**

Davis, Robert Gorham. 'Speak of the Devil,' *The New York Times Book Review* (March 25, 1972) 55. **633.**

Deanesly, Margaret. *The Lollard Bible* (Cambridge, 1920). **345, 357.**

'Débats et Combats'. *See* Soriano, M.

Debus, Allen. *The English Paracelsians* (New York, 1966). **472.**

    Science and Education in the Seventeenth Century: The Webster–Ward Debate (London, 1970). **275, 473, 550, 656, 681.**

    'The Chemical Debates of the Seventeenth Century,' *Reason, Experiment and Mysticism*, ed. M. L. Bonelli Righini and W. R. Shea (New York, 1975) 19–44. **275.**

    ed. *Science, Medicine and Society in the Renaissance* (Essays to Honor Walter Pagel) (New York, 1974). Includes articles by Keller, A.; Westfall, Richard.

Dechend, Hertha von. *See* de Santillana, G.

De Frede, Carlo. 'Per la Storia della Stampa nel Cinquecento in Rapporto con la Diffusione della Riforma in Italia,' *Gutenberg-Jahrbuch* (1964) 175–84. **311, 348.**

Degering, H. *Lettering: Modes of Writing in Western Europe from Antiquity to the Eighteenth Century* (London, 1929). **205.**

Delaissé, L. M. J. *A Century of Dutch Manuscript Illumination* (Berkeley, Calif., 1968). **259, 339.**

    Le Manuscrit Autographe de Thomas A Kempis et 'L'Imitation de Jésus Christ' (2 vol. Brussels, 1952). **12, 121, 391.**

    Book review of Millard Meiss' work, *The Art Bulletin* lii (1970) 206–12. **13.**

De la Mare, Albinia. 'Bartolomeo Scala's Dealings with Booksellers, Scribes and Illuminators, 1459–63,' *Journal of the Warburg and Courtauld Institutes* xxxix (1976) 237–45. **48–9.**

    'Messer Piero Strozzi, A Florentine Scribe,' *Calligraphy and Paleography. Essays Presented to A. J. Fairbank*, ed. A. S. Osley (London, 1965) 55–68. **13.**

    'The Shop of a Florentine "cartolaio" in 1426,' *Studi Offerti a Roberto Ridolfi* (Florence, 1973) 237–48. **47.**

    'Vespasiano and the Library of the Badia at Fiesole' to be published by the Warburg Institute. Forthcoming. **45.**

    'Vespasiano da Bisticci Historian and Bookseller' (unpublished doctoral dissertation, London University, 1965). **12–13, 45–6, 48–50, 217.**

Delany, Paul. *British Autobiography in the Seventeenth Century* (London, 1969). **229–30, 236, 366.**

D'Elia, Pasquale. *Galileo in China. Relations Between Galileo and the Jesuit-Scientist-Missionaries 1610–1640*, tr. R. Suter and M. Sciascia (Cambridge, Mass., 1960). **609.**

Delof, G. Turbet. 'Comment déjouait-on la censure en France au XVIIe siècle?' *Revue Française d'Histoire du Livre* III (1975) 113–15. **138.**

Delumeau, Jean. *Le Catholicisme entre Luther et Voltaire* (Paris, 1971). **314.**

DeMolen, Richard L. 'The Age of the Renaissance and Reformation,' *The Meaning of the Renaissance and Reformation*, ed. R. L. DeMolen (Boston, 1974) 1–25. **178.**
ed. *The Meaning of the Renaissance and Reformation* (Boston, 1974). Includes articles by DeMolen, R.; Reed, R. B.

Denholm-Young, N. *History and Heraldry 1254–1310* (Oxford, 1965). **134.**

Descartes, René. *A Discourse on Method*, tr. John Veitch, introduction A. D. Lindsay (Everyman's Library edn, 1912). **476.**

Deschamps, J. Book review, *Quaerendo* III (1973) 78. **391.**

Destrez, Jean. *La 'Pecia' dans les Manuscrits Universitaires du XIIIe et du XIVe Siècle* (Paris, 1935). **6, 13–14, 19, 103, 203, 216, 259.**

Deuel, Leo. *Testaments of Time: The Search for Lost Manuscripts and Records* (New York, 1965). **209, 211, 222.**

Deutsch, Karl. *Nationalism and Social Communication: An Inquiry into the Foundations of Nationality* (Cambridge, Mass., 1953). **118.**

Devereux, E. J. 'English Translators of Erasmus 1522–1557,' *Editing Sixteenth Century Texts*, ed. R. J. Schoeck (Toronto, 1966) 45–58. **357–8.**

Dibdin, Thomas F. *Typographical Antiquities or the History of Printing in England Scotland and Ireland...begun by the late Joseph Ames, augmented by William Herbert and Greatly Enlarged by the Reverend Thomas Frognell Dibdin* (4 vol. London, 1810). **ix, 378.**

Dibon, Paul. 'L'Université de Leyde et la République des Lettres au 17e Siècle,' *Quaerendo* V (Jan. 1975) 25–32. **137, 140, 409.**

Dickens, Arthur Geoffrey. *The Counter-Reformation* (London, 1969). **315, 353.**
The English Reformation (New York, 1964). **310, 324.**
Reformation and Society in Sixteenth Century Europe (New York, 1968). **303, 359, 373, 376, 394, 403.**
Thomas Cromwell and the English Reformation (London, 1959). **356.**

Dijk, S. J. P. von. 'An Advertisement Sheet of an Early 14th Century Writing Master at Oxford,' *Scriptorium* X (1956) 47–64. **82.**

Dijksterhuis, E. J. *The Mechanization of the World Picture*, tr. C. Dikshoorn (Oxford, 1961). **505–6.**
Simon Stevin (The Hague, 1943). **500.**
See also Forbes, R. J.

Diringer, David. *The Hand Produced Book* (London, 1953). **22.**
The Illuminated Book (London, 1958). **22.**

Dorsten, Jan van. *The Radical Arts* (London, 1973). Consulted but not cited.
Thomas Basson 1555–1613: English Printer at Leiden (Sir Thomas Browne Institute) (Leiden, 1963). **140.**
'Garter Knights and Familists,' *Journal of European Studies* 4 (1974) 178–88. **140, 143.**

Drachmann, A. G. Review, *Technology and Culture* 17 (Jan. 1976) 112–16. **589.**

Drake, Stillman, ed. and tr. *Discoveries and Opinions of Galileo* (New York, 1957). **458, 525, 526–7, 530, 644, 652–4, 658, 675–6, 681.**
'Early Science and the Printed Book: The Spread of Science Beyond the University,' *Renaissance and Reformation* (University of Toronto) 6 (1970) 38–52. **454, 524, 529, 540, 542, 546, 552, 622, 629.**

See also Rose, P. L.

Dreyer, J. L. E. *History of Astronomy, From Thales to Kepler* (rev. edn, New York, 1953). **617-18.**

Tycho Brahe (Edinburgh, 1890). **581, 583, 597, 624-5.**

Droz, Eugénie. 'Bibles Françaises après le Concile de Trente,' *Journal of Warburg and Courtauld Institutes* XXVIII (1965) 210-15. **334, 342-4, 349, 426.**

Dudek, Louis. *Literature and the Press* (Toronto, 1960). **153, 157.**

Dupree, Hunter. 'The Pace of Measurement from Rome to America,' *The Smithsonian Journal of History* III (1968) 19-40. **468.**

Dupront, Alphonse. 'Livre et Culture dans la Société Française au XVIIIe Siècle – Réflexions sur une Enquête,' *Annales: Economies Sociétés Civilisations* (1965) 867-98. **29, 149.**

Durand, Dana B. *The Vienna-Klosterneuberg Map Corpus: A Study in the Transition from Medieval to Modern Science* (Leiden, 1952). **21, 482, 512, 516.**

'Tradition and Innovation in 15th Century Italy: "Il Primato dell'Italia" in the Field of Science,' *Toward Modern Science*, ed. R. Palter (2 vol., New York, 1961) II, 25-48. **170, 488, 497, 584, 588.**

Durant, Will and Ariel. *The Story of Civilization*, Vol. 6 *The Reformation* (New York, 1957). **250.**

Durme, M. van, ed. *Correspondance Mercatorienne* (Antwerp, 1959). **110.**

Easton, J. B. 'The Early Editions of Robert Recorde's Ground of Artes,' *Isis* 58 (1967) 515-32. **533-4.**

Eastwood, B. S. Review of Lindberg's edition of Pecham, *Speculum* XLVII (1972) 324. **551, 590.**

Ebel, J. G. 'Translation and Cultural Nationalism in the Reign of Elizabeth,' *Journal of the History of Ideas* XXX (Oct.-Dec. 1969) 593-602. **360.**

Echeverria, Durand. *Mirage in the West* (Princeton, 1957). **149.**

Edgerton, Samuel. *The Renaissance Rediscovery of Linear Perspective* (New York, 1975). **192, 268.**

Edler de Roover, F. 'Cost Accounting in the Sixteenth Century,' *Accounting Review* 12 (1937) 226-37. **22, 383.**

'New Facets on the Financing and Marketing of Early Printed Books,' *Bulletin of the Business Historical Society* 27 (1953) 222-30. **22.**

'Per la Storia dell'arte della Stampa in Italia: come furono stampati a Venezia tre dei primi libri in volgare,' *La Bibliofilia* LV (1953) 107-15. **38.**

Eels, Hastings. *The Attitude of Martin Bucer toward the Bigamy of Philip of Hesse* (New York, 1924). **373.**

Egbert, Virginia Wylie. *The Medieval Artist at Work* (Princeton, 1967). **82.**

Ehrman, Albert. 'The Fifteenth Century,' in Ehrman and Pollard, *The Distribution of Books by Catalogue* (Roxburghe Club, Cambridge, 1965). **22.**

Ehrman, Albert and Pollard, Graham. *The Distribution of Books by Catalogue from the Invention of Printing to A.D. 1800* (Roxburghe Club, Cambridge, 1965). **58, 91.**

Eisenstadt, S. N. ed. *The Protestant Ethic and Modernization* (New York, 1968). Includes articles by Hooykaas, R.; Willems, E.

Eisenstein, E. L. 'The Advent of Printing and the Problem of the Renaissance,' *Past and Present* (Nov. 1969) 19-89. **xi.**

Febvre, Lucien and Martin, H.-J. *L'Apparition du Livre* (Paris, 1958). **5, 13, 15, 35-7, 44, 50, 54, 59, 71, 104, 117, 123, 138, 145, 149, 153, 203, 207, 223, 250, 392, 395, 399, 408, 415, 448, 454, 511, 645.**

The Coming of the Book, tr. David Gerard (London, 1976). **5.**

Fedou, René. 'Imprimerie et Culture: La vie intellectuelle à Lyon avant l'apparition du livre,' *Cinq Etudes Lyonnaises* (Histoire et Civilisation du Livre VI) (Geneva, 1966) 1–27. **179, 405.**

Fenn, Eric. 'The Bible and the Missionary,' *Cambridge History of the Bible*, Vol. 3. *The West from the Reformation to the Present Day*, ed. S. L. Greenslade (Cambridge, 1963) 383–407. **378.**

Ferguson, Arthur B. *The Articulate Citizen and the English Renaissance* (Durham, N.C., 1965). **135.**

Ferguson, Eugene. 'Leupold's *Theatrum Machinarum*,' *Technology and Culture* (1971) 64–6. **262.**

Ferguson, Wallace K. *The Renaissance in Historical Thought: Five Centuries of Interpretation* (Cambridge, Mass., 1948). **165-6, 175, 300, 305.**

'The Interpretation of the Renaissance: Suggestions for a Synthesis,' *The Renaissance: Medieval or Modern?* ed. K. H. Dannenfeldt (New York, 1959) 101–9. **165.**

Festugière, A. J. *La Révélation d'Hermès Trismégiste* (4 vol. Paris, 1944–54). **285.**

Feuer, Lewis. *The Scientific Intellectual* (New York, 1963). **611, 642, 661.**

Finegan, J. *Handbook of Biblical Chronology* (Princeton, 1964). **125, 287.**

Finley, M. I. 'Technical Innovation and Economic Progress in the Ancient World,' *The Economic History Review* XVIII (Aug. 1965) 29–45. **240, 251.**

Fisch, Max. 'The Academy of the Investigators,' *Science, Medicine, and History. Essays … in honor of Charles Singer*, ed. E. A. Underwood (2 vol. Oxford, 1953) I, 521–63. **667.**

Fischer, David Hackett. *Historians' Fallacies* (New York, 1970). **406.**

Fischer, Hans. 'Conrad Gesner (1516–1565) as Bibliographer and Encyclopedist,' *The Library*, 5th ser. XXI (Dec. 1966) 269–81. **98, 111.**

Fleckenstein, J.-O. 'Petrus Ramus et l'Humanisme Bâlois,' *La Science au Seizième Siècle* (Colloque de Royaumont 1957) (Paris, 1960) 119–33. **76.**

Forbes, R. J. and Dijksterhuis, E. J. *A History of Science and Technology* (2 vol. London, 1963). **120, 261.**

Ford, Franklin. *Robe and Sword* (Harvard Historical Studies LXIV) (Cambridge, Mass., 1953). **119, 136, 395.**

Foster, George. *Traditional Cultures and the Impact of Technological Change* (New York, 1962). **330.**

Foster, Kenelm. 'Italian Versions,' *Cambridge History of the Bible*, Vol. 3. *The West from the Reformation to the Present Day*, ed. S. L. Greenslade (Cambridge, 1963) 358–60. **348.**

'Vernacular Scriptures in Italy,' *Cambridge History of the Bible*, Vol. 2. *The West from the Fathers to the Reformation*, ed. G. W. H. Lampe (Cambridge, 1969) 452–65. **346.**

Foucault, Michel. *Madness and Civilization*, tr. R. Howard (New York, 1965). **433.**

Frank, R. G. 'Science, Medicine and the Universities of Early Modern England: Background and Sources,' *History of Science* (2-part article) XI (Sept. and Dec. 1973) 194–216, 239–69. **533-4.**

Frankl, Paul. *The Gothic: Literary Sources and Interpretations through Eight Centuries* (Princeton, 1960). **201.**

Franklin, Julian. *Jean Bodin and the Sixteenth Century Revolution in the Methodology of Law and History* (New York, 1963). **103, 200–1.**

Franklin, Ralph. 'Conjectures on Rarity,' *The Library Quarterly* (Chicago) 44 (1974) 309–31. **20.**

French, Peter. *John Dee: The World of an Elizabethan Magus* (London, 1972). **96.**

Frumkin, Maximilian. 'Early History of Patents for Invention,' *Transactions of the Newcomen Society for the Study of the History of Engineering and Technology* XXVI (1947–9) 47–56. **240, 251.**

Fuhrman, Otto W. 'The Invention of Printing,' *A History of the Printed Book*, ed. L. C. Wroth (New York, 1938) 25–57. **27.**

Furet, F. and Sachs, W. 'La Croissance de l'alphabétisation en France, XVIIIe-XIXe Siècles,' *Annales: Economies Sociétés Civilisations* (1974) 714–37. **414.**

Fussner, F. Smith. *The Historical Revolution: English Historical Writing and Thought 1580–1640* (London, 1962). **14, 113.**

Gabriel, Astrik. *The College System in the Fourteenth Century Universities* (Baltimore, Md., n.d.). **475, 536, 581, 622.**

Garlandia: Studies in the History of the Medieval University (Frankfurt, 1969). **608.**

Gade, J. A. *The Life and Times of Tycho Brahe* (Princeton, 1947). **581, 625.**

Gadol, Joan. *Leon Battista Alberti* (2nd edn, Chicago, 1973). **192, 268, 564.**

Galilei, Galileo. 'Letter to the Grand Duchess Christina' (1615), *Discoveries and Opinions of Galileo*, tr. and ed. Stillman Drake (New York, 1957) 175–216. **78, 527.** (*See also* entries under Drake.)

Gallick, Susan. 'A Look at Chaucer and His Preachers,' *Speculum* L (July 1975) 456–76. **236.**

Gandz, Solomon. 'The Dawn of Literature: Prolegomena to a History of Unwritten Literature,' *Osiris* VII (1939) 261–515. **9, 334.**

'The Invention of the Decimal Fractions and the Application of the Exponential Calculus by Immanuel Bonfils of Tarascon (c. 1350),' *Isis* XXV (May 1936) 16–45. **500, 563.**

Gardiner, Stephen. *The Letters of Stephen Gardiner*, ed. J. A. Muller (Cambridge, 1933). **68.**

Garin, Eugenio. *Italian Humanism: Philosophy and Civic Life in the Renaissance*, tr. P. Munz (New York, 1965). **100, 252, 475.**

Science and Civic Life in the Italian Renaissance, tr. P. Munz (New York, 1969). **502, 526, 528, 671.**

'A Garland for Gutenberg,' *Times Literary Supplement* (June 22, 1967) 561. **363.**

Gaskell, Philip. *A New Introduction to Bibliography* (Oxford, 1972). **4.**

Gautier, Théophile. Preface to *Mademoiselle de Maupin* (1835) tr. F. de Sumichrast, in *Paths to the Present*, ed. E. Weber (New York, 1960). **157.**

Gay, Peter. Introduction, *Deism: An Anthology* (Princeton, N. J., 1968). **323–4.**

The Enlightenment: An Interpretation (2 vol. New York, 1966). **209, 299, 491.**

The Party of Humanity (New York, 1964). **146.**

Geanokoplos, Deno J. *Greek Scholars in Venice: Studies in the Dissemination of Greek Learning from Byzantium to Western Europe* (Cambridge, Mass., 1962). **221, 223, 447.**

'Erasmus and the Aldine Academy of Venice, A Neglected Chapter in the Transmission of Greco-Byzantine Learning to the West,' *Greek-Roman-and Byzantine Studies* III, nos 2 and 3 (1960) 107–35. **223.**

Gedenkboek der Plantin-Dagen 1555–1955 (Memorial volume of the Plantin Celebration) (Antwerp, 1956). *See* Roover, R.

Geisendorf, Paul F. 'Lyons and Geneva in the Sixteenth Century: The Fairs and Printing,' *French Humanism 1470–1600*, ed. W. Gundesheimer (New York, 1969) 146–63. **411.**

Gelder, H. A. E. van. *The Two Reformations of the Sixteenth Century* (The Hague, 1961). **175.**

Geldner, F. *Die Deutschen Inkunabeldrucker* (2 vol. Stuttgart, 1968). Consulted but not cited.

'Das Rechnungsbuch des Speyrer . . . Grossbuchhändlers Peter Drach,' *Archiv für Geschichte des Buchwesens* (Frankfurt, 1962) V, 1–195. **22.**

Gerlo, A. 'The *Opus de Conscribendis Epistolis* of Erasmus and the Tradition of the *Ars Epistolica*,' *Classical Influences on European Culture A.D. 500–1500*, ed. R. R. Bolgar (Cambridge, 1971) 103–15. **190.**

Gerritsen, John. *See* Maslen, K. I. D.

Gerson, Jean, 'De Laude Scriptorum ad Fraters Coelestinos et Carthusienses,' *Joannis Gersoni . . . Opera Omnia*, ed. by L. E. Du Pin (5 vol. Amsterdam, 1706), II, cols 694–703. **14–15, 50.**

Geymonat, Ludovico. *Galileo Galilei*, tr. and ed. Stillman Drake (New York, 1965). **526.**

Giedion, Siegfried. *Space Time and Architecture* (Cambridge, Mass., 1941). **186.**

Gies, Dorothy. 'Some Early Ladies of the Book Trade,' *The Publishers Weekly* (Oct. 5, 1940). **46.**

Gies, Joseph and Frances. *Leonardo of Pisa and the New Mathematics of the Middle Ages* (New York, 1969). **236, 382, 467.**

Giesey, Ralph. Book review, *Bibliothèque d'Humanisme et Renaissance Travaux et Documents* XXXIII (1971) 207. **373.**

Gilbert, Neal. *Renaissance Concepts of Method* (New York, 1960). **102–3, 247.**

'The Early Italian Humanists and Disputation,' *Renaissance: Studies in Honor of Hans Baron*, ed. A. Molho and J. Tedeschi (DeKalb, Ill., 1971) 203–26. **473.**

Gilissen, John. 'Individualisme et Sécurité Juridique,' *Individu et Société à la Renaissance: Colloque International* April, 1965 (Brussels, 1967) 35–58. **104.**

Gille, Bertrand. *The Renaissance Engineers* (London, 1966). **243, 565.**

Gillispie, Charles C. *The Edge of Objectivity* (Princeton, 1960). **490, 576, 593, 677, 679–80, 682.**

Gilmore, Myron P. *Humanists and Jurists* (Cambridge, Mass., 1963). **104.**

The World of Humanism 1453–1517 (*The Rise of Modern Europe*, ed. W. Langer) (New York, 1952). **28, 78–9, 81, 183, 184, 187, 209, 210, 238, 289.**

'Italian Reactions to Erasmian Humanism,' *Itinerarium Italicum*, ed. H. Oberman (Leiden, 1975) 61–115. **67.**

'The Renaissance Conception of the Lessons of History,' *Facets of the Renaissance*, ed. W. Werkmeister (Los Angeles, 1959) 73–87. **104, 194–5, 218.**

Gingerich, Owen, ed. *The Nature of Scientific Discovery* (Copernican Symposium, Smithsonian Institution) (Washington, D.C., 1975). Includes article by Nelson, B.

Gossman, Lionel. *Medievalism and the Ideologies of the Enlightenment: The World and Work of La Curne de Sainte-Palaye* (Baltimore, 1968). **201, 338.**

Goudy, Frederick. *The Capitals from the Trajan Column at Rome* (New York, 1936). **82.**

Grabois, Aryeh. 'The *Hebraica Veritas* and Jewish-Christian Intellectual Relations in the Twelfth Century,' *Speculum* L (Oct. 1975) 613–34. **224.**

Grafton, Anthony T. 'Joseph Scaliger and Historical Chronology,' *History and Theory* XIV (1975) 156–85. **611.**

Graham, H. J. ' "Our Tong Maternall Marvellously Amendyd and Augmentyd": The First Englishing and Printing of the Medieval Statutes at Large, 1530–1533,' *UCLA Law Bulletin* XIII (Nov. 1965) 58–98. **105, 119, 360.**

'The Rastells and the printed English Law Book of the Renaissance,' *Law Library Journal* 47 (1954). **105.**

Graña, César. *Bohemian versus Bourgeois* (New York, 1964). **153, 156.**

Gravier, Maurice. *Luther et l'Opinion Publique* (Paris, 1942). **310–11, 354, 405.**

Gray, Hanna. 'Renaissance Humanism: The Pursuit of Eloquence,' *Journal of the History of Ideas* XXIV (1963) 497–514. **296, 473.**

'Valla's Encomium...and the Humanist Conception of Christian Antiquity,' *Essays in History and Literature Presented to Stanley Pargellis*, ed. Heinz Bluhm (Chicago, 1965) 37–51. **195, 323.**

Green, Lowell C. 'The Bible in Sixteenth Century Humanist Education,' *Studies in the Renaissance* XIX (1972). 112–34. **364.**

Greenslade, S. L. 'English Versions of the Bible A.D. 1525–1611,' *Cambridge History of the Bible*, Vol. 3. *The West from the Reformation to the Present Day*, ed. S. L. Greenslade (Cambridge, 1963) 141–74. **358.**

'Epilogue,' *Cambridge History of the Bible*, Vol. 3. 476–519. **343, 364, 374, 378.**

Gregg, Pauline. *Free-born John: A Biography of John Lilburne* (London, 1961). **362, 423.**

Grendler, Paul F. *Critics of the Italian World* (Madison, Wis., 1969). **137, 139, 228, 394, 399, 400.**

The Roman Inquisition and the Venetian Press 1540–1605 (Princeton, 1977). **348, 411, 671.**

'Francesco Sansovino and Italian Popular History 1560–1600,' *Studies in the Renaissance* XVI (1969) 139–80. **360.**

'The Rejection of Learning in Mid-Cinquecento Italy,' *Studies in the Renaissance* XIII (1966) 230–49. **228.**

'The Roman Inquisition and the Venetian Press 1540–1605,' *Journal of Modern History* 47 (March 1975) 48–66. **341, 348, 411, 671.**

Grendler, Paul and Marcella. 'The Survival of Erasmus in Italy,' *Erasmus in English Newsletter* (University of Toronto) No. 8 (1976) 2–22. **145, 416.**

Grimm, Harold J. Introduction to Ninety-Five Theses, *Career of the Reformer I* (*Luther's Works* XXXI, ed. H. T. Lehman) (Philadelphia, 1957) 19–23. **306–7.**

Grimm, Heinrich. 'Luther's "Ablassthesen" und die Gegenthesen von Tetzel-Wimpina in der Sicht der Druck- und Buchgeschichte,' *Gutenberg-Jahrbuch* (1968) 139–50. **306–8.**

Grossmann, Maria. *Humanism in Wittenberg 1485–1517* (Nieuwkoop, 1975). **221.**

'Wittenberg Printing, Early Sixteenth Century,' *Sixteenth Century Essays and Studies* (St Louis, Mo., 1970), I, 53–74. **307–8.**

Gruijs, Albert. 'Codicology or Archeology of the Book? A False Dilemma,' *Quaerendo* II (1972) 87–108. **10.**

Haas, K. H. de. *Albrecht Dürer's Engraving: Melancholia I, A Symbolic Memorial to the Scientist Johann Müller (Regiomontanus)* (Rotterdam, 1951). **247.**
Haebler, K. *The Study of Incunabula,* tr. L. E. Osborne, intro. A. W. Pollard (rev. edn, New York, 1933). **37, 169.**
Hahn, Roger. *The Anatomy of a Scientific Institution: The Paris Academy of Sciences 1660–1803* (University of California, 1971). **680.**
Hajnal, István. *L'Enseignement de L'Ecriture aux Universités Mediévales,* ed. László Mezey (2nd edn, Budapest, 1959). **14.**
Hale, J. R. *Renaissance Europe: The Individual and Society 1480–1520* (Fontana History of Europe, ed. J. H. Plumb) (New York, 1971). **28.**
Renaissance Exploration (New York, 1968). **477, 481.**
'Gunpowder and the Renaissance,' *From The Renaissance to the Counter Reformation,* ed. C. H. Carter (New York, 1965) 113–45. **554.**
'War and Public Opinion in the 15th and 16th Centuries,' *Past and Present* 22 (July 1962) 18–36. **136, 395.**
Haley, K. H. D. *The Dutch in the Seventeenth Century* (London, 1972). **138, 420, 645–7.**
Hall, A. Rupert. *The Scientific Revolution 1500–1800: The Formation of the Modern Scientific Attitude* (Boston, 1957). **263–4, 267, 467, 487, 517, 573, 578, 582, 639.**
'Can the History of Science be History?' *The British Journal for the History of Science* IV (1969) 207–20. **572.**
'Magic Metaphysics and Mysticism in the Scientific Revolution,' *Reason, Experiment and Mysticism,* ed. M. L. Bonelli Righini and W. R. Shea (New York, 1975) 275–82. **641.**
'On the Historical Singularity of the Scientific Revolution of the Seventeenth Century,' *The Diversity of History,* ed. J. H. Elliott and H. G. Koenigsberger (Ithaca, New York, 1970). 199–223. **494, 642.**
'The Scholar and the Craftsman in the Scientific Revolution,' *Critical Problems in the History of Science,* ed. M. Clagett (Madison, Wis., 1969) 3–24. **523, 537, 556–7, 570.**
'Science,' *The New Cambridge Modern History,* Vol. II. *The Reformation, 1520–59,* ed. G. R. Elton (Cambridge, 1958) 386–413. **72, 262.**
Hall, Basil. 'Biblical Scholarship: Editions and Commentaries,' *Cambridge History of the Bible,* Vol. 3. *The West from the Reformation to the Present Day,* ed. S. L. Greenslade (Cambridge, 1963) 38–93. **257, 328, 338, 369.**
'The Trilingual College of San Ildefonso and the Complutensian Polyglot,' *Studies in Church History* V, ed. G. J. Cuming (Leiden, 1969) 114–46. **331, 340.**
Haller, William. *The Elect Nation: The Meaning and Relevance of Foxe's Book of Martyrs* (New York, 1963). **128, 306, 361, 415, 421, 423, 425.**
Hammond, E. A. *See* Talbott, C. H.
Hannaway, Owen. *The Chemists and the Word: The Didactic Origins of Chemistry* (Baltimore, 1975). **102, 275, 474.**
Hanson, N. R. 'The Copernican Disturbance and the Keplerian Revolution,' *Journal of the History of Ideas* XXII (1961) 169–84. **510, 589.**

1974). **5, 6, 13, 15, 34, 37, 44, 50, 52, 55–60, 64, 80, 85, 168, 176, 206, 263, 316, 346–7, 360, 375, 399, 405, 587.**

'Bulla Super Impressione Librorum, 1515,' *Gutenberg-Jahrbuch* (1973) 248–51. **317, 347.**

'Pre-Reformation Censorship of Printed Books,' *The Library Chronicle* XXI (University of Pennsylvania, 1955) 100–5. **347.**

'Printing and the Spread of Humanism in Germany: The Example of Albrecht Von Eyb,' *Renaissance Men and Ideas*, ed. R. Schwoebel (New York, 1971) 23–39. **180, 372.**

Hodgart, Matthew. *Satire* (World University Library) (New York, 1969). **394.**

Hofer, Philip. 'Variant Issues of the First Edition of Ludovico Arrighi Vicentino's "Operina",' *Calligraphy and Paleography. Essays Presented to A. J. Fairbank*, ed. A. S. Osley (London, 1965) 95–107. **82.**

Holborn, Hajo. *Ulrich von Hutten and the German Reformation*, tr. Roland Bainton (New Haven, 1937). **243, 304.**

Holborn, Louise. 'Printing and the Growth of a Protestant Movement in Germany from 1517–1524,' *Church History* XI (June 1942) 1–15. **303, 354.**

Holmes, Margaret L. 'A Brief Survey of the Use of the Renaissance Themes in Some Works of the Lyonese Doctor ... Symphorien Champier,' *Cinq Etudes Lyonnaises (Histoire et Civilisation du Livre – VI)* (Geneva, 1966) 27–55. **523.**

Holt, J. C. *Magna Carta* (Cambridge, 1965). **119.**

Holznecht, Karl. *Literary Patronage in the Middle Ages* (1st edn, 1923; New York, 1966). **228.**

Hooykaas, Reijer. *Humanisme, Science et Réforme: Pierre de la Ramée 1515–1572* (Leiden, 1958). **543, 641.**

Religion and the Rise of Modern Science (Edinburgh, 1972; rev. edn, 1973). Consulted but not cited.

'Science and the Reformation,' *The Protestant Ethic and Modernization*, ed. S. N. Eisenstadt (New York, 1968) 211–39. **641–2, 650, 655, 657, 659–60.**

Horsky, Zdenek. 'Astronomy and the Art of Clockmaking in the fourteenth, fifteenth, and sixteenth centuries,' *Vistas in Astronomy* 9, ed. A. Beer (Oxford, 1967) 25–35. **589.**

Houghton, Walter. 'The History of Trades: Its Relation to Seventeenth Century Thought as Seen in Bacon, Petty, Evelyn, and Boyle,' *Journal of the History of Ideas* II (1941) 33–60. **558.**

Houzeau, J. C. and Lancaster, A. *Bibliographie Générale de l'Astronomie* (3 vol. Brussels, 1889). **590.**

Hoyaux, Jean. 'Les Moyens d'Existence d'Erasme,' *Bibliothèque d'Humanisme et Renaissance* V (1944) 7–59. **401.**

Hoyle, Fred. *Astronomy* (London, 1962). **466.**

Huffines, Marion L. 'Sixteenth Century Printers and Standardization of New High German,' *Journal of English and Germanic Philology* LXXIII (Jan. 1974) 60–72. **117.**

Hufstader, Anselm. 'Lefèvre d'Etaples and the Magdalen,' *Studies in the Renaissance* XVI (1969) 31–60. **331.**

Hughes, Barnabas, 'The Private Library of Johan Scheubel, sixteenth century mathematician,' *Viator* III (1972) 417–32. **587.**

ed. and tr. See Regiomontanus.

Hughes, H. Stuart. *History as Art and as Science* (New York, 1964). **117.**

Huizinga, Johan. 'The Problem of the Renaissance,' (1920), in *Men and Ideas: Essays by Johan Huizinga*, tr. J. S. Holmes and H. van Marle (New York, 1966) 243–88. **165, 226.**

Humphreys, K. W. *The Book Provisions of the Medieval Friars 1215–1400* (Amsterdam, 1964). **12, 90, 622.**

Hunt, R. W. 'The Library of Robert Grosseteste,' *Robert Grosseteste: Scholar and Bishop*, ed. Daniel Callus (Oxford, 1955) chap. 4. **92.**

Hunter, G. K. 'Elizabethans and Foreigners,' *Shakespeare Survey 17* (Cambridge, 1964) 37–52. **513.**

Huppert, George. *The Idea of Perfect History* (Urbana, 1970). **400.**

'The Renaissance Background of Historicism,' *History and Theory* v (1966) 48–60. **201.**

Hutchinson, G. Evelyn. 'Aposematic Insects and the Master of the Brussels Initials,' *American Scientist* (March–April 1974) 161–71. **264.**

Hutt, Allen. 'The Gothic Title-piece and the English Newspaper,' *Alphabet and Image* 3 (1946) 3–20. **207.**

Hyma, Albert. *The Christian Renaissance: A History of the 'Devotio Moderna'* (Grand Rapids, Mich., 1924). **175.**

Inalcik, Halil. *The Ottoman Empire: The Classical Age 1300–1600*, tr. N. Itzkowitz and C. Imber (London, 1973). **335.**

Individu et Société à la Renaissance. Colloque International (April 1965) (Brussels, 1967). **104, 229.** Includes article by Gilissen, J.; Mesnard, P.; and correspondence of Gilissen and Masai.

Innis, Harold. *The Bias of Communication* (Toronto, 1951). Consulted but not cited. *Empire and Communications* (Oxford, 1950). **114, 171.**

Irwin, Raymond. Introduction, *The English Library Before 1700*, ed. Francis Wormald and C. E. Wright (London, 1958) 1–14. **13.**

Iserloh, Erwin. *The Theses Were Not Posted* (London, 1968). **306.**

Issawi, Charles. 'Arab Geography and the Circumnavigation of Africa,' *Osiris* x (1952). **482.**

Itinerarium Italicum (in Honor of P. O. Kristeller) ed. H. Oberman (Leiden, 1975). Includes article by Gilmore, M.

Iversen, Erik. *The Myth of Egypt and its Hieroglyphs in European Tradition* (Copenhagen, 1961). **279–80, 282.**

Ivins, Jr., William M. *Prints and Books: Informal Papers* (Cambridge, Mass., 1926). **86.** *Prints and Visual Communication* (Cambridge, Mass., 1953). **53–4, 85–6, 108, 259, 262–3, 266–7.** *Three Vesalian Essays* (New York, 1952). **485.**

Ivy, G. S. 'The Bibliography of the Manuscript-Book,' *The English Library before 1700*, ed. Francis Wormald and C. E. Wright (London, 1953) 32–65. **14, 94.**

Jack, Mary Ann. 'The *Accademia del Disegno* in Late Renaissance Florence,' *Sixteenth Century Journal* VII (Oct. 1976) 3–21. **253.**

Jackson, Sydney L. 'Printed Books and the Mass Media: Some Sixteenth Century Views,' *Libri: International Library Review* (Copenhagen, 1968) vol. 18, 35–50. **348, 416.**

Karpinski, L. C. and Staubach, C. N. 'An Anglo Norman Algorism of the Fourteenth Century,' *Isis* XXIII (1935) 121–52. **467.**

Katzman, Natan. 'The Impact of Communication Technology: Promises and Prospects,' *Journal of Communication* (University of Pennsylvania) 24 (1974) 47–59. **39.**

Kearney, Hugh F. Introduction, *Origins of the Scientific Revolution* (Problems and Perspectives in History) (London, 1966). **683.**

'Puritanism and Science: Problems of Definition,' *Past and Present* 29 (July 1965) 104–10. **643, 646, 661, 664.**

'Puritanism, Capitalism and the Scientific Revolution,' *Past and Present* 28 (July 1964) 81–101. **688.**

Keele, K. D. 'Leonardo da Vinci's Influence on Renaissance Anatomy,' *Medical History* VIII (1964) 360–70. **551.**

Keller, Alexander G. 'Mathematical Technologies and the Growth of the Idea of Technical Progress in the Sixteenth Century,' *Science, Medicine and Society in the Renaissance*, ed. Alan Debus (New York, 1974) 11–27. **20, 27, 261.**

'A Renaissance Humanist Looks at "New" Inventions: The Article "Horlogium" in Giovanni Tortelli's De Orthographia,' *Technology and Culture* 11 (1970) 345–65. **20, 252.**

'Zilsel, The Artisans and the Idea of Progress in the Renaissance,' *Roots of Scientific Thought*, ed. Wiener and Noland (New York, 1957) 281–6. **558, 561.**
ed. *See* Besson, Jacques.

Kellett, C. E. 'Two Anatomies,' *Medical History* VIII (Oct. 1964) 342–50. **567.**

Kelley, Donald R. *Foundations of Modern Historical Scholarship* (New York, 1970). **103–4, 189, 191, 195, 201, 218.**

'Faces in Clio's Mirror,' *Journal of Modern History* 47 (Dec. 1975) 679–90. **218.**

'Martyrs, Myths and the Massacre: The Background of St. Bartholomew,' *American Historical Review* 77 (Dec. 1972) 1323–42. **133.**

Kemp, Martin. 'Dissection and Divinity in Leonardo's Late Anatomies,' *Journal of the Warburg and Courtauld Institutes* XXXV (1972) 200–25. **565–6.**

'A Drawing for the De Fabrica and some thoughts upon the Vesalius Muscle-Men,' *Medical History* XIV (July 1970) 277–88. **267.**

'"Il Concetto dell'Anima," in Leonardo's Early Skull Studies,' *Journal of the Warburg and Courtauld Institutes* XXXIV (1971) 115–34. **251, 473, 565.**

Kemsley, Douglas S. 'Religious Influences in the Rise of Modern Science,' *Annals of Science* XXIV (1968) 199–226. **696.**

Kenney, E. J. *The Classical Text: Aspects of Editing in the Age of the Printed Book* (Berkeley, Calif., 1974). **81, 108, 113, 209, 338.**

Kent, John. *See* Daniélou, J.

Kenyon, Frederick G. *Books and Readers in Ancient Greece and Rome* (Oxford, 1951). **15, 22, 334.**

Kermode, Frank. 'Between Two Galaxies,' *Encounter* 113 (Feb. 1963) 76–82. **x.**

Keuning, J. *Willem Jansz. Blaeu*, rev. and ed. M. Donkerslootde Vrij (Amsterdam, 1973). **480, 663.**

Khan, M. S. 'The Early Bengali Printed Books,' *Gutenberg-Jahrbuch* (1966) 200–8. **317.**

Kimble, George H. T. *Geography in the Middle Ages* (London, 1938). **580.**

King, M. D. 'Reason, Tradition and the Progressiveness of Science,' *History and Theory* 10 (1971) 3–32. **459.**

Kuhn, Thomas S. *The Copernican Revolution: Planetary Astronomy in the Development of Western Thought* (Cambridge, Mass., 1957). **113, 466, 512, 579-80, 592, 594-6, 598, 603-4, 609, 614-15.**
The Structure of Scientific Revolutions (rev. edn, Chicago, 1970). **189, 459, 461, 500, 597, 603, 605, 630.**
'The Function of Measurement in Modern Physical Science,' *Isis* 52 (1961) 161-93. **470, 605.**
'Science: The History of Science,' *International Encyclopedia of Social Sciences*, ed. D. L. Sills, xiv (Chicago, 1968) 74-83. **459.**
Kuhns, William. *The Post-Industrial Prophets: Interpretations of Technology* (New York, 1971). **41.**
Kulstein, David. 'Government Propaganda and the Press during the Second Empire,' *Gazette, International Journal for Mass Communications Studies* x (1964) 125-44. **150.**
Kurz, Otto. 'The Medical Illustrations of the Wellcome Manuscript,' *Journal of the Warburg and Courtauld Institutes* v (1942) 137-42. **267.**

Labarre, A. 'Un Atelier Mayençais d'Enluminure vers 1450-1500,' *Revue Français d'Histoire du Livre* iv (1974) 127-31. **54.**
Labrousse, Elisabeth. *Pierre Bayle* (2 vol. The Hague, 1963). **420.**
Lancaster, A. *See* Houzeau, J. C.
Langford, Jerome. *Galileo, Science and the Church* (rev. edn, Ann Arbor, Mich., 1971). **653, 672-3, 676.**
Larner, John. *Culture and Society in Italy 1290-1420* (New York, 1971). **232, 235.**
Laslett, Peter. *The World We Have Lost* (New York, 1965). **425-6.**
'Philippe Ariès and "La Famille",' *Encounter* (March 1976) 80-3. **131.**
Le Cinquième Centenaire de l'Imprimerie dans les Anciens Pays-Bas, catalogue of exhibition held in the Royal Library of Brussels (Sept.-Oct. 1973) (Brussels, 1973). **59.**
Le Livre (Catalogue of Bibliothèque Nationale Exhibition) (Paris, 1972). **374.**
Le Roy Ladurie, Emmanuel. *Les Paysans de Languedoc* (2 vol. Paris, 1966). **311, 415.**
Leavis, Q. D. *Fiction and the Reading Public* (London, 1939). **150, 352.**
Lecler, Joseph. *Toleration and the Reformation*, tr. T. L. Westow (2 vol. London, 1955). **442.**
Leclercq, Jean. *The Love of Learning and the Desire for God*, tr. C. Misrahi (New York, 1962). **297, 317, 456-7.**
Lee, Rensselaer W. *Ut Pictura Poesis: The Humanistic Theory of Painting* (rev. edn, New York, 1967). **254, 256.**
Lee, Sidney. *The French Renaissance in England* (Oxford, 1910). **349.**
Leff, Gordon. *Heresy in the Later Middle Ages: The Relation of Heterodoxy to Dissent c. 1250-1450* (2 vol. Manchester, 1967). **311.**
Lehmann-Haupt, Hellmut. *Gutenberg and the Master of the Playing Cards* (New Haven, 1966). **54.**
Peter Schoeffer of Gernsheim and Mainz (Rochester, New York, 1950). **13, 51-2, 55, 58-9, 206.**
'The Heritage of the Manuscript,' *A History of the Printed Book*, ed. Lawrence C. Wroth (The Dolphin no. 3) (New York, 1938) 3-23. **13, 22, 263.**
Leith, James. *Media and Revolution* (Toronto, 1968). **326.**

Lenhart, John M. *Pre-Reformation Printed Books: A Study in Statistical and Applied Bibliography* (Franciscan Studies no. 14) (New York, 1935). **44, 38, 169.**

Lenkey, Susan V. 'Printers' Wives in the Age of Humanism,' *Gutenberg-Jahrbuch* 1975, 331–6. **24, 87.**

Lenoble, R. *Mersenne ou la Naissance du Mécanisme* (Paris, 1943). **644.**

Lerner, Daniel. 'Toward a Communication Theory of Modernization' (1963 essay), reprinted in *Comparative Perspectives on Social Change*, ed. S. N. Eisenstadt (Boston, 1968). **414.**

Lerner, M. P. *See* Costabel, P.

Levy, Bernard S., ed. *Developments in the Early Renaissance* (Albany, New York, 1968). **175.**

Levy, F. J. 'The Making of Camden's Britannia,' *Bibliothèque d'Humanisme et Renaissance* XXVI (1964) 70–97. **110.**

Lewis, C. S. *The Discarded Image: An Introduction to Medieval and Renaissance Literature* (1st edn, 1964; Cambridge, 1974). **93.**

Lewis, John. *Anatomy of Printing* (London, 1970). **459.**

Leyden, William von. 'Antiquity and Authority,' *Journal of the History of Ideas* XIX (1958) 473–92. **191.**

Lievsay, J. L. *The Englishman's Italian Books 1550–1700* (Philadelphia, 1969). **417.**
 Venetian Phoenix: Paolo Sarpi and some of His English friends 1606–1700 (Lawrence, Kansas, 1974). **412.**

'The Life of Erasmus by Beatus Rhenanus' (1540), in *Christian Humanism and the Reformation: Selected Writings of Erasmus*, ed. and tr. John C. Olin (New York, 1965) 31–55. **180.**

Lilley, S. 'Robert Recorde and the Idea of Progress,' *Renaissance and Modern Studies* II (University of Nottingham, 1958) 3–38. **559–60.**

Lindberg, D. C. 'The Theory of Pinhole Images in the 14th Century,' *Archive for the History of the Exact Sciences* VI (1970) 299–325. **506.**
 tr. and ed. *John Pecham and the Science of Optics: Perspectiva Communis* (Madison, Wis., 1970). **551, 590.**

Ling, Wang. *See* Needham, J.

Little, Lester K. *See* Rosenwein, B. H.

Littleton, A. C. and Yamey, B. S., eds. *Studies in the History of Accounting* (London, 1956). Includes articles by Roover, Raymond de; Taylor, R. E.

Livre et Société dans la France du XVIIIe Siècle (2 vol. Paris, 1965). **29.**

Loodes, D. M. 'The Theory and Practice of Censorship in Sixteenth Century England,' *Transactions of the Royal Historical Society* (London, 1974) vol. 24, 5th ser., 141–57. **311.**

Lockwood, W. B. 'Vernacular Scriptures in Germany and the Low Countries before 1500,' *Cambridge History of the Bible*, Vol. 2. *The West from the Fathers to the Reformation*, ed. G. W. H. Lampe (Cambridge, 1969) 415–36. **346.**

Loewe, Raphael. 'The Medieval History of the Latin Vulgate,' *The Cambridge History of the Bible*, Vol. 2. *The West from the Fathers to the Reformation*, ed. G. W. H. Lampe (Cambridge, 1969). **328–9, 334.**

Lohne, J. A. 'Isaac Newton: The Rise of a Scientist 1661–1671,' *Notes and Records of The Royal Society of London* 20 (Dec. 1965) 125–39. **634.**

Loomis, L. H. 'The Auchinleck Manuscript and a Possible London Bookshop of 1330–1340,' *Publications of the Modern Language Association* 57 (1942), 595–627, **13.**

Lopez, Robert. 'Hard Times and Investment in Culture,' *The Renaissance: Six Essays* (New York, 1962) 29–55. **21.**

Lough, John. *Essays on the Encyclopédie of Diderot and d'Alembert* (Oxford, 1968). **147.**

An Introduction to Seventeenth Century France (London, 1960). **155, 395.**

Louis Philippe. *Mémoires de Louis Philippe* (2 vol. Paris. 1973). **19.**

Lovejoy, A. O. *The Great Chain of Being: A Study in the History of an Idea* (Cambridge, Mass., 1948). **215.**

Lowinsky, Edward. 'Music in the Culture of the Renaissance,' *Journal of the History of Ideas* IX (1954) 509–53. **249.**

'Music of the Renaissance as Viewed by Renaissance Musicians,' *The Renaissance Image of Man and the World*, ed. B. O'Kelly (Columbus, Ohio, 1966) 129–77. **249.**

Lowry, M. J. C. 'The "New Academy" of Aldus Manutius,' *Bulletin of the John Rylands University Library of Manchester* 58 (Spring 1976) 378–420. **222.**

'Two Great Venetian Libraries in the Age of Aldus Manutius,' *Bulletin of the John Rylands University Library of Manchester* 57 (Autumn 1974) 128–66. **222, 586.**

Luethy, Herbert. *From Calvin to Rousseau*, tr. S. Attanasio (New York, 1970). **403, 421.**

Luther, Martin. 'Against the Heavenly Prophets in the Matter of Images and Sacraments' (1525), *Luther's Works,* ed. C. Bergendorff and H. T. Lehmann, XL (Philadelphia, 1958) 99–100. **68.**

Lutz, Cora E. 'Manuscripts Copied from Printed Books,' *Essays on Manuscripts and Rare Books* (Hamden, Conn., 1975) 129–39. **51, 52.**

MacCaffrey, W. T. 'Elizabethan Politics: The First Decade 1558–1568,' *Past and Present* 24 (April 1963) 25–43. **395.**

McColley, Grant, Introduction, *The Defense of Galileo of Thomas Campanella* (Smith College Studies in History XXII) (Northampton, Mass., 1937). **668.**

'The Debt of Bishop John Wilkins to the "Apologia Pro Galileo",' *Annals of Science* IV (April 1939) 150–69. **668.**

McConica, James K. *English Humanists and Reformation Politics Under Henry VIII and Edward VI* (Oxford, 1965). **331.**

McDonald, E. E. 'The Modernizing of Communication: Vernacular Publishing in Nineteenth Century Maharashtra,' *Asian Survey* VIII (July 1968) 589–607. **317.**

McGuire, J. E. and Rattansi, P. M. 'Newton and the "Pipes of Pan",' *Notes and Records of the Royal Society* 21 (Dec. 1966) 108–43. **286, 572, 641.**

McIlwain, Charles. 'Medieval Institutions in the Modern World,' *The Twelfth Century Renaissance*, ed. Warren Hollister (New York, 1969) 72–81. **513.**

McKenzie, D. F. 'Printers of the Mind: Some Notes on Bibliographical Theories and Printing House Practices,' *Studies in Bibliography* XXII (Charlottesville, Va., 1969) 1–75. **11, 56, 393.**

McKerrow, R. B. 'Booksellers, Printers, and the Stationers Trade,' *Shakespeare's England* II (2 vol. Oxford, 1916) chap. 23, 212–39. **120.**

MacKinney, Loren. *Medical Illustrations in Medieval Manuscripts* (London, 1965). Consulted but not cited.

McLaughlin, Mary M. 'Survivors and Surrogates: Children and Parents from the Ninth to the Thirteenth Centuries,' *The History of Childhood*, ed. Lloyd de Mause (New York, 1974) 101–83. **431.**

McLean, Antonia. *Humanism and the Rise of Science in Tudor England* (London, 1972). **34, 35, 454, 511, 554.**

McLuhan, Marshall. *The Gutenberg Galaxy: The Making of Typographical Man* (Toronto, 1962). **16, 35, 122, 129, 151, 159, 186, 258.**

Understanding Media: The Extensions of Man (New York, 1965). **16, 159.**

McManners, John. *French Ecclesiastical Society under the Ancien Regime* (Manchester, 1960). **398.**

The French Revolution and the Church (New York, 1970). **352.**

McMullin, Ernan, ed. *Galileo, Man of Science* (New York, 1967). Includes articles by Bedini, S. A.; Boyer, Carl.

McMurtrie, Douglas. *The Book* (Oxford, 1943). **7, 167, 375-6.**

McNair, Philip. *Peter Martyr in Italy: An Anatomy of Apostasy* (Oxford, 1967). **348.**

McNally, R. L. 'The Ninety-five Theses of Martin Luther,' *Theological Studies* XXVIII (1967) 439-80. **306.**

McPherson, David. 'A Possible Origin for Mopsa in Sidney's Arcadia,' *Renaissance Quarterly* XXI (Winter 1968) 420-9. **259-60.**

Maas, Clifford. 'German Printers and the German Community in Renaissance Rome,' *The Library*, 5th ser. XXXI (June 1976) 118-26. **398.**

Machiavelli, Bernardo. *Libro di Ricordi*, ed. C. Olschki (Florence, 1954). **100.**

Machiavelli, Niccolò. *The Discourses of Niccolò Machiavelli*, tr. Leslie J. Walker (1950) with new introduction by C. H. Clough (2 vol. London, 1975). **100.**

Maddison, F. R. *See* Bedini, S. A.

Mahoney, Michael S. *The Mathematical Career of Pierre de Fermat (1601-1665)* (Princeton, N.J., 1973). **530, 532, 537, 552, 554.**

Major, J. Russell. 'Crown and Aristocracy in Renaissance France,' *American Historical Review* LXIX (April 1964) 631-45. **395.**

Malgaigne, J. F. *Surgery and Ambrose Paré*, tr. W. B. Hamby (Norman, Okla., 1965). **538.**

'The Man Behind the Sermon,' *Times Literary Supplement* (Feb. 27, 1964) 175. **337.**

Mandrou, Robert. *De la Culture Populaire aux 17e et 18e Siècles: La Bibliothèque Bleue de Troyes* (Paris, 1964). **130.**

'Le Livre: Ce Ferment,' *Revue Française d'Histoire du Livre* I (1971) 1-9. **29.**

'La Transmission de l'Hérésie à l'époque moderne,' *Hérésies et Sociétés dans l'Europe pré-industrielle, 11e-18e Siècles* (Colloque de Royaumont, 1962) ed. Jacques Le Goff (Civilisations et Sociétés 10) (The Hague, 1968) 281-9. **311.**

Mann, E. L. 'The Problem of Originality in English Literary Criticism, 1750-1800,' *Philological Quarterly* XVIII (1939) 97-118. **192.**

Mannheim, Karl. *Essays on the Sociology of Culture*, ed. and tr. E. Manheim (Oxford, 1956). **18, 154.**

Manuel, Frank. *The Eighteenth Century Confronts the Gods* (Cambridge, Mass., 1959) **282-3.**

Isaac Newton Historian (Cambridge, 1963). **611, 626.**

A Portrait of Isaac Newton (Cambridge, Mass., 1968). **283, 459, 555, 626-7, 633-4, 663, 679.**

Mardersteig, Giovanni. *The Remarkable Story of a Book Made in Padua in 1477*, tr. H. Schmoller (London, 1967). **56.**

Margolin, Jean-Claude. 'La Réalité Sociale dans l'Univers d'Albert Dürer,' *Individualisme et Société* (Brussels Colloquium) 215-56. **247-8.**

Marinoni, Augusto. Book review, *Technology and Culture* XIII (1972) 301–9. **566.**

Marks, Richard B. *The Medieval Manuscript Library of the Charterhouse of Saint Barbara in Cologne (Analecta Cartusiana* vol. 21–2) (Salzburg, 1974). **15.**

'The Scriptorium and Library of St. Barbara's Cologne,' lecture at Catholic University of America, July 9, 1974. **379.**

'The Significance of Fifteenth-Century Hand Corrections in the Düsseldorf Exemplars of Some of Therhoernen's editions of the Works of Werner Rolevinck,' *Gutenberg-Jahrbuch* (1977) 49–56. **316.**

Marrou, H. I. *A History of Education in Antiquity,* tr. George Lamb (1st edn, 1948; New York, 1956). **422.**

Marsak, L. M., ed. *The Rise of Science in Relation to Society* (New York, 1964). **493.**

Martin, H.-J. *Livre, Pouvoirs et Société à Paris au XVIIe Siècle* (2 vol. Geneva, 1969). **5, 135, 315, 333, 337, 349–50, 397, 408, 411, 414, 420, 646, 663, 680.**
See also Febvre, Lucien.

Masai, François. *See* Gilissen, John.

Maslen, K. I. D. and Gerritsen, John. Correspondence, *The Library* XXX (June 1975) 81–94, 134–6. **56.**

Mason, S. F. 'The Scientific Revolution and the Protestant Reformation,' *Annals of Science* IX (1953) 64–88. **641.**

Mathias, Peter. 'Who Unbound Prometheus?' *Science and Society 1600–1900,* ed. P. Mathias (Cambridge, 1972) 54–81. **554.**

ed. *Science and Society 1600–1900* (Cambridge, 1972). Includes articles by Mathias, P.; Rattansi, P. M.

Maunsell, Andrew. *Three Part Catalogue of English Printed Bookes* (London, 1595). **106, 107.**

Mayer, C. A. 'The Problem of Dolet's Evangelical Publications,' *Bibliothèque d'Humanisme et Renaissance* XVII (1955) 405–14. Consulted but not cited.

Mayor, A. Hyatt. *Prints and People* (New York, 1971). **489, 549, 588, 616.**

Mazlish, Bruce. *See* Bronowski, Jacob.

Mehl, James V. 'Ortwin Gratius: Cologne Humanist' (unpublished dissertation, University of Missouri, Columbia, Mo., 1975). **206.**

Meiss, Millard. *Painting in Florence and Siena After the Black Death* (Princeton, N.J., 1951). **297.**

Menninger, Karl. *Number Words and Number Symbols: A Cultural History of Numbers,* tr. Paul Broneer (rev. edn, Cambridge, Mass., 1969). **382.**

Menzel, Donald. Introduction to Pasquale D'Elia, *Galileo in China: Relations between Galileo and the Jesuit-Scientist-Missionaries 1610–1640,* tr. R. Suter and M. Sciascia (Cambridge, Mass., 1960). **648.**

Mersenne, Marin. *Les Nouvelles Pensées de Galilée,* ed. and introduction by P. Costabel and M.-P. Lerner (2 vol. Paris, 1973). **645.**

Merton, Robert K. *On the Shoulders of Giants: A Shandean Postscript* (New York, 1965). **121–2.**

Science, Technology and Society in Seventeenth Century England (rev. edn offset reprint, New York, 1970). **459–60, 478, 641, 661, 679.**

The Sociology of Science (Chicago, 1973). **506.**

Merton, Robert K. and Zuckerman, H. 'Patterns of Evaluation in Science: Institutionalisation, Structure and Functions of the Referee System,' *Minerva* 9 (1971) 63–102. **461–2, 667.**

Mesnard, Pierre. 'Le Commerce Epistolaire comme Expression Sociale de l'Individualisme Humaniste,' *Individu et Société à la Renaissance: Colloque International-1965* (Brussels, 1967) 15–21. **228–9.**

Metzger, Bruce M. *The Text of the New Testament, Its Transmission, Corruption and Restoration* (Oxford, 1968). **338, 373.**

Meyer, Carl S., ed. *Luther for an Ecumenical Age: Essays* (St Louis, Mo., 1967). Includes articles by Bluhm, H.; Schweibert, E. G.

Meyer, R. W. *Leibniz and the Seventeenth Century Revolution*, tr. J. P. Stern (Cambridge, 1952). **245.**

Meylan, Henri, ed. *Aspects de la Propagande Religieuse* (*Travaux d'Humanisme et Renaissance* XXVIII) (Geneva, 1957). **441.** Includes articles by Davis, N. Z.; Kingdon, R. M.

Michelangelo. *The Divine Michelangelo: The Florentine Academy's Homage on his Death in 1564* (a facsimile edition of the 'Esequie del Divino Michelangelo Buonarroti', Florence, 1564), introduction, tr., annot. Rudolf and Margot Wittkower (London, 1964). **254.**

Michelet, Jules. *Histoire de France: VII Renaissance* (16 vol.) (Oeuvres Complètes de J. M. 40 vol.) (Paris, Flammarion, 1893–99). **300.**

Middleton, W. E. K. *The Experimenters: A Study of the Accademia del Cimento* (Baltimore, 1971). **107, 665–6, 674.**

Milburn, R. L. P. 'The "People's" Bible: Artists and Commentators,' *Cambridge History of the Bible*, Vol. 2. *The West from the Fathers to the Reformation*, ed. G. W. H. Lampe (Cambridge, 1969) 280–308. **257, 355.**

Miller, C. William. *Benjamin Franklin's Philadelphia Printing 1728–1766: A Descriptive Bibliography* (American Philosophical Society Memoir: 102) (Philadelphia, 1974). **381.**

Miller, Edwin H. *The Professional Writer in Elizabethan England: A Study of Non Dramatic Literature* (Cambridge, Mass., 1959). **137.**

Miller, P. J. 'Eighteenth Century Periodicals for Women,' *History of Education Quarterly* (Fall 1971) 279-86. **134.**

Miner, Dorothy. *The Giant Bible of Mainz: 500th Anniversary: 4 April 1952*. Library of Congress Pamphlet, Washington, D.C. **82.**

Moeller, Bernd. *Imperial Cities and the Reformation: Three Essays*, tr. H. E. Midelfort and M. U. Edwards (Philadelphia, 1972). **366, 449.**

Mohl, Ruth. *The Three Estates in Medieval and Renaissance Literature* (New York, 1933). **394.**

Molho, A. and Tedeschi, J. ed. *Renaissance: Studies in Honor of Hans Baron* (DeKalb, Ill., 1971). Includes articles by Gilbert, N.; Kinser, S.; Nauert, C.; Strauss, G.; Zimmerman, T. P.

Molnar, Thomas. *The Decline of the Intellectuals* (New York, 1961). **153.**

Momigliano, Arnaldo. 'Ancient History and the Antiquarian' (1950), *Studies in Historiography* (New York, 1966) 1–40. **186, 190, 218, 325.**

Mommsen, Theodor E. 'Petrarch's Conception of the "Dark Ages",' *Speculum* XVII (April 1942) 226–42. **185, 294-5, 298.**

Monfasani, John. *George of Trebizond: A Biography and a Study of His Rhetoric and Logic* (Columbia Studies in the Classical Tradition I) (Leiden, 1976). **399.**

Monter, E. William. *Calvin's Geneva* (New York, 1967). **410.**

'Chronique: Trois Historiens Actuels de la Sorcellerie,' *Bibliothèque d'Humanisme et Renaissance Travaux et Documents* XXXI (1969) 205–13. **436.**

Montgomery, J. W. 'Cross Constellation and Crucible,' *Ambix* XI, no. 2 (June 1963) 65–87. **650.**

Montgomery, R. L. 'William Caxton and the Beginnings of Tudor Critical Thought,' *The Huntington Library Quarterly* XXXVI (Feb. 1973) 91–103. **457.**

Moody, Ernest A. 'Galileo and his Precursors,' *Galileo Reappraised*, ed. C. L. Golino (Berkeley, Calif., 1966) 23–44. **498, 503-4.**

See also Clagett, M.

Moran, James. 'William Caxton and the Origins of English Publishing,' *Gutenberg-Jahrbuch* 63 (1967) 61–5. **112.**

Moranti, Luigi. *L'Arte Tipografia in Urbino* (Florence, 1967). **49.**

Morison, Samuel Eliot. *Admiral of the Ocean Sea* (Boston, 1942). **583, 592, 610.**

The European Discovery of America: The Northern Voyages (Boston, 1969). **554.**

Vistas in History (New York, 1964). **x.**

Morison, Stanley. *Fra Luca Pacioli of Borgo San Sepolcro* (New York, 1933). **549.**

'The Learned Press as an Institution,' *Bibliotheca Docet: Festgabe für Carl Wehmer*, ed. S. Joost (Amsterdam, 1963) 153–79. **41, 340.**

Morley, Thomas. *A Plain and Easy Introduction to Practical Music (1597)*, ed. R. A. Harman, foreword by Thurston Dart (London, 1952). **244.**

Mornet, Daniel. *Les Origines Intellectuelles de la Révolution Française (1715–1787)* (1st edn, 1933; Paris, 1947). **148-9.**

Morris, Colin. *The Discovery of the Individual 1050–1200* (New York, 1973). **228.**

Moser, E. A., ed. *See Baroque and Rococo Pictorial Imagery.*

Mosher, Frederick. *See* Taylor, Archer.

Moule, H. T. *See* Darlowe, T. H.

Moxon, Joseph. *Mechanick Exercises on the Whole Art of Printing* (1683–4) ed. Herbert Davis and Harry Carter (London, 1962). **273, 625.**

Muir, P. *See* Carter, J.

Muller, Herbert. *Freedom in the Western World: From the Dark Ages to the Rise of Democracy* (New York, 1964). **467.**

Muller, J. A. *See* Gardiner, Stephen.

Mumford, Lewis. *Technics and Civilization* (New York, 1934). **21, 151.**

Murray, Alexander. 'Religion among the Poor in thirteenth-century France,' *Traditio* XXX (1974) 287–324. **63.**

Musper, Heinrich T. 'Xylographic Books,' *The Book Through Five Thousand Years*, ed. H. D. L. Vervliet (Brussels, 1972) 341–8. **54.**

Myconius, Friedrich. Selection from *Historia Reformationis* in *The Reformation*, ed. and tr. Hans Hillerbrand (New York, 1964) 43–4. **306.**

Nagel, E. Commentary, *Critical Problems in the History of Science* (conference held at Madison, Wis., Sept. 1957) ed. M. Clagett (Madison, Wis., 1959) 153–61. **505.**

Nardi, Bruno. 'La scuola di Rialto' (1963), *Saggi sulla Cultura Veneta del quattro e cinquecento* (Padua, 1971) 93–139. **547.**

Nasr, S. H. *Science and Civilization in Islam* (New York, 1970). **463.**

Nauert, Charles G. *Agrippa and the Crisis of Renaissance Thought* (Urbana, Ill., 1965). **276**

'The Clash of Humanists and Scholastics: An Approach to Pre-Reformation. Controversies,' *Sixteenth Century Journal* IV (April 1973) 1–18. **308, 331.**

'Peter of Ravenna and the "Obscure Men" of Cologne,' *Renaissance: Studies in Honor of Hans Baron*, ed. A. Molho and J. Tedeschi (DeKalb, Ill., 1971) 609–40. **308, 331.**

Needham, J. and Ling, Wang. *Science and Civilisation in China*, Vol. I. *Introductory Orientations* (Cambridge, 1954). **492.**

Science and Civilisation in China, Vol. III. *Mathematics and the Sciences of the Heavens and the Earth* (Cambridge, 1959). **609.**

Nelson, Benjamin. 'The Early Modern Revolution in Science and Philosophy: Fictionalism, Probabilism, Fideism, and Catholic "Prophetism",' *Boston Studies in the Philosophy of Science 1964/66*, ed. R. S. Cohen and M. W. Wartofsky (Dordrecht, Holland, 1968) 1–40. **672.**

'The Quest for Certitude,' *The Nature of Scientific Discovery* (Copernican Symposium, Smithsonian Institution) ed. Owen Gingerich (Washington, D.C., 1975) 363–72. **456.**

'Weber's Protestant Ethic,' *Beyond the Classics?*, ed. C. Glock and P. Hammond (Berkeley, Calif., 1974) 71–130. **378-9.**

Nesi, Emilia. *Il Diario della Stamperia di Ripoli* (Florence, 1903). **46.**

Newton, Isaac. *Sir Isaac Newton's Mathematical Principles of Natural Philosophy*, tr. A. Motte, 1729, appendix by Florian Cajori (Berkeley, Calif., 1934). **663.**

Niceron, Jean Pierre. *Mémoires pour servir à l'Histoire des hommes illustres dans la République des Lettres* (43 vol. Paris, 1729–45). **139.**

Nichols, S. G., Jr. 'The Interaction of Life and Literature in the *Peregrinationes ad Loca Sancta* and the *Chansons de Geste*,' *Speculum* XLIV (Jan. 1969) 51–77. **599.**

Nicolson, Marjorie Hope. *The Breaking of the Circle* (New York, 1962). **219.**

Science and Imagination (Ithaca, N.Y., 1956). **653.**

'English Almanacs and the "New Astronomy",' *Annals of Science* IV (Jan. 1939) 1–33. **677.**

Nock, A. D. Introduction, *Corpus Hermeticum*, ed. A. D. Nock, tr. A. J. Festugière (4 vol. Paris, 1945). **283.**

North, D. C. and Paul, T. R. 'An Economic Theory of the Growth of the Western World,' *The Economic History Review* XXIII (2nd ser. 1970), 1–17. **30.**

North, John. 'Medieval Background,' *Copernicus: Yesterday and Today* (conference held in Washington, D.C., Dec. 27 and 28, 1972) *Vistas in Astronomy*, ed. A. Beer and K. A. Strand, 17 (Oxford, 1975) 3–16. **464.**

Norton, F. J. *Italian Printers 1501–1520* (London, 1958). Consulted but not cited.

Printing in Spain 1501–1520 (Cambridge, 1966). Consulted but not cited.

'Nouvelles du Livre Ancien' (Fall, 1974) no. 1. **4.**

Nyhus, Paul L. 'Caspar Schatzgeyer and Conrad Pellican: The Triumph of Dissension in the Early Sixteenth Century,' *Archiv für Reformationsgeschichte* 61 (1960) 179–204. **328, 331, 341.**

Oakeshott, Walter. 'Some Classical and Medieval Ideas in Renaissance Cosmography,' *Fritz Saxl Memorial Essays*, ed. D. J. Gordon (London, 1957) 245–60. **512.**

Oastler, C. L. *John Day, the Elizabethan Printer* (Oxford Bibliographical Society Occasional Publication no. 10) (Oxford, 1975). **360-1.**

Oberhuber, Konrad. Introduction to *Early Italian Engravings from the National Gallery of Art* (Washington, D.C., 1973). **248, 254.**

O'Connell, Marvin. *The Counter Reformation 1559–1610* (The Rise of Modern Europe) (New York, 1974). **314.**

Oestreich, G. 'Die Antike Literatur als Vorbild der Praktischen Wissenschaften im 16 and 17 Jahrhundert,' *Classical Influences on European Culture AD 1500–1700*, ed. R. R. Bolgar (Cambridge, 1976) 315–25. **194.**

Offenberg, Adri. 'The First Use of Hebrew in a Book Printed in the Netherlands,' *Quaerendo* IV (1974) 44–54. **613.**

Olin, John C., ed. and tr. *See* 'The Life of Erasmus by Beatus Rhenanus.'

Olschki, C., ed. *See* Machiavelli, Bernardo.

O'Malley, C. D. *Andreas Vesalius of Brussels 1514–1564* (Berkeley, Calif., 1964). **267, 570.**
'Andreas Vesalius 1514–1564: In Memoriam,' *Medical History* VIII (Oct. 1964) 299–308. **573.**
See also Saunders and O'Malley.

Ong, Walter J., S.J. *The Presence of the Word* (New Haven, Conn., 1967). **41, 319.**
Ramus: Method and the Decay of Dialogue. From the Art of Discourse to the Art of Reason (Cambridge, Mass., 1958). **41, 92, 102, 275, 430.**
Rhetoric Romance and Technology (Ithaca, N.Y., 1971). **41, 92.**
'From Allegory to Diagram in the Renaissance Mind,' *Journal of Aesthetics and Art Criticism* XVII (June, 1959) 423–40. **92.**
'System Space and Intellect in Renaissance Symbolism,' *Bibliothèque d'Humanisme et Renaissance* XVIII (1956) 222–40. **92.**

Ore, Oyestein. *Cardano: The Gambling Scholar* (Princeton, N.J., 1953). **236, 662.**

Origo, Iris. *The Merchant of Prato* (rev. edn, London, 1963). **483.**

Ornstein, Martha. *The Role of Scientific Societies in the Seventeenth Century* (Chicago, 1928). **460, 644, 667-8, 676.**

Orr, M. A. *Dante and the Early Astronomers* (London, 1913). **483, 512.**

Ortelius, Abraham. 'Message to the Reader,' *Theater of the Whole World* (London, 1606) (Facsimile edn, Antwerp: Theatrum Orbus Terrarum Ltd, 1968). **88, 193, 227.**

Osley, A. S., ed. *Calligraphy and Paleography. Essays Presented to A. J. Fairbank* (London, 1965). Includes articles by de la Mare, A.; Hofer, P.; Wolpe, B. L.

Overfield, James. 'A New Look at the Reuchlin Affair,' *Studies in Medieval and Renaissance History* (University of Nebraska) VIII (1971) 165–207. **305.**

Owst, G. R. *Literature and Pulpit in Medieval England* (Oxford, 1966). **365.**

Ozment, Steven. *The Reformation in the Cities* (New Haven, Conn., 1975). **318.**

Pächt, Otto. 'Early Italian Nature Studies and the Early Calendar Landscape,' *Journal of the Warburg and Courtauld Institutes* XIII (1950) 13–47. **82, 233, 264, 492.**
'Notes and Observations on the Origin of Humanist Book Decoration,' *Fritz Saxl Memorial Essays*, ed. D. J. Gordon (London, 1975) 184–94. **204.**

Pagel, Walter. *Paracelsus: An Introduction to Philosophical Medicine in the Era of the Renaissance* (Basel, 1958). **286, 539, 657.**
'News, Notes and Queries,' *Medical History* VIII (1964) 78–83. **550.**
'William Harvey: Some Neglected Aspects of Medical History,' *Journal of the Warburg and Courtauld Institutes* VII (1944) 144–53. **528.**

Pagel, W. and Rattansi, P. 'Vesalius and Paracelsus,' *Medical History* VIII (Oct. 1964) 309–34. **472, 570-1, 573.**

Painter, George D. *William Caxton: A Quincentenary Biography* (London, 1976). **38.**

Palmer, Robert R. *Catholics and Unbelievers in 18th Century France* (Princeton, New Jersey, 1939). **325, 348.**

Palter, Robert. 'An Approach to the History of Early Astronomy,' *History and Philosophy of Science* I (1970) 93–133. **500, 603.**

Review of *Hypothesis and Perception* by E. E. Harris in *The Journal of Philosophy* (1973) 202–10. **268.**

ed. *Johannes Kepler 1571–1630*, Catalogue of Exhibition held Nov.–Jan. 1971–2 (University of Texas at Austin, 1971). **611, 630.**

Pannekoek, A. *A History of Astronomy*, tr. from Dutch (1st edn, 1951; London, 1961). **463, 583, 609.**

Panofsky, Erwin. *Albrecht Dürer* (2 vol., Princeton, 1945). **176, 197, 205, 248, 280.**

The Life and Art of Albrecht Dürer (1 vol. rev. edn, Princeton, N.J., 1955). **548, 549, 560.**

Meaning in the Visual Arts: Papers in and on Art History (New York, 1955). **188, 196.**

Renaissance and Renascences in Western Art (Uppsala, 1960). **165, 181–3, 186–7, 193–4, 200–2, 213, 215, 218, 258, 270, 293–4, 296.**

Studies in Iconology (New York, 1939). **186, 188, 196.**

'Artist, Scientist, Genius: Notes on the "Renaissance-Dämmerung",' *The Renaissance: Six Essays* (New York, 1962) chap. 6. **238–40, 249, 251, 267, 269–70, 284.**

'Erasmus and the Visual Arts', *Journal of the Warburg and Courtauld Institutes* XXXII (1964) 200–27. **174, 176, 295.**

Parent, Annie. *Les Métiers du Livre à Paris au XVIe Siècle (1535–1560)* (Geneva, 1974). **55–6, 60, 87, 540, 544.**

Parker, Anthony. 'The Difficult Publishing Art of Persuading Scientists to Sit Down and Write Books,' *Times Literary Supplement* (Sept. 7, 1971) 813–14. **461.**

Parkes, Malcolm B. 'The Influence of the Concepts of Ordinatio and Compilatio on the Development of the Book,' *Medieval Learning and Literature: Essays Presented to R. W. Hunt* (Oxford, 1976) 115–45. **92.**

'The Literacy of the Laity,' *The Medieval World*, ed. D. Daiches and A. Thorlby (*Literature and Western Civilization*, Vol. II) (London, 1972–6) 555–76. **62.**

Parsons, Edward. *The Alexandrian Library* (Amsterdam, 1952). **465.**

Paton, H. J. *See* Klibansky, R.

Pattison, Mark, *Isaac Casaubon 1559–1614* (2nd edn, Oxford, 1892). **73, 222.**

Paul, T. R. *See* North, D. C.

Paulus, Nikolaus. *Indulgences as a Social Factor in the Middle Ages* (New York, 1922). **376.**

Pedersen, Olaf. 'The Life and Work of Peter Nightingale,' *Vistas in Astronomy* 9 (ed. A. Beer) (1967) 3–11. **607.**

Penrose, Boies. *Travel and Discovery in the Renaissance 1420–1620* (New York, 1962). **74, 483, 512, 514–15.**

Peters, Edward M. 'Editing Inquisitors' Manuals in the 16th Century...' *The Library Chronicle* (University of Pennsylvania) XL (Winter 1974) 95–107. **87.**

Petrucelli, R. J. 'Giorgio Vasari's Attribution of the Vesalian Illustrations to Jan Stephan of Calcar,' *Bulletin on the History of Medicine* (Baltimore) XLV (1971) 29–37. **233.**

Pettas, William. 'The Cost of Printing a Florentine Incunable,' *La Bibliofila* LXXV (1973) 67–85. **50.**

Peyre, Henri. 'The Influence of Eighteenth Century Ideas on the French Revolution,' *Intellectual Movements in Modern European History*, ed. Franklin L. Baumer (*Main Themes in European History*, ed. B. Mazlish) (New York, 1965) 63–85. **148.**

Pfeiffer, Rudolf. *History of Classical Scholarship From the Beginnings to the End of the Hellenistic Age* (Oxford, 1968). **22, 465.**

Philip, Alexander. *The Calendar: Its History, Structure and Improvement* (Cambridge, 1921). **608, 610.**

Phillips, W. A. 'Faust,' *Encyclopedia Britannica* x (28 vol. 11 edn, London, 1910–11) 210–11. **50.**

Pintard, René. *Le Libertinage Erudit dans la Première Moitié du XVIIe Siècle* (2 vol. Paris, 1943). **644.**

Plant, Marjorie. *The English Book Trade* (London, 1939). Consulted but not cited.

Plumb, J. H. 'The Public, Literature and the Arts in the 18th Century,' *The Emergence of Leisure*, ed. M. M. Marrus (New York, 1974) 11–37. **131.**

Pocock, J. G. A. *The Ancient Constitution and the Feudal Law* (Cambridge, 1957). **201, 224.**

The Machiavellian Moment (Princeton, New Jersey, 1975). **189–90.**

Pollack, Michael. 'The Performance of the Wooden Printing Press,' *Library Quarterly*, vol. 42 (April 1972) 218–64. Consulted but not cited.

'Production Costs in Fifteenth Century Printing,' *Library Quarterly* xxxix (Oct. 1969) 318–30. Consulted but not cited.

Pollard, Graham. 'The University and the Book Trade in Medieval Oxford,' *Miscellanea Mediaevalia* iii (Berlin, 1964) 336–46. **14.**

See also Ehrman, Albert.

'Pontiff says Media Lead Youth Astray,' *The Washington Post* (Tuesday, May 5, 1970) A14. **355.**

Poole, H. W. *See* Berry, W. T.

Popkin, Richard. *The History of Scepticism from Erasmus to Descartes* (New York, 1964). **231, 326.**

The Portable Renaissance Reader, ed. and tr. J. B. Ross and M. M. McLaughlin (New York, 1969). **27, 166, 217, 320, 393.**

Post, R. R. *The Modern Devotion: Confrontation with Reformation and Humanism* (Leiden, 1968). **16, 346.**

Potter, G. R. 'Zwingli and His Publisher,' *The Library Chronicle* xl (Winter 1974) 108–17. **99.**

Pottinger, David. *The French Book Trade in the Ancien Regime 1500–1791* (Cambridge, Mass., 1958). **128, 145-7, 399.**

Poulle, E. *See* Hilliard, D.

Praz, Mario. *Studies in Seventeenth Century Imagery* (Rome, 1964). **280.**

Preus, R. *The Inspiration of Scripture* (Edinburgh, 1957). **319, 323, 326, 332.**

Price, Derek de Solla. *Science since Babylon* (enlarged edn, New Haven, 1975). **453-4.**

'The Book as a Scientific Instrument,' *Science* 158 (6 Oct. 1967) 102–4. **612, 691.**

'Gears from the Greeks: The Antikythera Mechanism,' *Transactions of the American Philosophical Society* 64 (Philadelphia, 1974) part 7, 1–70. **589.**

'Geometrical and Scientific Talismans,' *Changing Perspectives in the History of Science: Essays in Honor of Joseph Needham*, ed. M. Teich and R. Young (London, 1973) 250–64. **55.**

ed. *See* Chaucer.

'Veritas Filia Temporis,' *Philosophy and History: The Ernst Cassirer Festschrift*, ed. R. Klibansky and H. J. Paton (New York, 1963) 197–222. **143.**

Sayce, R. A. 'French Versions,' *Cambridge History of the Bible*, Vol. 3. *The West from the Reformation to the Present Day*, ed. S. L. Greenslade (Cambridge, 1963) 347–52. **351–2.**

Sayili, Aydin. *The Observatory in Islam and its Place in the General History of the Observatory* (Ankara: Turkish Historical Society Series) VII (1960). **463, 610.**

Schlegel, Dorothy. 'Freemasonry and the Encyclopédie Reconsidered,' *Studies in Voltaire and the Eighteenth Century* 90 (1972) 1433–60. **143.**

Schmidt, Herman A. P., S.J. *Liturgie et Langue Vulgaire: Le Problème de la Langue Liturgique chez les Premiers Réformateurs et au Concile de Trente* (Rome, 1950). **343–4, 348.**

Schmidt, Ph. *Die Illustration der Lutherbibel 1522–1700* (Basel, 1962). **68.**

Schmitt, Charles B. *A Critical Survey and Bibliography on Renaissance Aristotelianism 1958–1969* (Padua, 1971). **522.**

'Essay Review: A Fresh Look at Mechanics in 16th-Century Italy,' *Studies in the History and Philosophy of Science* I (1970–1). 161–75. **495, 522, 525, 546, 642.**

'The Faculty of Arts at Pisa at the Time of Galileo,' *Physis* XIV (1972) 243–72. **528.**

'Toward a Reassessment of Renaissance Aristotelianism,' *History of Science* XI (Sept. 1973) 159–94. **522.**

Book review, 'A Garin Compendium,' *Isis* 63 (Sept. 1972) 419–22. **667.**

Schmitt, Charles B. and Webster, C. 'Harvey and M. A. Severino: A Neglected Medical Relationship,' *Bulletin of the History of Medicine* XLV (1971) 49–75. **668.**

Schoeck, Richard J. 'Copernicus and Humanism,' paper given at a Folger Library Seminar, Spring 1974. **602.**

ed. *Editing Sixteenth Century Texts* (Toronto, 1966). Includes articles by Davis, N. Z.; Devereux, E. J.; Kortepeter, M.

Scholderer, V. *Fifty Essays in Fifteenth and Sixteenth Century Bibliography* (Amsterdam, 1967). **204.**

Schücking, Levin L. *The Puritan Family*, tr. Brian Battershaw (London, 1969). **425, 433.**

Schwartz, W. *Principles and Problems of Biblical Translations: Some Reformation controversies and Their Background* (Cambridge, 1955). **278, 339, 357.**

Schweibert, Ernest C. *Luther and His Times* (St Louis, Mo., 1950). **221, 307.**

'New Groups and Ideas at the University of Wittenberg,' *Archiv für Reformationsgeschichte* 49 (1958) 60–78. **94.**

'The Theses and Wittenberg,' *Luther for an Ecumenical Age: Essays*, ed. C. S. Meyer (St Louis, Mo., 1967) 120–43. **308.**

Scott, Geoffrey. *The Architecture of Humanism: A Study in the History of Taste* (London, 1924). **215.**

Scribner, R. W. 'The Social Thought of Erasmus,' *Journal of Religious History* VI (June 1970) 3–27. **372, 401.**

Seguin, J. P. *L'Information en France de Louis XII à Henri II* (Geneva, 1961). **135.**

Servetus, Michael. *Michael Servetus: A Translation of his Geographical, Medical, and Astrological Writings with Introduction and Notes* by D. C. O'Malley (Philadelphia, 1963). **566.**

Settle, Thomas B. 'Borelli, Giovanni Alfonso, 1608–1679,' *Dictionary of Scientific Biography* (14 vol. New York, 1970) II 306–13. **674.**

Seznec, Jean. *The Survival of the Pagan Gods: The Mythological Tradition and Its Place in Renaissance Humanism and Art*, tr. B. F. Sessions (rev. edn, New York, 1961). **195-8, 214-15, 258.**

Shackleton, Robert. 'The Encyclopédie and Freemasonry,' *The Age of the Enlightenment. Studies Presented to Theodore Besterman* (St Andrews, 1967) 223-40. **143.**

Shapiro, Barbara. *John Wilkins, 1614-1672 An Intellectual Biography* (Berkeley, 1969). **534, 555, 665.**

Shea, William. *Galileo's Intellectual Revolution: Middle Period 1610-1632* (New York, 1972). **527.**
See also Bonelli Righini, M. L.

Shearman, John. *Mannerism* (Pelican Style and Civilization Series) (London, 1967). **231.**

Shelby, Lon R. 'The Education of Medieval English Master Masons,' *Medieval Studies* (Toronto) XXXII (1970) 1-26. **65, 253, 553.**
'The Geometrical Knowledge of Medieval Master Masons,' *Speculum* XLVII (July 1972) 395-421. **65, 253, 537.**
'The "Secret" of the Medieval Masons,' *On Pre-Modern Technology and Science, Studies in Honor of Lynn White, Jr.* (UCLA Center for Medieval and Renaissance Studies publication) (Malibu, Calif., 1976) 201-19. **272.**

Shenker, Israel. 'Books as an Art Form Through Five Centuries,' *The New York Times* (Sept. 10, 1973). **48.**

Sheppard, L. A. 'Printing at Deventer in the Fifteenth Century,' *The Library* XXIV 5th ser. (1944) 101-19. **16, 346.**

Shera, J. H. 'An Epistemological Foundation for Library Science,' *The Foundations of Access to Knowledge: A Symposium*, ed. E. B. Montgomery (Syracuse, N.Y., 1968). **479.**

Sherman, Claire R. 'Some Visual Definitions in the Illustrations of Aristotle's *Nichomachean Ethics* and *Politics* in the French Translations of Nicole Oresme,' *The Art Bulletin* LIX (Sept. 1977) 320-30. **546.**

Sherrington, Charles. *The Endeavour of Jean Fernel* (Cambridge, 1946). **244, 249, 539, 540, 562, 567.**

Shipman, Joseph. 'Johannes Petreius, Nuremberg Publisher of Scientific Works, 1524-1550,' *Homage to a Bookman, Essays...for Hans P. Kraus* (Berlin, 1967) 154-62. **587, 650.**

Shumaker, Wayne. *The Occult Sciences in the Renaissance* (Berkeley, 1972). **191, 281, 284-5, 287-8, 290.**

Siebert, Frederick S. *Freedom of the Press in England 1476-1776, The Rise and Decline of Government Control* (Urbana, Ill., 1952). **120.**

Simone, Franco. *The French Renaissance*, tr. H. G. Hall (London, 1969). **294-5, 300.**

Simpson, Lewis. 'The Printer as a Man of Letters,' *The Oldest Revolutionary: Essays on Benjamin Franklin*, ed. J. A. Leo Lemay (Philadelphia, 1976) 3-21. **381.**

Singer, Charles, ed. and tr. *Galen on Anatomical Procedures* (Oxford, 1956). **567.**
'The Confluence of Humanism, Anatomy and Art,' *Fritz Saxl Memorial Essays*, ed. D. J. Gordon (London, 1957) 261-70. **538, 573.**
'Hebrew Scholarship in the Middle Ages Among Latin Christians,' *The Legacy of Israel*, ed. E. R. Bevan and Charles Singer (Oxford, 1927) 283-314. **224, 340.**

Singleton, C. S., ed. *Art, Science, and History in the Renaissance* (Baltimore, Md., 1967). Includes articles by Gombrich, E. H.; Waters, D. W.; Yates, F.

'Reuchlin's Philosophy, Pythagoras and Cabala for Christ,' *Archiv für Reformationsgeschichte* 47 (1956) 1–20. **278, 620.**

Sprat, Thomas. *History of the Royal Society* (1667) ed. J. I. Cope and H. W. Jones (St Louis, Mo., 1958). **283, 562, 563, 601, 669-70, 682.**

Stannard, Jerry. 'The Herbal as a Medical Document,' *Bulletin of the History of Medicine* XLIII (May–June 1969) 212–20. **265, 485.**

Starnes, DeWitt T. *Robert Estienne's Influence on Lexicography* (Austin, Texas, 1963). **91, 336.**

Staubach, C. N. *See* Karpinski, L. C.

Stavrianos, L. S. *The World Since 1500: A Global History* (Englewood, New Jersey, 1966). **516.**

Steele, Robert. 'What Fifteenth Century Books are About,' *The Library*, 2nd ser. IV (Oct. 1903) 337–55; V (Oct. 1904) 337–56; VI (Jan. 1905) 137–55; VIII (July 1907) 225–38. **169, 346, 436.**

Steinberg, S. H. *Five Hundred Years of Printing* (rev. edn, Bristol, 1961). **5, 7, 32-3, 44, 52, 59, 80-2, 89, 113, 117, 128, 138, 202, 204, 206, 259, 326, 359, 375, 392, 407, 440.**

Steiner, George. *After Babel: Aspects of Language and Translation* (Oxford, 1975). **287.**
'The Retreat from the Word,' *Kenyon Review* (Spring 1961) 187–216. **159.**

Steinmann, Martin. *Johannes Oporinus: Ein Basler Buchdrucker um die Mitte des 16. Jahrhunderts* (Basel, 1967). **442, 446, 570.**

Steneck, N. H. *The Scientific Press at the Time of Copernicus, 1530–1550* (Catalogue of Exhibition held at Ann Arbor, Michigan, April 3–5, 1973). **575-7.**

Stephenson, Carl. *A Brief Survey of Medieval Europe* (New York, 1941). **36.**

Stevens, Henry N. *Ptolemy's Geography A Brief Account of all the Printed Editions down to 1730* (London, 1908). **110.**

Stillwell, Margaret Bingham. *The Awakening Interest in Science During the First Century of Printing, 1450–1550. An Annotated Checklist of First Editions* (New York: Bibliographical Society of America, 1970). **461, 510-11, 548, 583, 585-6.**
The Beginning of the World of Books 1450 to 1470. A Chronological Survey of the Texts Chosen for Printing... With a Synopsis of the Gutenberg Documents (New York, 1972). **44, 50.**

Stimson, Dorothy. *The Gradual Acceptance of the Copernican Theory of the Universe* (New York, 1917). **614, 629-30, 677.**
Scientists and Amateurs, A History of the Royal Society (New York, 1948). **666.**

Stone, Lawrence. *The Crisis of the Aristocracy 1558–1641* (Oxford, 1965). **136, 395.**
Social Change and Revolution in England 1540–1640 (Problems and Perspectives in History, ed. H. F. Kearney) (London, 1966). **310.**
'The Educational Revolution in England, 1560–1640,' *Past and Present* 28 (July 1964) 41–80. **395.**
'Literacy and Education in England 1640–1900,' *Past and Present* 42 (Feb. 1969) 69–139. **61, 67, 330, 414.**
'The Massacre of the Innocents,' *The New York Review of Books* (Nov. 14, 1974) 25–31. **431.**

Strachan, James. *Early Bible Illustrations: A Short Study* (Cambridge, 1957). **64, 108 257.**

Strauss, Gerald. *Nuremberg in the Sixteenth Century* (New York, 1966). **308, 403-4.**
'The Course of German History: The Lutheran Interpretation,' *Renaissance:*

Studies in Honor of Hans Baron, ed. A. Molho and J. Tedeschi (DeKalb, Ill., 1971) 665–86. **305, 360.**

'A Sixteenth-Century Encyclopedia: Sebastian Münster's Cosmography and its Edition,' *From the Renaissance to the Counter-Reformation*, ed. C. H. Carter (New York, 1965) 145–63. **86, 102, 109.**

Strauss, Leo. *Persecution and the Art of Writing* (Glencoe, Ill., 1952). **147, 273.**

Struik, Dirk. 'Mathematics in the Netherlands During the First Half of the XVIe Century,' *Isis* 25 (1936) 46–53. **385, 500, 521, 530, 534.**

Stuewer, R. H., ed. *Historical and Philosophical Perspectives of Science* (Minnesota Studies v) (Minneapolis, Minn., 1970). Includes articles by Hesse, M.; Rosen, E.

Sutcliffe, E. F. 'Jerome,' *Cambridge History of the Bible*, Vol. 2. *The West from the Fathers to the Reformation*, ed. G. W. H. Lampe (Cambridge, 1969) 80–101. **328.**

Swerdlow, Noel. 'The Derivation and the First Draft of Copernicus's Planetary Theory,' *Proceedings of the American Philosophical Society* 117 (Dec. 31, 1973) 423–513. **583–4, 621.**

'On Copernicus' Theory of Precession,' *The Copernican Achievement*, ed. R. S. Westman (Los Angeles, 1975) 49–99. **578.**

Swierk, Alfred. 'Was bedeutet "ars artificialite scribendi"?' *Der Gegenwaertige Stand der Gutenberg-Forschung* (Stuttgart, 1972) 243–51. **168.**

Sykes, Norman. 'The Religion of the Protestants,' *Cambridge History of the Bible*, Vol. 3. *The West from the Reformation to the Present Day*, ed. S. L. Greenslade (Cambridge, 1963) 175–82. **327, 333.**

Sypher, Wilie. 'Similarities between the Scientific and Historical Revolutions at the End of the Renaissance,' *Journal of the History of Ideas* xxv (July–Sept. 1965) 353–68. **113.**

Tak, J. G. van der. 'Calcidius' Illustration of the Astronomy of Heracleides of Pontus,' *Mnemosyne* (The Netherlands) series iv, xxv, Fasc. 2 (1972) 148–56. **510.**

Talbott, C. H. and Hammond, E. A. *The Medical Practitioners in Medieval England: A Biographical Register* (London, 1965). **538.**

Talbott, John E. 'The History of Education,' *Daedalus* 100 (Winter 1971) 133–51. **61.**

Tavard, George H. *Holy Writ or Holy Church: The Crisis of the Protestant Reformation* (London, 1959). **319.**

Taylor, Archer. 'The Influence of Printing 1450–1650' (Lecture delivered Oct. 2, 1940, at the University of California, Berkeley) *Printing and Progress: Two Lectures* (Berkeley, 1941). **703.**

Taylor, Archer and Mosher, Frederick. *The Bibliographical History of Anonyma and Pseudonyma* (Chicago, 1957). **138.**

Taylor, E. G. R. *The Mathematical Practitioners of Tudor and Stuart England* (Cambridge, 1954). **110, 273, 530, 534, 583, 625, 633.**

Taylor, Henry Osborn. *Thought and Expression in the Sixteenth Century* (2 vol. New York, 1920). **73.**

Taylor, R. E. *No Royal Road: Luca Pacioli and His Times* (Chapel Hill, N.C., 1942). **514, 547.**

'Luca Pacioli,' *Studies in the History of Accounting*, ed. A. C. Littleton and B. S. Yamey (London, 1956) 175–85. **384, 547.**

Tory, Geoffroy. *Champ Fleury*, tr. George B. Ives (New York, 1967) (republication of Grolier Club edn, 1927). **203-4.**

Toulmin, Stephen. *Human Understanding* (Princeton, 1972). **461.**

Toulmin, S. and Goodfield, J. *The Fabric of the Heavens* (London, 1963). **465, 500.**

'Toward a New History of the New Science', *Times Literary Supplement*, Sept. 15, 1972, 1058. **521.**

Tracy, James D. 'Erasmus becomes a German,' *The Renaissance Quarterly* XXI (Autumn 1968) 281-8. **309.**

Trapp, J. B. 'The High Renaissance at Harvard,' *Times Literary Supplement*, Jan. 14, 1977, 41. **261.**

Trattner, W. I. 'God and Expansion in Elizabethan England: John Dee 1527-1583,' *Journal of the History of Ideas* XXV (Jan.–March 1964) 17-34. **274.**

Trénard, Louis. 'L'Histoire des Mentalités Collectives: Les Livres: Bilan et Perspective,' *Revue d'Histoire Moderne et Contemporaine* 15 (1968) 691-703. **29.**

'La Presse Française des Origines à 1788,' *Histoire Générale de la Presse Française*, ed. C. Bellanger *et al.* (4 vol. Paris, 1974) 27-376. **131, 134, 138, 147, 259.**

Trevor-Roper, Hugh R. *The Crisis of the Seventeenth Century: Religion, the Reformation and Social Change* (New York, 1968). **364, 388, 410, 418-19, 434, 436, 438-9, 449.**

'Desiderius Erasmus,' *Men and Events* [English title: *Historical Essays*] (New York, 1957) 35-61. **145, 401, 416.**

Review essay, *History and Theory* V (1966) 61-82. **281.**

Trimpi, Wesley. 'The Meaning of Horace's "Ut Pictura Poesis",' *Journal of the Warburg and Courtauld Institutes* XXXVI (1973) 1-34. **230, 256, 319, 322.**

Trinkaus, Charles. *In Our Image and Likeness, Humanity and Divinity in Italian Humanist Thought* (2 vol. Chicago, 1970). **298.**

'Humanism, Religion, Society: Concepts and Motivations of some Recent Studies,' *Renaissance Quarterly* XXIX (Winter 1976) 676-714. **298.**

Trithemius, Johannes. *In Praise of Scribes – De Lande Scriptorum*. **14-15, 50, 378.** *See* Klaus Arnold, ed.

Tuchman, Barbara. 'Hazards on the Way to the Middle Ages,' *The Atlantic Monthly* (Dec. 1975) 72-8. **236.**

Uhlendorf, B. A. 'The Invention and spread of printing till 1470 with special reference to social and economic factors,' *The Library Quarterly* II (1932) 179-231. **6, 44.**

Ullman, B. L. *The Origin and Development of Humanistic Script* (Rome, 1960). **45, 203, 205.**

Ullmann, Walter. *The Individual and Society in the Middle Ages* (Baltimore, 1966). **229.**

Underwood, E. A., ed. *Science, Medicine and History. Essays . . . In Honor of Charles Singer* (2 vol. Oxford, 1953). Includes articles by Arber, A.; Fisch, M.; Johnson, R. F.

Unguru, Sabetai. 'Witelo and Thirteenth century Mathematics: An Assessment,' *Isis* 63 (Dec. 1972) 496-508. **494.**

Updike, D. B. *Printing Types: Their History Forms and Use: A study in Survivals* (2 vol. Cambridge, Mass., 1937). **203, 224, 250, 588.**

Vaassen, Elgin. *Die Werkstatt der Mainzer Riesenbibel in Würzburg und Ihr Umkreis* (Frankfurt-am-Main, 1973). **54.**

Vann, Richard T., ed. *Century of Genius: European Thought 1600–1700* (Englewood, New Jersey, 1967). **460, 668.**

Vansina, Jan. *Oral Tradition: A Study in Historical Methodology*, tr. H. M. Wright (1st French version, 1961; London, 1973). **xiii, 9.**

Vasari. *Vasari's Lives of the Artists*, abridged and ed. by B. Burroughs (New York, 1946). **176.**

Venturi, Franco. *Utopia and Reform in the Enlightenment* (Cambridge, 1971). **142, 147.**

Vervliet, Hendrik D. L., ed. *The Book Through Five Thousand Years* (New York and Brussels, 1972). **178.** Includes articles by Musper, H. T.; Vervliet, H. D. L. 'Printing in the fifteenth and sixteenth centuries,' 355–82.
See also Carter, Harry.

Verwey, H. de la Fontaine. 'Les Caractères de Civilité et la Propagande Religieuse,' *Bibliothèque d'Humanisme et Renaissance Travaux et Documents* XXVI (1964) 7–27. **207, 430.**

'The Family of Love,' *Quaerendo* VI (1976) 219–71. **443, 447.**

'The First "Book of Etiquette" for Children . . .' *Quaerendo* I (1971) 19–30. **430.**

'The Netherlands Book,' *Copy and Print in the Netherlands*, ed. Wytze G. Hellinga (Amsterdam, 1962) 3–70. **169, 346, 414, 645.**

'Pieter Coecke van Aelst and the Publication of Serlio's Book on Architecture,' *Quaerendo* VI (1976) 166–94. **207.**

'Trois Hérésiarques dans les Pays-Bas du XVIe Siècle,' *Bibliothèque d'Humanisme et de Renaissance Travaux et Documents* XVI (1954) 312–30. **442, 446-7.**

'Willem Jansz. Blaeu and the Voyage of Le Maire and Shouten,' *Quaerendo* III (1973) 87–105. **481.**

Victor, J. M. 'The Revival of Lullism,' *Renaissance Quarterly* XXVIII (Winter 1975) 504–34. **315.**

Voët, Leon. *The Golden Compasses: A History and Evaluation of the Printing and Publishing Activities of the Officina Plantiniana at Antwerp* (2 vol. Amsterdam, 1969). **75, 100, 337, 408-9, 442, 446, 448, 647.**

Vogel, Kurt. 'Fibonacci, Leonardo,' *Dictionary of Scientific Biography* (14 vol. New York, 1970) IV 604–13. **236.**

Vorzimmer, Peter. 'Darwin, Malthus and the Theory of Natural Selection,' *Journal of the History of Ideas* XXX (1969) 527–42. **75.**

Vrij, M. de. *The World on Paper* (a descriptive catalogue of cartographical material published in seventeenth-century Amsterdam) (Theatrum Orbis Terrarum, Amsterdam, n.d.). **503.**

Vyer, O. van de. 'Original Sources of some early lunar maps,' *Journal for the History of Astronomy* II (June 1971) 86–97. **624.**

Wade, Ira O. *The Clandestine Organization and Diffusion of Philosophic Ideas in France from 1700 to 1750* (Princeton, 1938). **139.**

Wadsworth, James. *Lyons 1473–1503, The Beginnings of Cosmopolitanism* (Cambridge, Mass., 1962). **405.**

Walker, D. P. *The Ancient Theology* (Ithaca, New York, 1972). **125, 277, 281-2, 285, 644.**

Spiritual and Demonic Magic from Ficino to Campanella (London, 1958). **96, 438.**

'The *Prisca Theologia* in France,' *Journal of the Warburg and Courtauld Institutes* XVII (July–Dec. 1954) 204–59. **288.**

'A Secret Conspiracy Exposed,' *New York Review of Books* (Sept. 23, 1971) 42–4. **445.**

Walzer, Michael. *The Revolution of the Saints* (New York, 1968). **424-6.**

Wardrop, James. *The Script of Humanism: Some Aspects of Humanist Script 1460–1560* (Oxford, 1963). **203-4, 235, 298.**

Warner, Deborah H. 'The First Celestial Globe of Willem Janszoon Blaeu,' *Image Mundi* 25 (1971) 29–38. **599-601, 626.**

Warnke, Frank J. 'Mazzeo on the Renaissance,' *Journal of the History of Ideas* XXVIII (April–June 1967) 289–92. **165.**

Waters, D. W. 'Science and the Techniques of Navigation in the Renaissance,' *Art, Science and History in the Renaissance*, ed. C. S. Singleton (Baltimore, Md., 1967) 189–237. **583.**

Watson, Foster. *The Beginning of the Teaching of Modern Subjects in England* (London, 1909). **67, 487, 698.**

Watt, Ian. *The Rise of the Novel* (rev. edn, Berkeley, Calif., 1967). **316, 321.** *See also* Goody, J.

Watt, W. M. *The Influence of Islam on Medieval Europe* (Edinburgh, 1972). **463.**

Weber, Max. *The Protestant Ethic and the Spirit of Capitalism*, tr. Talcott Parsons (London, 1948). **378-81, 414, 427.**

Webster, Charles. *The Great Instauration: Science Medicine and Reform 1626–1660* (London, 1975). **120, 305, 362, 533, 656, 681.**

ed. *The Intellectual Revolution of the Seventeenth Century* (Past and Present Series) (London, 1974). **641.** Includes article by Espinasse, M.

Samuel Hartlib and the Advancement of Learning (Cambridge, 1970). **305.** *See also* Schmitt, C. B.

Wedgwood, C. V. 'Rural England under the Stuarts,' *History Today* (July 1968) 509–10. **426.**

Weil, E. 'William Fitzer the Publisher of Harvey's De Motu Cordis 1628,' *The Library*, 4th ser. XXIV (1944) 142–64. **529.**

Weil, G. E. *Elie Lévita: Humaniste et Massorète (1469–1549)* (Leiden, 1963). **224.**

Weisheipl, James A. 'Curriculum of the Faculty of Arts at Oxford in the Early Fourteenth Century,' *Medieval Studies* 26 (Toronto, 1964) 143–85. **536.**

Weisinger, Herbert. 'Ideas of History during the Renaissance,' *Renaissance Essays from the Journal of the History of Ideas*, ed. P. O. Kristeller and P. P. Wiener (New York, 1968) 74–94. **191.**

'Who Began the Revival of Learning?' *Papers of the Michigan Academy of Science, Arts and Letters* XXX (1944) 625–38. **185, 221.**

Weiss, Roberto. *The Renaissance Discovery of Classical Antiquity* (Oxford, 1969). **185, 218, 225.**

'Learning and education in Western Europe from 1470 to 1520,' *The New Cambridge Modern History*, Vol. I. *The Renaissance, 1493–1520*, ed. G. R. Potter (Cambridge, 1957) 95–126. **27.**

The Spread of Italian Humanism (London, 1964). **177.**

Weitzmann, Kurt. *Illustration in Roll and Codex: A Study of the Origins and Method of Text Illustration* (Studies in Medieval Illumination II, ed. A. M. Friend) (Princeton, 1947). **214.**

Westfall, Richard S. 'Newton and the Hermetic Tradition,' *Science Medicine and Society in the Renaissance*, ed. Allen Debus (2 vol. New York, 1973) I 183–98. **681.**

Westman, Robert S. Book review, *Renaissance Quarterly* XXVIII (Summer 1974) 221–3. **667.**

'The Comet and the Cosmos; Kepler, Mästlin and the Copernican Hypothesis,' *The Reception of Copernicus' Heliocentric Theory, Studia Copernica V*, Proceedings of a symposium organized by the International Union of the History and Philosophy of Science held in Toruń, Poland, 1972, ed. Jerzy Dobrzycki (Warsaw, 1972) 7–31. **598, 599, 602.**

'Kepler's Theory of Hypothesis and the "Realist Dilemma",' *Studies in the History and Philosophy of Science* III (1972) 233–64. **471, 588, 589.**

'Magical Reform and Astronomical Reform: The Yates Thesis Reconsidered,' *Hermeticism and the Scientific Revolution* (Clark Library Seminar, 1974) (Los Angeles, 1977) 5–91. **286, 641.**

'The Melanchthon Circle, Rheticus and the Wittenberg Interpretation of the Copernican Theory,' *Isis* 66 (June 1975) 165–93. **535, 650.**

'Three Responses to the Copernican Theory,' *The Copernican Achievement*, ed. R. S. Westman (Los Angeles, 1975) 285–345. **535, 581, 590, 618.**

ed. *The Copernican Achievement* (Los Angeles, 1975). Includes articles by Gingerich, Owen; Swerdlow, Noel; Westman, Robert; Wilson, Curtis; Wrightsman, Bruce.

White, A. D. *A History of the Warfare of Science and Theology* (2 vol. London, 1896). **642.**

White, Lynn, Jr. *Medieval Technology and Social Change* (rev. edn, Oxford, 1967). **20.**

'The Iconology of Temperantia and the Virtuousness of Technology,' *Action and Conviction in Early Modern Europe* (Festschrift to E. H. Harbison) (Princeton, 1969) 197–219. **251.**

'Jacopo Aconcio as an Engineer,' *The American Historical Review* LXXII (Jan. 1967) 425–45. **240, 243.**

'Pumps and Pendula: Galileo and Technology,' *Galileo Reappraised*, ed. C. L. Golino (Berkeley, Calif., 1971) 96–110. **538.**

Whitehead, A. N. *Science and the Modern World* (1st edn, 1926; London, 1938). **463, 472, 493, 615, 636, 637, 638.**

Whiteside, D. T. 'Before the Principia: The Maturing of Newton's Thoughts... 1664–1684,' *Journal for the History of Astronomy* I (1970) 5–20. **632, 634.**

'Newton's Marvellous Year: 1666 and All That,' *Notes and Records of the Royal Society of London* 21 (June 1966) 32–42. **633.**

ed. *The Mathematical Papers of Isaac Newton* Vol. I *1664–1666* (Cambridge, 1967). **245, 633.**

Whitmore, P. J. S. *The Order of Minims in Seventeenth Century France* (The Hague, 1967). **644, 667, 680.**

Whitteridge, Gweneth. *William Harvey and the Circulation of the Blood* (London, 1971). **262, 528–9, 535, 562, 574.**

Wiener, Carol Z. 'The Beleaguered Isle: A Study of Elizabethan and Early Jacobean Anti-Catholicism,' *Past and Present* 51 (May 1971) 27–62. **427.**

Wieruszowski, Helen. 'Burckhardt and Vespasiano,' *Philosophy and Humanism: Essays in Honor of P. O. Kristeller*, ed. E. P. Mahoney (New York, 1976) 387–405. **48.**

Wightman, W. P. D. *Science and the Renaissance* (2 vol. Edinburgh, 1962). **490, 494, 511, 582, 586, 598, 601.**

Science in a Renaissance Society (London, 1972). **533–4.**

Wiles, R. M. *Freshest Advices: Early Provincial Newspapers in England* (Columbus, Ohio, 1963). **131.**

Wilkinson, R. H. 'The Gentleman Ideal and the Maintenance of a Political Elite,' *Sociology of Education* xxxvii (Fall 1963) 9–26. **397.**

Willard, C. C. 'The Manuscripts of Jean Petit's Justification: Some Burgundian Propaganda Methods of the Early Fifteenth Century,' *Studi Francesi* 38 (1969) 271–80. **13, 46, 312.**

Willems, E. 'Cultural Change and the Rise of Protestantism in Brazil and Chile,' *The Protestant Ethic and Modernization,* ed. S. N. Eisenstadt (New York, 1968) 184–211. **415.**

Willey, Basil. *The Seventeenth Century Background* (London, 1942). **306, 336, 455, 471.**

Williams, George H. *The Radical Reformation* (Philadelphia, 1962). **444.**

Williams, Raymond. *Communications* (London, 1962). **61.**

   Culture and Society 1780–1950 (New York, 1960). **153.**

   The Long Revolution (New York, 1966). **61.**

Wilson, Arthur. *Diderot: The Testing Years, 1713–1759* (Oxford, 1957). **132, 700.**

Wilson, Curtis. 'From Kepler's Laws, so-called, to Universal Gravitation: Empirical Factors,' *Archive for the History of Exact Sciences* vi (1970) 89–170. **631-2.**

   'Newton and Some Philosophers on Kepler's "Laws",' *Journal of the History of Ideas* xxxv (April–June 1974) 231–58. **651.**

   'Rheticus, Ravetz and the "Necessity" of Copernicus's Innovation,' *The Copernican Achievement,* ed. R. S. Westman (Los Angeles, 1975) 17–40. **589, 604, 613.**

Wilson, N. G. *See* Reynolds, L. D.

Wilson, R. M. 'The Contents of the Medieval Library,' *The English Library before 1700,* ed. F. Wormald and C. E. Wright (London, 1958). 85–111. **211.**

Winetrout, Kenneth. 'The New Age of the Visible. A Call to Study,' *A. V. Communication Review* xii (Spring 1964) 46–52. **159.**

Winter, I. J. 'Mon Livre et Moi,' *Renaissance Quarterly* xxv (Autumn 1972) 297–307. **230.**

Winton, Calhoun. 'Richard Steele, Journalist and Journalism,' *Newsletters to Newspapers: Eighteenth Century Journalism,* ed. D. Bond and R. McLeod (Morgantown, W.Va., 1977) 21–30. **155.**

Wittkower, Rudolf. 'Individualism in Art and Artists: A Renaissance Perspective,' *Journal of the History of Ideas* xxii (July–Sept. 1961) 291–302. **232.**

Wittkower, Rudolf and Margaret. *Born Under Saturn* (New York, 1963). **232.**

Witty, Francis. 'Early Indexing Techniques: A Study of Several Book Indexes from the Fourteenth, Fifteenth and Early Sixteenth Centuries,' *Library Quarterly* xxxv (1965) 141–8. **90, 106.**

Wolf, A. *A History of Science, Technology and Philosophy in the 16th and 17th Centuries* (2 vol., rev. edn, New York, 1959). **491, 494.**

Wolpe, Berthold L. 'Florilegium Alphabeticum: Alphabets in Medieval Manuscripts,' *Calligraphy and Paleography, Essays Presented to A. J. Fairbank,* ed. A. S. Osley (London, 1965) 69–75. **88.**

Wolper, Roy S. 'The Rhetoric of Gunpowder and the Idea of Progress,' *Journal of the History of Ideas* xxxi (1970) 589–98. **21.**

Wood, Norman. *The Reformation and English Education: A Study of the Influence of Religious Uniformity on English Education in the Sixteenth Century* (London, 1961). **350, 357.**

Ziman, John. *Public Knowledge: The Social Dimension of Science* (Cambridge, 1968).
478.

Zimmerman, T. P. 'Confession and Autobiography in the Early Renaissance,'
Renaissance: Studies in Honor of Hans Baron (DeKalb, Ill., 1971) 121–40. **229.**

Zinner, Ernst. *Leben und Werken des Johannes Müller von Königsberg, genannt Regiomontanus* (Munich, 1938). **584.**

Zophy, J. W. *See* Buck, L. P.

Zoubov, V. P. 'Vitruve et ses Commentateurs du XVIe Siècle,' *La Science au Seizième
Siècle* (Colloque de Royaumont) (Paris, 1960). 69-90. **469.**

Zuckerman, H. *See* Merton, Robert K.

GENERAL INDEX

abacists versus algorists, 467n, 532
'Abbey of Free Will' (Rabelais), 393
Abbot of Sponheim, *see* Trithemius, Johannes
ABC books, 78, 89, 247, 432
Abelard, P., 230, 284
'The Abuses and Ignorance of Physicians', 541
Academiarum Examen (Braillier, P., London: J.Webster, 1654), 550n
Académie des Sciences, 679–80n
Accademia Venetiana, 675
accounting, 385, 542
  books, 65, 384
  bookkeeping, double-entry, 381–4, 548, 550, 554–5
  see also arithmetic; Pacioli, Luca
Aconcio, Jacopo, 103n
Acta Eruditorium (periodical), 138n
Actes and Monuments (Foxe, J.), *see Book of Martyrs*
'Ad Lectorum' (Osiander, A.), 651
Adages (Erasmus), 219n, 279, 280n
Adami, Tobias, 668n
Adams, Henry, x
Addison, Joseph, 670
Address to the Estates of the Empire (Sleiden, J., 1542), 305
Adelard of Bath, 210, 556, 588
The Advancement of Learning (Bacon, F., 1605), 338n
Advertisements from Parnassus (London, 1669) (English translation by Earl of Monmouth of Boccalini's *Ragguagli di Parnaso*), 669n
advertising, 52, 59–60, 145 (provided by *Index*), 156, 229, 234n, 240–1, 244, 376, 392, 406, 539, 553, 562, 587, 687
  see also blurbs; publicity
Aesopian language, 273, 674
Age of Reason (Paine, T.), 149n
Agricola (Bauer, Georg), 221, 242, 265, 469–70,

545, 555–6, 568, 571, 687
Agrippa, Henry Cornelius von Nettlesheim, 94–6, 276, 531
Albert of Brudzewo, 581n
Alberti, Leon Battista, 201n, 232n, 237–8, 243, 252, 255–6, 268n, 280, 283–4, 381, 548–9, 551n, 556, 564n, 604
Albertus Magnus, 513n, 552–3
alchemy, 76, 272, 274, 275n, 280n, 437, 474, 562–3, 641
  see also Paracelsus
Alciato, Andrea, 104
Alcuin, 80, 90, 316, 339
Aldine editions, *see* Aldus Manutius
Aldrovandi catalogue, 198
Aldus Manutius (Aldo Manucci), 48, 52n, 57, 178, 180, 218–24, 340, 393, 398, 409, 412–13, 441, 447, 545n, 691
Aldine editions, 175, 180n, 205, 221–3, 280n, 473, 569n, 691
Aldus' firm, 98n, 139, 198, 221n, 222, 279, 580
Alexander de Villedieu, 608n
Alexander the Great, 339
Alexandrian Museum and Library, xiv, 10, 89, 111, 195, 219, 465, 559n, 687
Alexandrian science, 193, 216, 220, 462–6, 469, 494–6, 505, 512, 516, 578, 580, 584–6, 593, 605–6
Alfonso X (The Wise, King of Castile and Leon), 500n, 603, 630n
Alhazen, 590n
allegory, 195–9, 260. 280n, 297, 457, 471
  see also mythography
Allen, P. S., 175–6, 401
Almagest (Ptolemy), 170n, 271, 288, 336, 382, 462–4, 466, 505, 510–11, 516, 523, 536–7, 581–2, 584–5, 594, 604, 612, 618, 621, 623, 629–30, 693, 695, 697, 701

Renaissance, 25, 27, 37, 73, 77, 163–302 (esp. 300n), 306, 368, 377, 410, 412–13, 418–19, 456, 459, 465n–6, 471, 474–5, 485, 488–98, 521–2n, 592, 594–5, 602, 683
see also classical revivals; 'rinascita'
renascences, see classical revivals
Renaudot, Théophraste, 133n, 246–7, 643n, 656, 665
Republic of Letters, xv, 128, 136–58 (137n history of term), 228–9, 397, 401, 409, 413, 420, 448, 619, 624n, 638, 645, 647, 653, 691
see also Commonwealth of Learning
Respublica Literaria Christiana (Grotius), 137n
Reuchlin, Johann, 94n, 221, 278, 305n, 331, 347, 367, 372n, 399n, 400, 447n, 620
Reuwich (or Rewich), Erhard (illustrator), 85–6, 266n
Revelation, see Bible, books of
Rhau-Grünenberg, see Grünenberg, Johannes
Rheticus, 525, 532n, 577, 581n, 582n, 583, 587n, 591, 593, 599, 607, 614, 617, 621n, 623n, 624n, 626n, 634, 637–8, 644, 649–50, 651n, 652, 654, 664, 694
Rhetorica (George of Trebizond, Venice, 1472), 399n
Rhetorica (Fichet, G.), 399n
Rhodes, 86n, 375n
Riccioli, Giovanni Battista, 624n, 629
Rice, Eugene, 325
Richelieu, Cardinal Armand Jean du Plessis de, 133n, 135, 441, 656n
Ridley, Nicholas, 68
Rienieri, Vincento, 630
'rinascita' (Petrarchan revival), 137n, 164, 172, 174–5, 177–8, 184–5, 194–5, 217–18, 294n, 298, 300, 306, 368
Ripa, Cesare, 662n
Ripoli press (convent of San Jacopo), 15n, 46
robe nobility, 147, 395
Robertson, H. M., 381
Robespierre, Maximilien François Marie Isidore de, 352
Rolevinck, Werner, 15n, 316
Rome (as an ecclesiastical centre), 178, 305, 348, 355, 390, 398–9n, 405, 412, 647–8, 656, 671, 682
Roriczer, Matthias, 65n
Rose, P. L., 675n
Rosen, Edward, 498, 501, 631, 641
Rosetta Stone, 69n, 77n, 563
Rosicrucians, 68–9n, 77, 97n, 125, 140–1, 274–6, 438, 529n, 534n, 669
Rostock, 625n
Rotterdam, 138, 401, 420, 646n
Rousseau, Jean-Jacques, 128n
Royal College of Physicians, 528n
The Royal Society (of London for Improving Natural Knowledge), 59n, 283, 337,

471, 476, 488, 494, 556, 559, 601, 619, 625, 634, 641n, 647, 664–70, 674, 679, 681, 694–6
Rudolph II, of Prague, Holy Roman Emperor, 474, 625n, 640
Rudolphine Tables, 461, 626, 628, 631–2, 661
Rutherford, Lord Ernest of Nelson, 562

Sacrobosco, Joannes de (John of Holywood), 537, 624n;
Sphaera, 510–12, 517, 533–4n, 590, 615n, 692
Sacy, Isaac le Maistre de, 351n
Saenger, Paul, 38n
Saggi (Papers of the Cimento), 666–7, 674
Saint-Evremond, Charles de Saint-Denis, 395n
Saint-Simon, Henri, 447
Salamanca, 386, 408, 444
'Salomon's House', 255n, 625n
Salusbury, Thomas, 631n, 677n
Salutati, Coluccio, 189, 203n, 205n, 251, 473
Samaritan language, 337
San Antonio di Castello (Venetian library), 548n
Santritter, J., of Heilbronn, 587n
Sanuto, Marco, 547
Sappho, 122
Sarpi, Paolo, 412–13, 418, 644n
Sarton, George, 27, 55, 72n, 75, 170n, 171n, 248n, 387, 484, 486, 507–9, 564–5, 591, 637, 642, 652n
Saumur, academy of, 278n
Savonarola, Girolamo, 236 285n, 316
Scaliger, Joseph Justus, 73–4, 200, 301, 611n
Schatzgeyer, Caspar, 327
Schedel, Hartmann, 197n
Scheiner, Christopher, 530n, 561n, 624n, 653n
Scheubel, Johan, 587n
Scheurl, Christoph, 308n
Schickard, Wilhelm, 642
Schioppo, Cristoforo, 52n
Schmuttermayer, Hans, 65n
Schoeffer, John, 96n
Schoeffer, Peter (Mainz printer), 31, 49, 51, 55n, 57–8, 85–6, 91, 95–6, 266, 484n
scholar-printers, xv, 4, 75, 85, 87, 98–9, 101, 104n, 139, 174, 177, 179–80, 221–4, 250–1, 277n, 279, 309, 320, 328, 331, 336–7, 356, 359–60n, 367n, 369–70, 399–400, 403n, 443–9 esp., 509, 521, 524, 542, 545, 561, 566, 569–70, 689, 692
see also Amerbach; Estienne; Oporinus; Plantin; et al
Scholarum Mathematicarum (Ramus), 624n
scholasticism, schoolmen, 212–14, 257, 294, 314–15, 457n, 459, 466, 472–3, 548, 595, 602